Rachel Morley is Lecturer in Russian Ci
of Slavonic and East European Studies, U
SSEES). She has written widely on early Russian and Soviet film.

Kino Series

Joint General Editors: Birgit Beumers & Richard Taylor

Editorial Board: Birgit Beumers, Julian Graffy, Richard Taylor & Denise J. Youngblood

Marina L. Levitina, *'Russian Americans' in Soviet Film: Cinematic Dialogues between the US and the USSR* (2015)

Rachel Morley, *Performing Femininity: Woman as Performer in Early Russian Cinema* (2017)

Forthcoming:

Oksana Sarkisova, *Screening Soviet Nationalities: Kulturfilms from the Far North to Central Asia* (2017)

Jamie Miller, *Propaganda and Popular Entertainment in the USSR: The Mezhrabpom Studio* (2018)

Julian Graffy, *Through a Russian Lens: Representing Foreigners in a Century of Russian Film* (2018)

Birgit Beumers, *The Cinema of the New Russia* (2019)

Rachel Morley

Performing Femininity

Woman as Performer
in Early Russian Cinema

BLOOMSBURY ACADEMIC
LONDON • NEW YORK • OXFORD • NEW DELHI • SYDNEY

BLOOMSBURY ACADEMIC
Bloomsbury Publishing Plc
50 Bedford Square, London, WC1B 3DP, UK
1385 Broadway, New York, NY 10018, USA
29 Earlsfort Terrace, Dublin 2, Ireland

BLOOMSBURY, BLOOMSBURY ACADEMIC and the Diana logo
are trademarks of Bloomsbury Publishing Plc

First published by I. B. Tauris
This paperback edition published in 2021

A catalogue record for this book is available from the British Library.

A catalog record for this book is available from the Library of Congress.

ISBN: HB: 978 1 7845 3159 1
PB: 978 1 3502 4286 9
ePDF: 978 1 7867 3058 9
eBook: 978 1 7867 2058 0

KINO: The Russian and Soviet Cinema Series

To find out more about our authors and books visit
www.bloomsbury.com and sign up for our newsletters.

Contents

List of Illustrations

List of Illustrations

General Editors' Preface

Cinema has been the predominant art form of the first half of the twentieth century, at least in Europe and North America. Nowhere was this more apparent than in Russia and the former Soviet Union, where Lenin's remark that 'of all the arts, cinema is the most important' became a cliché and where cinema attendances were until recently still among the highest in the world. In the age of mass politics Soviet cinema developed from a fragile but effective tool to gain support among the overwhelmingly illiterate peasant masses in the civil war that followed the October 1917 Revolution, through a welter of experimentation, into a mass weapon of propaganda through the entertainment that shaped the public image of the Soviet Union – both at home and abroad for both elite and mass audiences – and latterly into an instrument to expose the weaknesses of the past and present in the twin process of glasnost and perestroika. Now the national cinemas of the successor republics to the old USSR are encountering the same bewildering array of problems, from the trivial to the terminal, as are all the other ex-Soviet institutions, while Russia itself is now the world's sixth largest area for distribution. The present volume demonstrates that there was life in Russian cinema even before the 1917 Revolutions and that Soviet cinema did not come from nowhere.

Cinema's central position in Russian and Soviet cultural history and its unique combination of mass medium, art form and entertainment industry have made it a continuing battlefield for conflicts of broader ideological and artistic significance, not only for Russia and the Soviet Union, but also for the world outside. The debates that raged in the 1920s about the relative merits of documentary as opposed to fiction film, of cinema as opposed to theatre or painting, or of the proper role of cinema in the forging of post-Revolutionary Soviet culture and the shaping of the new Soviet man have their echoes in current discussions about the role of cinema *vis-à-vis* other art forms in effecting the cultural and psychological revolution in human consciousness necessitated by the processes of economic and political transformation of the former Soviet Union into modern democratic and industrial societies and states governed by the rule of law. Cinema's central position has also made it a vital instrument for scrutinising the blank pages of Russian and Soviet history and enabling the present generation to come to terms with its own past.

This series of books intends to examine Russian, Soviet and ex-Soviet films in the context of Russian, Soviet and ex-Soviet cinemas, and Russian, Soviet and ex-Soviet cinemas in the context of the political history of Russia, the Soviet Union, the post-Soviet 'space' and the world at large. Within that framework the series, drawing its authors from both East and West, aims to cover a wide variety of topics and to employ a broad range of methodological approaches and presentational formats. Inevitably this will involve ploughing once again over old ground in order to re-examine received opinions, but it principally means increasing the breadth and depth of our knowledge, finding new answers to old questions and, above all, raising new questions for further enquiry and new areas for further research.

The continuing aim of this series is to situate Russian, Soviet and ex-Soviet cinema in its proper historical and aesthetic context, both as a major cultural force and as a crucible for experimentation that is of central significance to the development of world cinema culture. Books in the series strive to combine the best of scholarship, past, present and future, with a style of writing that is accessible to a broad readership, whether that readership's primary interest lies in cinema or in political history.

Richard Taylor & Birgit Beumers

Acknowledgements

The research for this study was funded in part by a three-year scholarship from the Arts and Humanities Research Council (AHRC) and I am grateful for their generous support. A version of Chapter 7 appeared as 'Performing femininity in an age of change: Evgenii Bauer, Ivan Turgenev and the legend of Evlaliia Kadmina' in Robert Reid and Joe Andrew (eds), *Turgenev: Art, Ideology, Legacy* (Amsterdam and New York, 2010), pp. 269–316. I thank the original publisher, Koninklijke Brill NV, for granting me permission to re-publish this work here.

Birgit Beumers, Julian Graffy, Bryan Karetnyk, James Mann, Arnold and Svetlana McMillin, Milena Michalski, Anna Pakes, Luke Ponsford, Candyce Veal and Emma Widdis all supplied me with materials used in this study. I am grateful to them, and especially to Philip Cavendish for permitting me to use a number of the images that he acquired during research trips to *Gosfilmofond of Russia* to illustrate this study. I also wish to thank Erich Sargeant for enabling me to grab stills from a number of films held at the British Film Institute for the same purpose.

Some of the material included in this book has been presented at seminars hosted by the UCL SSEES Centre for Russian Studies, the UCL SSEES Russian Cinema Research Group, the Centre for Dance Research at Roehampton University and at conferences held at the Universities of Cambridge, Oxford and Surrey. Thanks to all who were present on those occasions, both for listening with interest and for responding with thoughtful and thought-provoking questions and suggestions. Special thanks to Vlad Strukov and Richard Marks, whose comments opened up new lines of enquiry. I am also grateful to Tim Beasley-Murray, Philip Cavendish, Pamela Davidson, Titus Hjelm, Robert Pynsent, Kristin Roth-Ey, Brooke Townsley, Emma Widdis and Peter Zusi, who read early versions of various chapters and offered valuable advice and suggestions for improvements. I am also indebted to the series editors, Richard Taylor and Birgit Beumers, and to Madeleine Hamey-Thomas and David Campbell at I.B.Tauris, for their helpful comments on the manuscript and their patience. Any errors that remain are, of course, my own.

Heartfelt thanks to De and Roy, for everything; to Brooke, for his constant support; and to Eve and May, who have borne with patience and generally good humour the fact my work on this book has often meant they have received less of my time and attention than they deserve.

Finally, I owe an enormous debt of gratitude to Julian Graffy, who introduced me to early Russian cinema and whose teaching inspired me to continue with research in this field. I wish to thank Julian for his boundless generosity in sharing with me so much of his knowledge, time and experience; for reading (multiple) drafts of this monograph with patience, enthusiasm and sensitivity; and for making many invaluable suggestions. I could not have asked for a better supervisor, reader or friend, and it is in recognition of this that I dedicate this book to him.

Note on Transliteration

Transliteration from the Cyrillic to the Latin alphabet is a perennial problem for writers on Russian subjects. We have opted for a dual system: in the text we use a simplified Library of Congress system (without diacritics), but we have departed from this system (a) when a Russian name has an accepted English spelling (e.g. Tchaikovsky instead of Chaikovskii, Chaliapin instead of Shaliapin, Yeltsin instead of Eltsin), or (b) when Russian names are of Germanic origin (e.g. Eisenstein instead of Eizenshtein, Meyerhold instead of Meierkhol´d). In the scholarly apparatus, which includes annotation, bibliography and filmography, we adhere to the Library of Congress system with diacritics for the specialist. The index cross-refers between main and subsidiary spellings.

Introduction

Rediscovering early Russian cinema: the story so far

[Evgenii] Bauer has died, but his work is alive and will live on for many years to come. Bauer is dead, but for many years to come his pictures will be shown and shown again on Russian screens; more and more copies of them will be made; they will finally find their way overseas and will gradually appear in all corners of the world. For a long time to come young directors will learn from the models of Bauer's creations, and many years in the future some cinema writer will extract his frayed films from the archives and use them to study closely the Bauer era of cinema, the mystery of his pictures' charm and the secret of their success with the general public.

Extract from an article published in *Cine-Gazette* [Kino-gazeta] in January 1918.[1]

The rediscovery in the late 1980s of 286 pre-Revolutionary Russian films at the Soviet State Film Archive [*Gosfilmofond of Russia*] and the screening of a selection of them in the *Silent Witnesses* programme of the eighth *Giornate del Cinema Muto* Festival, held at Pordenone in October 1989, are events of fundamental importance in the history of Russian and Soviet

1

film. Before that year, the accepted picture of Russian film-making during this period was fragmentary. Unable to view these films for themselves, film scholars had to content themselves with reading about them in the very few academic studies that were dedicated to this period of Russian film history.

In 1945 the size and shape of the early Russian film industry had become clearer, however, with the publication of Veniamin Vishnevskii's filmography of pre-Revolutionary cinema.[2] A monumental volume that identifies 1,716 Russian feature films made between 1907 and 1917, Vishnevskii's study remains an invaluable reference work for scholars of the films of this period. It is, however, by its very nature as a filmography, limited to reporting key facts about the films it enumerates: it gives their titles and subtitles, the names of the people who worked on them, those of the actors and the roles that they took, states the release date, if known, and identifies the production studio that made each film. Information about the films' content is by necessity, however, sparse or non-existent, restricted to the occasional brief sentence about a film's subject or its plot. As we would expect in a filmography, there is no attempt at critical analysis.

It was not until a decade and a half after the publication of Vishnevskii's volume that the first critical study of the pre-Revolutionary Russian film industry appeared. In 1960 the American film scholar Jay Leyda, who, as a student at the All-Union State Institute of Cinematography [Vsesoiuznyi gosudarstvenyi institut kinematografii (VGIK)] in Moscow in the 1930s, had been able to view the pre-Revolutionary films held there, published his history of Russian and Soviet film. Thus he became the first Westerner to attempt an informed analysis of Russian cinema before 1917, and one based on first-hand viewing experience.[3] As Leyda himself recognised, his account was neither comprehensive, nor unflawed; it was, however, 'a courageous starting point'.[4] The Thaw years also saw the publication of two books devoted to this period of film by the Soviet film historians Romil Sobolev[5] and Semen Ginzburg.[6] While these works remain untranslated, some of Ginzburg's observations and conclusions were made accessible to non-Russian-speaking scholars by the French film historian Georges Sadoul, who relied on Ginzburg's study for the details he included about early Russian cinema in later editions of the third volume of his *Histoire générale du cinéma*.[7] However, as the editors of the catalogue prepared to accompany the films' screening at Pordenone caution, Sadoul's account of pre-Revolutionary Russian film is highly subjective, coloured as it is by his ideological prejudices:

> Suffice it to remember that Sadoul despised the middle-class society of the tsarist period as well as its cinema, because they avoided 'the acute problems of that time', plunged into 'purely individualistic and often pathological events', in which he thought that 'death, passions, crimes, perversions, madness, mysticism, cosmopolitanism [*sic*], pornography reigned'.[8]

Sadoul's study was followed, in 1967, by that of another Frenchman, Jean Mitry.[9] Mitry also stressed the films' morbidity and 'delight in unhappiness', but unlike Sadoul he argued that this characteristic atmosphere *was* in fact a stark reflection of the social circumstances in which these films were made and, specifically, of 'the social pessimism due to the failure of the revolution in 1905'.[10]

And then there was silence. Nothing significant was published on the cinema of late Imperial Russia for almost a quarter of a century. As the British film historians Richard Taylor and Ian Christie noted in 1988: 'The existence of a distinctive Russian pre-Revolutionary cinema has been recognised at least since Leyda's preliminary account in *Kino*, but has still to be evaluated critically'.[11]

It is unsurprising, therefore, that the rediscovery of these films and their subsequent screening in the West led – as predicted in 1918 by the anonymous reviewer whose musings on the possible fate of Bauer's films are cited at the head of this Introduction – to a resurgence of scholarly interest not only in the films of Evgenii Bauer, the acknowledged major film-maker of the period, but also in this whole shadowy period of Russian film-making. The starting point for this evaluation was the aforementioned catalogue produced to accompany the 1989 screening of these films at Pordenone, *Silent Witnesses: Russian Films 1908–1919*. This encyclopaedic volume lists all the early Russian feature films preserved at *Gosfilmofond of Russia* and provides, in English and Italian, cast lists, excerpts from reviews and synopses published in contemporary film journals, biographies of the key figures in the early Russian film industry and brief critical notes, authored by the editors, on those films shown at Pordenone. A Russian version of this catalogue was published in 2002.[12] It contains additional material from contemporary journals and revised and expanded biographies of the key pre-Revolutionary film-makers and actors, but lacks the film notes written by the editors of *Silent Witnesses*.

The years that followed the Pordenone retrospective saw the publication of a growing body of work on the cinema of this period by such scholars as Mary Ann Doane, Jane Gaines, Mikhail Iampolskii, Rashit Iangirov, Viktor Korotkii and Neia Zorkaia. It is, however, the Russian film historian Yuri Tsivian who has emerged as the leading expert on the cinema of this period. Over the last two decades Tsivian has produced numerous books, articles, video essays, voice-over commentaries and a CD ROM on early Russian cinema and its cultural background, and has done more than any other commentator to shed light on the peculiarities and specificities of the early Russian film style and to chart their development and refinement. Too numerous to survey here, Tsivian's studies will be referred to in detail throughout this book, for his work, which is invariably both instructive and inspiring, has served as a springboard for many of the ideas developed in the present study.

The early 1990s also saw the publication of several interesting feminist/ Freudian responses to the films shown at Pordenone, most notably from the film scholars Heide Schlüpmann[13] and Miriam Hansen.[14] These have also informed the approach adopted in this study. Towards the end of the 1990s and into the 2000s, several notable American socio-cultural historians with an interest in late Imperial Russia also turned their attention to the cinema of this period. Most of their work addresses the question posed by Richard Stites in his review of the British Film Institute's ten-volume video anthology of early Russian cinema (1992), that is 'What do the films tell us about society and life in the twilight years of the empire?'[15] Thus, Denise J. Youngblood's book-length study of early Russian cinema focuses on 'fact and context, not theory and aesthetics'.[16] Another prominent contributor to this rich vein of scholarship is Louise McReynolds, whose most recent article on this subject explores seven Bauer films from a Lacanian perspective in order to argue that, as Mitry had suggested in 1967, the psycho-sexual morbidity of their plots reflects the social impotence and concomitant frustration that characterised the lives of most Russian men in the late Imperial age.[17]

Other commentators have focussed their analysis not so much on the films' narratives and plots as on the technical and aesthetic elements of the early Russian film style. Thus, Philip Cavendish, who privileges the role of the pre-Revolutionary camera operator, crediting him with playing a major role in the creation of the films' visual aesthetics, focuses his analysis of early Russian films on the meanings created by what he terms 'the poetics of the camera'.[18] Following Cavendish's lead, Natascha Drubek explores Bauer's aesthetic emphasis on lighting.[19] Alyssa DeBlasio similarly shuns the thematic approach and examines instead Bauer's innovative use of mise-en-scène in the creation of meaning.[20]

Thus, just over twenty-five years after the rediscovery of these extraordinary films, our understanding of early Russian cinema is much enhanced. However, with the exception of Youngblood, Cavendish and McReynolds, most recent commentators have focussed their critical attention solely on the films of Evgenii Bauer to the detriment of the work of other early directors. There are still, therefore, considerable gaps in our understanding of this period of film-making as a whole, some of which this present study intends to address.

Aims and approach

[…] woman is in a period of evolution; it is therefore difficult to create now a typical image of woman.
M. Moravskaia, 'Zhenshchina o sebe', 1915/16.[21]

This monograph sets out to explore the ways in which the figure of the female performer is represented in early Russian cinema during the period 1908–18. This subject grew out of my 2003 analysis of the representation of gender relations in sixteen films by Evgenii Bauer.[22] While researching that article, I was struck by how many of Bauer's female protagonists are cast as stage performers within the diegesis of his films. As I looked more widely at the extant corpus of early Russian films, I realised that the prevalence of this female type was not a phenomenon that was unique to Bauer; for, from the first Russian feature film, Vladimir Romashkov's *Stenka Razin* [Sten´ka Razin, 1908], via the increasingly sophisticated rural and urban melodramas of the mid-1910s, to Viacheslav Viskovskii's *The Last Tango* [Poslednee tango, 1918], one of the final films to be made before the collapse of the pre-Revolutionary film industry, the female performer is a ubiquitous figure. Many women give amateur performances, in forests, fields, villages or *kabinety*, the small rooms that could be hired for private parties in most urban restaurants. Others are cast as professionals and are shown either putting on their acts in the homes of the rich men and women who have engaged them or taking to the stage in theatres, dance halls and nightclubs, where they entertain a paying audience as actresses, opera singers and dancers of various types. Some also perform in private, in their bedrooms, their dressing rooms or before their mirrors. Thus, to borrow Moravskaia's phrase, cited at the head of this section, the 'typical image of woman' created by early Russian cinema is without question that of woman as performer. One of the main aims of this study is therefore to consider why this figure appeared in so many different films, by so many different early Russian directors, and to explore the various ways in which this persona is exploited by them.

On the most obvious level, the ubiquity of the female performer could be interpreted as a straightforward reflection of contemporary social reality, and my analysis will therefore consider the directors' representations of their female protagonists in the socio-historical context of the films' making. The late nineteenth and early twentieth centuries saw profound and rapid change in all layers of Russian society, but particularly in the social roles of women; in this social context, the performing arts represented one of the main spheres in which women could seek to transcend their traditionally prescribed social spaces of hearth and home and pursue a public profession that afforded them socially sanctioned 'visibility', enabled them to contribute to the cultural life of their society and, not least, gave them the opportunity to acquire financial independence. Moreover, towards the end of the nineteenth century, female stage performers in Russia began to enjoy higher status both in society and in their professional life. Unprecedented numbers of aspiring young women flocked to the theatre to pursue careers as *artistes* of various kinds – a phenomenon that the historian of Russian theatre Catherine M. Schuler terms 'the Nina Zarechnaia epidemic', alluding to Anton Chekhov's young actress heroine in his 1896 play *The Seagull* [Chaika][23] – as, in a reversal of the usual situation, the most successful female performers began to usurp their male counterparts in terms of both popularity and earning power. Personality cults arose around the most prominent *artistes*, whose lucrative audience appeal enabled them to command increasingly high fees for their performances.[24] In this respect, as Louise McReynolds has noted, in Russian society at this time 'the theater was an important site on many levels for registering the growing presence of females in public places.'[25]

This is, of course, only part of the story. Films are not merely social documents; they are also works of art. In Russia at the start of the twentieth century, cinema was an art form that was still very much in its infancy; the Lumière brothers had brought their cinematograph to Russia in May 1896, but native Russian film-making took longer to get going, with the first Russian production studios opening only in 1907. The period under consideration was thus not only an era of great social upheaval, it was also a time of immense artistic change, a new age during which a new artistic medium was born. The films made during this period therefore represent the first steps in the creation of this new art form. It is striking that the film-makers' explorations of cinematic technology and their attempts to develop a specifically cinematic language through which to express their themes and their concerns are bound up with their representations of the figure of the female performer to an extraordinary degree. Indeed, in the works of the greatest early Russian directors these two undertakings are inextricably linked. A second related aim of this monograph, therefore, is to consider the film-makers' representations of the female performer specifically through the prism of their attempts to experiment with and to explore the technological and aesthetic resources of film and thereby to develop a specifically cinematic language. In so doing, I shall attempt both to delineate the stylistic and aesthetic features that are most characteristic of early Russian film and to chart their development over the period under consideration.

These films did not, of course, either develop or exist in a cultural vacuum. My discussion will therefore also move beyond the world of cinema, to consider relevant features of the broader artistic and cultural landscape of early twentieth-century Russia and, indeed, of the literary, theatrical and artistic heritage out of which Russian film developed and on which early Russian directors so frequently drew.

In constructing a theoretical framework for this study, my preferred approach has been that of *bricolage*, in the sense accorded to the term by the French sociologist and anthropologist Claude Lévi-Strauss in *The Savage Mind* [La Pensée sauvage, 1962]; in other words, I draw on a variety of theoretical approaches, as suggested to me by the primary material under consideration, and on a range of different disciplines, including film theory, dance theory, gender theory, art history, literary criticism, feminist theory and general cultural theory. I also favour detailed analysis over broad comment, for the complexities of the films discussed in this study are such that only in-depth consideration can do them justice. Accordingly, this study does not seek to offer an exhaustive account of all the early Russian films that feature the figure of the female performer, but selects for analysis certain key examples of this widespread trope, treating them as illustrative case studies of this typical feature of early Russian film.

For these reasons, therefore, although the book is structured thematically and divided into seven chapters, each of which considers a different female performer archetype prevalent in the films of this period, the ordering of both the chapters and the discussion within them loosely follows a chronological framework.

Thus, Chapters 1 and 2 examine some of the earliest Russian feature films, made between 1908 and 1912, and a selection of the first filmic dancers. Specifically, Chapter 1 focuses on the representation of the first female performer in the first Russian feature film: the anonymous Persian princess of Romashkov's *Stenka Razin*. In addition to considering what this film reveals about the film-makers' understanding of gender roles in early twentieth-century Russian society, it also seeks to demonstrate that this anonymous woman, the first performer of Russian cinema, is a truly cinematic heroine and that, as such, her representation depends on and is executed by means of devices that are specifically cinematic. In so doing, this chapter takes the opposite view from that articulated by most previous commentators on this film, who have tended to deny its value as a work of cinematic art. Chapter 2, which examines the representation of other performer archetypes prevalent in films made between 1909 and 1912 – namely the peasant girl and her close sister, the nobleman's ward – continues my argument by considering how Romashkov's specifically cinematic representation of the Persian princess influenced and inspired later film-makers.

In Chapter 3, the focus moves from the rural melodrama to the urban, for it provides a close reading of a key film from the transitional year of 1913, Evgenii Bauer's earliest surviving work *Twilight of a Woman's Soul* [Sumerki zhenskoi dushi]. Drawing on the work of the psychoanalyst Joan Riviere as well as the gender theories of Simone de Beauvoir, Monique Wittig and Judith Butler, this chapter explores Bauer's representation of his first female performer protagonist, arguing that in this film Bauer directly engages with the question: 'What is a woman?' It also suggests that Bauer's heroine stands as a paradigmatic example of the so-called New Woman, who was making her presence felt in Russian society at this time. Finally, in considering how Bauer harnesses to his representation of his performer protagonist the technological and aesthetic opportunities afforded to him by the new medium of film, this chapter also seeks to demonstrate how far this new art form had advanced in sophistication in the five years since the release of the first Russian feature film, *Stenka Razin*.

This is also one of the aims of Chapter 4, which revisits the figure of the Persian princess, briefly considering the continued use of this persona in films made between 1914 and 1919 before focussing in detail on two films from 1914, Grigorii Libkin's *Stenka Razin* and Evgenii Bauer's *Child of the Big City* [Ditia bol´shogo goroda]. It considers how, as historical and rural melodramas were replaced by the urban melodrama, so the Persian princess metamorphosed into a new type of performer figure, and one more suited to representing the sophisticated early twentieth-century urban woman: the tango dancer [*tangistka*].

Chapters 5 and 6 both return briefly to the earliest years of the Russian film industry. Focussing on the dancing Gypsy girl [*tsyganka*], Chapter 5 explores how the first cinematic representations of this familiar nineteenth-century female figure, in films such as Vladimir Siversen's *Drama in a Gypsy Camp Near Moscow* [Drama v tabore podmoskovnykh tsygan, 1908] and André Maître's *The Gypsies* [Tsygane, 1910], differ from those that appear in two films made in 1915, Evgenii Bauer's *Children of the Age* [Deti veka] and Petr Chardynin's *The Love of a Councillor of State* [Liubov´ statskogo sovetnika].

Chapter 6 examines the figure of the ballerina, across the whole period under consideration, drawing on the memoirs of the American dancer Isadora Duncan, as well as on the work of dance historians and in particular on that of the feminist dance scholars Sally Banes, Ann Daly, Elizabeth Dempster and Christy Adair. The chapter begins with an analysis of the representation of the ballerina in one of Aleksandr Shiriaev's recently rediscovered puppet films, thought to have been made between 1906 and 1909, and continues with a discussion of Władysław Starewicz's animated-puppet comedy *The Cameraman's Revenge* [Mest′ kinematograficheskogo operatora, 1912]. Thereafter the chapter focuses on a series of feature films made between 1913 and 1918 by directors as varied as Boris Chaikovskii, Fedor Komissarzhevskii, Evgenii Bauer, Petr Chardynin, Iakov Protazanov and Vladimir Gardin. It suggests that the figure of the ballerina was in fact seen by most early Russian directors as a defunct archetype, ill-suited to representing the New Woman they wished to explore in their films, and demonstrates how the ballerina began to be replaced by a new type of performer, specifically the early modern dancer.

The final chapter of this study, Chapter 7, examines in detail the representation of the figure of the actress in Evgenii Bauer's 1915 film *After Death* [Posle smerti], now recognised as one of his most innovative and sophisticated works. This chapter examines the nineteenth-century literary, cultural and real-life heritage of Bauer's actress protagonist, and explores the complexity of the film's cinematic language and its importance to the representation of the female performer.

1

The Oriental Dancer

The first Russian feature film: the first steps towards the creation of a new art form

On 15 October 1908, Aleksandr Drankov's recently established St Petersburg production studio released what is now accepted as the first Russian-made feature film: *Stenka Razin*, subtitled *Brigands from the Lower Reaches* [Ponizovaia vol´nitsa] and also known as *Free Men of the Volga*. Billed as a historical drama, the film drew on the colourful legend of the eponymous Don Cossack, famed for leading a peasant revolt against Tsarist rule along the Volga at the end of the 1660s. According to Drankov's advance publicity material, it was to be 'a film the like of which has never before been seen in our cinematic repertoire!'[1]

Accounts of Drankov's film career typically focus on his personality, stressing his vulgarity and lack of education, and suggesting that his interest in film-making was motivated solely by financial concerns. Clearly, Drankov was an astute and competitive businessman, but there was more to him than this: he was a multi-talented figure – in Aleksandr Pozdniakov's words a 'one-man band' [*chelovek-orkestr*].[2] He started out in still photography, establishing a studio in St Petersburg and working as the Russian news photographer for several foreign newspapers, including the *Times*, the *London Illustrated News* and the Paris-based *L'Illustration*, and as the

11

official photographer of the State Duma. His first cinematic work was in making *actualité* programmes, and his connection with feature films came when he began photographing the Russian intertitles for French films distributed in Russia, using a second-hand Pathé camera. Moreover, by 1908 Drankov already had first-hand experience of feature film-making. For, although he himself advertised *Stenka Razin* as the 'first' Russian feature film, he had already produced a film in 1907: *Boris Godunov*, an adaptation of Aleksandr Pushkin's 1831 tragedy.[3] That same year he also filmed a theatre adaptation of Aleksei Tolstoi's 1862 novel, *Prince Serebrianyi* [Kniaz´ Serebrianyi].

Why did Drankov deny this earlier film in favour of *Stenka Razin*? This was in part, doubtless, because he was aware of the marketing value of the title of 'first film' and wanted to exploit it. A more significant explanation, however, is that *Stenka Razin* was a much more accomplished and sophisticated film than *Boris Godunov*. For this shrewd businessman was also conscious of his place in history. While keen to make as much money as possible from his film, Drankov was also driven by the desire to create a lasting work of cinematic art. In the run up to the release of *Stenka Razin* he commissioned advertising posters on which he announced the seriousness of his artistic aspirations:

> Having spent immense amounts of money and expended a great deal of work and time, I have focussed all my efforts on ensuring that this film, as far as its technical execution as well as its atmosphere and its performers are concerned, has reached the high level that befits its status as an epoch-making film in our cinematic repertoire.[4]

That Drankov genuinely aspired to technical and artistic excellence in *Stenka Razin* is also suggested by the quality of the collaborators he enlisted. Although little is known about the director, Vladimir Romashkov, and it seems that *Stenka Razin* was the only film he directed, the scriptwriter, Vasilii Goncharov, was an important creative figure who would go on to make an enormous contribution to Russian film, becoming a successful director in his own right.[5] Nikolai Kozlovskii, who worked alongside Drankov as the film's second cameraman, was (like Drankov) a former still photographer. He was also a serious artist and went on to work with

Evgenii Bauer, the most successful early Russian director; Philip Cavendish, in his study of pre-Revolutionary cameramen, describes Kozlovskii as 'an *actualités* specialist' and includes him in his list of the most 'intelligent and sophisticated' cameramen of the period.[6] The actors were professional theatre actors, as would become the norm in the early film industry. Finally, Drankov commissioned no less a figure than the famous composer Mikhail Ippolitov-Ivanov, then the director of the Moscow Conservatoire, to write a musical accompaniment to the film.[7]

This wealth of artistic talent and ambition ensured that, in modern parlance, *Stenka Razin* was an exceptionally 'slick' production, and when it was released it enjoyed immediate commercial and popular success. Audiences, used to French-made films which had dominated the Russian market since the Lumière brothers' cinematograph had arrived in Russia from France in 1896, loved the film's 'Russianness', the characters' wild drinking and especially its exploitation of two popular Russian folk songs: Goncharov had loosely based his scenario on the events recounted in the song *From the Island to the Deep Stream* [Iz-za ostrova na strezhen'], while in his musical accompaniment Ippolitov-Ivanov had drawn on the melody of another, *Down Along Mother-Volga* [Vniz po matushke po Volge], which, according to Drankov's publicity material for the film, was known by every Russian and sung everywhere, 'at concerts, among the *beau monde* and in poor peasant families'.[8] Jay Leyda recounts that enthusiastic cinema-goers would sing along with the songs while watching the film.[9] In his posthumously published memoirs, the Soviet film-maker Nikolai Anoshchenko writes evocatively of his experience of seeing the film in Moscow in 1908, when he was just thirteen years old, stating that both the occasion and the audience's enthusiastic response to the film were so powerful that the memory of it remained with him throughout his life.[10]

The film was also met with considerable critical acclaim. A journalist writing in the newspaper *The Stage* [Stsena] on 20 October 1908 declared that it marked 'the start of a new era' in the history of Russian film, and a reviewer writing in the same newspaper on 1 November 1908 recommended: 'Just watch *Stenka Razin*! It is still, of course, a far from perfect production, but even so the picture gives the viewer a very, very great deal.'[11] The reviewer for *The St Petersburg Cinema Herald* [Vestnik kinematografov v Sankt-Peterburge] lavished the greatest praise on the film, however:

> Among last week's new releases we would single out the film
> *Stenka Razin*. From the technical point of view it is excellently
> done. Mr Drankov has clearly achieved a perfect understanding
> of photography [...]. The view of the Volga and the flotilla of
> the brigands' boats is beautifully filmed; the scene in the forest
> is very interesting, as is the final moment [...].[12]

And yet, more recent responses to the film have been decidedly negative in their assessments of its artistic merit. This is typical of Soviet and
Western responses to the film and of responses written both before *Stenka
Razin* was screened at Pordenone in 1989 and subsequently. For example,
Eduard Arnoldi, writing on the fiftieth anniversary of the film's release,
summarises the numerous ways in which, in his view, the film-makers
demonstrate their lack of affinity for the new artistic medium: each of the
film's six sequences is filmed exclusively in long shot and set in the same
place of action; the film-makers rely on intertitles to convey meaning; the
film's sets and the acting are 'crude and primitive'; and because the actors
move too much and are positioned too far from the camera it is impossible to distinguish between them.[13] 'The film-makers proved themselves
to be vulgar profiteers', he concludes.[14] Leyda also sees the film primarily as a money-making venture, commenting that it proved 'a success in
every way known to our film industry today – it made money, and sent its
spectators away warm but empty.'[15] Writing on the film's eightieth anniversary, Andrei Chernyshev repeats Arnoldi's criticisms and pronounces
that this and, indeed, all other pre-Revolutionary Russian films prove that:
'Broadly speaking we are right when we call cinema an art born of revolution.'[16] Even Anoshchenko, who had retained such powerful memories
of seeing the film as a boy, concedes that when he showed the film to his
students at VGIK many years later he, like them, found it amusingly naïve
and clumsy.[17]

Throughout the 1990s, Western commentators rehearsed similarly
dismissive criticisms. For Peter Kenez it was 'not really a film, but a collection of tableaux [...] a clumsy product [in which] the modern viewer
can enjoy only pictures of the countryside, and perhaps be moved by
watching a significant moment in film history'.[18] Richard Stites describes
it as 'crudely acted by wildly gesticulating theater actors'.[19] Denise
Youngblood concedes that it tells 'a good enough story', but bemoans its

'simple retelling' of that story and its 'unimaginatively static camera'.[20] Most recently Alexander Prokhorov, while insisting he is not making negative value judgements, nevertheless implies that the film cannot be classed as 'art' when he cites it as the first example of the type of commercial lowbrow genre cinema that, in today's Russia, stands in opposition to quality art films.[21]

To be sure, some of these criticisms are not without justification. But, although *Stenka Razin* is unsophisticated by comparison even with Russian films made during the mid-1910s, it is not as crudely made as critics have suggested. On the contrary, this first Russian feature film deserves and repays consideration as a work of specifically cinematic art. Two recent commentators have acknowledged this, albeit to varying degrees. Neia Zorkaia, for example, has argued that the film's indubitable shortcomings are redeemed by its depiction of the natural setting, insisting that it has to be seen as an 'instructive' film in that it highlighted how well the new medium was able to capture the organic naturalness of the countryside and the 'tactile immediacy' of the physical world and the materials and textures that occur there.[22] It is this that leads her to conclude: 'The first film was thus also the first lesson in cinematic expressivity'.[23] Yuri Tsivian has demonstrated that many of the film's apparent errors in fact resulted not from the film-makers' incompetence or indifference to the new medium but, on the contrary, from Drankov's determination to learn, to develop his skill as a cinematographer and, specifically, to find ways in which to circumvent the numerous problems he had encountered while filming *Boris Godunov* in 1907.[24] This suggests that Drankov was not the hack many commentators have labelled him, but rather a striving, determined artist, who, together with a team of innovative collaborators, created in *Stenka Razin* a film that stands as a serious attempt to produce specifically cinematic art, as distinct from other art forms.

The Persian princess: the first female performer of Russian film

It is striking that the film-makers' attention to the specificities of the new artistic medium in which they were working is nowhere more obvious than in their representation of the film's only female protagonist, the Persian princess.

Hitherto overlooked by commentators, ignored in favour of the eponymous hero, this anonymous woman – the first heroine of Russian cinema and its first female performer – is a truly cinematic heroine in that her representation depends on and is executed by means of devices that are specifically filmic.

Moreover, despite the film's programmatic title it is the princess who stands at the centre of the film's thematic concerns. For this is not really a film about Razin, or at least not about Razin the historical figure.[25] The narrative does not focus on his heroic exploits and celebrated successes in battle. Instead, it relates his passion for the captured woman, which he celebrates with drink-fuelled revels, and which so infatuates him that he forgets his duty of leading the revolt. Angered by this, Razin's men plot against the princess, forging a letter that casts her as a traitor. Convinced of her infidelity and enraged by jealousy, Razin hurls the princess into the grey waters of the Volga where she is left to drown.

Evgeny Dobrenko's recent description of *Stenka Razin* as a 'historical *melodrama*' [emphasis added] is therefore more apposite.[26] For, in accordance with the demands of melodrama, *Stenka Razin* focuses on the protagonists' heightened emotions; in so doing it displays, albeit in embryonic form, the preference for psychology [*psikhologizm*] and emotions over action that, as Tsivian demonstrates, would become a distinctive characteristic of early Russian film melodramas in the 1910s.[27] Dobrenko's analysis of the film's genre is appropriate for another reason. As Louise McReynolds has noted, melodrama typically 'frames actions within contemporaneous social circumstances'.[28] Indeed, despite its veneer of history, this first Russian feature film is in fact extremely revealing about contemporary socio-psychological concerns, specifically the gender anxieties that unsettled early twentieth-century Russian society. One way of reading this film, therefore, is to see it as being about relationships between men and women, about the nature of gender roles and the state of gender relations in early twentieth-century Russia.

The objectified performer: 'blocking', visual pleasure and male fantasy

Details of plot emphasise from the outset that the status of the Persian princess within the diegesis of *Stenka Razin* is that of an object, a commodity; she is a spoil of war, captured during skirmishes with the Persians and held as the triumphant Razin's mistress. Her captor can therefore manhandle her, and as the film progresses Razin drags her from place to place with increasing violence, and forces her to do as he orders. The fact that the princess's name features neither in the film's title nor in its subtitle, both of which focus instead on the film's male protagonists, also serves to emphasise her insignificance. Moreover, as the alternative title of *From the Island to the Deep Stream* – the song on which Goncharov based the film's scenario – is *Stenka Razin and the Princess* [Sten´ka Razin i kniazhna], the exclusion of the princess from the film's titles appears to be deliberate.

The princess's insignificance is also suggested visually, however, both by the various ways in which the camera frames her and through the film-makers' careful use of 'blocking', that is the deliberate movement and placement of the protagonists within the frame. In the 1910s high-precision blocking would become, in the absence of a spoken text, a valuable tool of expressivity for early Russian film-makers and a key technique in their constant attempts to differentiate their new art form from the older art of the theatre. Film-makers soon realised that this device was far better suited to expressivity in film than in theatre: on a theatre stage the positioning of actors is also dictated by the need to ensure audibility but, as this is irrelevant on the silent screen, the positioning of characters within the frame is more flexible and can be used more meaningfully. Furthermore, in a cinema auditorium all spectators, regardless of where they are sitting in relation to the screen, share the same point of view, namely the single point of view of the camera, while, in a theatre, the view one has alters, depending on where one is sitting in relation to the stage. For these reasons, blocking was a fundamental part of early cinema's claim to originality and of early film-makers' search for cinematic specificity.[29]

Thus, in the film's opening sequence the film-makers use blocking to ensure that the princess is both excluded and marginalised by the camera. In the first moments of this sequence, entitled 'Stenka Razin's Revelry on the Volga', the frame is filled not by the characters whose revels we expect to witness, but by the river down which they are carousing. Moreover, as the boats gradually move towards the camera the princess remains marginalised by the composition of the frame: she appears, seated on the leader's right knee, only towards the end of the sequence and, furthermore, only at the extreme left-hand side of the frame. Indeed, at times she disappears from view completely, an effect created in part by the boat's motion on the water, but also by the cameraman's hesitant efforts to execute several horizontal panning shots.

By 1908 panning was already widely used in travelogue films and *actualités*, which both Drankov and Kozlovskii had worked on before turning to feature films. As Cavendish has noted, in early documentary films the panning shot was frequently used in order to emphasise the realism of the film's setting. Because such shots explore and reveal what lies beyond the edge of the frame, they ensure that 'the actors are no longer "imprisoned" by the frame' and show them to inhabit 'an "authentic" living space'.[30] Doubtless this was part of the film-makers' intention here, and they probably also sought to show off the size of their cast, which was so large that the actors could not all be easily held in the frame at any one time.[31] The contention that the panning shot is also intended further to marginalise the princess, if not to oust her from the frame completely, cannot be dismissed, however. It is only in the final, fleetingly held shot of the sequence that Razin and the princess are positioned both in the centre of the frame and relatively close to the camera. Moreover, the same visual/spatial marginalization is repeated at the start of the subsequent sequence, entitled 'Revelry in the Forest', when the princess is again positioned at the extreme left-hand edge of the frame on the very margins of the group of brigands.

Nevertheless, Tsivian argues that in both sequences this framing reveals not the film-makers' design, but the cameramen's inexperience; he sees the marginalization of the princess as an error, the result of Drankov and Kozlovskii's unfamiliarity with the Pathé camera they used for filming.[32] These cameras did not have a viewfinder, which made framing difficult, because the cameraman had no way of seeing the exact picture being filmed; as former still photographers, Drankov and Kozlovsii would have been more used to working with cameras that *did* enable one to see the image one was capturing. It may be that Tsivian overemphasises the camera operators' technical inexperience, however. After all, by the time he came to film *Stenka Razin* in the summer of 1908 Drankov had been using a Pathé camera for well over a year, both when photographing the Russian intertitles for the French films shown at a number of St Petersburg cinemas and when filming *Boris Godunov*.

Be that as it may, however, the contention that the marginalization of the Princess and her exclusion from the frame may not have been wholly intended does not in itself deprive either this positioning or this framing of significance or meaning. After all, 'bad framing' would only move the princess *more* out of shot than was originally planned; were the framing in those sequences 'better', she would still be positioned on the margins of the group composition. However, in his discussion of the forest sequence, Tsivian again argues that the film-makers arrived at this cinematically expressive means only by accident, suggesting that, as the director Romashkov is known to have worked in theatre before he made *Stenka Razin*, he may therefore have conceived these sequences in accordance with theatrical convention [*po-teatral´nomu*] since 'on the stage such a marginal position was not at variance with the protagonists' significance in the drama'.[33]

The theatrical origins of the film's subject cannot be denied. As Zorkaia has shown, there is much about it that reminds one of the traditional Russian folk play *The Boat* [Lodka], often described as an adaptation [*instsenirovka*] of the folk song *Down Along Mother Volga*.[34] However, *Stenka Razin* is not simply a piece of filmed folk theatre, as Zorkaia also stresses, describing it as 'a *cinematographic version*' [emphasis added] of *The Boat*.[35] Indeed, the way the forest sequence develops demonstrates the film's cinematographic nature. In this sequence Razin orders the princess to dance, and it is immediately striking that, as she prepares to perform, she moves both into the foreground and into the centre of the frame. Indeed, the film-makers emphasise this positioning by having some brigands step forward to spread a Persian rug on the ground, thereby creating a makeshift stage for her. The deliberateness of this action is arresting and there can be no doubt that here the princess's position is consciously controlled by the film-makers. Indeed, the apparently 'clumsy' framing of both the film's opening sequence and the opening shots of the forest sequence makes the careful framing of the dancing princess more striking.

This centralised, foregrounded positioning is expressive. On the one hand it serves to signal that, although the princess is a victim, she nevertheless also has considerable power and is highly significant in the film. For, in this respect, early cinematic conventions would diverge from theatrical conventions. Unlike on the early Russian stage, on the early Russian screen the main character is almost always positioned in the centre of the screen. This is a 'rule' formulated by Tsivian: 'On the silent screen [...] the main protagonist is the one who is in the centre and whose figure is most prominent.'[36] So, as Zorkaia notes: 'This can be considered a cinematographic "innovation" [*kinematograficheskaia novatsiia*]'.[37] Here the princess dominates the assembled men, the frame and the screen spatially, just as she dominates Razin's mind.

While Razin's obsession with the princess confers on her considerable power, its inevitable corollary is to weaken the ataman, and his weakness is, of course, also indicated spatially. In both of the film's early sequences Razin is also marginalised at the very edge of the frame, held, by his desire to be near the princess, away from the centre of the screen and the centre of the action, while this space is inhabited instead by the loyal men who represent the cause he has forsaken for his passion. Also significant is the fact that he alone remains marginalised during the entire forest sequence. He is positioned at the edge of the frame both during the princess's dance and after it, when her centre-frame position is taken over by a trio of Razin's men who together perform their own national dance and thereby emphasise both the princess's separateness and difference and the brigands' unity and solidarity.

However, while the princess's dance suggests both her importance in the diegesis and her power over Razin, it also serves, paradoxically, to reveal that her power is more apparent than genuine. In this connection, it is illuminating to apply to *Stenka Razin* Laura Mulvey's psychoanalytical analysis, proposed in 'Visual pleasure and narrative cinema', of the ways in which mainstream/classical cinema is structured according to the unconscious of patriarchal society, that is according to male fantasies of voyeurism and fetishism.[38]

In this article Mulvey elaborated the concept of the controlling 'male gaze' to express her conviction that in mainstream cinema the viewer, whether biologically male or female, is always encouraged to identify with the look of the film's male hero and therefore to see the heroine as a passive object of erotic desire. This is indeed what appears to happen when

20

the princess steps forward to dance. As she performs, in the centre and the foreground of the screen, the princess attracts the gaze not only of the male protagonists within the diegesis, who form an appreciative audience, but also of the viewers of the film. Moreover, her positioning encourages both them and us to observe her closely; she is on display, there to be looked at. In Mulvey's terminology, the princess is here framed by a scopophilic camera, according to which man is represented as spectator and woman as 'spectacle'. Mulvey used the term 'spectacle' to designate the subject/object relationship in which the (female) object of the look, whether the look of the camera or of protagonists within the film, is seen as being possessed, controlled and defined by the (male) subject or 'bearer' of the look. As Mulvey explains, Freud associated scopophilia with 'taking other people as objects', and saw it as an active source of pleasure.[39] In Mulvey's analysis, in this world, one that is 'ordered by sexual imbalance', pleasure in look-ing is split between 'active/male and passive/female', since 'the determining male gaze projects its phantasy on to the female figure which is styled ac-cordingly. In their traditional exhibitionist role women are simultaneously looked at and displayed, with their appearance coded for strong visual and erotic impact so that they can be said to connote *to-be-looked-at-ness* [em-phasis in original]'.[40]

It is not only the positioning of the actress that contributes to her rep-resentation as 'spectacle', however. Her costume also enhances her 'to-be-looked-at-ness'. For, what the viewer sees as the princess performs her national dance is a product of the male imagination: an image of woman as 'Other', structured according to a conventional and familiar male fan-tasy. Dressed in what to 'Western' eyes is a quintessentially 'Eastern' out-fit, consisting of loose trousers and flowing veils, all cut from the same diaphanous fabric, and with her long dark hair cascading down her back, the princess offers a tantalising vision of exotic femininity, who performs for the pleasure of men. She thus becomes an oriental cliché, a caricature of the typical oriental women, who in nineteenth-century Western artis-tic representations are, as Edward Said has shown, invariably linked with dance and, therefore, with 'unlimited sensuality' and who are 'usually the creatures of a male power-fantasy'.[41] As we shall see, like most Western con-ceptions of the Orient, the Persian princess therefore has 'less to do with the Orient than […] with "our" world'.[42]

The death of the dancer and the murderer's motives: homosociality and self-preservation

> To explore the subjection of women is also to explore the fraternity of men.
>
> Carol Pateman.[43]

In an illuminating article, Zorkaia explores how the motif of the Persian princess – or, more precisely, the motif of Razin's act of drowning the Persian princess – is treated in *lubok* versions, in folklore and in nineteenth- and early twentieth-century Russian literature, examining, among other ideas, how the representation of Razin's motives for killing the princess changes over time.[44] She concludes that from the mid-nineteenth century onwards each version of the princess's death always seeks to explain the murder by offering 'a psychological and often rather complex justification for Razin's brutal actions'.[45] What, then, do the film-makers suggest are the meaning of and the reasons for Razin's murder of the princess, and how do they communicate their interpretation of his motives to the viewer?

Zorkaia demonstrates that accounts of the legend produced during the first years of the twentieth century typically place an increased emphasis on its socio-political dimension, stressing Razin's status as the leader of a rebellion.[46] On the surface, Drankov's *Stenka Razin* appears to conform to this generalised tendency, for a socio-political reading does emerge from within its general historical/melodramatic framework. As befits a melodrama, a series of love triangles lies at the heart of the film's narrative. Unusually, however, the main triangles are not based around erotic rivalry; thus, one triangle brings into conflict Razin, the Persian princess and the Motherland in whose name Razin has always fought, symbolised by the river, the Mother-Volga. If the Persian princess represents Razin's personal pleasure and fulfilment, the Mother-Volga symbolises his self-sacrifice in the name of social duty. The conflict between these two feminine figures is made explicit in the film's final sequence, when an intertitle reproduces the speech he makes before throwing the princess into the river: 'Mother-Volga! You let me drink, you fed me, you rocked me to sleep on your waves. Accept my precious gift'. The Volga is also identified visually (that is, cinematically) as the most important figure in this triangle at the very start of the film, however: we recall

22

that the opening sequence begins with a lengthy long shot, in which the boats, positioned in the extreme background of the frame for the first twenty-five seconds or so of the ninety-five-second-long sequence, are barely visible on the vast expanse of the river. While commentators have repeatedly criticised the film for the 'clumsiness' of its 'overly-long' long shots, this perceived 'flaw' can be interpreted as a deliberate expressive device, especially when seen in the light of the precision blocking the film-makers employ in the subsequent sequences. For, by excluding the human protagonists from the frame almost entirely, the film-makers contrive to introduce and characterise the Volga and the Motherland it represents. Thus, the river overshadows the boats, dwarfing them and the people who sail in them and thereby stressing their comparative insignificance. Here, in other words, the river dominates the screen and, therefore, the viewer's attention in the same way, and for about the same length of time, that the princess will dominate the screen when she steps into the foreground to dance in the following sequence.

In order to arrive at this socio-political reading of the film, however, one has to overlook the details of what exactly prompts Razin to kill the princess. A reading that takes account of these important facts forces the viewer to focus on a different triangle, namely that between Razin, the princess and the brigands. Again, this triangle and the balance of power within it are given visual representation for, while Razin and the princess are invariably marginalised at the edge of the frame, the brigands tend to dominate it, both by their being positioned in the centre and/or foreground of the frame and by their sheer number: we recall how, in the forest sequence, the three brigands replace the princess on the oriental rug and perform their national dance. To be sure, in their association with Razin and in their concern that he is neglecting his duty while dallying with the princess, the brigands are also linked to the values of the Motherland. Their concern to wrest their leader from the clutches of this woman is, however, prompted too by their fear that her presence among them threatens to destroy their male solidarity. The ringleader's rousing speech emphasises that the brigands' plot is motivated not by their sense of social duty alone, but also by their strong personal feeling that they have been abandoned by their leader/father figure and that their place in his affections has been usurped by the princess.[47]

It is therefore inevitable that the power the princess's femininity/sexuality exercises over Razin also proves to be her undoing. By distracting the ataman from his role as the brigands' leader, the princess threatens the men's way of life. Seen in the early twentieth-century context of the film's making, an era of profound social change in Russia, their response is predictable, a reflection of the contemporary social fear that a powerful woman posed a threat to the increasingly unstable patriarchal order. It is in order to subdue the power of this 'enchantress' [*charovnitsa*] and to nullify the threat she poses that the brigands plot to engineer her death.

There is also a second anxiety at work in the film, however, and one on which the brigands play: Razin's private sexual fear that this beautiful woman might, through her infidelity, humiliate and emasculate him. Indeed, this dread exists in Razin even before he is shown the brigands' forged letter: the film's fourth tableau is introduced by the title 'Jealousy is awakened' and shows the ataman confronting the princess with suspicious questions about her feelings for him, the violence of his emotions already clear as he casts her to the ground. Thus, when Razin's men bring the princess's alleged crimes to light in their forged letter,[48] it is really, at an unconscious level, the problem of her femininity/sexuality that is being uncovered. For Mulvey, the female protagonist, even when cast as a passive spectacle, remains in essence a problematic, even dangerous figure:

> in psychoanalytic terms, the female figure poses a deeper problem. She also connotes something that the look continually circles around but disavows: her lack of a penis, implying a threat of castration and hence unpleasure. [...] Thus the woman as icon, displayed for the gaze and enjoyment of men, the active controllers of the look, always threatens to evoke the anxiety it originally signified.[49]

Mulvey identifies for the male unconscious 'two avenues of escape from this castration anxiety', that is to say, two ways in which the spectator can be assured of retaining a sense of pleasure throughout the film.[50] The first she terms 'sadistic voyeurism', whereby pleasure is assured through the narrative and the film's dénouement, which typically sees the male protagonist 'ascertaining guilt (immediately associated with castration), asserting control, and subjecting the guilty person through [*sic*] punishment or forgiveness'.[51]

24

In other words, pleasure 'depends on making something happen, forcing a change in another person, a battle of will and strength, victory/defeat'.[52] The second avenue, which she terms 'fetishistic scopophilia', ensures pleasure by turning the represented woman into a fetish so that she becomes 'reassuring rather than dangerous'; the physical object of beauty is built up so that it becomes 'something satisfying in itself'.[53] It is perhaps an indication of the depth of the anxiety that Russian men felt in the early twentieth century that the film-makers here prefer the first avenue of escape to the second.

It is also significant to the reading of the film as addressing contemporary gender issues that neither the brigands' murderous plot nor Razin's anxiety about the princess's infidelity features in the lyrics of the song *From the Island to the Deep Stream*. These psycho-sexual concerns were 'invented' by Goncharov for his scenario, and they are indeed very much issues of his time.[54] As Zorkaia has shown, while overt erotic overtones began to appear in depictions of the Persian princess's appearance and to be used to explain her power over Razin in the early 1890s, it was not until the start of the twentieth century that the erotic element of the plot came to the fore.[55] It is telling that the Russian poet Marina Tsvetaeva would, in her 1917 triptych of poems entitled 'Stenka Razin', similarly interpret Razin's murder of the Persian princess as being motivated by his desire for revenge for her lack of sexual interest in him. In the second poem of the triptych, Razin – casting himself as the princess's 'eternal slave' – asks her to lie closer to him, a request that the princess meets with indifference and a muttered sigh of longing for her oriental lover, Dzhal-Eddin.[56] As the following couplet makes clear, in Tsvetaeva's interpretation of the legend, Razin's decision to kill the princess is directly related to her spurning him:

> 'You couldn't get along with our bed,
> So get along, dog, with our baptism!'[57]

As Zorkaia puts it: 'Tsvetaeva adds the nuance that the ataman has some sort of male failing/lack: his vulnerability (his inferiority complex)'.[58] These nuances can also be discerned in Drankov's filmic version of the legend.

From fantasy figure to femme fatale:
the Persian princess and 'Salomania'

The Young Syrian: How beautiful is the Princess Salomé tonight!
The Page of Hérodias: You are always looking at her. You look
   at her too much. It is dangerous to look at people in such a
   fashion. Something terrible may happen.
The Young Syrian: She is very beautiful tonight.

Oscar Wilde, *Salomé*, 1893.[59]

Also significant is the fact that none of the earlier versions of the princess's fateful encounter with Razin, including the song on which the film's scenario was based, depicts her as a dancer; this role was invented for her by the film-makers. In having their oriental heroine dance for Razin's pleasure the film-makers contrive to add a further, more specific layer of 'myth' to their capacious female persona who, in dancing, evokes very precisely a second Eastern princess and one who was, moreover, very much in vogue in Russia in the first decade of the twentieth century: Salome, daughter of Herodias, who, legend has it, danced for the pleasure of one man and in so doing brought about the death of a second.

As has been widely documented, an unprecedented interest in the so-called Salome theme emerged in all forms of European art in about 1860, and it remained a central artistic concern, if not obsession, into the second decade of the twentieth century.[60] Each new artistic representation of Salome's story inspired another and these inter-connected works of art became so numerous that they are now conventionally treated together as a unitary 'cultural text' of that period. As commentators invariably note, it was primarily turn-of-the-century male artists who found the Salome theme so fascinating; they also agree that their interest in it can be explained by the myth's relevance to and resonance with both modish 'decadent obsessions: murder, incest, female sexuality and the mysterious Orient'[61] and contemporary socio-psychological fears about changing gender roles and gender relations. As Lawrence Kramer puts it:

> In general, the Salome craze, like the science and medicine of its
> day, sought to legitimise new forms of control by men over the
> bodies and behaviour of women. [...] As commonly understood
> in contemporary scholarship [Salome] stands, or rather dances,

as the extreme personification of patriarchal fears of female sexuality, fears so disruptive that they compulsively play themselves out in a scenario of fetishism and castration. [...] It seems clear enough that the Salome craze constituted an effort to normalise, by means of aesthetic pleasure, the epidemic male neurosis that coupled sexual potency with loathing and dread of women.[62]

Thus, Kramer concludes, Salome came to stand 'as a castrating femme fatale [...] as a monstrous sexual icon [and] as focal point for the representation of a bundle of instabilities produced by the fin-de-siècle gender system'.[63]

In early twentieth-century Russia, the work that arguably had the greatest impact on the resurgence and development of the Salome theme was Oscar Wilde's 1893 play *Salomé*. A cult of Wilde existed among Russian Symbolists and Decadents: in 1904 the poet Konstantin Balmont published his translation of Wilde's *Salomé* and by 1908 five further Russian translations of the play had been published.[64] Wilde's depiction of Salome was unlike any before it, and he added to her figure a number of new features which would be seized on and developed by later artists in their versions of this enticing female figure: first, the idea that it was Salome herself, rather than her mother, Herodias, who asked Herod to reward her dance with the head of John the Baptist; second, the suggestion that she did so because John – or Jokanaan as Wilde names him – had spurned her desire for him; third, the name, and implicitly, therefore, the nature of Salome's dance;[65] fourth, Wilde also added the detail of Salome's murder by Herod; finally, in the hieratic repetitions of the Page's prophetic warning to the Young Syrian that he should not look at Salome – cited at the head of this section – Wilde also emphasised the idea that the act of looking at a beautiful 'unveiled', overtly sexual woman is dangerous.[66]

Between April 1907 and November 1908 there were three attempts to stage Wilde's *Salomé* in the Russian capitals. In April 1907 Vladimir Nemirovich-Danchenko, the co-founder of the Moscow Art Theatre, had his application to stage the play rejected by the censor. In early October 1908, however, Nikolai Evreinov, the director of Vera Komissarzhevskaia's St Petersburg theatre company, known by his contemporaries as 'the Russian Oscar Wilde', received permission to begin rehearsing Wilde's play. Concurrently, a version of *Salomé* was being organised by Ida Rubinstein, a rich and ambitious young woman who would go on to make her name as a dancer with Sergei Diaghilev's *Ballets russes*.[67] Both these proposed productions were banned by the Russian Orthodox Church before they could be performed before the general public. Rubinstein did not abandon her desire to embody Salome on stage, however. On 3 November 1908, she performed a mimed version of the play before a private audience at the Mikhailovskii Theatre in St Petersburg.[68] She also transformed her 'Dance of the Seven Veils' or 'Dance of Salomé' into a stand-alone act, performing it at the St Petersburg Conservatoire on 20 December 1908.

Although Mikhail Fokin had originally choreographed Rubinstein's version of Salome's dance, when Rubinstein took her interpretation of it out of the context of Wilde's play and made it stand as a performance in its own right, she joined the ranks of a growing number of European and North American female dancers who had self-choreographed Salome dances in their repertoires. The first solo dancer to present a Salome piece was Loie Fuller in March 1895. This was not well received, however, and it was only after the premiere, in Dresden on 5 December 1905, of Richard Strauss's opera *Salome*, whose libretto was based on a German translation of Wilde's play, that 'Salomania' began in earnest.[69] In the following years, Salome found her way onto the stages of musical halls all over Europe and North America. The exotic dancer Ruth St Denis and the dancer-courtesans Mata Hari and La Belle Otéro all performed their own versions of it, and in November 1907 Fuller premiered a second Salome dance, entitled 'La Tragédie de Salomé'. It was the Canadian-born Maud Allan who made the Salome dance her own, however. A self-taught dancer who began performing in 1903, Allan made her debut as Salome at the Karlstheater in Vienna on 26 December 1906. This twenty-minute-long dance, entitled 'The Vision of Salome', brought Allan international fame and fortune. In 1906 she was immortalised in this role by the German Art Nouveau painter Franz von Stuck, who took her as his model for his painting *Salome*, and between 1906 and 1909 she took her dance around the world, from Paris, to Prague, Bucharest, Leipzig and, by the royal appointment of King Edward VII, to London and thence, in late 1909, to North America and Russia.

Why did so many early twentieth-century female performers embrace the figure of this classic femme fatale? Jane Marcus sees Salome's dance as the New Woman's art form, similar to the tarantella danced by Nora in

Henrik Ibsen's 1879 play *A Doll's House* [Et dukkehjem]; both heroines, she notes, 'are reluctant to perform their ritual obeisance to their masters, but in the end, choose the degrading act rather than find no means at all of self expression.'[70] Toni Bentley suggests that for early twentieth-century women this dance represented an unprecedented form of liberation:

> The great paradox of the veil – that which conceals yet invites revelation – is crucial to the meaning of Salome's dance. [...] Wilde's Salome unveil[s] herself, in a defiant act of will, controlled not by others but by her own hand. It is in her dance that the veils of concealment – of chastity, of marriage, of mourning, of sex, of the harem – are discarded. Salome has broken through the male-imposed laws that attempt to hide the female object of desire. She is autonomous and her dance is a profound tear in these veils of concealment.[71]

Moreover, although Wilde gave Salome's dance a name, he did not describe or prescribe the details of that dance; the stage direction introducing it states simply: 'Salomé dances the dance of the seven veils'.[72] The precise nature of the dance was, therefore, left to the performer, who was free to improvise. It was doubtless this freedom of interpretation that made the figure of Salome and her dance so popular. Indeed, it is striking that while the costumes worn by these early twentieth-century Salome dancers were all remarkably similar, their performed interpretations of the Salome story were all very different.[73] Thus, Salome made it possible for female performers to author their own dances, and her story provided them with the perfect vehicle through which to explore tensions that arose from such contentious contemporary issues as female autonomy, female power, female sexuality and female desire. Embodying the figure of Salome on stage therefore came to stand as a powerful statement both of these women's awareness of their power and of their defiance of a patriarchal model of society that sought to deny them the right to exercise that power. In other words, the Salome craze enabled early twentieth-century women to dramatise for themselves, and for their audiences, their desire for various kinds of emancipation.[74]

It is unlikely that Drankov and his fellow film-makers were unaware of these female performers and of the Salome craze. Indeed, Arnoldi might be thought to allude to a connection between their Persian princess and the Salome dancer when he notes that in *Stenka Razin* 'the princess dances "the Persian national dance" (in the manner of a nightclub act!)'.[75] However, as Arnoldi's intention is to disparage, he does not develop this observation. Whether or not Drankov and his team of film-makers were directly influenced by these real-life Salome dancers, however, this was the cultural backdrop against which their Salome-esque Persian princess made her appearance on the Russian screen and, willy-nilly, all the richly allusive associations of both the Salome archetype and the early twentieth-century Salome dancer therefore attach to her figure. It is little wonder, therefore, that the Persian princess, like Wilde's Salome before her, had to die.

Ultimately, then, in *Stenka Razin* all's well that ends well. The homosocial bonds that bind Razin to his comrades prove more deep-rooted than his ephemeral erotic desire for the Persian princess. In the film's final sequence, the great leader therefore rids himself of his female impediment choosing homosocial solidarity – an important defining feature of patriarchy – over erotic love.[76] In so doing, he also eliminates the threat that this beautiful and overtly sexual woman poses to his own insecure sense of self. Thus, as the princess disappears under the grey waters of the Volga, the patriarchal status quo is restored and Razin's male potency also remains intact. Through Razin's voyeuristic and sadistic control over the princess, our hero reaffirms both his own mastery and, by proxy, that of the (implied male) spectator. As we would expect, the film-makers signal both these facts by having Razin finally occupy his rightful place in the (approximate) centre and the (relative) foreground of the frame throughout the film's final sequence. It is also telling that a contemporary publicity poster for the film emphasised this triumphant final sequence over all others.[77]

The spectator's response: triumph, or tragedy?

There is perhaps little reason to doubt that contemporary audiences would have responded to the princess's death with cheers rather than tears – indeed, it is easy to imagine the spectators' delight at her demise, for everything about the film's ending conveys a sense of triumphalism: danger has been averted, order has vanquished chaos, Russian citizens have defeated a foreign interloper, male pride and male solidarity have been restored. However, if – to reverse Carol Pateman's eloquent observation, cited at the head of an earlier section in this chapter – to explore the fraternity of men is also to explore the subjection of women, the question inevitably arises of whether different spectators might have responded to the film's ending in different ways; specifically, how might the contemporary *female* spectator have responded to the film's dénouement? Would the actual woman in the audience have seen the princess's death as a triumph, or as a tragedy? Would she, like the male members of the audience, have identified with the male ego ideal of Razin and, therefore, have applauded the death of the princess along with both the film's male protagonists and, we can assume, its male spectators? Or would the film's ending have left her feeling alienated, perhaps, even, threatened?

While these questions are, of course, impossible to answer definitively with fact, a theorised answer can be suggested, again by drawing on Mulvey's analysis of the ways in which mainstream cinema works. One of the most frequent of the numerous challenges levelled at Mulvey's theory of the 'male gaze' has been that it ignores the experience of the female spectator.[78] In 1981, Mulvey therefore addressed these objections.[79] Drawing again on Freud's thinking – this time his ideas about the existence of a pre-Oedipal 'phallic phase' in girls (associated with activity), which is later repressed when they develop their 'femininity' – Mulvey argued that the female spectator *is* able to identify with the male position, and indeed actively enjoys having the opportunity to do so. As Freud noted, during many women's lives there are frequent regressions to this phallic phase, leading their behaviour to alternate between 'passive' femininity and regressive masculinity. Mulvey argues that the female spectator can therefore temporarily accept 'masculinisation' – that is, identify with the active masculine position – in memory of her active phase. In Mulvey's analysis, therefore, the effect of the objectification of the Persian princess would be to force the female spectator to become temporarily masculinised and, thus, to identify with the male ego ideal of Razin.[80]

We can therefore conclude of Drankov's *Stenka Razin* what Mulvey concluded of classic Hollywood films of the 1930s, 40s and 50s and argue that the 'magic' of this first Russian feature film arises in large part 'from its skilled and satisfying manipulation of visual pleasure' and from 'the way in which it codes the erotic into the language of the dominant patriarchal order'.[81] The male narrative perspective is privileged in this film and the female perspective is ignored, or at least supressed. The film-makers' representation of their female protagonist can therefore be said to reflect the unconscious of the dominant patriarchal order of early twentieth-century Russia. They do not seek to challenge either traditional images of femininity or traditional gender roles. In *Stenka Razin* the power that the Salome-esque Persian princess gains while dancing proves to be no more than the power of a beautiful object to entrance and captivate. It does not confer on her any agency or control over her fate. Thus, like innumerable Salomes and Persian princesses before her, she – the first female performer of Russian film – remains 'a creature of legend [...], serving men's ideas, desires, and fears about the erotic woman'.[82]

2

The Peasant Girl and the Boyar's Ward

Like *Stenka Razin*, many of the earliest Russian feature films had rural settings and, accordingly, their protagonists were frequently cast as peasants, with the figure of the beautiful young peasant girl often standing at the centre of the film. In the years that followed 1908, Drankov's film would provide the template for the way in which the peasant girl was represented, for, as in this earlier film, the peasant girl's allure is invariably communicated by having her dance. Called upon to provide amateur dance performances for an audience made up mostly, if not solely, of male spectators, the peasant girl is, like the Persian princess before her, repeatedly cast as a natural performer. Moreover, these performances are without fail used in the same way as in *Stenka Razin*: to represent these women, who are usually from a lower social class than the men who watch them dance, as accessible objects of both scopophilic and sexual desire. Thus, Vasilii Goncharov's *Vanka the Steward* [Van'ka-kliuchnik, 1909] features a group of dancing peasant girls and maids who do not appear in the text of the folk song on which the film's scenario is based and whose sole function in the film is to enable the film-makers to highlight the lasciviousness of the old prince and his drunken nobleman friend: in two of the film's four tableaux these men are shown delighting in the young women's dancing to the extent that they find it difficult to refrain from touching them. Similarly, in *The Dashing*

Merchant [Ukhar´-kupets, 1909], variously attributed to Goncharov, Kai Hansen, Maurice Gache [Moris Gash] and Mikhail Novikov, the eponymous merchant is so struck by the beauty of a young peasant girl whom he happens to see dancing that he persuades her drunken father to sell her to him.

For all these similarities, however, there are also some important differences between these films and *Stenka Razin*, not least as regards the film-makers' stance in relation to their protagonist. In *Stenka Razin* the film-makers identified unequivocally with the male narrative perspective and the male gaze, and, by various means, they encouraged their viewers to do likewise. In both *Vanka the Steward* and *The Dashing Merchant*, however, the male protagonists are uniformly represented in negative terms, as loathsome sexual predators. That is not to suggest that these films explore or even put forward the female narrative perspective, however. For, while the women who dance in these films are shown to be victims of the patriarchal assumptions of their male counterparts, they remain throughout little more than convenient devices, exploited as a means of characterising the male protagonists by the film-makers, who appear to have no interest either in representing events from their point of view or in exploring their psychology.

Moreover, other early Russian films continued to use the trope of dancing to represent their female protagonist as a dangerous femme fatale who poses a grave threat to the well-being of any man foolish enough to become involved with her. Consider, for example, Goncharov's *The Water Nymph* [Rusalka, 1910]. Based on Pushkin's 1829–32 drama of the same title, which itself drew on motifs from a traditional Russian fairy tale, *The Water Nymph* tells the story of a peasant girl who is seduced by a prince. Eventually tiring of the affair and seeking to marry a woman from his own class, the prince attempts to pay off his lover and her father, a poor miller, with expensive jewels. The devastated girl refuses to be either placated or consoled, however, and throws herself into the river, where she drowns. She returns as a ghost almost immediately, however, and haunts the prince relentlessly, appearing both at his wedding feast and in his bedchamber on his wedding night. Eight years pass, but the prince proves unable to forget the peasant girl; driven to distraction by her vengeful and unforgiving spectre, he finds himself drawn to the mill where she had lived. There he encounters first her father, reduced to madness by his daughter's untimely death, and then the young girl herself. Dressed in flowing robes and with flowers in her hair, she has become a water nymph. She and her fellow nymphs dance before the prince and thereby succeed in enticing him to follow them into the water. The film's extraordinary final sequence shows the prince lying dead on the riverbed, forever reunited with his triumphant peasant lover, who (watched by a group of approving *rusalki*) caresses his hair tenderly.[1]

Other films from this period would offer a more balanced and nuanced view of the performing girl, however, among them Petr Chardynin's *Vadim* [1910].

Olga: dancing and desire

> Do you like dance?… Well, I have a little girl – she's a marvel… and how she dances!… She burns, she doesn't dance!… I am no monk, and nor are you, Vasilich…
> Mikhail Lermontov, 'Vadim', 1832–34.[2]

> Olga entertains the drunken guest with her dancing.
> Intertitle from the restored version of Chardynin's *Vadim*.

As we saw in Chapter 1, the male tendency to treat the female dancer as a passive object of scopophilic pleasure, fantasy and desire was expressed cinematically in the first Russian feature film, *Stenka Razin*. The power of the Persian princess's dance sequence, and especially the significance and effectiveness of the expressive cinematic device of blocking that was discerned, if not consciously adopted, by Drankov and his fellow film-makers, are suggested by a brief sequence that appears in a film made two years after *Stenka Razin*, namely Petr Chardynin's *Vadim*, which was made at the Khanzhonkov production studio, where Goncharov – author of the scenario on which Drankov had based *Stenka Razin* – was by this time working.

Like Mikhail Lermontov's 1832–34 story of the same title, on which the film's scenario was based, Chardynin's film focuses on the attempts of the eponymous hero to secure vengeance on behalf of his father, a minor member of the landed gentry who, many years earlier, had been ruined by the more powerful boyar Palitsyn, a fact that subsequently led to his death.

In order to escape punishment for his actions Palitsyn had undertaken to act as the guardian of Vadim's three-year-old sister, Olga, who, as she grows into a young woman, remains unaware that it was Palitsyn who killed her father.

It is at this point that the film's action begins. As a contemporary reviewer writing in the journal *Cine-Phono* [Sine-fono] in 1910 put it: 'Years pass; the young Olga grows into a real beauty, and Palitsyn, already now in his declining years, is secretly preparing her for shameful pleasures.'[3] As this film has survived without intertitles, it is impossible to know whether this intention was communicated to the viewer verbally, via an intertitle, or not. What is clear, however, is the fact that such an intertitle, had it existed, would have been superfluous, for Palitsyn's nefarious intentions towards Olga are communicated visually in a striking sequence that occurs near the start of the film when Olga, like Drankov's Persian princess before her, is also cast in the role of reluctant performer for a group of drunken men. As Palitsyn sits drinking with a friend, he sends his wife to summon Olga to dance. In the next sequence, which takes place in Olga's bedroom, the boyar's wife roughly rouses Olga from her bed and orders her to change and prepare to perform. This is clearly a regular occurrence in Palitsyn's household. As Olga begins reluctantly to dress, the camera cuts back to the drawing room, where Palitsyn and his guest are still drinking. As his wife ushers a group of musicians into the room, Olga enters from the left-hand side of the frame. She bows towards Palitsyn and his guest and then begins to dance, moving, as she does so, from the edge of the frame to the centre, where she too performs on a carpet 'stage'.[4]

The viewer, like the men, is again placed in the position of voyeur, while the young female protagonist provides the 'spectacle'. Both men are clearly entranced by the girl and, as Olga dances, Palitsyn's guest can restrain himself no longer: he leaves his seat, moves towards Olga and attempts brutally to kiss her. It is significant that this detail does not feature in Lermontov's original story, in which Olga is required to tolerate only the men's 'drunken eyes, which audaciously explore her charms',[5] but was added by Chardynin. When Olga pushes him away and runs, distraught, to her room, the wife's only thought is to apologise to the guest. Palitsyn, however, similarly aroused by her performance, follows Olga to her room and attempts in his turn to force himself on the young woman. His embraces are interrupted only when his wife enters and surprises him; shaking her fist at Olga, whom she clearly holds responsible for her husband's behaviour, she marches Palitsyn from the room. As Chardynin's film progresses, Olga proves to be more fortunate than the Persian princess, however. She finds happiness in love with a man her own age, Palitsyn's son Iurii, and the film ends, unusually, with the young couple preparing to live happily ever after.[6]

While the very different fates that await Drankov's Persian princess and Chardynin's Olga undoubtedly suggest a shift towards the adoption of the female narrative perspective, which (according to Miriam Hansen) differentiates early Russian film from the early cinemas of other countries,[7] more relevant to the present discussion is the fact that Chardynin here employs the same cinematic strategies that Drankov and his collaborators had used in *Stenka Razin* and for exactly the same reasons: to focus the viewer's attention on his young female protagonist, to characterise her as an object of (male) desire and to reveal both the power she holds over the male protagonists and her concomitant paradoxical vulnerability.

Furthermore, it is not inconceivable that Chardynin's construction of this sequence was inspired by the dance sequence in the earlier *Stenka Razin*. Chardynin's connection with the Russian film industry began in 1908 when he joined Khanzhonkov's studio in Moscow as an actor. He started working as a director for Khanzhonkov in 1909 and remained there until he joined Dmitrii Kharitonov's rival production company early in 1916. As his career progressed, Chardynin would acquire the reputation of being a prolific creator of films that were invariably hugely popular with audiences. He did not, however, ever attain the artistic recognition that other early directors, such as Evgenii Bauer and Iakov Protazanov, enjoyed. Indeed, it is perhaps no exaggeration to say that, whereas Bauer was considered the supreme innovator of early Russian film, Chardynin was viewed as its supreme imitator. In his memoirs, Khanzhonkov refers to him, perhaps unfairly, as being 'without invention',[8] while, in their reviews of his films, contemporary critics repeatedly commented – not always negatively, it must be said – on his tendency to recycle from film to film, and with only the most minor alterations, formulae, be they themes, character types, settings, plot situations or even costumes, that had proved popular or successful in earlier films, both his own and those of other directors. It cannot be denied that the sequence in which Chardynin's Olga dances bears a striking resemblance to the Persian princess's performance in *Stenka Razin*. Indeed, there is only one significant difference between the two sequences: while the latter is set outdoors, Chardynin has Olga dance indoors. As Chardynin's successful and almost ubiquitous use of outdoor locations in *Vadim* was noted by most contemporary reviewers,[9] the indoor location makes the dance sequence stand out as different from the rest of the film. By situating Olga's performance indoors Chardynin adds a stylised or 'staged' feel to it, reinforcing the sense of its being, by 1910, a recognised cinematic 'set piece'. This perhaps also explains why contemporary commentators uniformly omitted to highlight it in their descriptions of the film's merits: in the early years of the Russian film industry, reviewers tended to concentrate on what was felt to be new or innovative in the film under consideration. Ultimately, then, Chardynin's ostensible borrowing of many of the details of the sequence in which Drankov's Persian princess danced is perhaps the clearest indicator of all that the makers of the first Russian feature film deserve to be considered cinematic artists and that their female protagonist, the Persian princess, can lay claim to be not only the first dancer of Russian film, but also its first truly cinematic heroine.

Lusha: dancing, incest and suicide

The figure of the dancing peasant girl reappeared two years later in an extraordinary film that deserves to be better known.[10] As its eloquent title suggests, *The Incestuous Father-in-Law* [Snokhach, 1912] tells a shocking story. Lusha, a young peasant woman, is married to Ivan, an ineffectual drunkard (played by the future 'King' of the Screen, Ivan Mozzhukhin[11]). Lusha's life takes a turn for the worse when her beauty attracts the amorous attentions of her father-in-law. As is to be expected, all Lusha's vigorous attempts at resistance prove futile: as Ivan lies beside her in a drunken stupor, her father-in-law rapes her in the field she has been ploughing.[12] Rumours circulate, villagers gossip, Lusha's mother-in-law advises her to save her soul through prayer. Ivan does nothing and the patriarch continues to pursue Lusha. Summoned by him to a night-time assignation, Lusha hangs herself, thereby driving her father-in-law to madness.

Numerous facts about the making of *The Incestuous Father-in-Law* remain unverified: the director is unknown and the film is variously attributed to Aleksandr Ivanov-Gai and/or Petr Chardynin; commentators disagree about the identity of some of the actors, and the cameraman, Aleksandr Ryllo, remains an obscure figure. Yet this film displays an almost precocious cinematic sophistication. As Denise Youngblood has observed, this film (to which she refers by the title *The Daughter-in Law's Lover*):

> is among the first signs we have of the 'paradigm shift' in Russian cinema – from a filmed *tableau* or 'attraction' to a movie that is a *movie*, consistently articulated in a cinematic idiom.
>
> [It] is not a rudimentary filmed play, but a story that can be told much more effectively on the screen than on the stage. Its themes of violent sex, incest, death are integrated not just through what is *shown* on the screen, but also by how these scenes are cut and edited [emphasis in original].[13]

Moreover, many of the specifically cinematic expressive devices discerned in relatively crude form in Romashkov's *Stenka Razin* also occur in this later film. Specifically, the use of blocking, the exploitation of natural, outdoor settings and the use of different types of shot and of camera movement are all refined and developed in this film in ways not evidenced in other films made either before or during 1912. As we shall see, the film-makers' treatment of both the female and the male protagonists and of the theme of relations between them is also more complex than in earlier films.

Blocking

If the father-in-law first becomes aware of his attraction to Lusha while watching her at work in the fields one day, it is, predictably, not until he sees her dance that his desire becomes overwhelming. The dance sequence is one of the most innovative, powerful and precisely constructed sequences in the film, but the debt it owes to Drankov's staging of the princess's dance in *Stenka Razin* is also clear.

Their work over for the day, the villagers are in the mood for entertainment. Arranged in a semi-circle that leaves a discreet stage-like space in front of them, they call insistently on Lusha to dance. Although she thrice invites her husband to partner her, Ivan refuses each request, moving away from his wife to the extreme left-hand side of the group composition and the frame, thereby leaving Lusha to take centre stage on her own. As she moves into the foreground she, like so many female dancers before her, automatically becomes the focus of everybody's attention, protagonists and viewers alike. Lusha dances with such vitality and energy that the viewer, as engrossed in her performance as are the peasants, does not notice that her father-in-law is in the audience; although he is standing in the very middle of the watching crowd, he is often obscured from view by the dancing girl. The viewer is therefore surprised when he suddenly stands, moves to the front of the frame and, shedding his hat and jacket, prepares to do what Lusha's ineffectual husband had refused to do and accompany Lusha in her dance.

Exhilarated by their performance, the father-in-law cannot restrain himself from succumbing to his desire for the young woman: he seizes his daughter-in-law round the waist and, lifting her off the ground, kisses her full on the lips, knocking off her headscarf, that traditional symbol of a peasant woman's married state,[14] in the process. Lusha, although unable to react for a moment, is horrified and clutches her head in her hands. Ivan looks on dumbly, barely registering a reaction. There is a momentary lull in the dancing, but the musicians do not break beat and then another peasant woman takes to the floor, attracting the attention of the villagers. That of the viewer, however, is fixed on the film's three central protagonists and the drama that is beginning to unfold between them. Unlike the other villagers, Ivan, his father and Lusha all remain motionless, as if petrified by both the horror and the import of what has just occurred.

The father-in-law's stolen kiss obviously prefigures his subsequent rape of his daughter-in-law. His imminent usurpation of his son's position is also indicated more subtly, however, through the very precise positioning of the three key protagonists in the frame at this point: Ivan and his father are both standing on the extreme left-hand side of the screen, with Ivan in the background and a couple of steps further into the middle of frame than the father, who is closer to the front of the frame, but on its extreme left-hand side. Lusha, meanwhile, is standing in the foreground, on the extreme right-hand side; she is on a diagonal line from Ivan, her increasingly estranged husband, but directly opposite her father-in-law. In this way, the nascent triangular relationship between father-in-law, daughter-in-law and son/husband is given visual representation within the frame and on the screen.

Moreover, as Lusha and her father-in-law are positioned on the same level and in the foreground of the frame, the film-makers also contrive to indicate that it is they who constitute the new 'couple'. This is further emphasised when the protagonists then move in a way that, although subtle, is nevertheless carefully planned and deliberately intended by the film-makers. Ivan takes a slow step towards his wife, but then he pauses; he looks across at his father and, surprisingly, takes a slow step backwards, away from Lusha. Pulling on his hat, he looks down at the ground and turns away from his wife. As Ivan retreats in this way, his father takes one very deliberate step towards Lusha, blocking Ivan from the viewer's line of sight as he does so. In this way the director indicates that, as the father here asserts his presence over Ivan's both visually and spatially, so he will soon assert his power over his wife's body. Lusha, doubtless aware that she can hope for nothing good from either of these men, looks away from them both, down at the ground, anxiously touching and tidying her exposed and loosened hair.

This all takes only a few seconds and at the same time the dancing continues, but the film-makers succeed in conveying an enormous amount to the viewer simply by means of the way in which they position the actors within the frame and choreograph their movements and gestures both within the frame and in relation to each other. The complicated, high precision blocking employed here by the makers of *The Incestuous Father-in-Law* attains a level of sophistication rarely met in films from 1912, but it also clearly develops from the early use of this technique in *Stenka Razin*.

Privileging the female narrative perspective: natural settings and the mobile camera

In other ways, however, *The Incestuous Father-in-Law* is very different from *Stenka Razin*. The thoughtful, exploratory way in which this later film represents its central protagonists contrasts sharply with the schematic characterisation in *Stenka Razin*, and it also differs in its narrative perspective, at least in its earliest sequences. Whereas in the earlier film the viewer was encouraged to identify with Razin and to see the Persian princess through his eyes and those of his fellow brigands, in *The Incestuous Father-in-Law* the film-makers continue to develop that tendency of Russian film from the 1910s, observed also in Chardynin's *Vadim*, of shifting towards privileging the narrative perspective of the victimised female protagonist. Thus, throughout much of *The Incestuous Father-in-Law*, the film-makers strive to encourage the viewer to identify with Lusha and to sympathise with her helpless plight.

One of the key methods that the film-makers employ in this aim is a sustained exploitation of the expressive potential of the film's natural settings, and especially of natural light and shade, for in this thirty-minute-long film only one sequence is set indoors. Indeed, their treatment of nature and the elements (most notably, wind) in their telling of Lusha's terrible tale is almost Tarkovskian. Thus, for all the breath-taking beauty and depth of some of the landscape shots, in this film nature is never merely an attractive backdrop. Instead it functions variously to establish mood and atmosphere, to mirror the protagonists' states of mind and to foreshadow their ultimate fates.

It is significant that Lusha is the protagonist whose perspective on and position in the world is most often conveyed through natural imagery. Also striking is the fact that the visual and, therefore, the affective characteristics of the natural world through which Lusha moves change dramatically as the film progresses. In the film's early sequences, Lusha is framed by a nature that is shown to be fecund, luxuriant and beneficent. Thus, she and her husband lie in a beautiful meadow, cushioned by long grass and wild flowers. Later, as she goes about her daily tasks, bare-legged and bare-footed, far from appearing oppressed by her labours, she exudes strength, energy and vitality. She also takes a sensual pleasure in her surroundings, stretching luxuriously as she enjoys the warmth of the sun on her bare limbs. After the dance sequence and the father-in-law's stolen kiss, however, the natural world that surrounds Lusha gradually undergoes a transformation, as does her relationship with it. The balmy sunshine disappears, replaced by a relentless wind, and the natural surroundings themselves are also increasingly represented as hostile and harsh: the soft grass of the film's early sequences is, for example, replaced by the parched furrows of fields that appear so barren that the viewer doubts they will ever yield a harvest despite all Lusha's efforts with the plough.

Similarly, during Lusha's post-rape journey to a soothsayer, the hopelessness of her situation, her powerlessness and her distraught emotional state are all evoked by the landscapes through which she moves and by the way they are photographed. Deep in shade, Lusha struggles to steer a boat along a river flanked with dense trees and bushes. Although the current does not appear strong, the boat repeatedly drifts in the opposite direction from that in which Lusha seeks to guide it. Eventually, however, she succeeds in mooring the boat. Then, as she steps from it onto the overgrown riverbank, something extraordinary happens: the camera begins to move, panning slowly from left to right, following her progress. The riverbank is steep, and as Lusha climbs she moves out of the frame. Escape is impossible, however. A quick editing cut, and the camera is lying in wait for her at the top of the slope. This combination of cinematic devices is repeated twice in quick succession, creating almost unendurable tension. Although it seems, at times, that Lusha might escape the camera's gaze, ultimately she cannot; in this way, the camera ceases to be a passive observer of events, becoming an antagonist, a sinister double of the implacable, predatory father-in-law.

The camera continues to track Lusha as she toils towards the deserted mill that is home to the soothsayer, struggling through an almost surreal landscape of steep inclines strewn with oversized rocks and boulders, dead trees, derelict buildings and other obstacles. In this and other sequences that occur after Lusha's fateful dance, the young woman is shown to be oppressed by a hostile and malevolent natural environment that stands as a vivid symbol of the social and cultural customs that enslave her; as Hansen puts it, in these post-dance sequences, Lusha is 'dwarfed by the conspiracy between the world of things (the parched furrows, the relentless wind, the huge rocks and rubble on the way to the mill) and the social conditions of partriarchy'.[15] It is impossible for the viewer not to look upon her with both pity and foreboding.

Lusha: from victim to author of her own fate

It is made obvious cinematically, in the ways described above, that no matter how fervently the viewer might will Lusha to escape, she cannot; on her return to the village, her father-in-law continues to pursue her and she is unable to resist his advances. As Youngblood puts it: 'By raping his son's wife, the father [...] is "only" taking what is his according to village custom'.[16] For this was, apparently, the reality facing many young peasant women at this time. In his 1879 work *A History of the Russian Woman* [Istoriia russkoi zhenshchiny], the historian S. Shashkov stressed, in his evaluation of the mechanics of *snokhachestvo*, the daughter-in-law's complete powerlessness to refuse her father-in-law's attentions. As Henrietta Mondry, summarising Shashkov, puts it:

> the entire family of in-laws, including the woman's own husband, put pressure on the young daughter-in-law to enter into sexual relationships with the father-in-law as an act of submission to the despotic demands of the patriarch of the peasant family. Such is the fear of the patriarch by his household that a young woman refusing to become a *snokhachka* is tyrannized and humiliated by the rest of the family.[17]

Lusha is, however, so determined to resist that she devises a way out of her situation, resorting to what Heide Schlüpmann terms 'the ultimate refusal', namely suicide.[18] In this resolutely unsentimental film, the suicide sequence is nonetheless intended to shock. It begins when Lusha, dressed in a simple white nightgown and with her long hair flowing loose, leaves the family's hut in the stillness of a misty night. The viewer knows she is on her way to meet her father-in-law, for in the previous sequence he had ordered her to do so, dismissing her entreaties that he leave her alone as nonsense. Moreover, as Lusha sets off her mother-in-law suddenly appears at the door and addresses her angrily: 'I know, you debauched woman, who you are going to meet...' Lusha looks at her sorrowfully and with regret, but says nothing and sets off into the mist with a determined gait. The film-makers then cut to show the father-in-law as he furtively approaches the storehouse he had designated as their meeting place. As he nears the door, he looks repeatedly over his shoulder, checking that nobody is watching him, and he is still looking over his shoulder as he makes to open the door. An editing cut suddenly reverses the viewer's perspective: we are now inside the hut, looking at the other side of the door that we know the father-in-law is about to open.

At this point there is minimal lighting and the inside of the hut is effectively in complete darkness; the viewer can see only the few thin shafts of light that are filtering in through the ill-fitting door. As the father-in-law opens the door, however, light floods into the hut and the viewer realises that it is not empty: Lusha is hanging dead from the ceiling. The viewer sees the young woman's body before the *snokhach* does, as he is still looking over his shoulder as he enters the hut.[19] He therefore bumps into her limp corpse. Realising immediately what his daughter-in-law has done, the *snokhach* runs from the hut in horror. The viewer is not granted such immediate escape, however, for the camera holds its view of Lusha's dead body, which is visible only from the waist down, for seven seconds, thereby forcing the viewer to contemplate and reflect on her fate. Moreover, it is significant that the sight that confronts the viewer is not the stuff of scopophilic pleasure on which s/he might feel inclined to let his/her gaze linger, but rather the ugly reality of Lusha's death, for the film-makers refuse to aestheticise either her dead body or her dank surroundings. Indeed, the dark storehouse in which she hangs stands as a powerful symbol not only of the grave that awaits her, but also of the oppressive, life-denying social situation in which this vibrant young woman had been constrained and stifled.

However, as Schlüpmann's description of Lusha's suicide suggests, Lusha's act cannot be seen as a passive acceptance of defeat. Instead it is represented by the film-makers, understood by the other protagonists and intended by Lusha as both an act of defiance and an attempt at communication. Throughout the film we watch Lusha as she struggles to defy her father-in-law's will and escape his attentions, and we also see her attempt, on numerous occasions and always without success, to communicate with her relatives – with Ivan, with her mother-in-law and with her father-in-law himself – to enlist their support for her resistance of the patriarch and to persuade them of the wrongness of what he is forcing her to do. Paradoxically, Lusha's suicide enables her to accomplish what she could not while alive and to succeed in both these aims. For, as Elisabeth Bronfen has argued persuasively, in those narratives, cultures and societies that connect femininity inextricably with the body and with objectification, it is the feminine body itself that enslaves women.[20] This is the case in the world represented in *The Incestuous Father-in-Law*, where Lusha's sufferings are shown to be caused by such apparently inalterable facts as her gender, the physical beauty of her body and the social and cultural assumptions of the time and the place into which she was born. The only way in which she can make herself the subject of her life is, therefore, to 'deny' or 'eradicate' her body in suicide.[21] In this way, Lusha's moment of self-destruction becomes, paradoxically, an act of self-construction and self-affirmation. As Bronfen puts it:

> The choice of death emerges as a feminine strategy within which writing with the body is a way of getting rid of the oppression connected with the feminine body. Staging disembodiment as a form of escaping personal and social constraints serves to criticize those cultural attitudes that reduce the feminine body to the position of dependency and passivity, to the vulnerable object of sexual incursions.[22]

In hanging herself, then, Lusha, by her own hand, transforms her body from a source of pleasure into an object of terror. She denies the *snokhach* what he demands as his right, namely her body, and in this way challenges not only his patriarchal assumptions about the nature and role of women, but also his patriarchal authority and, indeed, his very sense of self.

The 'full scene' and the *snokhach*: from victimiser to victim

Lusha's suicide is, therefore, a powerful and eloquent act. It reveals her to be a strong, determined young woman who is not content to submit passively to the entrenched patriarchal law of *snokhachestvo*. Yet, *The Incestuous Father-in-Law* does not end with the held shot of Lusha's corpse. Instead, alerted, we assume, by the patriarch's screams, Ivan and his mother arrive, cut Lusha's body loose and carry her corpse back to their hut. As he leaves the storehouse Ivan casts his father a look full of disgust, clearly blaming him for his wife's death. It is striking, however, that the camera does not follow Ivan as he carries Lusha away from the site of her death, as the viewer might have expected. Instead it remains behind, fixed on the father-in-law, who then steps closer to the camera. This is an interesting movement, and it seems intended to suggest that from now on it is the *snokhach* who will be at the centre of the film's attention, as had been indicated by the film's eloquent Russian title. And indeed this is exactly what happens, for far from ending with Lusha's death the film continues for almost five full minutes, during which time the camera tracks the *snokhach* as relentlessly as both it and he had earlier tracked Lusha.

Thus, we follow him as he returns to the hut where Ivan has laid out his wife's body and we watch as he attempts to express his remorse to his son, who can only recoil from him in horror. We look on as the old patriarch then seeks forgiveness from a different source; bowing his head before the icon that hangs in the corner, he appears to pray. On turning away from the icon he is visibly shocked by the presence of Lusha's corpse and is unable to bring himself to touch her, although he seems to want to do so. Instead, he runs out of the hut and away from the village. The camera, of course, follows him in his flight and the film's final sequence shows him staggering along a windswept riverbank. Barefoot, crazed and haunted by what has happened, he stares, unseeing and unmoving, at the river, clearly reliving in his mind the terrible events of that night and petrified by their horror.

On first watching, these final five minutes might be felt by the modern viewer to weaken the overall impact of the film, for after the tension, dynamism and innovation of the preceding twenty-five minutes they appear slow-paced and conventional. This filmic 'coda' may also appear to be at odds with the preceding narrative, which, as we have seen, is so concerned with presenting events from Lusha's point of view. As Hansen has noted, however, this shift to the male narrative perspective is not completely unexpected, for the film-makers had granted the *snokhach* 'a modicum of subjectivity' early in the film, when they detailed his 'initial recognition of his son's failure toward Lusha' in the intertitle: 'Her soul is miserable, she does not love my Ivan'.[23]

This verbal indicator is not, however, the only way in which the film-makers pave the way for this shift to the old man's perspective. The sequence referred to by Hansen also conveys his subjectivity visually, that is cinematically. Early in the film, Lusha and her husband are shown arguing. Is she complaining about his neglect of her, about his excessive drinking, or about his reluctance to help her in the fields? Whatever it is, Ivan refuses to listen; all he wants to do is sleep. The next sequence shows Lusha trying, unsuccessfully, to wake him. Her father-in-law appears and attempts to rouse his lazy son in his turn. His anger is also directed at Lusha, however, since she, after all, had also been shirking, and he orders her back to her work in the field. Lusha obeys, but she is obviously still upset by her disagreement with her husband and pauses beneath a tree to collect herself before rejoining her fellow workers, who can be seen in the background. Her father-in-law, noticing her tears, appears to be genuinely concerned for Lusha's wellbeing; he approaches her and attempts to console her, stroking her head in a fatherly gesture of comfort, before gently encouraging her to return to her work. Reassured, Lusha does indeed return to the field, leaving her father-in-law standing by the tree. He watches the young woman walk away and it is at this point that we see the intertitle. The film-makers then cut back to the father-in-law, who is still standing by the tree. For a moment he is motionless, but then, suddenly, he places his hand on his heart, as if in physical pain, and staggers backwards, seeking support from the tree trunk. There he remains, the expression on his face conveying shock and horror at the emotions he is experiencing. The camera holds this shot for several seconds, thus enabling the viewer to witness the moments in which his thoughts turn from fatherly concern to sexual interest.

What the viewer here sees is an early attempt at conveying a character's psychology on screen. Of course, by 1912 this interest in psychology was not in itself new; indeed, it was already one of the most distinctive features of early Russian film, which had valued the depiction of psychology over action almost from its inception: as we saw in Chapter 1, the first Russian film, *Stenka Razin*, already displayed this preference, albeit in quite crude form. As the 1910s progressed, however, Russian film-makers would develop very definite ideas about how best to evoke their characters' psychology, with the pace and quality of acting coming to be seen as fundamental to the evocation of the characters' psychology on screen: the so-called 'Russian style' of acting was defined by its adherence to a 'doctrine of immobility', a conscious aesthetic programme according to which the camera would linger at length on the actors, who were required to convey emotion by shunning action and movement in favour of inaction and near motionlessness. Such scenes eventually became known as 'full' scenes, a term coined by the actress Olga Gzovskaia, and were defined thus by a film theorist writing in the journal *The Projector* [Proektor] in 1916:

> A 'full' scene is one in which the actor is given the opportunity
> to depict in stage terms a specific spiritual experience, no mat-
> ter how many metres it takes. The 'full' scene involves a com-
> plete rejection of the usual hurried tempo of the film drama.
> Instead of a rapidly changing kaleidoscope of images, it aspires
> to *rivet* the attention of the audience on to a single image [em-
> phasis in original].[24]

What we have in this sequence, then, is an embryonic 'full' scene, through
which the film-makers attempt to convey to the viewer the struggle that is
going on in the patriarch's mind and to enable him/her to witness not only
the birth of the father-in-law's incestuous desire for Lusha, but also the pain
that this realisation causes him. The sequence therefore effectively represents the father-in-law as a man who is conflicted about his feelings and
desires, and suggests that we should perhaps attempt to understand rather
than merely condemn him. The film's final five minutes also serve the same
function, a fact that is all the more striking because in ending in this way
The Incestuous Father-in-Law stands out as atypical of its time and place of
production. As Hansen has noted, typically the characteristic catastrophic
endings of Russian melodramas are not buffered by a moment of recognition, remorse or mourning: 'A suicide would typically be followed by the last
title, "The End", rather than, say, a reaction shot of an implicated character'.[25]
Here, however, we get five minutes of reaction and we watch, in all its grim
progression, the development of the father-in-law's remorse, which leads
him neither to repentance nor to forgiveness, however, but only to madness,
to a fearful disorientation and, significantly, to the loneliness of a hostile,
windswept wilderness, far from the security of the village society that had
bestowed on him the rights that Lusha so dramatically denied him.

Thus, although the film-makers clearly favour Lusha's point of view
throughout the film, repeatedly showing her to be, as Hansen puts it,
'the subject of suffering or, rather, object of a triple oppression through
poverty and hard work, sexual abuse and village opinion', that is not
to say that the father-in-law is 'the only villain or, for that matter, only
a villain'.[26] The film-makers emphasise the hopelessness of the young
woman's situation, but they also reveal the discrepancy between the
old man's assumed social power and his actual impotence and failure.
And, moreover, they show the effect that the patriarch's awareness of this

discrepancy, forced on him by Lusha's final act of defiance and denial, has on him: this once strong man proves unable to cope with the young woman's rebellion. The film's final five minutes therefore make it impossible for the viewer not to feel at least some sympathy for his plight, for ultimately, to cite Hansen again, they show the male subjectivity to be 'irreparably damaged, compromised by the violence inherent in the [man's] social role'.[27]

In these ways, then, in *The Incestuous Father-in-Law* the weakness of the male protagonist that was implied but ultimately overcome in *Stenka Razin* is not only stated explicitly but also shown to be insurmountable. As in the earlier film, the cause of the patriarch's problems is shown to be a young woman who dances. Unlike the Persian princess, however, who four years previously was murdered on screen by her vengeful and frightened male counterparts, Lusha has the strength of character to take matters into her own hands. Unwilling to submit passively to the outdated nineteenth-century tradition that makes of her little more than a possession to be used and abused in accordance with the will of the patriarch who owns her, she rebels. If this is a progress of sorts from 1908, it is of course, however, not unambiguous. That this young woman can assert her independence from the man who seeks to possess her only by committing suicide inevitably attenuates her moment of triumph over the *snokhach*, reducing it to a sombre and distressing Pyrrhic victory.

3

The Opera Singer

The first professional female performer: Evgenii Bauer's Vera Dubrovskaia[1]

The year in which the sophisticated film *The Incestuous Father-in-Law* was made proved to be a significant transitional year in Russian cinema in other ways, for it was in 1912 that Evgenii Bauer entered the world of film. Since the rediscovery of his films at the end of the 1980s, Bauer has come to be seen as the major Russian film-maker of his era, and as a figure of fundamental importance not only in the history and development of Russian film, but also in world cinema. Accordingly, his work will be central to this and to following chapters. A student of the Moscow College of Painting, Sculpture and Architecture [Moskovskoe uchilishche zhivopisi, vaianiia i zodchestva], Bauer had worked as an actor, a caricaturist, a satirical journalist and a portrait photographer and was already well known as a theatre set designer when he was engaged, in the autumn of 1912, to design the sets for Drankov and A. Taldykin's 1913 production *The Tercentenary of the Rule of the House of Romanov, 1613–1913* [Trekhsotletie tsarstvovaniia doma Romanovykh, 1613–1913], which was directed by Aleksandr Uralskii and Nikolai Larin. Bauer subsequently worked as a director both under them and for Pathé before joining Aleksandr Khanzhonkov's rival company at the end of 1913, where he remained until

51

his untimely death from pneumonia in June 1917.[2] Bauer quickly rose to become Khanzhonkov's leading film-maker and was reputedly the most highly paid director in Russia. Despite the brevity of his cinematic career, Bauer's output was prodigious. He directed at least eighty-two films, of which twenty-six are currently known to be extant. As the following chapters will seek in part to demonstrate, the range and number of Bauer's surviving films make it possible both to gain a sense of the recurrent features of style and theme that make a 'Bauer film' instantly recognizable and to trace the development of Bauer's method and thematics.[3]

We are aided in this by the fact that among Bauer's extant films is his directorial debut for Khanzhonkov, *Twilight of a Woman's Soul*, which was released on 26 November 1913. Photographed by Nikolai Kozlovskii, the cameraman who in 1908 had worked alongside Drankov on *Stenka Razin*, this film demonstrates how far the new art form of cinema had advanced in sophistication in the five years since the release of the first Russian feature film. It also exemplifies the shift occurring in Russian cinema at this time, with rural settings being replaced by urban settings. But *Twilight of a Woman's Soul* is notable for another reason: it marks a change in the way the female performer is represented in Russian film, for Bauer's heroine, Vera Dubrovskaia (Nina Chernova), takes to the stage of her own volition, thus becoming the first professional female performer in Russian film. This fact is significant for, as we shall see, in this way Bauer is able to invest the trope of performing with alternative meanings from those it was accorded in films made before 1913. In this film Bauer directly addresses the fundamental question that would be made famous by the French feminist writer Simone de Beauvoir in 1949: 'What is a woman?'[4] The trope of performing is central to Bauer's exploration of this question.

'Becoming' a woman, 1: objectification, idealisation and enculturation

> One is not born a woman: one becomes a woman. No biological, psychic or economic destiny defines the figure that the human female assumes in society; it is civilisation as a whole that constructs this intermediary product between the male and the eunuch that is called the feminine.
>
> Simone de Beauvoir.[5]

52

> We [women] have been compelled in our bodies and in our
> minds to correspond, feature by feature, with the *idea* of nature
> that has been established for us [emphasis in original].
>
> Monique Wittig.[6]

Bauer's Vera does not become a stage performer until the end of *Twilight of a Woman's Soul*. However, from the film's earliest sequences Bauer exploits both the trope of the stage and the idea of performing in more abstract and general terms in his representation of his female protagonist. This is especially striking in the sequence in which he introduces Vera to the viewer. We first meet the young woman in her bedroom, in a carefully constructed shot (Figure 3.1). In recent years, this frame has been the focus of several extended analyses of Bauer's cinematic art, with commentators agreeing that it exemplifies many of the stylistic features that make Bauer's films instantly recognisable.[7] Perhaps most striking is the extraordinary attention paid to the details of the set design. Even when he worked in theatre Bauer's complex and innovative set designs were his trademark,[8] and he

Figure 3.1. Vera sits alone in her bedroom (Bauer, *Twilight of a Woman's Soul*, 1913)

soon also made the field of cinema set design his own.[9] Concerned to overcome the flatness of the cinema screen, Bauer constantly experimented with new ways to enhance the depth and stereoscopic quality of his sets by using carefully placed columns, furniture, staircases, curtains, partition walls or plants to divide the space into different planes, both horizontal and vertical. Indeed, his sets are so distinctive that the Soviet director Lev Kuleshov, who worked as art director on several late Bauer films, talks of 'the Bauer method' of set building.[10] This attention to detail is neither gratuitous nor insignificant. Although no doubt partly intended as impressive backdrop, Bauer's sets and the objects he places within them are always more than mere ornament; instead they function meaningfully, being used to highlight aspects of character and/or of theme. Bauer's sophisticated 'blocking' and his fondness for treating his actors as one more element of the mise-en-scène, to be carefully posed, both in relation to the camera and to each other, are also often mentioned in contemporary reviews of his films.[11] We see all these carefully thought-through elements of style at work in this introductory shot of Vera.

What does Bauer communicate about Vera here? First, he signals her centrality to the film and his concerns. As the figure placed in the centre of the frame, it is clearly Vera on whom Bauer intends the viewer to focus. In addition to her positioning, Vera's motionlessness enables, indeed encourages, the viewer to observe her closely: it is again a scopophilic camera that here presents Vera to the viewer. Although somewhat distant, separated from the viewer by the flimsy gauze curtains that are drawn almost completely across the set, she is on display, there to be looked at, a fact Bauer emphasises by having his cameraman hold the shot for almost ten seconds.

Moreover, the frame is structured according to a specifically male gaze, with man as the (active) spectator and woman as the (passive) 'spectacle'; Vera is here 'taken as an object' and 'styled' to reflect the 'phantasies' of the 'determining male gaze'.[12] The nature of these 'phantasies' is predictable: Vera here represents a virtual compendium of clichéd, nineteenth-century patriarchal assumptions about woman. In Russia in 1913, the obsession with the figure of the eternal feminine – expressed perhaps most fully in the early verse collections of the Symbolist poet Aleksandr Blok – had peaked and was, for many artists, a legitimate target for satire. The Futurist poets Aleksei Kruchenykh and Velimir Khlebnikov had, for example, recently written in a poetic manifesto the disparaging comment that 'lately, people have sought to transmute woman into the eternal feminine, the Beautiful Lady; in this way, *a skirt* has become something *mystical* [emphasis in original]'.[13] And indeed, posed in the middle of the extravagant 'kingdom of gauze and lace' that is her bedroom,[14] this is indeed how Vera is represented: beautiful, passive, chaste and pure, she is the embodiment of the 'passivity, submissiveness, pliability, softness' that, for the future Soviet politician and sexual theorist Aleksandra Kollontai, was the essence of the outdated image of the 'eternal feminine'.[15]

The gauze curtains drawn across the middle of the set serve to emphasise Vera's detachment from the outside world, the sphere of public activity. They evoke 'the veil of the hymen',[16] and they also stand as a literal representation of what Luce Irigaray describes as the 'metaphorical veil of the eternal feminine'.[17] The lighting is also evocative: as the space in front of the curtains is in complete darkness, in contrast the well-lit background where our heroine sits appears even brighter, and Vera is bathed in an unearthly light that suggests her ethereality. Her delicate, virginal nature is further suggested by the fragile, transparent curtains themselves and by the diaphanous gown she is wearing. The whiteness of the curtains, of the bed linen and of Vera's dress also evokes associations of purity and innocence, as do the vases of flowers that decorate her bedroom. Vera is transformed into a 'woman in white'.

Thus, from the very beginning of the film, and long before we see the male protagonists' responses to and treatment of her, Vera is represented both as a mysterious and enticing object of erotic contemplation and as the epitome of nineteenth-century male fantasies of the perfect woman. She is held in a state of what Simone de Beauvoir would later term 'immanence': a closed-off, dead-end interior domain in which women are passive, static and imprisoned.

Subsequent sequences set in Vera's bedroom offer similarly idealised and abstracted images of the young woman. Thus we watch Vera as she sleeps and dreams. Although Vera's erotic appeal is heightened in this sequence – her thick black hair cascades down her back – her loose white nightgown is, for all its vague sensuality, a reminder of her virginal purity. This is emphasised when, at one point, Vera kneels by her bed and appears to pray; this pose, combined with her attire and the bright lighting, lends Vera an aura of saintliness. When she takes to her bed through illness, she is also depicted in the same evocative poses and attire, pale, wan and vulnerable but no less beautiful and desirable. Later in the film, Vera is also shown before her mirror, contemplating her beauty and daydreaming of her lover, Prince Dolskii, while a maid brushes her hair. Familiar from many portraits of women throughout the history of art, this pose leads the spectator to focus on what the art historian Elizabeth Prettejohn describes as 'the talismanic parts of the female body […]: eyes, lips, hands, rippling hair'.[18] Again the spectator is encouraged to view Vera through male eyes for, as Prettejohn goes on to suggest, drawing on the work of the feminist art critic Griselda Pollock, these 'symbols of eroticism' refer 'not so much to the characteristics of the depicted woman as to those of male desire'.[19]

These clichéd formulations of Vera's femininity do not express Bauer's directorial perception, however. It is characteristic of Bauer's sophistication that he is able to suggest that these idealised, conventional and outdated images of femininity exist primarily in the minds of his male protagonists. One way in which Bauer implies this is by introducing a male protagonist in the frame in such a way that his voyeuristic tendencies are highlighted. Thus, as Vera sits daydreaming in her bedroom at the start of the film, she is observed unawares not only by the viewer, but also by the manservant sent to summon her to the ball. The servant enters the dark foreground of the frame and stands silhouetted, his back to the camera, apparently taking advantage of the opportunity to observe Vera for a moment, before eventually making his presence known to her. The fact that he remains in the dark space of the frame throughout the sequence transforms him into a faceless and vaguely menacing figure.[20]

This technique recurs throughout the film, with a more sinister example occurring after Vera's first philanthropic visit to the workman, Maksim Petrov. Moved by the poverty of his attic garret, Vera had knelt by Petrov's side and bandaged his wounded hand. Struck by her beauty and mistaking her compassion for erotic attraction, Petrov is overcome by desire for the young woman, who, even in this early sequence, is identified in an intertitle as the 'victim of deception'. He therefore sets a trap for her: playing on her sympathy, he writes to Vera, announcing that he is near death and begging her to visit him again. Petrov delivers this duplicitous letter himself, climbing through the open window of Vera's bedroom at night. Unable to

Figure 3.2. Petrov parts the gauze curtains and enters Vera's bedroom (Bauer, *Twilight of a Woman's Soul*, 1913)

resist the sight of the 'sleeping beauty', however, he lingers, looking at the young woman through the gauze curtains, as the manservant had done before him; then he parts the curtains, enters Vera's bedroom and again stands watching her 'unawares' (Figure 3.2). In his violation of Vera's intimate space, Petrov displays the same patriarchal self-confidence as during his subsequent rape of her, an act that is symbolically pre-figured in this sequence.

Bauer's method in these examples is subtle. In addition to casting the male protagonists as voyeurs in this way, he uses other means to distance himself from the film's initial representation of Vera. Most notably, he self-consciously highlights the stylised and constructed nature of the introductory shot of her in her bedroom by incorporating the trope of the stage visually into his set design (Figure 3.1). The gauze curtains, for example, both recall the stage curtains of any theatre and 'lay bare' the concept of the so-called 'fourth wall', that imaginary barrier at the front of the stage in a proscenium theatre, through which the audience observes the action that is taking place in the fictional world of the performance they are watching. Thus, in addition to their other symbolic values, the curtains also function to draw attention to the artificiality, or the 'constructedness', of both Vera and her surroundings. The way in which the shot is lit, which, as Yuri Tsivian notes, 'is very unusual, even for 1913, the year in which lighting effects were much in vogue',[21] also contributes to the creation of this 'theatrical' effect, for it replicates the way in which in a theatre the on-stage performers are illuminated by the footlights, while the members of the audience, seated in the stalls, find themselves in darkness. This stark, theatrical effect is highlighted by the fact that at other times in the film's first reel the same set is, as Cavendish observes, 'presented naturalistically, with the foreground generously illuminated, and the vantage point of the camera slightly altered'[22] (Figure 3.3). Bauer also reproduces the spectatorial and spatial relationship of the theatre audience and the performer in the figures of the men who at various times stand in the dark foreground of the frame,

Figure 3.3. Vera's bedroom, presented naturalistically (Bauer, *Twilight of a Woman's Soul*, 1913)

on the other side of the curtains/'the fourth wall', and watch Vera. By incorporating overtly theatrical elements into his set design for Vera's bedroom in these ways, Bauer further emphasises that what he is offering to the viewer is not an objective, 'truthful' representation of this young woman, but rather a reconstruction of how she appears when viewed through the prism of the male protagonists' subjectivity. In other words, Bauer here creates a representation of Vera as a social, cultural and ideological gender construct. This is what, to use the terminology proposed by Simone de Beauvoir, woman had 'become' in Russia at the start of the twentieth century: a passive, pure and idealised object of erotic contemplation, a locus of male fantasies about perfect femininity. Or, in Monique Wittig's words: 'only a myth'.[23]

'Becoming' a woman, 2: agency

The women of today are actively overthrowing the myth of femininity; they are beginning to affirm their independence concretely.

Simone de Beauvoir.[24]

If gender is the variable cultural interpretation of sex, then it lacks the fixity and closure characteristic of simple identity. To be a gender [...] is to be engaged in an ongoing cultural interpretation of bodies and, hence, to be dynamically positioned within a field of cultural possibilities. Gender must be understood as a modality of taking on or realizing possibilities, a process of interpreting the body, giving it cultural form. In other words, to be a woman is to become a woman; it is not a matter of acquiescing to a fixed ontological status, in which case one could be born a woman, but, rather, an active process of appropriating, interpreting, and reinterpreting received cultural possibilities.

Judith Butler.[25]

Bauer also shows, however, even in the film's earliest sequences, that there is more to Vera herself than this fossilised feminine image suggests. For it is striking that in addition both to stressing the encultured 'constructedness' of Vera's persona and the state of 'immanence' in which she exists, and to characterising this as a male-defined image, Bauer also takes care to reveal, by various means, Vera's dissatisfaction with her present identity and way of life. Tsivian has analysed, for example, how in the initial sequence in Vera's bedroom Bauer uses light and ambience – and specifically the title metaphor of 'twilight' – to evoke Vera's depressed state of mind, her sense of social alienation and her frustration with the closed-off emptiness of her life.[26] Moreover, several times Bauer has Vera walk over to the large window in her bedroom, whereupon she opens the shutters wide, letting light flood in, and gazes out at the world beyond.[27] The symbolism is clear: Vera wants to escape the claustrophobic confines of her bedroom, to become something and someone other than a beautiful, trapped object. She wants to explore the world outside her bedroom window. She desires, to use de Beauvoir's terminology again, 'transcendence'.

Bauer also emphasises this by harnessing Nina Chernova's considerable acting talent. Using subtle gestures, body language and facial expression, Chernova effectively conveys Vera's consciousness of existing within the confines of an imposed set of rules and restrictions. There is her reluctance to attend her parents' ball, for example, and her obvious boredom with the social niceties that are required of her once she is there. Although Vera accepts an invitation to dance from one of the many insistent admirers who crowd round her, Chernova's acting makes it clear that she cannot wait for it to be over. Once it is, she excuses herself and retreats behind a row of ornate pot plants, which serve as markers of her parents' wealth and class, to a space that is, as Tsivian observes, 'as solitary as Vera's bedroom had been'.[28]

Bauer clearly sympathises with Vera in this sequence and he also expresses his approval of her restlessness. Typically, he does so cinematically: by means of a subtle camera movement that aligns the camera with his heroine; as Vera cannot remain still, neither can his camera. Thus, towards the end of the ball sequence, after Vera has retreated from the public gaze, she sits first on one chair for a moment before standing and walking to another. As the young woman moves, something remarkable happens: the camera – which in 1913 was still almost entirely static, except in a few rare cases – follows her. As we saw in Chapter 2, in *The Incestuous Father-in-Law* the camera's pursuit of Lusha had functioned as a symbol of the way in which the eponymous male protagonist had relentlessly pursued the film's heroine. In this case, however, the camera movement is of an entirely different order. Instead, it is emblematic of the fact that in this film Bauer is concerned to represent the point of view of his female protagonist as the dominant narrative perspective. For, Bauer's camera movement here functions as a gesture of solidarity and encouragement between the director and his female protagonist. As Tsivian puts it: 'We may not quite feel it today, but on the part of the author and therefore the viewer, this was a gentle, sympathetic gesture, as if it were saying: "The others may not know how you feel, but I'm with you; I'm on your side."'[29]

Vera's desire to transcend her status as a 'woman in white' and her search for a new identity are also stressed by her enthusiastic acceptance of her mother's suggestion, the day after the ball, that she accompany her on philanthropic visits to the poor. Although philanthropy was one of the few social activities allowed to women by the patriarchal order of the time, Vera's willingness to embrace this social role is significant, for it suggests an alternative understanding of what it means to become a woman, one that is broader and, indeed, more positive than that expressed in the film's early sequences. For, as Judith Butler elaborated, in a series of articles published in the late 1980s, an important connotation of the verb 'to become' is the idea of purposefulness, or 'personal agency'.[30] This interpretation has profound implications. As Moya Lloyd puts it: 'As a way of thinking, the idea of becoming a gender poses a challenge to the idea that gender is passively produced by patriarchy or forced on subjects by the phallogocentric symbolic'.[31] Instead, for Butler, 'to *become* a woman is a purposive and appropriative set of acts, the acquisition of a skill […] a self-reflexive process [emphasis in original]'.[32] In other words, 'becoming' a woman is a process of self construction and can, therefore, be seen as containing 'emancipatory potential'.[33]

'Becoming' a woman, 3: encountering opposition

[W]hat sense does becoming a gender have in a world where gender relations appear to be firmly established and deeply entrenched? What kind of freedom is this?

Judith Butler.[34]

When Vera sets out into the world that she has so far only glimpsed from her bedroom window, however, Bauer stresses the difficulties she encounters in her attempts to construct an identity for herself and become her own kind of woman; her strength and determination are repeatedly put to the test, to some extent in her relationship with her mother, who fails either to understand or to be sympathetic to her daughter's desire for something more than marriage and a conventional life, but primarily in her encounters with the film's two male protagonists. What is striking is the fact that, although they belong to different social classes, both men are wedded to equally outmoded views of what a woman is and what she should be. Predictably, they both do their best to impose their views on Vera.

Vera and the workman

For the workman Maksim Petrov a woman is a vulnerable sexual object to be used and abused at will. His 'symbolic defloration' of Vera in her bedroom has been discussed.[35] Consider also the construction of the sequence in which Vera, tricked by Petrov's claim that he is near death, visits his garret alone. Many elements of the mise-en-scène function to characterise Vera as the innocent victim of a dangerous male predator. With her simple dress, shawl-covered head and basket of provisions and medicine, Vera is cast as an urban Little Red Riding Hood, an innocent young girl, threatened by a wolf. Petrov's predatory nature is further communicated through the various camera angles from which Bauer constructs the sequence, and in this way Bauer again contrives to indicate that this view of Vera reflects not his own perceptions of women, but those of his male protagonist. Thus, the camera stalks Vera (as it had Lusha in *The Incestuous Father-in-Law*), as, keeping close to the wall, she walks nervously along the deserted street towards Petrov's garret; tension mounts when the camera cuts to Petrov's leering face, as he leans out of the window to observe Vera's approach. In the next shot the camera adopts Petrov's rapacious perspective on the young woman in what Tsivian describes as an 'amazing, long, hawk-eye point-of-view shot', looking down on Vera and framing her as his helpless prey, heading unwittingly into his trap.[36] Maksim's lower-class status is significant for, as Heide Schlüpmann notes, Bauer thus suggests (surprisingly, perhaps, given the proximity of the 1917 Revolutions) that in early twentieth-century Russian society, social power is not grounded in class but 'is defined above all in terms of gender, of sexually specific violence.'[37]

As Bauer shows us, however, Petrov's assessment of Vera's weakness and vulnerability is misguided, for she is made of stronger stuff than he allows: despite appearing traumatised and incapable of action immediately after Petrov has raped her, Vera soon rouses herself and fights back; refusing to be a passive victim, she avenges herself on her rapist by killing him. Significantly, she uses one of his own tools. Thus, in this man/woman encounter, it is the woman who survives.

Vera and the prince

Months pass. Tortured by the memory of these disturbing events, Vera reverts to spending most of her time in her bedroom. Eventually, however, she meets and falls in love with a man from her own class, Prince Sergei Dolskii. Throughout their courtship, Bauer reveals Dolskii's firm attachment to nineteenth-century assumptions about how women should be. In sound patriarchal fashion, Dolskii believes that a woman should be passive: when Dolskii and Vera first meet she is marginalised visually, invited to sit (passively) on a chair positioned at the very edge of the frame and to watch Dolskii as he steps into the centre to demonstrate his prowess at the (active, if not phallic) male pastimes of target shooting and fencing.

For Dolskii, a woman should also be vulnerable: Vera is at her most appealing to him when she is lying ill and wan in bed. Indeed, her invalidism appears to render her even more attractive to Dolskii, who visits her sick bed faithfully. In his study of distorted images of women in fin-de-siècle culture, Bram Dijkstra explores the taste for paintings of bed-ridden women and explains the cult of feminine invalidism as a product of male fantasies about the perfect women, for, he observes, there was no 'better guarantee of purity […] than a woman's pale, consumptive face, fading, in a paroxysm of self-negation, into nothingness.'[38]

Most important, however, a woman, if she is to make a suitable wife, should be pure, both sexually and morally. Laura Engelstein describes how, in the tabloid newspapers that sprang up in Russia in the early twentieth century, widowers would advertise for 'the perfect second wife (under thirty, "without a past")'.[39] The overriding importance of a woman's sexual purity is revealed by the fact that in her letter to Dolskii, Vera, who is desperate not to have any secrets from her fiancé, omits any mention of her murder of Petrov, simply confessing, euphemistically: 'Something unspeakably awful happened – I belonged to another'. The letter remains unread, however, for Dolskii is not at home when it is delivered. The wedding therefore goes ahead and Vera is faced with the task of confessing her past to her husband in person. Again, her account focuses on her rape, of which part is shown visually, as a flashback. Although Vera does subsequently mime the fact that she stabbed Petrov, the damage has already been done by her account of her rape. Dolskii recoils from Vera in horror and revulsion, revealing the emptiness of his repeated promises to her that nothing that had happened in her past could ever diminish his love for her. The reality is that he cannot cope with the fact that the woman he thought he had married – a society *belle* 'with a spotless reputation'[40] – is not in fact pure. As Youngblood comments: 'Dolskii saw Vera's victimisation and revenge as moral degradation rather than as moral triumph'.[41] In the eyes of this patriarchal male protagonist, Vera is now a Fallen Woman.

Vera is shocked and stung by Dolskii's reaction to her confession. Indeed, it is striking that in Bauer's eyes there appears to be little difference between the physical violence Petrov inflicts on Vera and the psychological suffering that Dolskii causes her: in a telling 'trick' shot earlier in the film, he links the two men visually, superimposing Petrov's leering face on Dolskii's. Just as she did after her rape, however, Vera again takes her life into her own hands and refuses to be the passive victim of her male counterpart's prejudices. She responds to Dolskii's rejection of her with pride and determination, neither pleading for forgiveness nor allowing him to berate her. Instead she takes a step back from him, looks at him for a moment and then pronounces a damning assessment of his conduct: 'You are pitiful, Prince!' Then she acts: she puts on her coat and walks away from Dolskii and their marriage. She does not look back.

'Becoming' a woman, 4: on stage – imitation, masquerade and performing gender

Dolskii regrets losing Vera almost immediately, and he tries to track her down. All he learns from the private detective whom he hires at considerable expense, however, is that she has gone abroad, and the two years he spends travelling himself also prove fruitless. But Bauer lets the viewer in on Vera's secret: she has created a new identity for herself, earned fame and, we assume, fortune by building a career as the operatic performer Ellen Kay [Kei]. The next twist in the plot therefore comes as no surprise to the viewer. Shortly after his return to Russia, one of Dolskii's friends invites the despondent prince to accompany him to the opera. As Dolskii settles himself in his box at the theatre, he is amazed to recognise Vera in the famous diva he sees on the stage.

In early twentieth-century Russian society and culture, however, the position of the professional female performer was still a conflicted one. It is therefore not immediately clear whether Bauer intends Vera's new status to be seen as the realisation of her desire for a meaningful life, or whether it in fact suggests something less positive about the avenues open to her as a Russian woman at the start of the twentieth century. Indeed, there are several reasons why it is impossible for the viewer not to feel some unease about Vera's choice of vocation. First, performing on stage was not a new sphere of social activity for Russian women, but had, like philanthropy, long been considered an acceptable way for women to participate in public life. As Catherine M. Schuler documents in her study of the Russian actress in the Silver Age: 'Unlike Western European theatre, Russian theatre had never excluded women from the stage on moral and religious grounds or for reasons of social convention'.[42] Moreover, in the eyes of the early twentieth-century Russian public, the female stage performer was still not completely dissociated from the prostitute and the *demi-mondaine*. Indeed, Schuler observes: 'Russian actresses were more constrained than most by their association in the minds of the public with prostitution'.[43] Sexual patronage was still a fact of life for most Russian female performers, even those who received high salaries and worked in the Imperial Theatres, and contemporary Russian critics frequently accused theatre entrepreneurs and directors of treating their female performers like 'living goods' [*zhivoi tovar*].[44] Indeed, Bauer seems to stress the fact that Vera's new career means that she is destined to end the film as she began it: as an object gazed at by men. This status is suggested by the shot that homes in on five glossy publicity photographs of Vera in her new identity, which emphasises that in becoming a famous female performer she has also become a commodity, or, as Louise McReynolds puts it, 'an article of mass consumption'.[45] This is also implied by Dolskii's reaction to seeing Vera on stage: in another example of male scopophilia, he seizes his opera glasses in order to observe Vera more closely.

Other more disturbing views about why women were especially suited to a stage career were also current in early twentieth-century Russian society. Dijkstra suggests that the sudden abundance of and enthusiasm for starring female performers in turn-of-the-century Europe was due, at least in part, to misogynous beliefs about the nature of sexual difference.[46] Dijkstra demonstrates how the turn-of-the-century male's belief in woman's 'inherently passive nature' and 'ignorance' led to the conviction that 'it was part of woman's nature to imitate incessantly. Her passive nature made her incapable of original thought or action, but she had a protean capacity to take on whatever form she was given to imitate'.[47] According to Dijkstra, 'the idea that woman was inherently an imitator, not an originator, [became] one of the most pervasive clichés of Western culture', and it thus came as no surprise that:

> Because of her propensity for imitation, the stage came to be seen as the place where woman could best express her contribution to the cultural life of civilised society. For what was acting if not a form of imitation? It is by no means an accident that the years around 1900 were years of triumph for actresses everywhere. [...] But it was not because they were seen as particularly original that the actresses became celebrated. Instead, they were seen as unusually successful in exploiting the imitative bent of 'women's nature'.[48]

While, as Schuler puts it, Dijkstra 'does not specifically identify Russia as a polestar of international misogyny',[49] a significant number of the so-called scientific treatises on the subject of essential sexual difference that Dijkstra cites were translated and sold in Russia during this period.[50] Moreover, Linda Edmondson has shown that such essentialist attitudes did characterise discourse on emancipation and sexuality in turn-of-the-century Russia and that in their battle against female emancipation and sexual equality, conservative Russian males, like their European counterparts, took to using scientific 'facts' about woman's 'nature' as ammunition.[51] A pervasive theory in early twentieth-century Russia, for example, 'purported to prove the built-in inferiority of women by revealing that the female brain was smaller than the male and that the entire structure and functioning of the female reproductive system negated the possibility of intellectual or artistic effort'.[52] This, it was felt, 'denied the possibility of a "true" woman being capable of (or even desiring to be capable of) sustained intellectual endeavour, sound and rational judgement, or creativity in anything other than reproduction, self-adornment and a little music, drawing or needlework'.[53]

Considered in the light of this socio-cultural background, Vera's new status as a female performer therefore begins to appear invidious. For it seems that the stage was in fact viewed as one more place in which Russian women could be held in check, contained in an area considered 'suitable' for them by patriarchal society, encouraged to exploit 'essential' feminine characteristics and thereby prevented from entering other spheres of activity traditionally seen as 'male'. That performing is shown to be Vera's chosen way of participating in public life is thus, at least on the surface, highly suspect as a statement of female emancipation.

Moreover, the role in which Vera is cast also suggests her continued imprisonment in outdated male myths of femininity, for she 'imitates' a classic nineteenth-century female protagonist, appearing in Giuseppe Verdi's *La Traviata* (1853) as the eponymous fallen woman, Violetta Valéry, Verdi's consumptive courtesan.[54] The precise scene that Vera is shown performing is also significant: Bauer chooses to show us the opera's closing sequence, in which Violetta succumbs to her illness in the arms of her distraught lover, Alfredo.

Focussing on the libretti and the plots of key nineteenth-century operatic works, the French philosopher and cultural critic Catherine Clément has argued that nineteenth-century opera – 'this spectacle thought up to adore, and also to kill, the feminine character' which tells and retells the story of women's 'undoing' – is a misogynous art form that perpetuates the pernicious 'models, ideas, feelings, ways of loving' of an outmoded social order, requiring either the domestication or, more usually, the death of the female protagonist, as a way of containing them and thus rendering them innocuous.[55] McReynolds makes a similar point when she observes that 'dying on stage was an especially feminine action'.[56] Moreover, 'these staged deaths were coded by the dominant morality: sexually innocent women did not perish in this manner'.[57]

Indeed, Dolskii's reaction to seeing Vera on stage appears to confirm these interpretations, for all his hopes of resurrecting his relationship with her are immediately awakened. However, his reaction has little or nothing to do with Vera, the 'real' woman with whom he was once involved, and everything to do with the fictional character he sees her embodying on stage, and all the rich cultural associations of both the life and the death of Verdi's heroine. Susan Sontag has identified the multifarious uses of tuberculosis as metaphor and she summarises the essential contradictions between them, thus:

> The metaphor of TB [...] described the death of someone [...] thought to be too 'good' to be sexual: the assertion of an angelic psychology. It was also a way of describing sexual feelings – while lifting the responsibility for libertinism, which is blamed on a state of objective, physiological decadence or deliquescence.[58]

In addition to these central metaphorical uses, tuberculosis was repeatedly represented as 'the prototypical passive death' and 'the disease of born victims'.[59] It was also seen as 'a redemptive death for the fallen'.[60] The similarity between these metaphoric associations of tuberculosis and the ideals of womankind favoured by Dolskii is striking. Vera's stage death from this disease thus enables him to see her as he did before her revelations about her past: as passive, vulnerable and, most importantly, pure. In other words, seeing 'Vera' die from consumption onstage confirms Dolskii in all the misguided preconceptions about her nature as a woman that led to their separation in the first place.

Vera's stage performance also enables Dolskii to believe that Vera will be prepared to forgive him for deserting her, in the same way that the character she plays on stage forgives her errant lover. Similarly, other recurrent associations of tuberculosis enable him to believe that she will welcome his declaration of love. For tuberculosis was also understood as 'the disease of love', caused by 'hopes blighted', by 'thwarted' or 'renounced' love, but also by an excess of passion.[61] Tuberculosis was imagined to be an aphrodisiac and was thought to intensify sexual desire.[62] As Sontag puts it: 'While the standard representation of a death from tuberculosis places the emphasis on the perfected sublimation of feeling, the recurrent figure of the tubercular courtesan indicates that tuberculosis was also thought to make the sufferer sexy'.[63]

The stage role in which Vera is cast is thus the perfect representation of femininity for Dolskii. It does not represent any challenge to hegemonic gender ideology, nor threaten the established sexual hierarchy. Instead, it centres on nineteenth-century male myths about the nature of woman and 'perfect' femininity. For the various and contradictory applications of the metaphor of tuberculosis enable him to retain his ideals of femininity intact and to believe that, as his wife has been purged of her sin, she is once more suitable for his erotic attentions. It therefore comes as no surprise to the viewer that at the end of the performance Dolskii rushes backstage to Vera's dressing room, confesses undying love and begs her to take him back.

Again, then, it seems that, far from offering the female protagonists a means of escape, the stage functions instead as a bastion of tradition, where women are trapped in the endless representation of male-created images of femininity that reinforce oppressive, patriarchal values and ideals of 'perfect' femininity or represent them in misogynous and limited (and limiting) terms. Thus, the stage has a 'comforting' function for the male protagonists: it ensures that a safe, albeit erotically charged, distance exists between the male protagonists and the female performers to whom they are attracted.

A more productive way of reading Vera's status as an operatic performer specialising in nineteenth-century roles, however, and one that fits better with Bauer's own views, is through the prism of the concept of 'the masquerade'. Elaborated by the psychoanalyst Joan Riviere in 1929 and taken up by the French psychoanalyst and psychiatrist Jacques Lacan and the thinker Luce Irigaray, 'masquerade' refers to the idea that femaleness ('womanliness') is a conscious display of conventionally defined femininity that seeks to 'mask' a woman's possession of subjectivity (in Riviere's terminology, 'masculinity') and functions as a form of defence against the 'reprisals' a woman expects to suffer (from men/society), if she is found to possess this quality.[64] Riviere built her theory round the behaviour of one of her female patients, an intellectual who was widely respected for her ability, but who in order to compensate for the supposed (socially understood) 'masculinity' of her professional self/identity would, after giving a public lecture, begin to behave in an exaggeratedly 'feminine' way towards male members of her audience, 'flirting and coquetting with them in a more or less veiled manner'.[65] It may be, therefore, that, like Riviere's anonymous patient, Vera (who has, after all, suffered at the hands of the reactionary Dolskii, who was unable to value the subjectivity/'masculinity' she displayed in defending herself against the rapist Petrov) now seeks refuge in 'safe' representations of femininity in order to 'mask' the fact that she is not a 'typical' (passive, dependent) woman, but one who can stand on her own two feet and who has successfully built a life of her own.[66]

This may appear to be a gloomy assessment, for as Mary Ann Doane has noted, Riviere does not theorise 'masquerade' as something 'joyful' or 'affirmative', but rather 'as an anxiety-ridden compensatory gesture, as a position which is potentially disturbing, uncomfortable, and inconsistent, as well as psychically painful for the woman'.[67] However, there exists a crucial difference between Riviere's patient and Bauer's Vera, namely that what the former did unconsciously and in life, Vera does *consciously* and *on stage*. This difference, of course, highlights the fact that her 'behaviour' is clearly marked as an act, a performance. Put simply, *it is not Vera's real life*.

Parker Tyler has written of the Hollywood actress Greta Garbo that she '"got in drag" whenever she took some heavy glamour part, whenever she melted in or out of a man's arms, whenever she simply let that heavenly flexed neck [...] bear the weight of her thrown back head'.[68] While it would of course be an exaggeration to claim that Bauer has Vera 'get in drag', she can nonetheless be said to do here what Stephen Heath describes Marlene Dietrich as doing in the numerous films in which she is cast as a cabaret performer, that is she 'wears all the accoutrements [of femininity] *as* accoutrements, does the poses as poses, gives the act as an act [emphasis in original]'.[69] In other words, what Bauer shows us in the sequence of Vera on stage as Violetta Valéry is intended to be, as in the film's second sequence in Vera's bedroom, another demonstration of an encultured representation of woman.

Bauer alerts the viewer to this fact in several ways. First, he offers an unmediated, 'factual' view of Vera on stage that stresses her identity as a performer. Thus, Vera is shown in long shot, a framing that enables Bauer to emphasise not her as an individual, but the whole theatre setting of which she is simply one constitutional part: we see the stage on which she sits, the 'flat' theatrical set in which she is placed, the props, the edge of the curtain on the left hand side of the stage and the silhouettes of the conductor and members of the orchestra in their places in the orchestra pit. Bauer also emphasises the artificial, 'assumed' nature of Vera's on-stage character by showing her dressed to play a different role in an earlier sequence when, three times, she steps out from behind the heavy stage curtains to take a bow before her appreciative audience; their figures, as they stand to applaud Vera, are again visible as silhouettes in front of the stage, as the manservant's and Petrov's had been in the earlier bedroom sequences. In their design, their construction and their lighting these sequences there-fore both recall the film's second sequence, in Vera's bedroom; and again they both leave the viewer with the same sense that Bauer is here demon-strating – at a distance – a socially constructed representation of woman. Showing Vera backstage in her dressing room further reminds the viewer that she is a performer, not the character we see on stage.

The 'factual' nature of these sequences is further emphasised when the viewer is offered a contrasting point of view on the performer, this time mediated through Dolskii's perspective. Thus, the initial long shot of Vera on stage in *La Traviata* is immediately followed by a shot seen from Dolskii's perspective, a fact Bauer indicates by including the outline of his opera glasses in the frame and thorough the shot's closer framing, which replicates the magnifying effect of Dolskii's glasses. The most striking con-sequence of this closer framing is that all the naturalistic details of the theatre setting – the stage, the set, the orchestra, the lighting and the cur-tains – are excluded from the frame, which is filled instead by the figures of Vera and her male counterpart. This is a telling alteration of perspective, for it reveals that, unlike Bauer, Dolskii is incapable of distinguishing be-tween Vera, the woman with whom he was once involved, and Violetta, the woman whom she is 'imitating' on stage.

'Becoming' a woman, 5: off stage – new womanhood and feminism

'I am a living human being and I want to live a human life, with all its flaws; I find it unbearable to be looked upon as a sort of abstracted being, albeit the most ideal [...]. You have dragged me away from life and set me apart, somewhere on high, where it is cold, frightening and [...] boring.' The Beautiful Lady has rebelled!

Liubov Dmitrievna Mendeleeva-Blok in an unsent letter to her husband, the Symbolist poet Aleksandr Blok, 1902.[70]

However, while seeing 'Vera' die from consumption on stage confirms Dolskii in all his misguided preconceptions, Bauer suggests something different about her to the viewer. Significantly, the film does not end with Vera on stage. After the performance, Dolskii rushes to Vera's dressing room and begs her to take him back. The viewer perhaps expects Vera to welcome him back into her life. After all, a previous sequence has stressed her continuing love for Dolskii by picturing her gazing at his photograph, which she keeps in a locket, worn round her neck even when she is in costume. Moreover, the acts of forgiving and of gratefully accepting a faithless man's declaration of love are – to use Butler's terminology – two powerful regulatory 'norms' of feminine behaviour, as exemplified not only by the ending of *La Traviata*, but also by countless other nineteenth-century works of art in all media. Vera's actual response is therefore unexpected, for she rejects Dolskii, announcing clearly and deliberately: 'It is too late, Prince! There was a time when I loved you. Now my love has died'.

In going against these nineteenth-century 'gender norms', Vera displays the full extent of her potential for agency and action. Refusing to continue to 'reiterate' outmoded conceptions of femininity, she resists them (without even pausing to consider the potential negative consequences of this refusal) and, as she has done throughout the film, instead follows her own mind. Thus, if Butler is correct that the fundamental character of such gender norms is their 'iterability' in 'the daily social rituals of bodily life',[71] then Vera can be said to have shattered several nineteenth-century gender norms and replaced them with a new norm of feminine behaviour for the new twentieth century, namely that a woman can claim for herself those rights previously reserved only for men by the patriarchal order. In other words, the twentieth-century woman can now start to live, love and work independently, as she herself chooses. Even more significantly, she will not allow her actions to be dictated by her feelings; she will not give in to her love for a man who, she knows, cannot accept her for who she is. As de Beauvoir might have put it, Vera has achieved 'transcendence'. That this is a momentous achievement is a fact of which Vera herself is aware; as Youngblood notes, 'Although she is emotionally shaken by [Dolskii's] renewed declarations of love, she is proud of her control over her emotions, and her discipline in refusing to jettison her career for this unworthy lover'.[72] For, as Schuler has documented, 'during the nineteenth and early twentieth centuries, all but a few Russians accepted without question the notion that gender is determined by nature and therefore immutable'.[73] Bauer uses Vera to prove that this majority view is wrong.

The fate of Prince Dolskii is also revealing. Rejected by the self-sufficient 'Ellen Kay', he reflects for a moment on his 'ruined life' before shooting himself through the heart. Thus, in a final rewriting of the ending of *La Traviata*, Bauer reverses male and female gender roles: in his film it is the woman who lives, and the man who dies. The ending of Bauer's film also perhaps alludes to one of the best-known male/female relationships in nineteenth-century Russian culture, for it recalls Tatiana's famous rejection of Pushkin's Evgenii Onegin, except in one significant respect: unlike Tatiana, Vera has no husband to whom she has to remain loyal. More significant than either Vera's financial independence or her successful career, then, is the emotional independence she has achieved. As Vera is neither angel nor excused libertine, neither born victim nor redeemed sinner, so she is no man's wife; instead she is shown by Bauer to be a determined agent of her own destiny. This makes her unique among his female performer protagonists, for – as we shall see – none of her successors acquires both emotional and financial independence and self-sufficiency.

In Bauer's 1916 film *A Life for a Life* [Zhizn´ za zhizn´] an intertitle informs us: 'Under the influence of love, a woman forgets everything'. Vera is the exception who proves this rule, being the only young woman who does not allow love to rule her life. According to Aleksandra Kollontai, this makes Vera a true New Woman. In her 1913 article 'The New Woman' ['Novaia zhenshchina'], Kollontai argued that it was not only traditional marriage and financial dependence that held women 'in captivity', but also women themselves, or, more precisely, the female psychology. As Kollontai saw it, in her quest for liberation the New Woman faced obstacles not only from a hostile social order and the reactionary men who controlled it, but also from her innermost self. The main enemy of the New Woman was, she argued, female heterosexual love and desire: 'The power of past centuries still has a strong hold even over the soul of the new, free woman. Atavistic feelings interrupt and weaken new experiences, outlived conceptions still hold in their persistent clutches the feminine spirit that thrusts towards freedom'.[74] This ability for women to 'put love in second place' is also the 'key to happiness' identified by the popular writer Anastasiia Verbitskaia in her blockbuster novel, *The Keys to Happiness* [Kliuchi schast´ia, 1910–13], which was brought to the cinema screen by the directors Iakov Protazanov and Vladimir Gardin in a two-part film released just over a month before Bauer's *Twilight of a Woman's Soul*, on 7 October and 28 October 1913. However, unlike Vera, Mania – the heroine of Verbitaskaia's melodrama, who is often seen as a quintessential New Woman – proves unable to live by this precept; the film concludes with her suicide, caused in no small part by the death (also by suicide) of the man with whom she is hopelessly in love. 'The woman in me is stronger than the *artiste*. I am powerless in the face of love', Mania writes in her suicide letter.[75]

Bauer also stresses Vera's New Woman status in another way. Vera renames herself, choosing a foreign name – Ellen Kay – to symbolise her escape from her restrictive past. This name is not chosen by chance, however, for it bears an additional layer of significance, containing within it a barely cloaked allusion to a real-life woman, namely the Swedish suffragist and feminist Ellen Key (1849–1926).[76] In 1911, the Italian poet Ada Negri described Key as the 'liberator of woman's soul'.[77] It can be no coincidence that Key's monograph, *Love and Marriage* [Kärleken och äktenslapet, 1904, published in Russian as Liubov´ i brak in 1907],[78] influenced Kollontai's 1913 formulation of the New Woman, of which Vera stands as a paradigmatic example.[79] For Vera also displays many of the qualities that her namesake advocated for modern women: specifically, 'a finer knowledge of self, a stronger consciousness of personality [...] this determination of individualism [that] makes it impossible for the modern woman to be fired by the ideal of Griselda, if for no other reason because she feels how all-suffering meekness increases injustice'.[80] It is, therefore, ironic that the Swedish censors banned Bauer's film because they were shocked by his portrayal of his female protagonist.[81]

Thus, in his first surviving feature film as director, inspired by the example of Ellen Key, a woman ahead of her times in so many ways, Bauer also proves himself to be ahead of his field, not only in terms of his artistic mastery – his consummate use of the expressive potential of all elements of mise-en-scène and of cinematic technology – but also as regards his themes and his understanding of the challenges that faced Russian women as they struggled to take advantage of the possibilities for social change offered by modernity. For, in charting Vera's progress as she 'becomes' a woman, asserting her agency and transforming herself from the encultured object of the male gaze to the independent subject of her own freely created narrative, Bauer enthrals his viewers with a 'bravura tale of female independence'[82] that is already, even at this early point in his directorial career, told in the confident, innovative and specifically cinematic language that would become the hallmark of his distinctive authorial style. Moreover, at the end of this film we are shown an example of a quintessential New Woman, as defined by Kollontai: 'Before us stands woman as personality, before us stands a human being possessing a characteristic value, with her own individuality, who asserts herself – in short, a woman who has broken the rusted fetters of her sex'.[83] In this respect, Vera Dubrovskaia would prove to be an almost impossible act to follow.

4

From the Oriental Dancer to the Tango-Woman

> There must be something to 'Salome' because we recognise 'her'
> in so many different guises [...], but this is not Woman veiled
> and unveiled again and again, this is intertextuality.
>
> Megan Becker-Leckrone.[1]

Grigorii Libkin's *Stenka Razin*

In spite of the increasing preference among directors and viewers for urban melodramas set in the twentieth-century present, early Russian cinema proved unable to forget its first anonymous performer heroine. The suggestive figure of the oriental dancer recurs throughout Russian films of the 1910s and is increasingly conflated with the more general Salome archetype. In many of these later films the oriental dancer is used simply (although not always unironically, or without humour) as a convenient shorthand indicator of – or, to adapt Becker-Leckrone's terms, an interfilmic referent to – existing cinematic representations of fatal femininity. Thus, in Mikhail Bonch-Tomashevskii's *The Mother-in-Law in the Harem* [Teshcha v gareme, 1915], Robert Reinols's engaging *Baldy in Love with the Dancer* [Lysyi vliublen v tantsovshchitsu, 1916], Iosif Soifer's *Aziade* (1918), Fedor Komissarzhevskii and Boris Chaikovskii's *The Stage Set of Happiness* [Dekoratsiia schast'ia, 1918], Petr Chardynin's

A Tale of Precious Love [Skazka liubvi dorogoi, 1918] and *The Song of Persia* [Pesn´ Persii, 1919, director unknown], to name but a few films that offer examples of this tendency, the oriental dancer retains many of the associations she had first acquired in Drankov's *Stenka Razin* and is not explored in depth.

More revealing, however, is a second film about Stenka Razin and the Persian princess, directed by Grigorii Libkin and also entitled *Stenka Razin* (1914). Only three of the film's seven reels have survived, but the detailed synopsis published in the journal *Cine-Phono* enables the modern viewer to fill in the gaps.[2] Like Drankov before him, Libkin focuses on Razin's infatuation with the beautiful Persian princess. While this time she is at least given a name (Fatma), which suggests some progress towards autonomy, this film in fact does little to develop Drankov's representation of the oriental dancer, and Fatma remains a quintessential example of this stereotypical paradigm. Thus a scopophilic camera presents the princess as a beautiful, passive object of erotic contemplation. We first see her reclining on a couch in her court, like so many nineteenth-century odalisques before her. Tapestries decorate the walls and, as the princess admires her numerous bracelets, so the viewer admires her: she is merely one of the many beautiful objects that adorn her boudoir. When Razin captures Fatma during his battle with her father, he therefore treats her as he would any other plunder, seizing her and placing her securely in his tent before resuming the fight. Indeed, a schematic outline of the film, published as part of a trade advertisement in an earlier edition of *Cine-Phono*, summarises this part in precisely this way: 'Razin's spoils of war – the Persian Princess – Part 3'.[3] Razin also makes this comparison explicit in the words he utters before drowning the princess: as the Volga gave him silver, gold and other riches, so he now offers the river the 'great gift' of Fatma's life.[4]

As in Drankov's film, the male protagonists are shown to have the same voyeuristic tendencies as the film-makers' camera. Thus when Semen Alatyrets, the young brigand sent to inform Razin of the men's desire to return home, happens upon the sleeping princess in the ataman's tent, he stands and gazes at her intently. In thrall to her beauty, he later takes advantage of Razin's absence and enters his tent uninvited, so that he may again observe the sleeping princess, whose erotic appeal is heightened in this sequence by the simple white, sleeveless nightgown in which she is dressed.

Razin is also, of course, captivated by Fatma's beauty and twice persuades the princess to dance before him and his men. As she dances, dressed in gauzy veils and with her long hair flowing loose, Fatma bears a strong resemblance to the oriental dancer imagined by Drankov six years previously. At the end of her performance, the ataman is overcome by his desire for this alluring young woman. As the *snokhach* had done with Lusha in *The Incestuous Father-in-Law*, he sweeps her up in his arms and embraces her passionately in full view of all his men, prompting one of them to comment: 'Stepan! Cossack freedom comes to an end, once women are given power'.[5] This observation has a profound effect on Razin. It brings him to his senses and re-awakens his sense of male pride: as Drankov's Razin had done before him, he therefore immediately hurls Fatma into the Volga. As in Drankov's film again, then, it is in dancing that the princess is shown to be not only at her most powerful and dangerous but also at her most vulnerable.

Indeed, Libkin does not merely repeat the various negative elements of Drankov's portrayal of the Persian princess, but in fact formulates them even more explicitly. The belief in woman as a malign influence is expressed directly in the film's prologue, when Razin encounters the sorceress Alena, who issues him with a warning: 'Beware of this woman! She will be the ruin of you and of your entire cause'.[6] Repeatedly recalled by Razin at significant moments, Alena's portentous words become the film's leitmotif. They express a truth apparently accepted even by Fatma herself for, when Razin tells her about the sorceress's prediction, she declares that in order to save him she will happily accept death. Indeed, the veracity of Alena's words is borne out by the way the narrative develops, for while Romashkov's male protagonists dealt easily with the threat posed by the first Salome-esque dancer of Russian film, in this later film they are less successful. In this connection it is significant that Libkin's *Stenka Razin*, unlike Drankov's, does not end with the princess's death, but instead continues for three more reels in which the film-makers chart Razin's gradual downfall. The princess is, from the outset, implicated in this process. Indeed, Razin's first serious mistake is to have surrendered to his desire for the captive princess, for in taking her as his lover he arouses the jealousy of the brigand, Alatyrets. Fatma's beauty is therefore shown to set men against men; both Razin and this young man allow their actions to be governed by their desire for her, and the acts they commit are shown to be destructive not only of them-selves, but also of their fellow brigands. Thus, 'under the influence of irre-sistible passion', Alatyrets is driven to kill the Cossack whom Razin had charged with guarding the princess, in order to gain access to her presence, which proves, Razin sadly concludes, that 'the woman's beauty is in fact ruining his entire cause'.[7]

Ultimately, Alatyrets turns even against his leader. Having vowed to avenge the princess's death, he defects to the Streltsy, joining their attack on Razin in the town of Simbirsk. During the ensuing battle Alatyrets and Razin come face to face. Seeing the young man reminds Razin of the princess; he freezes and Alatyrets, taking advantage of Razin's distraction, wounds him. Like the ataman, however, Alatyrets is also marked by Fatma's fatal 'curse': Razin's brother rushes to Razin's aid and kills Alatyrets.

Moreover, although dead, the Persian princess does not vanish from the film, but makes two further appearances as a beguiling figure who haunts Razin's dreams. Razin's obsession with the princess continues to bring dis-aster. Visited by his wife, Nastia, he spurns her love, confessing to his pas-sion for the princess. Angered by this revelation, Nastia threatens Razin before running away. Razin ignores her, however, retreating into dreams of Fatma, who remains alive and acquiescent in his mind. It is an error for which he pays dearly, for his wife reveals his hiding place to the authorities, who send soldiers to capture him. As he is conveyed to Moscow, Razin learns that his men have also been defeated. Once more Fatma is linked to Razin's misfortune. Held in stocks overnight, he dreams of his oriental lover, who appears before him in her white nightgown. On waking, Razin is taken to his place of execution and beheaded before a large crowd of onlookers, his severed head displayed for all to see. By repeatedly conjuring the Persian princess at such significant moments, the film-makers continu-ally suggest that she is responsible for the ills that befall the ataman and his fellow men. Put simply, this bewitching, Salome-esque dancer costs Razin his head.

Or does she? That Fatma is responsible for these terrible events is cer-tainly the opinion of the film's protagonists and arguably also that of the film-makers themselves. There is, however, a significant problem with this view of Fatma as a Salome figure, for she neither seeks nor desires Razin's death. On the contrary, she is passively respectful of his male authority, referring to him as her 'master', and, mindful of the patriarchal hierarchy, she values her own life less than his. However, while Fatma in fact has little influence over the events depicted in the film, another female protagonist does, namely Razin's wife. For Nastia is everything Fatma is not: unlike the passive and compliant princess, Nastia is driven by strong feelings of her own, and she is both able and willing to act on them. Thus, from the moment Razin spurns her love, she – like Wilde's Salome – is motivated only by her desire to take revenge on him for this rejection. It is Nastia who alerts the authorities to Razin's whereabouts, she who brings about his capture and she, therefore, who causes his head to roll. Although she neither dances nor looks the part, Nastia, as a strong, independent woman, is in fact more of a Salome than the stereotypical Fatma. Razin's error was perhaps, therefore, not to have recognised that this apparently 'ordinary' Russian woman was far more 'dangerous' than the Persian princess, for all her alluring oriental sexuality, could ever be.

Writing of the development of the literary motif of the Persian princess, Neia Zorkaia notes: 'Continual migrations, transplantations, metamorphoses and alterations would prove to be characteristic of this secondary character'.[8] As in Russian literature, so in Russian film: the Persian princess, with her femme fatale allure, proved a malleable figure. As the 1910s progressed, the archetype of the fatal oriental dancer began to develop, to take on other more contemporary forms and to appear in Russian film in altered 'guises', in particular that of the tango dancer [*tangistka*].

Evgenii Bauer's *Child of the Big City*

The most complex use of the figure of the Salome dancer occurs in a film made slightly earlier than Libkin's *Stenka Razin*: Evgenii Bauer's *Child of the Big City*, which was released on 5 March 1914. Photographed by Boris Zavelev, the cameraman with whom Bauer worked on almost all subsequent films, *Child of the Big City* tells the tale of an ambitious young seamstress who improves her lot by captivating a rich gentleman whom she ruins and then abandons, driving him to suicide. This early Bauer film, for which Bauer wrote the original scenario in addition to serving as both director and art director [*khudozhnik-dekorator*], features two of the most memorable dance performances in early Russian cinema. While the first recalls those of both Drankov's and Libkin's Persian princesses, the second is striking in its novelty: at the end of the film Bauer's female protagonist performs a lengthy tango routine. The tango had arrived in Russia from Paris in the late autumn of 1913, and in March 1914 there was no more fashionable (or controversial) dance that this.[9] As we shall see, Bauer exploits the precise cultural significance of these two very different dance forms to tell a complex story of male fear and female dynamism that taps into contemporary concerns about both changing gender roles and relations, and the profound social changes ushered in by modernity. He also concentrates on these performances his continuing exploration of the narrative possibilities afforded by the developing cinematic technology. As a result, they both also reveal much about Bauer's approach to the new art form of cinema, which he was already, after less than two years in the industry, making his own.

Child of the Big City opens with the orphaning of Manka/Mania, the eponymous child, whose mother dies from tuberculosis in the dirty basement they call home. Nine years pass. Bauer's heroine has blossomed into a beautiful young woman and now works in a sewing workshop. Mania's dissatisfaction with her life is clear, however, as is her flightiness. Her mind wanders from her tasks as she gossips with her workmates, and her frustration can be read on her face when she is framed in medium close-up, sitting by the workshop window and looking wistfully at the Moscow streets below.[10] The cause of her dissatisfaction is explained in an intertitle: Mania is transfixed 'by dreams of a make-believe life, full of luxury and wealth'.

Bauer's hero, Viktor Kravtsov, is similarly dissatisfied with life and prone to dreaming. The focus of his idealistic fantasies is not, however, money (of which he has plenty), but his desire to find the perfect woman. Tired of the 'cultured' women of his own social class, he is seeking, an intertitle informs us, the love of 'an unspoilt young creature'.

In the next sequence, hero and heroine meet. Hatbox in hand, Mania is out on an errand, but work is not what occupies her attention as she walks down the Moscow streets. Instead, she stands staring at the display in an extravagant flower shop, then gazes into a jeweller's window and bursts into tears of frustrated longing. Viktor and his friend, the more pragmatic and worldly wise Kramskoi, have already been watching Mania for some time. Seizing their opportunity, they attempt to comfort her, with Kramskoi wasting no time in inviting her to dine with them. Initially feigning reluctance,

Mania soon accepts and the three of them repair to the private room [*kabinet*] of a restaurant where, predictably, Kramskoi attempts to seduce the young woman.[11] Mania resists, but the way the sequence develops reveals that her protestations were motivated not by moral scruples, but by sexual preference; when Kramskoi leaves, Viktor attempts to seduce Mania in his turn. He encounters no resistance.

It can be no coincidence that Bauer names his confident male protagonist after the nineteenth-century Russian realist artist Ivan Kramskoi, whose most famous work is his 1883 portrait of a knowing and challenging 'Unknown Woman' ['Neizvestnaia'].[12] By thus linking Viktor's friend with this realist artist, Bauer both emphasises Kramkoi's matter-of-fact approach to women and underlines Viktor's naïve idealism in this regard. While Kramskoi immediately sees Mania for what she is – a pragmatic working-class girl who dreams of a good life and will do anything to achieve it – the idealistic Viktor is taken in by her performance of innocence and vulnerability. Believing he has at last found an 'unspoilt creature', Viktor sets Mania up as his mistress. Thus he enables Mania's dreams to come true, for through him she goes up in the world. While Mania signals her improved social status and her new sense of self by changing her name to the foreign Mary [Meri], Bauer indicates her rise from working-class poverty to high-society luxury visually in an innovative low-angle location shot – that again demonstrates his awareness of the expressive possibilities of mise-en-scène – of the huge art nouveau staircase that Mary climbs to reach the fashionable nightclub to which Viktor takes her. It is here that the film's first dance sequence occurs.

Mary and the Salome dancer

As Viktor studies the menu and discusses his order with the waiter, Mary – already very obviously bored by her rich lover – sips champagne and flirts with her numerous admirers. Drunken revellers cavort on the dance floor behind them, and the stage curtains in the background part to reveal a black velvet backdrop and the undulating arms of a barefoot Salome dancer who moves slowly to the centre of the stage. So much action is taking place in the frame at this point that the viewer does not initially pay more than glancing attention to the dancer. This changes, however, when the camera suddenly begins an extended track-in, advancing slowly yet deliberately over the heads of the nightclub-goers towards the dancer. The track-in lasts for almost one minute, an extraordinarily long time at this point in the history of film. Indeed, in every respect, this camera movement was hugely innovative. Although the extended track-in would become, in Tsivian's words, Bauer's 'favourite camera movement', it was without precedent in Russian films in 1914.[13]

This shot is also remarkable for the way in which it testifies to the superlative self-consciousness that is the hallmark of Bauer's directorial style. The activization of the camera was one of the key ways in which early Russian film succeeded in freeing itself from the theatrical conventions that had shaped its aesthetics in its earliest days.[14] That Bauer elects to demonstrate the stunning mobility of his camera in the diegetic context of a theatre has to be seen as a self-aware challenge to and rejection of this theatrical heritage. You might think you are watching a stage performance, Bauer seems to be saying in this sequence, but do not forget that you are in fact watching a film.

No doubt part of the function of this shot was also to impress the viewer with the depth and three-dimensional quality, or 'stereoscopy', of the set, for as the camera moves forward the cameraman, Zavelev, takes the viewer with him, into and over the different planes and levels of the glamorous set, from the dais where Mary and Viktor sit, over the lower dance floor and, finally, to the raised stage itself. As we saw in Chapter 3, however, in Bauer's films technical innovation is never included simply to impress, but always used meaningfully to contribute to the film-makers' evocation of mood, character or theme. Indeed, as Philip Cavendish has rightly noted: 'Such tracking shots [...] are intended to be discursive, and possess a syntagmatic function'.[15] The challenge for the viewer, then, is to unravel the meanings expressed by this technically and aesthetically innovative cinematic sequence. Specifically, why does Bauer want the viewer to focus on the performance that is taking place in the background of the frame? The dancer is not a protagonist in the film's diegesis; she plays no role in the plot. Were it not for the track-in she would remain just another component of Bauer's complex and many-layered mise-en-scène, contributing to the cinematic illusion that this glamorous nightclub is 'real'.

One meaning that is clear is that the track-in is intended to connect Mary and the dancer. A striking feature of this sequence is the fact that although the camera is moving towards the dancer on the stage, Bauer does not allow the viewer to forget his female protagonist; throughout most of the track-in the camera also keeps Mary in view, in the bottom right-hand corner of the frame (Figure 4.1). This effect is strengthened by the fact that the track-in also includes a (rather crude) jump cut that brings Mary back into sight after the camera has gone past her. Mary and the dancer are further linked because, as the camera tracks in, they are the only two female characters facing the camera. They are also on approximately the same level within the set: the dancer performs on a raised stage, and Mary is seated at a table on a dais that is separated from the dance floor by a flight of steps. Furthermore, the sensation that Mary, like the dancer, is putting on a performance (for the male guests who surround her) is also very strong. Oblivious to the stage performance behind her, Mary throws streamers and confetti at the men, raises her glass in their

Figure 4.1 As Mary flirts with her admirers, the camera tracks in on an exotic Salome dancer (Bauer, *Child of the Big City*, 1914)

direction and casts them coy but seductive glances from under fluttering eyelashes.

In all these ways, then, but especially by means of the precise construction of the track-in, Bauer links Mary with the figure of the Salome dancer. Having established this link, the camera then cuts to an extended full-length shot of the performer. There it remains, fixed on the dancer for a full thirty seconds (an usually long time) as she performs her solo routine (Figure 4.2). Everything about this shot forces the viewer to observe her performance closely, from her centralised position in the frame (as in Drankov's *Stenka Razin*) to the set design; the plain black backdrop against which the performer dances – striking in a film that privileges cluttered sets and highly patterned backdrops – ensures that there is nothing in the background to distract the viewer's attention from her. Study her well, Bauer exhorts: this female performer will shed light on Mary.

However, while it is clear that this sequence and the figure of the Salome dancer are intended to contribute to the film's characterisation of Mary, precisely what they suggest about her is less easy to state with certainty, for

Figure 4.2. The Salome dancer (Bauer, *Child of the Big City*, 1914)

the questions arise both of whose view of Mary the sequence expresses and of what Bauer seeks to communicate about her by linking her the figure of the Salome dancer.

Mary through Mary's eyes?

Cavendish has suggested that the camera's extended track-in serves to evoke Mary's perspective.[16] Arguing that the unusual height of the camera and its unexpected movement combine to evoke 'the dizzy excitement' she is experiencing as she enjoys 'the pleasures of affluence for the first time', he proposes that the track-in should be read as a 'quasi point-of-view-shot' in which the camera evokes Mary's worldview.[17]

This reading is suggestive, but not unproblematic. First, it overlooks the fact that Bauer's view of Mary has been, from the start of the film, coolly detached and appraising; he, like the knowing Kramskoi, has no illusions about this young woman's character. Second, and more importantly, however, it stops short of considering the relevance of the 'subject' of the track-in. In any track-in shot it is not only the movement of the camera that bears meaning; the precise nature of the subject towards whom the camera moves is also significant, and, indeed, Bauer emphasises this by following the track-in with the extended full-length sequence of the dancer's performance.[18]

What do we notice as we watch the dancer? First, her eloquent costume: in almost all its details, it recalls those worn by the real-life Salome dancers Ida Rubinstein, Ruth St Denis, Mata Hari, La Belle Otéro, Maud Allan *et al.*, who were so in vogue in Russia, as in Europe and North America, in the first decade of the twentieth century. Indeed, a reviewer, writing in the Khanzhonkov production company's journal *Cinema Herald* [Vestnik kinematografii] in 1914, praised this sequence precisely because it drew on this trend, noting:

> We must dwell on [the] beautifully performed Eastern dance, in which the wonderful gracefulness of [the dancer's] arms is striking; their undulating, snake-like movements have something in common with the expressive grace of the famous English [*sic*] dancer Miss Maud Allan.[19]

As we saw in Chapter 1, for the many early twentieth-century female performers whose repertoire featured a Salome dance, embodying the figure of that legendary femme fatale on stage enabled them to dramatise
for themselves, and for their audiences, their desire for various kinds of
emancipation. It was the New Woman's art form. Is this what Bauer here
seeks to evoke? Is this Mary's view of herself as New Woman? If we read
the track-in as representing Mary's perspective, this is what we have to
assume.

However, there are a number of problems with this reading, not least
the fact that it ignores the precise significance of the Salome dancer in
the cultural landscape of Russia in early 1914. When *Child of the Big City*
was released on to Russian cinema screens in March of that year, almost
six years had elapsed both since Drankov's Persian princess had appeared
on Russian cinema screens and since Ida Rubinstein had stunned St
Petersburg with her Salome routine. Moreover, the Russian Salome dance
craze was over almost as soon as it had begun. In late 1909, when Maud
Allan toured Russia with her 'Vision of Salome', her performances were
met at best with indifference and at worst with derision. As the dance
historian Toni Bentley describes it: 'Russia had little tolerance for what
critics dismissed as a "caricature" of Isadora [Duncan, the American dan-
cer], and Maud's tour was all empty houses and snickering reviews'.[20] By
1914, then, the Salome dancer had long been considered out-moded by
Russian audiences. Indeed, the 'datedness' of this persona did not pass
unnoticed by more astute (and less partisan?) contemporary critics. In
an article published in 1914 in *Cine-Journal* [Kine-zhurnal] – according
to Denise Youngblood, 'an important trade journal that was less biased
than most'[21] – one reviewer wrote that, although *Child of the Big City* was
the best film released by the Khanzhonkov production company to date,
Bauer had let himself down by including such an unoriginal and hackneyed set piece:

> The inclusion of the so-called 'Indian dance' also suggests he
> has no taste – who needs such banality and tastelessness? And
> then again, why should this dance be referred to as 'Indian'?
> It could just as well have been called Egyptian, or Syrian, or
> Turkish, etc, etc. It is totally lacking in style![22]

However, although the reviewer does not consider this possibility, it is highly unlikely that Bauer, one of the most culturally aware directors of this period, did not realise that the Salome dance would appear hackneyed, tasteless and out-of-date. It must therefore be assumed that he intended it to create precisely this effect. This undermines the suggestion that Bauer intends the Salome figure to be seen as a representation of Mary's self-image, for, as we shall see, she is nothing if not up-to-date. Indeed, this film can be read as the story of her creation of a twentieth-century self.

It is not only the outdatedness of the Salome dancer that suggests that this sequence is not intended to represent Mary's self-image, however. Other elements of the dancer's performance point to the fact that Bauer here seeks not to evoke the positive 'emancipated' associations of the figure of the female-created early twentieth-century Salome dancer, but to conjure up the older and more negative values of the Salome archetype propagated in nineteenth- and early twentieth-century art. In other words, Bauer here presents the Salome figure – and, therefore, Mary – from a more generic, and old-fashioned, 'male' point of view.

Mary through 'male' eyes: from ancient mythologies to new archetypes of fatal femininity

> Woman's [...] advance in society is not a voyage from myth to truth but from myth to new myth.
>
> Camille Paglia.[23]

> As lithe as a serpent, pale to the point of transparency, with almost holy eyes and dissolute lips. This is the tango-woman [zhenshchina-tango].
>
> 'The New Eve' ['Novaia Eva'], 1914.[24]

That the track-in represents a male perspective on Mary is, in fact, strongly implied by the very movement of the camera as it homes in on the dancer; it functions to draw the viewer's attention to the exotic dancer and to encourage the viewer to observe her closely. As in Drankov's *Stenka Razin*, therefore, a scopophilic camera here frames the Salome dancer and the sequence is structured according to a specifically male gaze, with man positioned as spectator and woman as 'spectacle'. As in the earlier film again, the dancer's costume heightens her 'to-be-looked-at-ness', and suggests the exotic 'Otherness' and sensuality of a male-imagined femininity. Moreover, unlike in *Stenka Razin*, in the central section of this sequence the dancer's diegetic audience is entirely excluded from the frame. In this way, the dancer is extracted and abstracted from the film's diegetic context. This emphasises the fact that, despite its importance to the film's thematics, this sequence does not contribute anything to the film's plot line. In other words, it 'embellishes' the film but adds no narrative facts. In existing outside the film's diegesis, the dancer's performance therefore stands as an example of how, as Laura Mulvey has argued, in classical cinema 'woman's visual presence tends to work against the development of a story line, to freeze the flow of action in moments of erotic contemplation'.[25] What the viewer gets in this sequence, then, is yet another image of woman as an object, displayed for the viewer's pleasure.

Seen in its contemporary context, this camera movement also, however, serves to remind that the male gaze can, in Elaine Showalter's words, be 'both self-empowering and self-endangering'.[26] Moreover, drawing on the research of the film historian Tom Gunning, Tsivian has documented that in the early 1900s the track-in was often misread by viewers, who responded to it as being not the activization of the camera towards the subject, but rather that of the subject towards the camera.[27] In support of this reading Tsivian cites a passage from the memoirs of the Spanish-born film-maker Luís Buñuel:

> I shall never forget my horror, which was shared by the whole audience, when I saw a track-in for the first time in my life. A head bore down upon us from the screen, getting larger and larger as if it was going to swallow us up. I could not for one moment imagine that it was the camera that was being brought closer to the head [...]. What we saw before us was a head getting nearer, becoming monstrously enlarged.[28]

Even in the 1910s, this apprehension coloured the viewer's reception of the track-in. As Tsivian explains:

> Of course, in the 1910s no viewers still believed that the head was actually getting bigger, instead of getting nearer. But the

attendant effect of 'a head bearing down upon us from the screen', described in Buñuel's memoirs, was still very much there. *The track-in imparted extra energy to the subject, which made it impending, menacing, even aggressive. In the 1910s these connotations were still part of the track-in and not only conditioned its reception but also determined its usage* [emphasis added].[29]

Indeed, there are other 'menacing' and 'aggressive' features in Bauer's representation of the Salome dancer. The black backdrop creates an ominous, funereal atmosphere, and Bauer includes a striking, unfamiliar detail in his design for the dancer's costume: her extraordinary talon-like false nails. These nails transform the dancer's elegant, undulating arms into menacing fanged serpentine creatures and, in this way, evoke the spectre of the *vagina dentata* – commonly linked with Salome in nineteenth-century art – that both Showalter and Paglia see in Aubrey Beardsley's 1894 drawing 'John and Salome'.[30] They also recall the extraordinary set design that the theatre director Nikolai Evreinov and his designer Nikolai Kalmakov created for their 1908 production of Wilde's *Salomé*. According to Spencer Golub, the play's main action was located 'inside a giant scenic vagina', a mise-en-scène that stripped away 'all pretense of illusion and metaphor' and 'literally made a spectacle of gender consumption (the vagina dentata)'.[31] As William Tydeman and Steven Price also note, this set design would have served 'to signify visually the "castrating woman" whom many have detected in Wilde's Salome'.[32] All these details and their contemporary cultural associations combine to suggest that the Salome dancer is here intended less as a positive representation of the twentieth-century Salome dancer as New Woman than as an archaic nineteenth-century model of the femme fatale, that familiar source of male fear.

The link between Mary and the nineteenth-century figure of Salome is stressed subtly throughout the rest of the film. In a subsequent sequence set in Mary's home (paid for by Viktor, no doubt, but furnished by his lover, the tasteless knick-knacks that clutter her rooms, and the clutter itself, being emblematic of her greed and hunger for material possessions), Bauer suggests Mary's predatory nature by including in his mise-en-scène an extraordinary bearskin couch, on which she reclines like a huntress delighting in showing off a trophy. This pose evokes the figure of the odal-isque, a common oriental fantasy figure in nineteenth-century literature and art. As Oksana Bulgakova has demonstrated, in the period under con-sideration 'the vogue for oriental beauties introduced a new pose [...]: that of reclining'.[33] Mary's body language – both in this sequence and in a later sequence when she lies on a chaise-longue, indulging herself in erotic fanta-sies about Viktor's valet (Figure 4.6) – therefore also serves to re-emphasise her kinship with the figure of the Persian princess, who is framed reclining sensuously in both Drankov's and Libkin's films, on an oriental rug in the former, and on a divan in the latter.

It is, however, in the film's final sequence that both the negative asso-ciations of the Salome archetype and the link between Mary and this fig-ure are made explicit, when Mary dances and Viktor dies. This sequence begins when the impoverished, lovesick Viktor arrives at Mary's house to deliver a letter that pleads for one final meeting. As Viktor hands the letter to Mary's doorman, Bauer cuts inside to the drunken dinner party where Mary and her new lover are preparing to entertain their guests. As befits such a defiantly and self-consciously New Woman, Mary performs a new style of dance: the tango.[34]

Described by Tsivian as 'disturbingly libidinous', the tango arrived in Russia from Paris in the late autumn of 1913 and was an immediate *succès de scandale*.[35] This new dance inspired intense discussion, and open debates about it were held in both Moscow and St Petersburg in early February 1914.[36] Most Russian commentators agreed that its defining char-acteristic was its tragic and vaguely sinister sexual nature. Thus Mikhail Bonch-Tomashevskii, in his 1914 *Book about the Tango: Art and Sexuality* [Kniga o tango: iskusstvo i seksual´nost´], commented: 'Yes, the tango is sexual. Imperceptible motions are saturated with the electric current of feeling. [...] The tango lends its rigid mould to the sexuality of our age'.[37] The theatre critic Homo Novus wrote:

> The tango is serious, the tango is tragic [...]. The tango is never performed *aus reiner Tanzlust* [...]. It tells the sad story of desire, with its painful joys and sweet torments. [...] The tango tells the story of experience, after-taste, resentment; it tells us about the fatality of sexual drive.[38]

The official Holy Synod newspaper, *The Bell* [Kolokol], meanwhile, published an article that condemned the tango as a form of 'dry perversion'.[39]

While a modern approach to sexuality is, therefore, already implicit in Mary's chosen dance form, Bauer heightens the sensual atmosphere of her performance through his mise-en-scène: a heavy black velvet curtain, discreetly patterned with embossed roses (perhaps referencing the thorned roses of Beardsley's Salome image), is drawn three-quarters of the way across the set, putting the viewer in the position of frustrated voyeur by allowing only brief glimpses of Mary as she dances. It also recalls the backdrop against which the anonymous Salome dancer performed in the earlier nightclub sequence, reminding the viewer of the link between Mary and the Salome figure. The curtain has another function, however, for it creates two distinct planes of action: the space behind it, which is shown to belong to Mary and her guests, and that in front, which is the maid's domain – as she bobs about, attempting to attract Mary's attention to deliver Viktor's letter, the maid dares not step behind it. The curtain thus represents the social divide separating Mary and her upper-class entourage from the maid. By showing Mary to be the only character who frequents both spaces, Bauer reminds the viewer of Mary's humble origins and also contrives to represent her as mobile, dynamic and transgressive. The curtain has a final significance: it evokes a traditional theatre stage, especially when, after the maid has left, Mary draws back the curtain with a flourish before resuming her dance. In all these ways, Bauer succeeds in emphasising the fact that what we are watching is as much a performance as the Salome dance we watched earlier in the film.

The arrival of Viktor's letter interrupts Mary's performance, but it elicits from her only a sneer and, in a gesture that enables Bauer neatly to illustrate the complete shift in the balance of power in his protagonists' relationship, Mary reverses society's traditional gender roles and gives her maid three roubles for Viktor, hoping this will rid her of him. Then, without giving him another thought, she resumes her tango performance. Bauer cuts briefly to his hero, who throws Mary's money to the ground. Then, his illusions finally shattered by Mary's insulting gift, Viktor raises a pistol to his head. At this dramatic point in the narrative Bauer unexpectedly cuts away from his hero, however, and returns his attention to Mary. For well over a minute, the camera looks on (in an innovative high-angle shot)

Figure 4.3. Mary tangos with her new lover (Bauer, *Child of the Big City*, 1914)

as she and her new lover tango (Figure 4.3). It is only when Mary and her guests leave to continue dancing at Maxim's, a fashionable Moscow tango club that had opened in December 1913, that we discover that Viktor has indeed shot himself.

Tsivian has suggested that, if judged in purely cinematic terms, the final extended tango routine may appear both 'laborious' and '[i]nept by narrative standards', for, when Bauer finally cuts back to Viktor, any suspense the viewer might have felt about his impending suicide has 'completely gone'.[40] However, the length of the tango performance is not necessarily incompatible with the creation of suspense and it might, on the contrary, be felt to intensify the shock of Viktor's death. Dominique Nasta cites this sequence as an example of how early film melodramas would 'introduce musical occurrences at precise psychological keypoints, so as to increase the visuals' emotional impact'.[41] The exotic tango music that would have been supplied by the cinema accompanist would have delighted contemporary audiences. Swept away by enjoyment of the fashionable dance sequence, viewers would have been jolted out of that enjoyment when the sequence

93

was brought to an end by the abrupt cut to Viktor's corpse. Indeed, the more reflective among them might have been shocked by the ease with which they had been seduced by both Bauer and Mary into forgetting about Viktor. In this analysis, the sequence is effective precisely because of its length, for, as Nasta continues: 'The audience *must* perceive aurally the tango's sensuous rhythmics in order to fully experience the shock of the victim's subsequent suicide [emphasis in original]'.[42]

Maiia Turovskaia includes Mary in her discussion of the murderess in the Russian and Soviet cinematic tradition, considering her to be responsible for Viktor's death even though, as she acknowledges, 'she kills without recourse to a weapon'.[43] Indeed, that this sequence suggests that Mary bears some responsibility for Viktor's death is difficult to deny. For, when one takes into account the contemporary cultural associations of the tango, it acquires a wealth of meanings: the tango's significance as a dance of tragic and vaguely sinister sexuality combines with Bauer's earlier linking of Mary and the Salome dancer, his evocative, expressive mise-en-scène and his euphemistic cross-cutting between Mary, as she dances, and Viktor, as he prepares to kill himself, to suggest that Mary is the cause of Viktor's death. It is also significant that Viktor shoots himself not in the heart, but in the head, an act that links his fate to that of Wilde's unfortunate Jokanaan.

The way in which Mary reacts to Viktor's lifeless body is also significant. In a macabre inversion of the expected, her initial shock at discovering Viktor's corpse on her doorstep turns not to grief or remorse, but first to irritation and then to absolute indifference. Announcing that discovering a dead body is thought by many to be a sign of good luck to come, Mary urges her companions to hurry lest they arrive late at Maxim's 'where gaiety and wine await us […]'.[44] Then she lifts up her gown and, revealing a dainty foot clad in an elegant tango slipper, she steps over Viktor's body. As she does so, the camera homes in for an extra-diegetically lengthy close-up of her foot and her skirt, which momentarily obscures Viktor's head from view, thereby severing it visually if not physically from his body (Figure 4.4).

If these facts were not enough in themselves to connect Mary unambiguously to the mythical figure of Salome, Bauer also ensures that even the way in which she moves in the later parts of the film draws attention to this connection, for when she walks, she does so *à la tango*. Tsivian

94

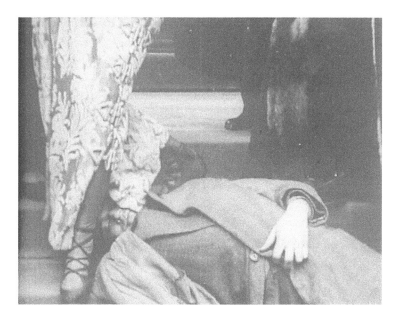

Figure 4.4. Mary steps over Viktor's corpse, revealing her tango slipper (Bauer, *Child of the Big City*, 1914)

cites Ernestine Carter, who describes the 'tango walk' as consisting, significantly, of 'tight delicate steps, reminiscent of Salomé's movements when constrained by jewelled anklets'.[45]

Bauer also indicates Mary's responsibility for Viktor's death in another, more subtle way, however. By homing in for a close-up of her foot as she steps over Viktor's corpse and by making this close-up extra-diegetically lengthy, Bauer very deliberately stresses Mary's action of stepping over the corpse in both space and time. In this way he contrives to link his heroine to the most famous murderer of nineteenth-century Russian literature, Dostoevsky's Rodion Raskolnikov, who repeatedly – twenty four times, in fact[46] – uses transitive verbs meaning 'to step over' (*pereshagivat'/pereshagnut'* and *perestupat'/perestupit'*) as a metaphor for committing a crime against morality. In Part 3, Chapter 5 of *Crime and Punishment*, when Raskolnikov meets the chief detective for the first time, Porfirii questions him about the theories behind his article 'On Crime' ['O prestuplenii'], whereupon Raskolnikov declares: 'The "extraordinary person has the right [...] to permit his conscience *to step over...* certain obstacles, but only if it is absolutely necessary for the fulfilment of his idea on which, quite possibly, the welfare of all mankind may depend [emphasis added].'[47] Using it figuratively here, Raskolnikov later uses this verb more literally:

> if, for the sake of his idea, such a person has *to step over a corpse* or through blood, he is, in my opinion, absolutely entitled, in accordance with the dictates of his conscience, to permit himself to wade through blood, all depending, of course, on the nature and scale of his idea – note that, please. [emphasis added] (p. 200).

In these ways, then, Mary the *tangistka* is presented as a contemporary Salome, a murderess. Bauer appropriates the classic nineteenth-century figure of the femme fatale and modernises her – making her a tango dancer – in much the same way that Aubrey Beardsley imagined Wilde's Salome in 1890s dress, thereby suggesting that there is a Salome for every age.[48]

However, Bauer's representation of Mary is more nuanced than his intertextual appropriation of the negative associations of the Salome archetype suggests on the surface. It is characteristic of the complexity of his thematics and of his artistic sophistication that Bauer is able both to suggest and to persuade that this essentially misogynous view of Mary as a dangerous femme fatale – a contemporary Salome – belongs not to him but to his male protagonist. In other words, as the following section will demonstrate, it is in *Viktor's* mind that Mary exists in this extreme and outdated guise.

Mary through Viktor's eyes

How does Bauer convey this? Let us return to the track-in sequence. While the perception of woman as 'fetish', or as an erotic object of contemplation, is undeniably created by the camerawork in the track-in sequence, it does not necessarily express Bauer's directorial point of view. Instead it can be seen as conveying that of his male protagonist, for the way the camera here treats the dancer – and by extension Mary – is similar to the way in which Bauer shows Viktor to behave towards women generally and towards Mary in particular.

Typically, Bauer uses details of mise-en-scène to reveal early in the film Viktor's unconscious attitudes towards women and, in particular, his view of them as sources of visual pleasure. In the set Bauer designed for his study, Viktor's tendency to objectify, to fetishise and to aestheticise women is writ large, for this would-be Pygmalion is surrounded with artistic representations of his feminine ideal (Figure 4.5). The fact that these neo-classical statuettes depict half-naked women (even the base of his desk lamp is embellished by the form of a scantily clad woman) also, however, suggests a deep-rooted erotic interest in worldly, sexual women that his stated preference for an 'unspoilt' woman attempts to deny. So, too, does his photograph album that contains portraits of the knowing society *belles* he affects to dislike.[49] At the same time, this mise-en-scène also reveals Viktor's profound fear of women. The numerous statuettes, photographs and other artefacts that fetishise the female form provide Viktor with a 'safe' and manageable version of the women he desires but finds so threatening. It is therefore unsurprising that after Mary has left him Viktor seeks refuge from the truth about her by venerating her photograph.[50]

Figure 4.5. Viktor's study (Bauer, *Child of the Big City*, 1914)

97

These many artistic representations of the feminine form also, however, function as a *mise-en-abîme* of the ways in which Mary is framed and held as spectacle by the voyeuristic gaze of Bauer's male protagonist. Again Bauer reveals that Viktor has this tendency early in the film. As he and his friend Kramskoi stroll through the Moscow streets, they encounter Mania and stop to admire her beauty. She, however, is initially oblivious to their gaze, and has eyes only for the luxury goods on sale in the shops she must pass. In this sequence Bauer ironically equates the longing gazes of his male and female protagonists, for, though the objects of their gazes may be different, they are both expressive of desire.[51] Thus, as seen through Viktor's eyes, Mania is as much an object to be admired and, ultimately, bought, possessed and consumed as the luxury goods she admires in the shop windows.

Bauer's inclusion in his representation of the Salome dancer of such details as the ominous black backdrop and the dancer's hideous, femme fatale talons also links this misogynous, nineteenth-century view of the Salome archetype with Viktor, for he is nothing if not firmly wedded to the nineteenth-century past. Bauer makes this fact clear through his complex use of intertextuality in this film (for which, we recall, he wrote the original script). Bauer's intertextuality typically takes two forms: he draws widely on the common topoi of the nineteenth-century Russian literary tradition that recur from text to text and from author to author – specifically, the prototypical male and female protagonists, their conventional relationships and other staple motifs and themes – and he also makes extremely precise and sustained reference to several key texts of this tradition. In other words, Bauer slots his twentieth-century cinematic protagonists into the familiar and prototypical personae, relationships and situations of the classic nineteenth-century Russian literary tradition and charts their progress through this world.[52] Thus, from the first time we meet Viktor, he is situated firmly within the nineteenth-century Russian literary tradition. Introduced to the viewer as an idealistic but unhappy young man, world-weary and tormented by a romantic disillusionment, he is immediately cast as a twentieth-century Moscow version of the nineteenth-century literary type of the naïve and intense 'Petersburg dreamer'. In this, Bauer's filmic hero joins a long line of nineteenth-century literary heroes. Bauer's allusion to this general nineteenth-century literary type subsequently

narrows into a direct reference to a specific nineteenth-century protago-
nist, however, namely Piskarev, the naïve and idealistic hero of Nikolai
Gogol's story 'Nevsky Prospect' ['Nevskii prospekt', 1835], with whom
Viktor is repeatedly linked. Indeed, the two men share so many traits that
Viktor at times appears to be Piskarev's double.

Their similarity is especially striking in their attitudes to women. Thus
like Viktor, whose tendency to objectify, to fetishise and to aestheticise has
already been noted, Piskarev is shown to aestheticise women: he describes
his beloved as 'the very image of Perugino's Bianca' and fantasises that, had
she not existed in reality, but instead been 'the creation of an inspired artist', he would have been able to worship her as he chose.[53] Both men also
idealise the objects of their infatuation. As Piskarev loses himself in dreams
and opium-induced visions of the prostitute, so Viktor sits daydreaming of
Mary. Both protagonists construct fantasy images of the women they love
that have little to do with reality and again coincide to a remarkable degree.
In his favourite dream, Piskarev casts the prostitute as his faithful wife, and
pictures her devotedly watching him at work before 'she leant her delight-
ful little head on his chest [...]' (p. 24). Viktor similarly constructs a passive, compliant and faithful lover who is content to adore and be adored, as
she too rests her head on his chest in a superimposed shot that, it is clear,
emanates from Viktor's mind. Gogol states outright that these images are
false, noting that in Piskarev's dreams the prostitute always appears 'in a
guise completely contrary to reality' (p. 24); Bauer underlines the diver-
gence cinematically. In addition to the superimposed shot described above,
a skilfully constructed sequence shows Mary, reclining odalisque-like on
her chaise-longue, indulging herself in erotic daydreams. As an image
of Viktor's valet fades in, superimposed in the centre of the frame, Mary
arches her back and reaches out to him ecstatically. Throughout this sequence, one of Viktor's statuettes can be seen on a stand behind Mary, a
constant, ironic reminder of the gap between Viktor's ideal image of his
lover and the self-image (and desires) of the real woman with whom he is
involved (Figure 4.6).

Later, when Viktor surprises Mary and his valet in an embrace, he
raises his gun and shoots at her. The bullet, however, misses, and instead
shatters Viktor's reflection in the mirror. This telling misaim is symbolic of
something the viewer already knows: the ideal woman whom Viktor loves

Figure 4.6. The juxtaposition of idealised aesthetic image and real self-image: the faithless Mary indulges herself in erotic daydreams of Viktor's valet (Bauer, *Child of the Big City*, 1914)

has no existence except as a projection of his own psyche. An act of inadvertent self-destruction, this also, of course, prefigures Viktor's suicide, a further indication of Viktor's status as Piskarev's double.

The numerous links between Piskarev and Viktor serve both to undermine Viktor and to discredit his view of Mary as a Salome-esque femme fatale. There is another reason why we should not take Bauer's use of the Salome archetype too earnestly, however. In addition to exaggerating the nineteenth-century associations of this archetype, Bauer also stresses the artificiality and unreality of the Salome figure, and he does so through his careful choice of actress: the role of the oriental dancer is played by Bauer's wife, Lina Bauer (née Ancharova), also known by the pseudonym Emma Bauer. Bauer and Lina had met and married sometime in the 1890s, when Bauer began working as a set designer for Lentovskii and Aumont's Winter Garden theatre groups. Lina was already well known as a dancer and a comedienne at that time and, moreover, the role of dancer in *Child of the Big City* was not her first screen role; she had also appeared in an earlier film, *Bloody Glory* [Krovavaia slava, 1913], co-directed by Bauer and Vitalii Brianskii. She would therefore have been familiar to many contemporary viewers and would have brought important extra-diegetic associations to the role of the Salome dancer, affecting the way in which contemporary audiences responded to the dance sequence. Thus, for those viewers who recognised her, the mystique of the fearsome Salome persona would have been diluted, if not dissipated completely, for instead of a femme fatale they would have seen in this sequence the well-known estrada performer, Lina Bauer herself, performing a cameo role in her husband's film! Indeed, the actress seems aware of this fact; throughout her dance a smile plays on her lips, and she enjoys the bow she takes at the end.

Moreover, even for viewers who did not know Lina by reputation, the artifice of the sequence would have been clear. To be sure, the dancer's exotic costume is striking, but it does not hide that fact the dancer is clearly not a nubile young oriental girl, but a plump, middle-aged Russian woman – Zorkaia describes Lina as a 'luxuriant Blonde'[54] – who is playing at being exotic. Put simply, Lina Bauer is no Ida Rubinstein; her Salome is far from being the 'ferocious chthonian female' that Paglia discerns in nineteenth-century representations of Salome.[55] Her dance is a perfor-mance, a routine, nothing more. It is telling that many of the revellers in the nightclub do not even bother to watch the show closely. It is 1914 and they have seen it all before.[56]

That the link between Mary and the figure of Salome is the product of Viktor's deluded mind is again made explicit in the film's closing sequence. Viktor clearly considers himself to be Mary's victim, and the ways in which Bauer suggests she might bear some responsibility for his death have been outlined. However, Maiia Turovskaia adds an important and insightful attenuation to her discussion of Mary as murderess [*zhenshchina-ubiitsa*], describing the murder weapon thus: 'The weapon turns out to be the very feelings of her former beloved'.[57] It is not, then, Mary who poses the lethal threat to Viktor; rather the threat springs from his own psychology, from his inability to adapt either practically or emotionally to changing gender roles and from his paralysing fear that these changes, as they erode his authority, his previous certainties and his preferred way of life, will lead inevitably to the annihilation of the male self. For the weak-willed Viktor, as for Piskarev before him, it is less frightening to die than to confront this.

101

Neia Zorkaia has argued that *Child of the Big City* proves how inaccurate it is to consider Bauer a film-maker who was always on the side of the female protagonist, her view being that in this film 'all his sympathy is reserved for the simple young rich man, who has fallen sincerely in love with this "vamp", a plebian, an orphan from a sewing workshop'.[58] However – like Gogol, who dismisses Piskarev as 'completely ridiculous' (p. 17) – Bauer does not in fact sympathise with his suffering hero; instead he repeatedly mocks Viktor's delusions and romantic aspirations. While Bauer's reaction to Viktor's death may not be as dismissive as that of Wilde's Herod to the suicide of the love-sick Young Syrian – he observes, 'It is ridiculous to kill onself'[59] – even at the end of the film he withholds sympathy from his male protagonist, and ultimately he achieves this through his sustained appropriation of nineteenth-century prototypes. For, by linking Viktor very closely to one 'ridiculous' and long outdated nineteenth-century hero (Piskarev), Bauer contrives to sideline his male protagonist; he becomes one-dimensional, a cardboard cut-out, and is therefore incapable of engaging the viewer's interest. Floundering in nineteenth-century clichés, Viktor does not stand still, but actually regresses. Although a man of the twentieth century, he has yet to learn the lessons Gogol drew from the fate of Piskarev nearly eighty years previously.

Mary through Bauer's eyes: the tango-woman as an emblem of the new age

> [W]hen social structures change, so do the cultures that hold societies together. When this occurs, new 'modal types of personality' emerge, 'bearers of the new culture'.
>
> Philip Rieff.[60]

Ultimately, then, the figure of the Salome dancer and her association with Mary can be seen to function as part of Bauer's strategy for undermining his regressive male protagonist and his outdated attitudes to women. In a number of ways, this dancer comes to stand as an ironic comment on Viktor's view of himself as Mary's victim not least because by the end of the film Mary has moved on, adopting her own persona and one, moreover, that is right up to date. As we have seen, in Russia in early March 1914 there was no more fashionable figure than the tango-woman. Mary's choice of this persona therefore again serves to highlight her dynamism, her adaptability and her malleability. The fact that Elena Smirnova, the actress who plays Mary, was herself a famous *tangistka* would also have strengthened the sense of Mary's absolute modernity for contemporary viewers. Smirnova's fame as a tango dancer was at its height in 1914, and her association with the new dance form was so strong that she had been invited to host the 'Tango Evening' held at the *Stray Dog* [*Brodiachaia sobaka*] cabaret in St Petersburg on 12 January 1914. In 1915 Aleksandr Tolmachev would dedicate to her a poem entitled 'To a Tango Dancer' ['Tangistke'].

Thus, in the same way that Bauer reveals his self-consciousness by casting his wife, Emma Bauer, in the role of the Salome dancer, so he exemplifies his sophisticated playfulness in his choice of this well-known *tangistka* for the role of Mary. Moreover, the set design of the private room to which Kramskoi and Viktor take Mania early in the film also draws the viewer's attention to this fact, for it includes a poster across which is emblazoned, in capital letters, SMIRNOVA (the actress's surname). While it is not possible to make out precisely what this poster is advertising – it is located not on the wall of the room itself, but behind the heavy doors that separate it from the rest of the restaurant, meaning that the viewer glimpses it only when the door is opened – it seems likely that it is an advertisement for one of the actress's real-life tango performances. The style of acting Smirnova adopts at the end of this sequence is also significant, for the embrace that leads to Mania and Viktor's first kiss clearly bears the hallmarks of tango choreography.

For the alert viewer, then, these carefully controlled details of both set design and acting style also serve to undermine Viktor: how can he not recognise that Mania is not a nineteenth-century figure, but a modern tango-woman, Bauer seems to ask with playful incredulity. It is therefore entirely fitting that this modern woman should chose to end the film not with the Viktor, but with the character played by Leonid Iost, himself a famous tango dancer [*tangist*] in life. Thus, as Mary steps out to tango the night away with him she is the very image of modernity, an emblem of the new age in which she lives and dances, and a 'bearer' of its 'new culture', to borrow Philip Rieff's eloquent phrase, cited at the head of this section.[61]

What was the nature of this 'new culture', however? The 'tangomania' that engulfed Russia at this time was much more than a simple dance craze: it was a quest for a new lifestyle, a sort of popular modern philosophy, an ideology, even. One of its key tenets was the promotion of self-indulgent consumption: Tsivian has documented that, from as early as September 1913, even before the dance itself had been introduced to Russia, numerous articles and advertisements appeared in the Russian press exhorting consumers to dress the part; they could choose from tango slippers, tango skirts, tango dresses, tango suits, tango make-up and even 'those items of one's toilet which may only be named on your laundry bill'.[62] They could even drink tango champagne and eat tango chocolates.[63] The dance was also associated with social and political upheaval, for, according to the Russian media, in Europe the tango had become 'a political issue, dividing atheists from believers, rightists from leftists, progressives from conservatives'.[64]

As we have seen, Mary is portrayed as an enthusiastic and avaricious consumer. Viewed through Bauer's eyes, however, perhaps the most striking and disturbing trait of the modernity Mary embraces and represents is its absolute amorality. Although Mary's action of stepping over Viktor's corpse may appear to link her with Dostoevsky's Raskolnikov, the resemblance is ultimately shown to be misleading and wholly superficial. For, while Dostoevsky's gloomy intellectual murders to test out a serious – albeit naïve – moral theory, Mary does not ruin Viktor in pursuit of any Dostoevskian moral agenda. Despite the fact that the 'nature and scale of her idea' are frivolous and selfish – she does not want Viktor's suicide to ruin her night out – Mary steps over the obstacle that lies in her way (Viktor's corpse) without the slightest twinge of conscience. Moreover, after the murder, Raskolnikov is tormented first by his belief that he did not succeed in 'stepping over' and therefore failed to prove himself a great man, and, ultimately, by his recognition of the awfulness of his crime. Unlike him, however, Mary is not in the least tormented by the part she might have played in a person's death. Indeed, she does not even reflect on whether she bears some responsibility for it. The moral concerns central to Dostoevsky's novel and his protagonists are therefore ignored. Bauer's female character behaves badly – commits 'moral suicide' and 'moral murder', the core of both Sonia's and Raskolnikov's dilemmas – without any sense of guilt, without any punishment or retribution, either from without or from within, and without any repentance.[65] For, while Dostoevsky's novel begins with the crime and goes on to chart the process of Raskolnikov's repentance, Bauer's film ends abruptly with the 'crime' itself. Bauer therefore deliberately rejects the conventional nineteenth-century 'moral' ending, both by showing that Mary is not shocked into guilt and repentance at the sight of Viktor's lifeless body, and especially by declining to explore her reaction to her crime over time.[66]

Moreover, Mary's act of stepping over Viktor's corpse also has a more modern antecedent, a sequence in a film that was made in November 1913 and released in January 1914, just two months before *Child of the Big City*. Entitled *Drama in the Futurist Cabaret No. 13*, this twenty-minute-long film was directed by Vladimir Kasianov and conceived and performed by the members of the group of artists who called themselves *The Donkey's Tail* [Oslinyi khvost] together with other Futurist writers and artists: Konstantin Bolshakov, David Burliuk, Natalia Goncharova, Vasilii Kamenskii, Mikhail Larionov, Boris Lavrenev, Vladimir Mayakovsky and Vadim Shershenevich are all thought to have participated in its conception and realisation.[67] While no prints of this film have survived, contemporary reviews have enabled film historians to piece together a synopsis.[68] From them we learn that the film featured both a solo (!) tango – 'The Futurist Tango' – and a tango-like *apache* dance, dubbed the 'Futuredance of Death' [*futurtanets smerti*], performed on a table by a man and a woman chosen by drawing lots.[69] Both dancers are armed with crooked daggers and during the dance one partner must try to kill the other. Tsivian describes what happens next:

> Eventually, the woman dancer is killed and, bare-breasted, is taken out into the cold. Violating the rite announced by an intertitle 'A Futurefuneral', the killer kisses his victim before throwing her corpse into the snow and is exiled from Futurism on the grounds of sentimentality. The exile kills himself at the outer door of the cabaret, whereupon, in a scene suspiciously similar to the closing sequence of Yevgenii Bauer's *Child of the Big City* made some five [*sic*] months later, one by one the rest of the Futurists indifferently step over the corpse of the transgressor.[70]

Like Viktor, then, the male dancer's fatal transgression was that he was not 'modern' enough, that he was too wedded to 'outdated' ways of feeling and behaving. His forward-looking colleagues therefore have no room for him in their world of the future, as Mary has no room for the old-fashioned Viktor in the early twentieth-century present. His death is therefore nothing to be mourned, it is an inevitability.

In these ways, then, Bauer suggests in this film – through the figure of the amoral *tangistka* – that the old, nineteenth-century codes of morality are being undermined and dismissed as invalid in the new century. In the twentieth-century city that appears on his screen, we witness crime without reason, crime without punishment and, most shockingly, crime without remorse. The moral certainties of the old century and its classic literature have collapsed, but nothing has taken their place; what remains is an amoral vacuum, where self-interest is the only criterion for action. Bauer also suggests a similarly disruptive shift in gender relations. Here, as in Bauer's earlier *Twilight of a Woman's Soul*, the old male certainties about women are shown to have lost all validity. Bauer again stresses that his twentieth-century cinematic heroine is very different from the conventional nineteenth-century literary heroine, and his rejection of the various clichés that surrounded her makes it clear that such mythologies have no lasting or permanent relevance, either for him or for the twentieth-century woman he seeks to portray in this film. By contrast, like Bauer's Prince Dolskii before him, Bauer's Viktor appears to be stuck in the past; unwilling or unable to change, he attempts to relate to his female counterpart as the heroes of nineteenth-century literature once did. As Bauer shows, such anachronistic behaviour renders him 'superfluous' to the requirements of the dynamic, exacting and disturbing twentieth-century woman we watch on the screen. The ending of Bauer's film thus reverses that of Drankov's *Stenka Razin*, where the innocent Persian princess is murdered by the jealous Razin. Here, the victim who lies dead is the cuckolded man, while the unfaithful woman – Bauer's dynamic, amoral and aggressively modern *tangistka* – ends the film alive and well. Moreover, unlike Libkin's Nastia in his *Stenka Razin*, Mary is not wronged by Viktor, nor is she either vengeful or desirous of his death. She is simply supremely indifferent.

Evgenii Bauer's *Silent Witnesses* [Nemye svideteli]

Bauer again drew on the rich allusiveness of the figure of the tango dancer as an emblem of the amorality of the new age in another film from 1914, *Silent Witnesses*, released almost two months after *Child of the Big City*, on 29 April 1914. This film initially seems to repeat the plot trajectory of *Child of the Big City*. Thus, a wealthy aristocrat, Pavel Kostyritsyn, seduces Nastia, his young maid. Unlike Mary, however, Nastia falls deeply in love with her master, which leads her to reject her fiancé from her own class, the neighbours' lackey. Pavel is in love with a woman from his class, however, the stunningly beautiful New Woman Ellen, played by the celebrated tango dancer Elza Kriuger.[71] When Ellen accepts his proposal of marriage he therefore loses interest in Nastia, whom he had seduced simply in order to pass a moment of drunken boredom and to relieve the feelings of powerlessness and frustration caused by Ellen's blatant infidelity. Like Mary, however, Ellen is presented as an indifferent, amoral New Woman. She accepts Pavel's offer of marriage because she needs his money, and she has no qualms about continuing her affair with the dashing Baron von Rehren after her engagement.

Although no sequences in this film show her dancing the tango, Ellen's tight-fitting dresses and the way she moves reveal her to be as much of a tango-woman as Mary. When she walks, she, like Mary, does so *à la tango*. Tsivian analyses Ellen's movements and her body language in the sequence in which she accepts Pavel's marriage proposal, and suggests that Bauer – who often used 'mood music' on the set to inspire his actors and create the right atmosphere – choreographed the sequence around common tango steps, thus:

> She approaches him, takes his hand (the tango ethos entails the equality of the sexes), makes a step and freezes, looking at him (intertitle: 'Yes, I agree'), makes another step, so that their joint arms [*sic*] are now bent and their legs crossed, and freezes again, her eyes looking straight into his.[72]

Furthermore, Tsivian speculates that the 'exquisitely designed' dresses Kriuger wears in this film were the special tango dresses that the Russian avant-garde artist Natalia Goncharova is known to have designed for her, noting that 'the costume designer is not credited for this film, [and] the usual practice of production companies in the 1910s was to let film stars wear their own costumes in modern dramas, rather than designing costumes for each film'.[73]

However, as regards its representation of the protagonists, *Silent Witnesses* has none of the ambivalence of the earlier *Child of the Big City*; in fact it is exceptional among Bauer's extant films, for it is the only work that consistently foregrounds class concerns and in which the protagonists are unequivocally divided into 'good' and 'bad' solely on the basis of their class. Thus, while the members of the 'downstairs' class, including the poor lackey whose proposal the misguided Nastia rejects, are shown in a uniformly positive light, the tango-woman, Ellen, and the other members of the 'upstairs' class to which she belongs are all portrayed negatively.

The fate of the tango dancer in later pre-Revolutionary films

Tangomania continued in Russia almost to the end of the decade under consideration.[74] Indeed, one of the final films to be made before the pre-Revolutionary film industry was dismantled was Viacheslav Viskovskii's symbolically entitled *The Last Tango*, which was released on 31 May 1918.[75] In this film, based on motifs from a tango romance, 'Beneath the Burning Sky of Argentina' ['Pod znoinym nebom Argentiny'], made popular by the singer Iza Kremer,[76] the role of the tango dancer, Chloe, was played by the Queen of the pre-Revolutionary screen, Vera Kholodnaia, and that of her tango partner and lover, Joe, by Osip Runich, one of the industry's Kings. By 1918, however, it was the participation of these great film stars that drew audiences to see the film, for the dance itself had become little more than a familiar set piece and, consequently, was rendered almost meaningless: I. Surguchev, writing in the newspaper *News of the Season* [Novosti sezona] in 1918, commented that the film was worth watching despite the 'meaninglessness [*neznachitel'nost'*] of the "tango" itself'.[77] Indeed, it is also telling that the film's final dance sequence had greater success when it was abstracted from the film and performed live by Kholodnaia and Runich at a charity concert held in Odessa on

8 February 1919.[78] Thus, seen in early 1914 as an icon of the new age, by the end of that decade both the tango and the figure of the tango dancer had already come to be viewed as empty, if not dead, images, emblems only of the decadent, irrelevant and meaningless pre-Revolutionary past in which they had been born.[79]

5

The Gypsy Dancer

Sources of the myth

The films discussed in Chapters 2 and 4 all feature elements that derive from and develop both the thematic concerns explored in Drankov's *Stenka Razin* and the cinematic devices employed to express those concerns. In particular, their depictions of their young female protagonists have much in common. In all of them, they are shown to be at their most desirable when dancing, and the underlying assumption is that women are somehow inherently suited to perform before men and that when they display themselves in this way, they do so for men's enjoyment and sexual gratification. Dancing is therefore seen as being an innate part of woman's nature, her duty, or even her *raison d'être*.

These assumptions also colour the early representation of another dancer protagonist prevalent in the films of this period, namely the Gypsy dancer. The ubiquity of the figure of the Gypsy [*tsyganka*] reflects, in part, the so-called 'Gypsy mania' [*tsyganshchina*] that engulfed all strata of Russian urban culture and society at the start of the twentieth century. This infatuation with Gypsies and Gypsy culture was not new, however. Anthropologists and cultural historians trace the beginning of the singular Russian fascination with the figure of the Gypsy performer to the latter half of the eighteenth century, when Count Aleksei Orlov, a favourite of

Catherine the Great and the brother of one of her lovers, brought Gypsy serfs from Moldavia to Moscow and founded Russia's first private Gypsy choir in 1774. In 1807, Orlov freed the singers and they became the first professional Gypsy chorus in Russia. Orlov's Gypsies often performed at Catherine's soireés and thus initiated a major cultural trend that saw Gypsy singers become de rigueur in the homes of every important member of the Russian nobility.[1] The trend continued into the nineteenth century and spread to the emergent merchant class: Gypsies provided the entertainment in the large out-of-town inns and restaurants that became the fashionable evening haunts of well-to-do Russian urban dwellers in the years following the Napoleonic Wars. Later in the century, Gypsy performers were also the star attractions of the floorshows mounted in such modish city restaurants as the Strelna and the Iar in Moscow.[2]

Even in the earliest Gypsy choruses the women played the main roles and would often dance as well as sing.[3] Some Gypsy women, most notably Stepanida Soldatova and Tania (Tatiana Dmitrievna Demianova), both originally members of Orlov's choir, became famous as solo performers. Similarly, in the 1880s the Gypsy singer Vera Zorina achieved star status with her performances at the Strelna. Unlike Soldatova and Tania, Zorina was not a true Gypsy, but neither ethnic nor musical authenticity were important considerations for the nineteenth-century Russian consumers of Gypsy performances. The most popular songs from the Gypsy repertoire, so-called Gypsy romances, were not Gypsy at all, but had Russian lyrics that offered glamorised and romanticised versions of Gypsy life as Russians liked to imagine it rather than as real Gypsies lived it. They were set to music composed by Russians in an approximation of what was generally considered to be 'Gypsy style'.[4] This indifference to ethnic accuracy and fixation on Gypsy stereotypes continued into the early twentieth century. Thus, among the numerous female performers who achieved fame and celebrity status as 'Gypsy' singers in early twentieth-century Russia there was only one, Varia Panina, who was a truly ethnic Gypsy.[5]

This preference for stylised and romanticised versions of Gypsies and their way of life also characterises the way the *tsyganka* has been represented in Russian literature. Like Gypsy music, Gypsy personae and motifs began to appear in Russian literary works in the late eighteenth century. Two of the great poets of Catherine's reign, Gavrila Derzhavin and Ivan

Dmitriev, wrote verses on Gypsy themes. It was nineteenth-century Russian writers – poets, dramatists and novelists, Romantics and Realists alike – who seized most enthusiastically on the figure of the *tsyganka*, however, with Aleksandr Pushkin leading the way. His narrative poem, *The Gypsies* [Tsygany, 1824, published in 1827], though not the first work of Russian literature to place a Gypsy heroine at its centre, was one of the most influential treatments of this persona and inspired many other literary and musical works with Gypsy heroines, and not only in Russia.[6]

By the beginning of the twentieth century, therefore, the *tsyganka* was a familiar female figure. Typically represented in nineteenth-century Russian and European art as strong-willed, free-spirited, independent and assertive, sexually uninhibited and disdainful of accepted moral and social laws, bewitchingly beautiful, dangerous and frequently, therefore, better off dead, the figure of the Gypsy woman was thus a well-established typology of the enigmatic and dangerous feminine 'Other', that, in Elisabeth Bronfen's words, makes of this persona 'a static allegorical figure for difference'.[7] The *tsyganka* was, moreover, an archetype of which early twentieth-century Russian film-makers were well aware. Indeed, an elaborate and intricate familiarity with nineteenth-century literary and cultural models of the *tsyganka* underpins early Russian filmic representations of this female persona; as we shall see, three specific inter-related nineteenth-century works of art, whose characterisations of the central female protagonists and representations of the male protagonists' reactions to them share many similarities, had a direct influence on early twentieth-century Russian film-makers, namely Pushkin's *The Gypsies*, Prosper Mérimée's novella 'Carmen' (first published, without Chapter 4, in 1845; second edition, including Chapter 4, published in 1846) and Georges Bizet's 1875 opera of the same title, with libretto by Henri Meilhac and Ludovic Halévy.[8]

Re-enacting nineteenth-century myths: the first films on the Gypsy theme

The first feature film produced by Aleksandr Khanzhonkov's Moscow studio was *Drama in a Gypsy Camp Near Moscow*. Written, directed and photographed by Vladimir Siversen, it was released on 20 December

1908, a little over two months after Drankov had released his *Stenka Razin*. Like this earlier film, *Drama in a Gypsy Camp Near Moscow* was shot entirely outdoors, this time at a real Gypsy camp, and its cast was made up from the Gypsies who were living there. Khanzhonkov's explanation that his choice of location and subject matter was motivated by his desire to be the first in Russia to release a film on an everyday [*bytovoi*] theme demonstrates the ubiquity of Gypsies in Russian life and culture at this time.[9] This comment also suggests a documentary style approach to the subject and implies a desire to create a factual filmic record of real Gypsies and their real lives. Indeed, contemporary commentators responded to the film in just this way; in a 1908 edition of the newspaper *The Stage* a reviewer observed: 'The picture [...] introduces us to the life and *moeurs* of Gypsies near Moscow'.[10] More recent critical responses to the film have also highlighted its 'realism': Ian Christie compares it favourably to Drankov's *Stenka Razin*, commenting that Siversen's film has 'a *plein air* freshness and authenticity (it uses real Gypsies) that *Stenka Razin* lacks';[11] Paolo Cherchi Usai states that the film 'insists on an atmosphere drawn from real life';[12] while, echoing Semen Ginzburg's description of it as 'half-ethnographic, half-acted film',[13] Denise Youngblood categorises it as 'a kind of early docudrama'.[14]

As the film has been preserved without intertitles and not in its entirety,[15] it is difficult for today's viewer to grasp the narrative significance of the events and actions depicted and to understand fully the relationship between the film's two central protagonists, a beautiful *tsyganka* and a young Gypsy man, who is her lover. In the film's opening sequence the *tsyganka* awaits him, and when he arrives they embrace. The camera then cuts to the camp, where all the Gypsies, including the *tsyganka*, are asleep. The viewer next sees her lover creep into the camp, awaken the young woman and, after much protestation on her part, he eventually persuades her to leave the camp with him. Once they are alone, he pleads with her about something, but she resists his entreaties. They then argue and the young man stabs the *tsyganka*, who falls dead to the ground, where she is subsequently discovered by a group of Gypsies. Meanwhile, the murderer commits suicide, throwing himself from a cliff top onto the rocks below. The film's final shot focuses on his lifeless body.

113

A review of *Drama in a Gypsy Camp Near Moscow*, published in *Cine-Phono* in 1908, enables us to fill in the gaps in the narrative.[16] From the synopsis given there we learn that the *tsyganka*, Aza, having received marriage proposals from two admirers, accepts that of a Gypsy named Aleko. This, presumably, is what we watch in the extant film's opening sequence. An important central section, described in detail in the review, does not appear in the surviving print of the film, however: the spurned rival, refusing to accept defeat in love and knowing Aleko's weakness for gambling, persuades Aleko to join a game of cards during the wedding celebrations. Having lost all his money, Aleko bets his remaining possession, a horse, but he also loses this to his rival, who proposes one last hand in which the stake will be Aleko's new wife. Aza begs Aleko not to go ahead with the game, but he does, and once more loses to his rival, who thus wins the right to Aza's hand. Outraged that Aleko could treat Aza with so little respect, the Gypsies banish him from the camp, whereupon night falls and the Gypsies settle down to sleep. This is the setting for the extant film's second sequence, and it is clearly, then, the regretful Aleko whom we see creeping back to the camp, attempting to explain his actions, begging Aza to leave the camp and her new husband to be with him and, finally, murdering her when she refuses.

Although some details of plot are clearly obscured in the extant print of the film, it is nevertheless obvious that *Drama in a Gypsy Camp Near Moscow* offers a highly stylised and conventional representation of the Gypsies and of gender relations among them. Indeed, the Gypsies' self-conscious awareness of the camera and their obvious discomfort at being filmed remind the viewer that although the people we see on the screen are ethnically real Gypsies, here they are nevertheless playing at being Gypsies; they are not enacting scenes from their everyday lives, but performing, for the benefit of the camera, stereotypical 'Gypsy' roles invented by the (non-Gypsy) scriptwriter. As Khanzhonkov recalled: 'The Gypsies were terrorised by the camera. Siversen only had to turn the handle for the Gypsies' faces to freeze with terror [...] they squinted at the camera in horror.'[17] Moreover, the Gypsies chosen to 'star' in the film were selected for their conformity to stereotype, as Khanzhonkov himself acknowledged: the Gypsy camp 'had everything we needed', he wrote in his memoirs, 'a young Gypsy girl who danced with such suppleness and a handsome Gypsy with a demonic face'.[18] The conventionality of the film's representation of the *tsyganka* is particularly striking. The opening sequence begins with a portrait shot of the young Gypsy woman; awaiting her lover in a meadow full of wild flowers, and dressed in swirling skirts ornamented with coins, a loose blouse, flowing scarves and with flowers in her long black hair, she is a familiar and stereotypical sight: the beautiful, passionate, free-spirited and seductive Gypsy.

In both Mérimée's novella and Bizet's opera, Carmen's unconstrained sexuality is explicitly linked to her proclivity for dancing; indeed, her dance is portrayed as being akin to a seduction technique. Mérimée's Don José first realises he is in love with Carmen when he watches unobserved as she performs before an audience of lewdly appreciative officers. Unable to catch more than partial glimpses of Carmen as she dances, Don José is overcome by jealousy and the desire to attack the men who are able to enjoy Carmen's performance to the full. On this occasion, his jealousy is assuaged when Carmen gives him a private dance performance that acts as a prelude to their spending the night together for the first time, as it does in Bizet's version of their story ('I am going to dance in your honour' ['Je vais danser en votre honneur'], Act II). Moreover, in Bizet's work it is Carmen's promise that she will dance with Don José at Lillas Pastia's tavern that persuades the young soldier to forget his orders and allow Carmen to escape. In Mérimée's novella, the Gypsy's predilection for dancing is taken to be further proof of her sexual availability and immorality also by the frame narrator, who notes disapprovingly that Gypsy women 'go about dancing for money', performing 'dances that strongly resemble those which are forbidden at our [Parisian] public balls during the Carnival'.[19]

Although we see no dancing in the surviving fragment of the film, Khanzhonkov and Siversen clearly intended to convey the *tsyganka's* sexual appeal by having her perform Gypsy dances. The section of Khanzhonkov's memoirs cited previously makes it clear that this was one of the criteria that Khanzhonkov applied when selecting the specific Gypsy for the role; moreover, he later refers to her as 'the dancing beauty' [*krasavitsa-pliasun'ia*], notes that the film's scenario featured 'dancing, endless dancing' and describes how difficult it proved to capture on film the spontaneity of Gypsy dance.[20]

The film's deliberately scripted and highly melodramatic plot contains many other features familiar from the nineteenth-century literary and operatic works with Gypsy heroines, and not only the name Aleko, which links it unambiguously with Pushkin's *The Gypsies*. Thus the prize of the *tsyganka's* love once again costs the male protagonists dear. The extremity of the passions she arouses in the men – in the words of a contemporary reviewer: 'Passionate, invincible love [...], jealousy that leads to a crime'[21] – sets them against each other and leads Aleko to rash action. For, although in Siverson's film Aza does not take a new husband of her own volition, Aleko nonetheless blames her for this 'infidelity' and behaves in the same way as Pushkin's Aleko and Mérimée and Bizet's Don José before him: first he pleads with the *tsyganka* to remain faithful and then, when this fails to yield the desired result, he resorts to violence against her.

There is, however, some evidence that the film-makers wanted to portray the *tsyganka* sympathetically as the victim of her lover's obsession and jealousy. This is suggested cinematically, in the film's central sequence, when the spurned Aleko pursues the Gypsy across the field, before stabbing her. As he chases after her, so too does Siversen's camera, which executes a horizontal panning shot that looks ahead to the way in which Ryllo's camera would symbolically and very deliberately pursue Lusha in *The Incestuous Father-in-Law* four years later. Ginzburg instructs the modern viewer not to overestimate the significance of this camera movement by seeing in it an innovation in film language, however.[22] Arguing that its use here was, on the contrary, simply dictated by the cameraman's inexperience and lack of skill, he dismisses the panning shot as nothing more than a necessary and hasty attempt to reframe, claiming that 'the camera operator V. Siverson had recourse to a panning shot only so that the moment of the murder [...] did not occur outside the edge of the frame'.[23] While Philip Cavendish argues that this panning shot does more than Ginzburg allows, suggesting that it functions not only to keep the main protagonists in the centre of the frame but also to show them 'to inhabit an authentically rural space', he stops short of according it a diegetic significance.[24] Yet, as the camera follows the film's female protagonist, its movement mimics that of the murderous Aleko and conveys his intention of hunting down the *tsyganka* who, whether by accident or by design, in this sequence is characterised cinematically, by the movement of the camera, as the helpless prey of this implacable hunter.

Ultimately, however, as in both *Stenka Razin* and *The Incestuous Father-in-Law*, it proves to be the fate of the male protagonist that most concerns the film-makers. Thus, the camera leaves the young woman where she lies, dead, in the field, focussing instead in the film's closing shots on Aleko as he jumps to his death on the rocks by the Moscow river, whereupon the camera homes in for a final, emblematic shot of his corpse. This recalls the ambiguous ending of Pushkin's *poema* in which certain details combine not only to attenuate the *poema's* condemnation of Aleko's conduct, expressed directly in the old man's final, dignified speech, but also to create sympathy for him and to suggest to the reader that he, like the old man himself, is a victim of the *tsyganka's* cruelty: there is the description of how Aleko falls slowly to the ground, as if dead himself, when the Gypsies have finished burying Zemfira; the final evocative image that likens Aleko to a wounded crane, left behind to die by the rest of the flock; and his absence from the concluding scene of the *poema*, which suggests his figurative death.[25] Indeed, in his socio-biological reading of *The Gypsies*, which sees the problem of female promiscuity as 'the unstated but obvious central issue of the whole work', Leighton Brett Cooke suggests that the *poema's* concluding couplet serves a similar mitigating function, arguing that, with its close association of fate and 'passions', it implies instead that such passions are ineluctable and thus insists on the commonality of the male emotional response to female infidelity.[26] Commenting that Pushkin's approach in *The Gypsies* reminds him of Freud's dictum that 'anatomy is destiny', Cooke continues:

> In our modern understanding, the passions are fateful and ineluctable because they are encoded in our common genetic heritage. They are triggered by relationships such as comprise the major themes of the poema: sexual attraction, exogamy, pair-bonding, kin altruism, reciprocal altruism, infidelity, male sexual jealousy and aggression.[27]

In this film, then, as Louise McReynolds puts it, 'sex overwhelmed cultural accuracy'.[28] The first Russian film to feature the *tsyganka* therefore exploits this archetypal figure in a wholly conventional manner.

117

Khanzhonkov and Siversen tap into the contemporary Gypsy mania in an attempt to add popular appeal to their film, but they also take advantage of all the rich cultural associations that the *tsyganka* had acquired throughout the nineteenth century, similarly portraying her as a dangerous and disruptive element, who, as in Pushkin's *The Gypsies* and Mérimée and Bizet's *Carmen*, makes rivals out of former friends, destroys the harmony of the male community and who should, therefore, be destroyed in her turn.

The same is true of the way in which the *tsyganka* is represented in André Maître's *The Gypsies* (1910), an adaptation of Pushkin's famous *poema*, scripted by Czesław Sabiński and photographed by the French cameramen Georges Meier and Toppi. A contemporary reviewer, writing in *Cine-Phono*, stresses how faithful this screen adaptation is to Pushkin's *poema* and advises those readers who have forgotten what happens in this great work of nineteenth-century Russian literature to re-read it. He then revises this recommendation, however, continuing: 'In fact, there's no need to read it. Watch this film and this will be enough, so brightly and so beautifully is Pushkin's *poema* reproduced in it'.[29] Be that as it may, however, as the detailed synopsis published in the same edition of *Cine-Phono* reveals,[30] Maître's film adaptation narrows considerably the depth and range of reference of Pushkin's *poema*, in much the same way as does the socio-biological interpretation of his work provided by Cooke. For the film focuses solely on the fateful sexual relationship between Aleko and Zemfira, while the role of the old man is reduced to only two brief appearances at the beginning and the end of the film.

For Ginzburg, the film derives less from Pushkin than from Bizet, however. He suggests that Maître, who, he claims, did not speak Russian and had never read Pushkin, saw in Sabiński's scenario 'a cruel "exotic" melodrama, something akin to a Russian variant of the libretto of the opera *Carmen*', a fact that for him explains why this film focuses primarily on the portrayal of sexual passion.[31]

In these ways, then, the earliest representations of the *tsyganka* found in Russian film appear clichéd and outdated. They rely solely on pre-existing nineteenth-century versions of this female persona and are therefore unable to tell us anything new about the *tsyganka* and her significance in early twentieth-century Russia.

Modernising and undermining the nineteenth-century myths of the *tsyganka*

By comparison with the figures of the Persian princess and her updated alter ego the *tangistka*, the *tsyganka* features in very few films made during the mid- to late 1910s. Moreover, most of the films in which she does feature do not seek to explore this female archetype either in any depth, or through the prism of contemporary concerns. Instead, like Siversen in *Drama in a Gypsy Camp Near Moscow* and Maître in *The Gypsies*, they rely on the well-established nineteenth-century associations of the figure of the wild, promiscuous and fatal Gypsy dancer of the Russian steppe. Chardynin's drama *Gypsy Romances* [Tsyganskie romansy, 1914] continues this trend and it therefore remains, as Vishnevskii puts it, a film 'with a far-fetched and trite plot'.[32] Other examples include Reinols's comedy *Baldy among the Gypsies* [Lysyi u tsygan, 1916], Chardynin's *Still, Sadness... Still...* [Molchi, grust'... molchi..., 1918], Viskovskii's *The Last Tango* [1918], Sabiński's *The Living Corpse* [Zhivoi trup, 1918], an adaptation of Lev Tolstoy's 1910 play of the same name, and the Kharitonov studio's *Aza the Gypsy* [Tsyganka Aza, 1919, director unknown].

More interesting, therefore, are those few films from this period that either subvert or adapt these nineteenth-century traditions. Typically, these are films that feature the *tsyganka* less as a character in her own right, but rather as a symbol or a means of characterisation of one of the film's female protagonists. Also striking is the fact that in them the *tsyganka* typically appears in a new guise, that of the professional, non-ethnic, urban Gypsy performer. In this way, a new and intentional level of artifice attaches to the figure of the Gypsy dancer that had been lacking, in intention if not in fact, in earlier, more conventional filmic representations of the *tsyganka*. While this development must be attributed at least in part to the shift in emphasis from the rural melodrama to its urban counterpart that occurred during this period, it also suggests that the sophisticated Russian directors who came to the fore in the 1910s did not consider the essentially nineteenth-century model of the Gypsy dancer to be a useful persona through which to explore their twentieth-century concerns. For these reasons, then, in some Russian films made after 1914 the figure of the *tsyganka* begins to take on different meanings.

The *tsyganka* as *dikovinka*: Evgenii Bauer's *Children of the Age*

This shift in the symbolic associations of the *tsyganka* is visible in Bauer's *Children of the Age*, which was released on 3 October 1915. This film tells the story of Mariia Nikolaevna (played by the future 'Queen' of the screen, Vera Kholodnaia), a young woman who is happy with her modest life as the wife of a low-ranking bank clerk and the mother of their baby until, while out alone one day in Moscow's glamorous and ultra-modern shopping arcades, she meets by chance an erstwhile school friend, Lidiia Verkhovskaia. Clearly a woman of considerable wealth and, apparently, one who lives independently, for and by herself, the glamorous Lidiia befriends Mariia. The young woman embraces with enthusiasm the exciting new social life that friendship with Lidiia opens up before her, and eventually the lure of social status and material wealth proves irresistible: at the end of the film Mariia leaves her husband, taking their baby with her, to become the live-in mistress of the wealthy and much older businessman Lebedev, to whom Lidiia had introduced her. This act of betrayal causes her husband to commit suicide.

The figure of the dancing *tsyganka* appears in several of the film's early sequences, when Lidiia invites Mariia and her husband to attend an elaborate soirée at her home. As the out-of-place couple arrives at the party, the viewer sees in the background the Carmen-esque Gypsy dancers whom Lidiia has hired to entertain her guests. The camera neither foregrounds the Gypsy dancers nor lingers on their performance, however, and they thus become simply part of the mise-en-scène, one more element of Bauer's opulent backdrop. To be sure, part of the function of the *tsyganki* in this sequence is to heighten the sense of the film's verisimilitude, to create a naturalistic depiction of Lidiia's soirée and to evoke the fashionable high society in which she moves. This being a Bauer film, however, the viewer should assume that the Gypsy dancers, like all other elements of Bauer's evocative mise-en-scène, are intended to do more than merely create a surface image of reality. For it is not only objects that take on symbolic significance in Bauer's films; as Alyssa DeBlasio has noted, 'Actors often become just one of the many layers of background: fulfilling the same roles as *dikovinki*, they blend in with the tapestry of fabrics and arrangements of palms'.[33] *Dikovinka*, a Russian word which literally means something unusual, exciting or surprising (a 'wonder', or 'marvel') was the term used by Lev Kuleshov to describe the objects that Bauer characteristically chose to dominate the décor of particular sets.[34] Carefully arranged and often, although not exclusively, situated in the foreground of the frame, the *dikovinka*, which at its most effective has both diegetic and non-diegetic import, assumes a special symbolic significance, highlighting aspects of character or theme.[35] Like the numerous photographs and statuettes that decorate Viktor's study in Bauer's *Child of the Big City*, therefore, the Gypsy dancers who entertain Lidiia's guests are exploited by Bauer as an important and revealing signifying detail, and one that serves several possible functions.

Louise McReynolds has observed that a reading that reduces *Children of the Age* to its basic plotline suggests that Bauer sought 'to excoriate Kholodnaia's character, Mariia', to condemn her for her 'personal fallibilities' that make her, if not evil, then at the very least ' "deceitful" and "shallow"' in her decision to leave her husband for Lebedev.[36] It could be, then, that Bauer intends the presence of the *tsyganka* in this sequence to symbolise his female protagonist's fatal femininity, to alert viewers to the New Woman's Gypsy-like fickleness and propensity for sexual infidelity and to prepare them for the tragic fate that awaits Mariia's husband. After all, these essentially nineteenth-century associations of the *tsyganka* were still current in Russian culture in the 1910s, whether 'low-brow' or high. Mania Eltsova, the unconventional and sexually liberated dancer heroine of Anastasiia Verbitskaia's best-selling popular novel, *The Keys to Happiness*, for example, is frequently both cast as a *tsyganka* in her on-stage performances and likened to one when off stage by the many men with whom she enters into relationships and who see her as a dangerous and destructive femme fatale. When she rejects the amorous advances of her dance partner, Nils, for example, he accuses her of playing with his feelings like the inconstant Gypsy she embodies on stage. On this occasion, Mania refuses to accept this comparison, exclaiming, 'Do you really not understand that life is one thing and the stage another?'[37] At other times, however, she applies the image of the *tsyganka* to herself, most typically when explaining why she will not marry. Similarly, intent on seducing the recalcitrant Garald at a masked ball, she 'disguises' herself as a Gypsy, reassuring him that he need not worry that she seeks fidelity from him.

Such archetypal images of the *tsyganka* are also frequently encountered in the works of the Symbolist poet Aleksandr Blok.[38] Thus, in 'To the Muse' ['K muze', 29 December 1912], the poet draws on the image of the *tsyganka* as the archetypal faithless lover in his lament to his Muse that 'her terrible caresses' were:

> More treacherous than the northern night,
> And more intoxicating than golden champagne
> And more fleeting than a gypsy woman's love.[39]

It is also telling that, even in the complex and multi-layered poems contained in Blok's ten-poem cycle *Carmen* [Karmen, 1914], the rhyme that occurs with most frequency and which also concludes the final poem of the cycle is that of 'Carmen/betrayal' [*Karmen/izmen*].[40]

As always in a Bauer film, however, the director's representation of his female protagonist's actions is more subtle and nuanced than it may at first seem. Thus, as the film progresses, it gradually becomes clear that Bauer does not use the *tsyganka* simply as an uncomplicated negative shorthand 'double' of Mariia. Indeed, the assumption that he might have intended this association is attenuated, if not undermined entirely, by the fact that even in this early sequence he suggests that Mariia should be seen less as a victimiser than as a victim by revealing her to be the target of Lidiia's and Lebedev's callous and self-serving machinations. Bauer has already hinted, earlier in the film, that Lidiia has no genuine interest in getting to know Mariia: in a telling sequence, Mariia is reduced to just another name in Lidiia's little black book, and when she first visits Mariia at home, lorgnette in hand, Lidiia reveals herself to be repulsed by their baby, who she fears might soil her fine clothes, entirely indifferent to Mariia's husband and disdainful of their modest flat and simple way of life. The viewer cannot help but wonder why she pursues her friendship with Mariia so determinedly. However, during the sequences set at Lidiia's soirée Bauer makes it explicit that Lidiia's motives for befriending Mariia are deeply questionable. Indeed, here it becomes clear that Lidiia is seeking to procure her as a mistress for Lebedev, the wealthy, dissolute man, who, the viewer suspects, is perhaps not only Lidiia's friend but also the 'benefactor' who supports her lavish lifestyle.[41] A more persuasive interpretation of the significance of the Gypsy dancers, therefore, is one that sees them as a comment not on Mariia's character, but on that of the film's other female protagonist, Lidiia. After all, it is she who hires them and it is in her home that they perform.

The contention that it is Lidiia who is linked to the *tsyganka* is also strengthened by the fact that Mariia has a *dikovinka* of her own: her sewing machine. In nineteenth-century Russian literature and culture sewing and sewing machines were pervasive and powerfully suggestive tropes that were repeatedly used as both the means and a symbol of the fallen woman's moral and spiritual redemption.[42] Thus, before Mariia allows herself to be corrupted by Lidiia and Lebedev, she is shown to spend much of her time sewing. Moreover, when Lidiia calls on her for the first time, she has to clear her sewing patterns from the table before they can take tea. After she has succumbed to the temptations of Lidiia's lifestyle, however, Mariia starts to lose interest in this activity. A telling moment occurs during Lidiia's next visit. Excluded from the women's conversation, Mariia's husband retreats to the background of the frame; he picks up from the floor a piece of material, looks sorrowfully at his wife, and replaces it on the abandoned sewing machine. Like Mariia's husband, the sewing machine remains behind when she moves in with Lebedev.[43]

Thus, as the Gypsies dance, Lidiia takes Mariia by the arm, excluding the young woman's husband and soon contriving to separate Mariia from him completely. When the two women walk past a group of elegant gentlemen, Lidiia neither stops nor makes any introductions, but one of the men is alert to their presence. This, the viewer will soon discover, is Lebedev. That Lidiia's walking past him with Mariia is a pre-arranged signal is beyond doubt: on seeing Lidiia the businessman immediately turns and stares after the two women, before rising from his seat and craning his neck to gain a better view of them. Meanwhile, Lidiia leads Mariia away from the main party to an elegant and isolated conservatory, where a table is already set for an intimate *tête à tête* with a bottle of champagne and, significantly, only two glasses. Bauer cuts back to the main party, where Mariia's husband is a forlorn figure, ill at ease and indifferent to the Gypsy dancers and the fine food that Lidiia's other guests are enjoying. The camera then cuts back to Lidiia and Mariia and the viewer is unsurprised when Lebedev also enters the conservatory and invites Mariia to sit and drink with him. Also predictable is the fact that Lidiia then finds herself obliged to take her leave and return to the party, where she interrupts the Gypsies' performance to invite the rest of her guests to take to her rowing boats and participate in a decadent and lengthy carnival on the lake. That this is a pre-planned diversion is suggested by Bauer's eloquent cross-cutting, which repeatedly takes the viewer between the 'public' face of Lidiia's soirée – that is, the gaiety of the lively guests and the *tsyganki,* who are all assembled on the boating lake – and the hushed privacy of the conservatory, where Lebedev plies Mariia with champagne, kisses her hand (gallantly at first, but with increasing insistence) and, in a crudely disguised attempt to get closer to her, pretends to read her palm.

The viewer's conviction that Lidiia has set Mariia up as prey for Lebedev is confirmed in subsequent sequences. Each time Lidiia invites the young woman to accompany her on an outing, whether for a walk in the park or a picnic in the countryside, they 'unexpectedly' run into the businessman; and, each time they do so, Lidiia contrives to leave Mariia alone in his company, whereupon she is obliged to defend herself from Lebedev's increasingly violent amorous advances. Lidiia's fakery is also stressed, for when Mariia confides her fear of Lebedev to her Lidiia displays no compassion for her 'friend'; instead, as exasperated by Mariia's refusal to submit to his demands for physical favours as is the businessman himself, Lidiia dismisses her tears with barely concealed anger and a threat that Lebedev wields great influence at the bank where her husband works.

The link between Lidiia and the *tsyganka* is finally made explicit, however, when Lidiia performs an impromptu dance routine for her friends during their picnic in the countryside. It is significant that it is on this occasion that Lebedev, frustrated beyond endurance by Mariia's repeated rejection of his amorous advances, eventually loses his patience and rapes her. Lidiia makes no secret of her satisfaction at this development, laughing in delight when, after noticing Mariia's hat and shawl lying abandoned on the grass and, apparently, hearing noises coming from the bushes, she realises that Lebedev is finally getting his way with the young woman. The viewer is reminded of Blok's poem 'In the Restaurant' ['V restorane', 19

April 1910], which concludes with an image of a dancing *tsyganka* who stands as a mocking indictment of the lyric persona's vain hope that there is any possibility of genuine love between him and the beautiful woman, a prostitute most likely, whom he admires from across the room:

> But from the depths of the mirrors you threw me glances
> And, as you glanced, called out: 'Catch!..'
> But a necklace jangled, a gypsy woman danced
> And screeched to the dawn about love.[44]

Mariia is similarly unlikely to find love in the cynical company of Lebedev and Lidiia, as the following sequence emphasises, for while the first rape scene takes place off screen, Lebedev's second attack on Mariia, which occurs in his car, is captured by the camera. Bauer renders this violent scene more disturbing by implicating male society as a whole in Mariia's rape. Having succeeded in breaking free of Lebedev's violent embrace, Mariia jumps from the car and runs to the nearest group of passers-by, all of whom are male. Despite her obvious distress and fear, these men accept Lebedev's misogynistic explanation that she's hysterical, and allow Lebedev to force Mariia back into the car where he continues his assault. Brutalised and traumatised, Mariia is no longer able to resist.

These sequences combine to stress, of course, that Mariia's sexual infidelity is not entered into freely. She does not succumb to Lebedev without putting up a fight and it is only at the very end of the film, after she has been repeatedly pursued, harassed and twice raped by Lebedev and after her husband, thanks to the businessman's connivances, has lost his job at the bank, that Mariia finally abandons her resistance and leaves her husband to move in with her 'lover'. Moreover, in the sequence in which Mariia moves in with Lebedev, Bauer emphasises the young woman's powerlessness, her vulnerability and her lack of freedom. When Mariia arrives at Lebedev's home, he and his friends are already celebrating. Lebedev's guests applaud when Mariia enters the room. The young woman appears shy and uncomfortable, but Lebedev is solicitous; he pours Mariia a glass of champagne and then proposes a toast ('To Mariia's new-found happiness!'), whereupon there is cheering, laughter and more applause. Mariia, however, looks far from happy and, when Lebedev tries to take her hand in his, she screws it up into a fist so that he cannot. Moreover, she stands apart, on the fringes of the happy group and, instead of engaging with the assembled merrymakers, gazes away from them, straight into the camera. The expressions on her face and in her eyes speak of deep despair. Mariia appears oppressed, both by the space in which she finds herself and by the people who inhabit it. A reviewer writing in *Cinema* in 1915 drew attention to how well Kholodnaia conveyed these emotions.[45] Thus the viewer is left feeling that for Mariia this is a far from happy ending. Indeed, the following sequence confirms and emphasises this, for it reminds the viewer that, in Lebedev's eyes, Mariia is not an individual, a person, but simply a beautiful possession, an object that he seeks to possess; we watch as he summons Mariia's husband to his office and, in the presence of his lawyer, offers him a significant sum of money to relinquish any claim over his wife and their child.

In these ways, then, Bauer presents Mariia not as the embodiment of a fatal femininity, but as a real, albeit flawed, woman. Moreover, she is also shown to be a victim, and the 'choices' and 'decisions' she makes in her life are not emblematic of her freedom, but merely the inevitable corollary of the weakness and powerlessness of her lowly social status and her gender. As she acknowledges to her husband when she tells him she is leaving him for Lebedev: 'This is stronger than me'. We therefore see Bauer attaching new associations to the figure of the *tsyganka*. The gypsy dancers who feature in this film are, after all, professional urban performers; as such, it is unlikely that they are authentic, ethnic Gyspies. The *tsyganka* thus comes to stand as a symbol of Lidiia's high-class fakery and lack of authenticity. She, like the Russian performers who embraced the Gypsy persona, is false, inauthentic. As the film's title stresses, so, by extension, is the new age of which Lidiia is a product.

The *tsyganka* as New Woman: Petr Chardynin's *The Love of a Councillor of State*

If Bauer engages with the persona of the *tsyganka* only *en passant* in *Children of the Age*, however, a striking, original and sustained use of this female archetype occurs in Petr Chardynin's *The Love of a Councillor of*

State. In this film, released just over a month after Bauer's *Children of the Age*, on 10 November 1915, Chardynin engages with the familiar, already rather tired image of the *tsyganka* on various levels and, in so doing, contrives to create a complex and unusual representation of his film's central female protagonist.

Like *Children of the Age*, Chardynin's film tells the story of a young woman who enters into a relationship with an older man, not because she is in love with him, but because she is attracted by the increased social status and material security that such a match will bring her. Like *Children of the Age* again, this film also presents events from the female narrative perspective. There the similarities end, however, for while Bauer halts his narrative when Mariia moves in with Lebedev, thereby suggesting that Mariia cannot hope to escape from this unequal and unhappy match, Chardynin's film focuses instead on portraying how the protagonists' relationship develops after their marriage. In so doing, he imagines a very different fate for his female protagonist from the one that Bauer implies is the lot of his unfortunate Mariia.

The centrality of the Gypsy persona to Chardynin's representation of his female protagonist is made explicit from the very start of the film, even before its narrative proper begins. From at least 1911 it was the convention for directors to introduce the main actors and actresses to the viewer by including a series of non-narrative portrait shots among the credit titles. Chardynin appears to work within this convention, for the first shot that appears on screen is a medium close-up of Vera Karalli, the actress cast in the central female role of the dancer, Lola. The viewer's expectations are disrupted, however, by the fact that Karalli is the only actor to be introduced in this way. The viewer expects the cameo of Karalli to be followed, at the very least, by portraits of Vladimir Elskii and Marfa Kassatskaia, the actors playing the eponymous State Councillor and his mother, who were both well known and highly respected. Moreover, Chardynin's portrait of Karalli differs subtly from the norm in another way: it introduces not Karalli as Karalli the actress, nor even Karalli as Lola, but instead shows Karalli playing Lola playing Carmen; the actress is dressed in a Spanish Gypsy costume consisting of patterned headscarf, flamenco-style dress and fringed shawl, and she holds in her hand a red rose. Thus, even before the film's narrative has begun, Chardynin's central female protagonist is linked to a nineteenth-century cultural archetype and her representation is thus situated firmly within that tradition.[46]

Moreover, as the film progresses, it becomes clear that Bizet's *Carmen* and, therefore, by extension, Mérimée's novella and Pushkin's *The Gypsies*, function as crucial subtexts to it. There are also many echoes of Blok's *Carmen* poems, though of course many differences as well. Thus, in the first part of the film we witness a performance by a touring opera troupe, whose star attraction is the dancer Lola, that reproduces many of the details of scenes from Bizet's opera. The supporting cast, with men dressed as toreadors and the women as Spanish Gypsy dancers, watch as Lola and her male partner perform a dramatic and fast-paced dance that speaks of desire and wild passion. At one point Lola, dressed in a tightly fitting flamenco-style dress, throws a red rose to her partner, as Carmen throws a flower to Don José in both opera and novella, thereby indicating her sexual interest in the hero. Moreover, as the dance progresses it becomes a battle for power and dominance between the two performers, and it is the female dancer who emerges triumphant: with a defiant flourish of her beautiful arms, she casts her partner's hand from her shoulder, turns her back on him and steps forward, away from him, to the front of the stage, where she stands gazing out over the audience, her head thrown back in a gesture of proud self-assertion and independence.

The dancer's performance makes a strong impression on von Brück, the eponymous Councillor of State who, like the lyric persona in Blok's 'As the ocean changes colour...' ['Kak okean meniaet svet...', 4 March 1914] is overwhelmed 'By the appearance of Carmensita' (p. 227). He sends Lola a bouquet of flowers and goes backstage to visit her in her dressing room. After presenting her with a box of chocolates (an example of the type of comically bathetic detail that is the hallmark of this entertaining and sub-tly satirical film), he cajoles from her a white flower that, despite his staid mother's obvious disapproval, he wears in his buttonhole with visible pride. It is significant that Lola does not offer the flower to him of her own accord.

That night, von Brück finds himself unable to sleep. Tormented by the memory of Lola's appearance at the theatre, he re-imagines her public per-formance as a private act of seduction aimed solely at him; in von Brück's fantasy – which Chardynin indicates by superimposing the female per-former in the top half of the frame, as Bauer had superimposed Viktor's valet during the sequence detailing Mary's erotic day-dreaming in his *Child of the Big City* – Lola dances before him, now moving slowly and without any male partner and any audience other than himself; she blows a kiss to him before handing him, unbidden, her red rose, that conventional symbol of passion and, in the context of *Carmen*, of sexual interest.

The next day, unable to concentrate on his work, von Brück writes a lengthy letter to Lola, in which he declares his love and asks her to leave the stage, become his wife and share his 'quiet family life'. Thus Lola is shown to occupy his mind when he is both awake and asleep and to distract him from his 'duty', leading him to behave out of character: his mother complains that he is acting 'like a little boy', and an intertitle informs us that von Brück's writing such a letter is 'completely incompatible with his respectable way of life'. The upheaval that Lola's appearance causes in von Brück's daily routine is also signposted in the film's opening intertitle, which describes how with the unexpected arrival of the theatre troupe the town's 'quiet, sleepy life' is disturbed. The effect that the dancer has on the State Councillor thus mirrors that of Carmen on Don José in Mérimée's novella; he stresses the impossibility of forgetting Carmen and repeatedly discovers that she occupies his thoughts so completely that he forgets everything he once considered important, including his mother and his duty as a soldier. It also recalls that of Carmen/Delmas on the lyric persona/Blok in the poem 'Snowy spring is raging…' ['Bushuet snezhnaia vesna…'] (p. 231).

Lola is also shown to have some of the defining characteristics of the nineteenth-century *tsyganka* whom she embodies on stage. Before he sees her perform, von Brück encounters the dancer when he goes to the theatre to purchase tickets. As he leaves the box office he is covered by a shower of torn paper that Lola, amid much laughter, has thrown at her friend, the violinist Surdinskii. This brief scene immediately characterises Lola as a lively, vivacious woman who is indifferent both to social niceties and to social rank, for she makes no apology for showering one of the town's most important personages with paper and merely laughs all the more. While on this occasion von Brück finds Lola's vivacity refreshing and engaging (in this sequence he himself laughs for the first and only time in the film), after their marriage he attempts to stifle her *joie de vivre*; he objects to Lola's attempting to enliven a gathering he holds for his and his mother's friends by playing the piano, grabbing her arm roughly and all but dragging her from the piano stool in an effort to prevent her from performing. His mother is similarly exasperated by Lola's ignorance of and indifference to social norms and, during one of several interminable family meals, repeatedly pushes the young woman's elbows off the table.

Lola's status as a member of a touring troupe of performers also suggests that she, like Carmen in all her guises and Pushkin's *tsyganki*, Mariula and Zemfira, is at heart a nomad. Indeed, after her marriage Lola finds it impossible to settle into her new life as a provincial wife. The film-makers repeatedly convey the stifling confinement that such a marriage represents to Lola by various means. The shot of a formal photographic portrait of von Brück and Lola on their wedding day emphasises the captivity that the dancer now finds herself in and, while Karalli's nuanced acting – which was highly praised by contemporary reviewers[47] – effectively conveys the dancer's restlessness and boredom, the film-makers nevertheless underline her dissatisfaction in a superfluous intertitle, thereby suggesting how significant a feature of Lola this restlessness is: 'Lolla [*sic*] cannot bear her husband's grand air, or his mother's affectation or, in general, their whole way of life, which is so measured, monotonous and dreary'.

The notepaper on which von Brück pens his marriage proposal is similarly emblematic of the restrictive life that awaits Lola, for it is decorated with a pair of plump turtledoves. These domesticated birds, which contentedly co-exist for life as a mating pair, with the female dove refusing to take another mate should her first mate die, have long been seen as a symbol of devoted, everlasting love and fidelity. They therefore function as an ironic reference to Pushkin's and Bizet's comparisons of their free-spirited Gypsies to a wild bird that resists all attempts to confine it;[48] they are also an ironic comment on the nature of Lola's relationship with her future husband. For, despite choosing to abandon her career to marry von Brück, whose letter of proposal had made it clear that Lola would have to leave the stage once she became his wife, Lola discovers that she is not the type of woman who can exist in tranquil, provincial domesticity with her mate; imposing such a life on her is like trying to cage a wild bird, a similarity that a contemporary reviewer of the film drew attention to in an article published in the journal *Pegasus* [Pegas] in 1915, describing Lola as a striking *Bohémienne* possessed of 'all the charm of a wild bird, loving freedom [*svoboda*] before anything and touchingly languishing in captivity'.[49]

Lola does not in fact fade away, however. Instead, she rebels against von Brück's repeated attempts to cage her. She retains her strength of character and her desire for independence, remaining true to her conviction that she is the only person who has the right to make decisions about how she lives her life; it is ironic that it is this attitude that led to Lola's accepting von Brück's proposal in the first place, in the face of her mother's obvious reservations.[50] Thus we watch as Lola stands up to her domineering husband on numerous occasions: by twice shrugging off the clumsy physical caresses with which he attempts to make amends for his harsh and demeaning treatment of her; by refusing to dispose of her Gypsy costume and donning it in her room while he is at work in order to perform Gypsy dances secretly, for nobody other than herself, before the mirror (Figure 5.1); by inviting her former music-hall colleagues to drink wine with

Figure 5.1. Lola performs in her Gypsy costume in the privacy of her bedroom (Chardynin, *The Love of a Councillor of State*, 1915)

131

her in von Brück's absence; and by persuading him to allow Surdinskii to come and play music with her, a concession that annoys von Brück's suspicious mother, who does not let the performers out of her sight and follows them from room to room as they search for pieces of sheet music. Finally, it is telling that when Lola eventually acknowledges and expresses her love for Surdinskii, she does so by accepting his invitation to perform in a concert he is organising, irrespective of the fact that, in so doing, she creates a scandal that rocks the whole town.

On learning of Lola's intention to perform again, von Brück, who sees the stage as the place where 'accessible' women put themselves on display, imperiously announces (pompously referring to himself in the third person): 'Mr von Brück forbids you to dance!' And he then issues his wife with a strident ultimatum: 'Either dance, or remain the wife of Mr von Brück'. This confrontation mirrors that between Pushkin's Aleko and Zemfira, when Aleko, enraged by the words of Zemfira's wild songs, repeatedly orders her to stop singing. Unsurprisingly, Lola, like Zemfira, defies her husband and rises to his challenge: without even pausing to consider her decision, she proudly declares 'I will dance'. Then she leaves the room, calmly packs her few belongings and walks out of von Brück's house, his life and their marriage. She pauses at the gate, but this is not a mark of her hesitation; instead in this moment, as she breathes in deeply, as if tasting the freshness of the air for the first time, Lola savours her newfound freedom. When she sets off down the road with her suitcase, she, like Vera in Bauer's *Twilight of a Woman's Soul*, does not look back.

Lola's determined flight from patriarchal domesticity comes as no surprise to the viewer, for the turtledove is not the only bird with which she is associated in the film. In an intertitle, not included in the restored print of the film, von Brück rebukes his wife as follows: 'Stop playing "Chizhik". You are compromising yourself and undermining my prestige'.[51] The most likely context for this remark is the dull tea party hosted by von Brück and his mother, at which Lola attempts to play the piano[52] (Figure 5.2). The noun *chizhik* (a siskin, a type of finch), rendered as it is in inverted commas and capitalised, is undoubtedly the title of the piece of music that Lola begins to play, and refers most probably to a nineteenth-century folk song with the following lyrics:

Siskin, siskin, where've you been?
On the Fontanka, drinking vodka.
Drank one glass, drank a second,
My head starting spinning.
They tried to catch the siskin
And put him in a cage.
No, no, I don't want that,
I'll fly out of the cage.
This cage is not for me,
This cage is for the nightingale![53]

It is not difficult to see why von Brück objects to Lola's attempt to perform this song before his friends. With its references to vodka drinking, drunkenness and defiant escape, it is hardly appropriate background music for the staid tea party he and his mother are hosting. Moreover, it will remind everyone present of Lola's former career as a music-hall performer.

Figure 5.2. Lola attempts to enliven the von Brücks' dull tea party by playing music-hall tunes on the piano (Chardynin, *The Love of a Councillor of State*, 1915)

133

Thus, like the siskin of the song, and like Mariula, Zemfira and Carmen, Lola rebels against von Brück's attempts to cage her. It is significant that the film's final sequence features Lola's triumphant return to the stage. Surprisingly, however, she does not perform the Gypsy dance with which she has been associated throughout the film. Instead, dressed in a tutu and partnered by two male dancers, she performs a lively, light-hearted dance piece, identified by a contemporary film reviewer, writing in *The Projector*, as 'a comic polka'.[54] The polka has an interesting history. Thought to have been 'invented' one Sunday afternoon in 1834 by a Bohemian peasant girl, Anna Slezakova, who devised it for her own amusement, its quickness and liveliness meant that it soon came to be seen as representing a new, informal style of social dancing.[55] These associations make it the perfect vehicle through which Lola can declare her newly reclaimed freedom. She has chosen to return to the stage for her own satisfaction and enjoyment; that her choice goes against all the rules of polite, middle-class society is of no relevance to her. It is striking that in Chardynin's representation of Lola's status as a stage performer, there is none of the ambiguity that was discerned in Bauer's earlier *Twilight of a Woman's Soul*. The stage is her element, and she performs there on her own terms.

Thus, while Chardynin undoubtedly takes nineteenth-century texts featuring the *tsyganka* as subtexts for his film and the nineteenth-century figure of the *tsyganka* as a model for Lola, he does not remain faithful to their representation of the Gypsy archetype, but adapts their themes and their concerns in order to comment on pressing social concerns of the early twentieth century. Indeed, contemporary reviewers of the film were unanimous in their praise of this film as social commentary. An article published in *The Projector* described the film as containing 'great vividness and truthfulness'.[56] A reviewer writing for *Pegasus* was most effusive, however, declaring the film to be:

> a genuine everyday [*bytovaia*] comedy, possibly the first seen on our screens. Its content is everyday life [*byt*] and psychology; its comedy is more internal than external […].
>
> Mr Chardynin, having given us a picture that is beautiful, and full of real life and of subtle humour, has begun a new trend in cinematographic art. It is clear that the screen is just as productive a field for serious comedy and social satire as are books.[57]

Contemporary commentators also agreed that it was von Brück who was the object of Chardynin's satire, and, specifically, his narrow-minded petty-bourgeois worldview [*meshchanstvo*] and the outmoded patriarchal assumptions about gender roles and gender relations that he attempts to impose on Lola. As Carlo Montanaro notes: 'It is an entirely feminine film'.[58]

It is clear, then, that Lola is not a twentieth-century *tsyganka* for anyone other than her possessive, patriarchal husband and his disapproving mother. No man lies dead at the end of the film, for Lola is no dangerous femme fatale but simply an impoverished dancer, reasonably talented but of no great renown, who works to support herself and her mother and who enjoys touring and performing many different kinds of role on stage. The freedom that Lola achieves at the end of the film is not the *tsyganka's* freedom [*volia*] – that is, an elemental free will, linked in nineteenth-century Gypsy texts with fickle female sexuality – but rather the twentieth-century New Woman's freedom [*svoboda*], a more structured, ordered liberty from established social law and rule. As Montanaro puts it: 'The character of the dancer reflects above all the wish for emancipation and independence, even when being dependent could lead to higher social status and acquiring bourgeois privileges'.[59]

Thus, while there are some similarities between the stories of Bauer's Mariia in *Children of the Age* and Chardynin's Lola in *The Love of a Councillor of State*, the fates of the female protagonists are ultimately shown to be very different. Mariia ends the film passive and helpless, trapped in an unequal and unhappy relationship in which she is valued not as an individual but only as a beautiful object. By the time she moves in with Lebedev she has, as Youngblood puts it, 'given up – on herself and on her past life. No one will help her'.[60] Lola, on the other hand, proves herself to be made of sterner stuff; able to act on her own behalf, she escapes the confines of her unhappy marriage and lives a life of her own choosing. As a contemporary reviewer noted: 'The poor dancer proves to be sufficiently strong to tear herself out of the maelstrom'.[61] What also differentiates these two female protagonists is the fact that only Lola is cast as a performer. Indeed, it is striking that both Montanaro and the anonymous reviewer cited above refer to Lola not simply as a woman [*zhenshchina*], but as a dancer [*tantsovshchitsa*]. In this way the figure of the dancer is invested with a number of positive associations, coming to stand as a signifier of those character traits usually associated with the New Woman, namely strength of character, the desire for independence, both economic and emotional, and the ability to achieve these aims. Thus, unlike Blok, who, as Osip Mandelshtam suggests, had ensured, only one year previously in his lyric cycle *Carmen*, that the Carmen story retained the status of myth accorded to it by Merimée's and Bizet's nineteenth-century works of art on that theme,[62] in *The Love of a Councillor of State* Chardynin subverts the nineteenth-century figure of the *tsyganka*, matter-of-factly normalising and domesticating this myth. In so doing, he creates an unusual and original film about a brave and determined twentieth-century woman.

6

From the Ballerina to the Early Modern Dancer

Ballerinas – the most beautiful and the most desired women in the capital.

Anastasiia Verbitskaia, *The Keys to Happiness*.[1]

A powerful cultural symbol and a potent image of femininity, the ballerina had dominated classical Russian ballet since the 1830s and had been the object of personality cults throughout the nineteenth century in life and in art of all media. Although enthusiasm for classical ballet was waning in Europe at the start of the twentieth century, it remained overwhelmingly popular in Russia; as Ann Kodicek has documented, in the season 1899–1900, twenty-six different ballet productions were staged in St Petersburg alone.[2] Indeed, the ballerina's popularity in Russian culture and society more generally was also at its height during the first decades of the twentieth century, as reflected in the fact that some of the most popular ballerinas began to perform solo at this time.

Among them was the legendary Anna Pavlova. One of the most mythologised Russian performers, Pavlova came to be seen as the quintessential ballerina. Her famously weak feet and delicate physique left her unable to master some of the showy, virtuosic techniques popular at the time, but Pavlova turned her physical weakness into her greatest strength, creating a unique performance persona that relied on her fragility for its

137

power. 'Slim, straight, agile as a reed [...] ethereal and ephemeral,' wrote the Russia dance critic Valerian Svetlov of her in 1906, 'she seemed as fragile as a porcelain statuette'.[3]

   Pavlova's signature role was *The Dying Swan* [La Mort du cygne], a solo piece created for her by the future *Ballets russes* choreographer Mikhail Fokin, in 1905 or 1907.[4] Although other ballerinas would perform their own versions of this dance, it remained firmly associated with Pavlova's name and image, both during her lifetime and after her death. The dance historian Sally Banes's description of Pavlova's style of dancing is typical in that it uses this dance as a point of reference for general comments about her style, thus: 'Her head often canting flirtatiously, her body often snuggling into itself (like the swans with which she was forever associated after dancing Fokine's *The Dying Swan* in 1907), [Pavlova] created an image of the ballerina as lyrical, childlike, and ultrafeminine'.[5]

   In this way, the ballerina, perhaps more than any other female performer figure encountered in early Russian film, exists as a pre-established complex of idealised associations, acquired over several centuries. As Roger Copeland notes: 'The popular stereotype of the ballerina – woman as virginal, disembodied, sylphide – [...] dominated ballet from the heyday of Taglioni to that of Pavlova'.[6]

Early Russian film representations of the ballerina

The world of Russian ballet was resolutely elite, however. Patronised by the Tsar and members of his court, it was accessible exclusively to the nobility. As such, it might be seen as standing in opposition to the emerging film industry, which from its earliest days was committed to providing accessible popular entertainment. It is therefore perhaps unsurprising that, on the evidence of both Vishnevskii's filmography and the corpus of pre-Revolutionary Russian films screened at Pordenone in 1989, the ballerina does not feature as protagonist in any Russian feature film made before 1912.

   In 1995, however, this accepted fact of early Russian film history was re-written, when the documentary film-maker, film historian and producer Victor Bocharov discovered an extraordinary collection of animated films that had been made between 1906 and 1909. These films, which were premiered in their restored versions at the twenty-seventh *Giornate del Cinema Muto* Festival, held at Pordenone between 4 and 11 October 2008, revealed that the ballerina was in fact present as a protagonist in Russian-made films even before the Persian princess appeared on the screen.

The man who made these films was Aleksandr Shiriaev, a member of the Russian Imperial Ballet at the Mariinskii (Marinsky) Theatre in St Petersburg, where he worked for over fifty years in various roles: as the troupe's leading character dancer, as an assistant to the great choreographer Marius Petipa and as a gifted ballet teacher. Shiriaev was fascinated by the challenges of dance notation and saw in cinema the perfect medium for recording the choreography of his elusive art, so difficult to describe in words.[7] In 1904 he therefore wrote to the management of the Imperial Ballet, requesting financial assistance to enable him to purchase a movie camera and film stock so that he might record the leading dancers of the day as an aid to staging and rehearsing future ballet productions. The managers, considering the still photographs of famous dancers that hung in the halls of the Mariinskii to be sufficient record of their greatness and, perhaps, looking with disdain upon the then low-brow medium of cinema, turned down his request. Undaunted, Shiriaev purchased a camera by his own means, returning from a trip to London with a 17.5mm Biokam.[8]

The manufacturers of this early camera advertised it as being capable of photographing 'everything in motion,'[9] and Shiriaev took them at their word, for he proceeded to make an astonishing number of films that were impressive in their variety: live records of character dances, performed by Shriaev and his wife, Natalia Matveeva, on a specially constructed open-air stage at the Ukrainian farm where they spent their summers; home movies; staged comedies involving members of his family; trick films; and animated puppet films.[10] It is these puppet films that are most relevant to the present study. As many of them reproduce scenes from the classical ballets that were in the Mariinskii's repertoire, it is in them that the figure of the ballerina features most prominently.

Aleksandr Shiriaev's *The Artist Pierrots* [P´ero-khudozhniki]

One of the most interesting of Shiriaev's films, from the perspective of the representation of the ballerina, is *The Artist Pierrots*, a five-and-a-half-minute-long film made in 1906 or 1907 that combines both drawn-illustrated and puppet animation. Described in its introductory intertitle as a 'comic picture', it stars three puppets that Shiriaev made from wire covered with papier-mâché and which were highly flexible and could be moved into almost any position.

The film's narrative is based on that of the comic *pas de trois* that the Russian choreographers Nikolai and Sergei Legat created for their staging of Josef Bayer's one-act ballet *The Doll Fairy* [Die Puppenfee, 1888] at the Mariinskii in 1903. The curtain rises to show an empty stage. A Pierrot enters, carrying a pot of paint and two long-handled paintbrushes. He is followed on to the stage by a second Pierrot and, after some clowning, the pair begin to paint a picture of a one-storey brick house on to the back-drop, while each tries surreptitiously to daub the other's suit with paint. After a slapstick sequence in which they succeed in covering themselves and each other with what remains of the paint, the Pierrots are startled to see smoke rising from the chimney. A window opens to reveal a ballerina, who then opens the door and comes out. As the ballerina dances for the astounded Pierrots, performing a series of *pirouettes en pointe*, she is remarkably life-like. Each Pierrot wants the ballerina for his own. They vie for her attention and compete for the privilege of partnering her. After one Pierrot goes down before her on bended knee, his friend resorts to violence, throwing his rival through the window into the house. On bended knee in his turn, he declares his love to the ballerina. But the ballerina rejects him, shaking her head and admonishing him gently, as one would a young child, by wagging her finger at him. As the other Pierrot escapes from the house, their fight for her attention begins anew, but the ballerina will have none of it. Positioning herself between the two Pierrots, she makes it clear that she will belong to neither of them. She will, however, perform for them both, and the Pierrots watch as she dances, again *en pointe* throughout. It is a sight that causes them both to fall to their knees. The ballerina's performance comes to an abrupt end, however, when she suddenly dances back into the house. The door closes behind her. Distraught, the Pierrots open the windows to look for her. She is nowhere to be seen, however, and instead two ugly rag dolls jump up at them. The Pierrots fall to the ground in fright and the painted house vanishes from the backdrop. As no paint remains in their bucket, they can neither recreate the magical house nor re-summon the beautiful dancer. Reunited by their loss, the Pierrot-artists leave the stage arm in arm, as friends.

Thus in the first Russian film to feature a ballerina protagonist, we see that this iconic figure is portrayed in similar ways to the female personae explored in earlier chapters, for, as with the Persian princess, the peasant girl and the *tsyganka*, her portrayal derives from pre-existing nineteenth-century representations. The relationship between ballerina dolls and their creators was one that ran throughout the tradition of classical ballet, receiving its fullest and most influential treatment in Arthur Saint-Léon's *Coppélia* (1870), which Petipa had restaged in St Petersburg in 1884. In Shiriaev's film, although the ballerina is ultimately unattainable, and certainly powerful, she, like Coppélia before her, nevertheless lacks autonomy and remains the creation of the men who admire and desire her. She is also, in some sense, their captive. After all, she is at liberty to perform on the stage only after they have painted the house from which she emerges, which, we can assume, bestows on them the power both to keep her from the stage and to summon her on to it. Finally, as in many of the films already discussed in this study, the male protagonists are also shown to be better off without her, for her presence sows discord between them and undermines their friendship.

Where this charming puppet film differs most from the other early Russian films discussed so far in this study, as regards its representation of its female dancer protagonist, is in its mode of discourse: it is, after all, a comedy film. Accordingly, it is characterised by a ludic vitality and a gentle affection, with Shiriaev's hapless Pierrots evoking neither apathy nor dislike in the viewer. Nor are the rights and wrongs of their reactions to and treatment of the ballerina explored in any depth, not least because Shiriaev's interest in film lay in exploring not contemporary social concerns, but the new medium's ability to capture the movements and the choreography of specific set pieces from the nineteenth-century ballet repertoire. As we shall see, however, in the decade that would follow the ballerina would

become one of the most important, complex and conflicted female personae featured in the sophisticated acted melodramas produced by the great
Russian directors of the 1910s.

From the feminist perspective: later filmic representations of the ballerina

> The ballerina is 'not simply an innocuous, isolated theatrical
> image' but an icon of femininity which not only reflects but
> inscribes gender behaviour in everyday life.
>
> Elizabeth Dempster.[11]

If the ballerina is a relatively unexplored figure in the earliest years of
Russian film-making, in the period 1912 to 1919 she is remarkable for her
ubiquity. Moreover, she appears in films of all genres. Filmed ballets became hugely popular in the 1910s: in 1913 Iakov Protazanov made two
short ballet films, *Moment musical* [Muzykal´nyi moment] and *A Chopin
Nocturne* [Noktiurn Shopena], with the Bolshoi dancers Ekaterina Geltser
and Vasilii Tikhomirov, and Kai Hansen produced a full-length version of
Coppélia. The ballerina also began to appear as a protagonist in Russian
feature films, however, and she retained her appeal as a female persona
until the final years of the decade under consideration.

As the 1910s advanced, so the ambition and sophistication of early
Russian film-makers grew. Their understanding of the myriad narrative
possibilities offered by cinematic technology developed and, as they began
to exploit and explore these possibilities in their films, so they were able to
examine their central thematic concerns in greater depth and to tell their
protagonists' stories with increasing complexity. After 1912, the female
protagonists' performances also began to play a much greater role, occu-
pying more screen time and being shown both with more precision and
in greater detail than in earlier films. The way in which the film-makers
exploited their female protagonists' performances also developed. Thus,
even more than in films made before 1912, their dances are used as an
important means of characterisation. They continue to reveal a considerable amount about the men who enjoy them (as we saw in the case of
Dolskii's response to Vera's performance of *La Traviata* in Bauer's *Twilight*

of a Woman's Soul), but they also begin to be used to communicate more about the women themselves who perform them. This is especially true in the case of those protagonists who are cast as dancers in films made after 1912, for the act and the art of dancing are repeatedly represented as being adopted consciously and actively by many female protagonists as a form of self-expression. In other words, their dance becomes their voice.

The appropriateness of this interpretation is encouraged by established theoretical approaches employed in the field of dance scholarship. While dance is an art form that traditionally makes no use of spoken words, dance scholars frequently speak of the 'textuality' of dance, and in so doing advocate an approach to this art form that sees it as a system of readable and comprehensible signs. Susan Leigh Foster, for example, in her seminal work *Reading Dancing: Bodies and Subjects in Contemporary American Dance*, argued against the idea that dancing – and by extension, the role of dancers and choreographers – should be seen as a mute, idealised form of bodily expression, suggesting instead (by adopting semiotic analysis), that dancing can be 'read', like other texts, as an organised semantic structure.[12] Thus, the dancer's body becomes a sign within a system of representation that varies between choreographers and historical periods. By extension, the body's movement in dance can therefore be seen as an act of writing. Elizabeth Dempster has developed Foster's idea, suggesting that dance can also be seen as equivalent to speech, for dances, like spoken words, 'have no existence except though the body/bodies which produce and reproduce them'.[13]

Whichever comparison one prefers, however (dance as writing or dance as speech), they both suggest that dance is a substitute for language, indeed, is itself a form of language, and posit that when a woman dances her dancing body creates a text that can be read and understood in the same ways as a written or spoken text. The author of the text is either the choreographer or the dancer, depending on the form of dance. It thus becomes important, when considering the representation of the female dancer in Russian films made after 1912, to pay close attention to the dance form accorded to, or chosen by her. In Dempster's words, the viewer is required to 'watch a little how she dances' in order to learn more about her.[14]

What, then, does the choice of ballet suggest about the protagonists who perform this style of dance? In recent years feminist practitioners of and commentators on dance have argued that many of ballet's defining characteristics, in particular the way it deploys the female body and the roles in which it traditionally casts women, make it a highly oppressive dance form for the women who perform it. Ann Daly, for example, suggests that classical ballet is 'one of our culture's most powerful models of patriarchal ceremony'.[15] Dempster, focussing on the 'lengthy and rigorous training' that ballerinas undergo in order to acquire a 'long established lexicon' of highly stylised steps, argues that in ballet 'the female dancer enjoys a very limited degree of autonomy with respect to the deployment and representation of her body in performance' and concludes that 'this training process is the female dancer's initiation into a patriarchal symbolic order, that is into the language of the father'.[16] For feminist critics, then, the ballerina is oppressed and repressed by the patriarchal institution of which she accepts to be part.[17] Indeed, Dempster sees the ballerina as little more than a puppet, a persona that classical ballets frequently require her to assume, reduced by the traditional roles she performs to being 'a dependent, contingent object, lacking autonomy, lacking the capacity to speak or otherwise represent itself and lacking a transcendent symbology and function'.[18]

On the surface, then, the ubiquity of the ballerina in films from this period appears invidious, for what are the ballerinas whom we watch on screen able to say of any value in the 'texts' produced by their bodies, if, by the very nature of the dance form at which they excel, they are trapped into simply representing and re-representing age-old, male-created and male-pleasing images of femininity? As the following sections will demonstrate, however, between 1912 and 1919 Russian directors exploited this cliché-drenched female archetype in complex and surprising ways. Indeed, what is striking about films featuring the ballerina is the fact that they share the following characteristics: a carefully constructed and maintained disjuncture between the way in which the film's male protagonists are shown to respond to the ballerina heroines and the film-makers' representation of their female protagonists; and a determination on the part of the film-makers both to distance themselves from the attitudes and responses of their male protagonists towards the ballerina and to examine their responses to her critically.

Władysław Starewicz's dragonfly-ballerina

The first ballerina to appear in a Russian film made during the period 1912 to 1919 was not in fact a human figure, however. On 27 October 1912, Władysław Starewicz released *The Cameraman's Revenge*, an animated-puppet comedy in which he replaced human actors with insects. The film charts the adventures of Zhukov, a lascivious beetle-businessman who makes a trip to St Petersburg, telling his wife he is going there to work. In fact he spends the evening at a dance club, *The Jolly Dragonfly* [Veselaia strekoza], where the star attraction is a beautiful dragonfly-ballerina.[19] As Zhukov and the other members of the audience sit enjoying their drinks, the stage curtains part and the dragonfly-ballerina makes her dramatic entrance on stage: flying down from above, she lands gracefully on the tips of her 'toes' and gives a dazzling display of *en pointe* dancing. Exploited throughout the history of ballet as a powerful means of characterisation, *en pointe* dancing features in all the ballets in the classical repertoire, functioning always to convey the unearthly powers and empyreal delicacy of ethereal female characters – fairies, sylphs, sprites, nymphs, ghosts, magic birds and enchanted dolls – who appear in their narratives. As a technique that minimises the ballerina's contact with the ground, *en pointe* dancing enables the ballerina to create an impression of weightlessness, as she appears to float magically across the stage.

The dragonfly-ballerina's performance captures the attention of all the (obviously male) insects in the audience. As a 1912 reviewer comments: 'Zhukov could not take his eyes from the stage, where, gracefully writhing her slender figure, the famous dancer Mlle Dragonfly was performing her seductive [obol'stitel'nyi] dance.[20] Likewise, 'the customer seated next to him also gazes passionately at the dancer.[21] In this way, Starewicz replicates, mockingly, the conventional male (viewing subject)/female (viewed object) dichotomy that is characteristic of Russian films from this period that feature female performers. Moreover, he also suggests that to see is to desire: a grasshopper, struck by the dragonfly-ballerina's beauty, invites her to drink with him after her performance. This displeases Zhukov, who attacks his rival. Emerging victorious from their scuffle, the beetle seduces the ballerina himself and, in the next sequence, drives his conquest to the *Hôtel d'Amour*. The grasshopper, who has of course guessed Zhukov's next move, arrives at the hotel before them, however. He, it turns out, is the eponymous cameraman. He sets up his movie camera and films the illicit liaison, capturing the couple's arrival at the hotel and filming through the keyhole as the beetle and the dragonfly-ballerina sip champagne and enjoy the intimate surroundings of their hotel room. Then, in what may perhaps be the earliest example of a film plot that features the phenomenon now referred to as 'revenge porn', the grasshopper – a projectionist as well as a cameraman – uses the resulting footage to avenge himself on his rival, screening his film on the evening when Zhukov visits the cinema with his beetle-wife. Furious on discovering her husband's infidelity, she (who has herself been enjoying an illicit affair with a dashing grasshopper-artist) strikes him with her parasol. As he flees his wife's blows, Zhukov crashes through the cinema screen on which his tryst with the ballerina had been displayed for all to see, ripping a hole in it and shattering the image, an act that could perhaps been seen as evidence of his naïve (for 1912) belief that in this way he can destroy the visual evidence of his infidelity.[22]

In this entertaining film, then, the classical, nineteenth-century characterisation of the ballerina as a fragile, weightless and ethereal creature is made literal (in her representation as a dragonfly, that most delicate of insects) and thereby downgraded and ridiculed. In this way, Starewicz constructs a remarkable parody of the conventional image of the ballerina. The film's final sequence goes even further, however: by having his beetle-hero shatter the screen on which the ballerina had been projected, Starewicz seems to suggest that the ballerina cannot be considered an appropriate female persona for the twentieth century, for as this is the age of the new cinematic technology, so it is the era of the New Woman. This original filmic parody, made as early as 1912, suggests just how banal and hackneyed an image of femininity the ballerina had become even by the early 1910s.

Boris Chaikovskii's *A Ballerina's Romance* [Roman baleriny, 1916]: the ballerina as 'real' woman

The directors of acted feature films made after 1912 were similarly critical of the conventional nineteenth-century associations of the ballerina persona and also targeted the typical male response to her as an object of erotic contemplation, intended to satisfy their scopophilic fantasies and physical desires. For, while Starewicz's dragonfly-ballerina accepts without demur the amorous advances of the male insect-spectators, subsequent ballerina protagonists reject the masculine assumption that their status as a stage performer makes them accessible, sexual objects.

A new thematic trend that began in the mid-1910s and continued almost to the end of that decade therefore saw Russian directors striving to represent their ballerina protagonists first and foremost as modern, twentieth-century women who find themselves oppressed and victimised by the nineteenth-century associations of the ballerina archetype. Thus, in several films from this period, the ballet school is represented as a hierarchical and patriarchal institution and the ballerina as its powerless victim. In his 1916 film *A Ballerina's Romance*, for example, Boris Chaikovskii shows ballerinas training at the barre under the watchful eye of the ballet master, as he would later do in *The Stage Set of Happiness*, the film he made with Fedor Komissarzhevskii in 1918. Several times in this later film the ballet master touches the dancers, moving their arms or legs into the 'correct' position. It is telling that on one occasion a ballerina appears irritated by this physical contact and brushes his hand away from her leg.

It is in Chaikovskii's *A Ballerina's Romance* that these patriarchal attitudes are portrayed most shockingly, however.[23] This film tells the story of a young ballet student, Elena M., who commits suicide. After her death, Elena's diary is discovered and its entries reveal the reasons for her action. Elena's parents, having fallen on hard times, decide to marry their daughter to Satarov, a wealthy businessman who has proposed to Elena on numerous occasions. Repulsed by the idea of marrying a man she hates, the resourceful Elena devises an alternative solution to her family's financial problems: she persuades her parents to postpone the marriage until after she has completed her studies at ballet school, intending that, once qualified, she will pursue a career as a professional ballerina and thereby both retain her independence and support her family financially. We watch as Elena takes her final ballet examination, willing her to succeed. However, although her performance cannot be faulted, the director of the ballet school refuses to pass her, an act of revenge on Elena, who had once spurned his romantic advances. With all hope of a dancing career dashed, marriage to Satarov is the only remaining option. Faced with this bleak reality, Elena prefers to end her own life.

Although the fate of Chaikovskii's Elena is unquestionably tragic, it can nevertheless be argued that she at least had some choice over how to live her life, even if, like the peasant Lusha in *The Incestuous Father-in-Law*, she was able to exercise that choice only by committing suicide. Unlike Elena and Lusha, the heroines of two of Bauer's 'ballerina' films are not permitted even this measure of autonomy by the relationships in which Bauer situates them.

Mad love. From idolatry through necrolatry to murder: two films by Evgenii Bauer

Cult-objects are prisoners of their own symbolic inflation.

Camille Paglia.[24]

But what if the object began to speak?

Luce Irigaray.[25]

Daydreams

Bauer's *Daydreams*, released on 10 October 1915, is an adaptation of *Bruges-la-Morte*, a novel written by the Belgian Symbolist Georges Rodenbach in 1892. Described by Paolo Cherchi Usai as 'perhaps [the] best' of all Bauer's surviving films,[26] *Daydreams* tells the story of the ill-fated relationship between a ballerina and the recently bereaved Sergei Nedelin. The film is also known by the alternative title *Deceived Dreams* [Obmanutye mechty] and, as its eloquent title and subtitle make clear, Nedelin is a dreamer and a fantasist. Predictably, the objects of his fantasies are the film's two heroines.

The ideal: the dead wife
From the very beginning, Bauer emphasises Nedelin's tendency to worship and idealise women by showing him to be immersed in a cult of his

dead wife, Elena (N. Chernobaeva). The film's prologue, which pictures him weeping by her deathbed, presents Elena as a beautiful vision in white; with her lace-trimmed nightgown, the huge bouquets of white flowers that surround her and her alabaster skin, she is the embodiment of a fragile and ethereal beauty. In his study of distorted feminine images in late nineteenth- and early twentieth-century European art, Bram Dijkstra explains the turn-of-the-century cult of the beautiful female corpse as the *reductio ad absurdum* of patriarchal ideals of passive, virtuous and therefore desirable womanhood.[27] The documentary footage of the actress Vera Kholodnaia's funeral (1919) is perhaps animated by the same obsession; Helena Goscilo comments that 'Kholodnaia's funeral as immortalized on film [...] seemed to validate Edgar Allen Poe's notorious claim that "the death of a beautiful woman is, unquestionably, the most poetical topic in the world."'[28] The prologue to *Daydreams* is not simply 'poetical', however; it is also deeply disturbing, for it ends with Nedelin cutting off Elena's long plait. The violence implicit in this fetishising act hints at a darker side to Nedelin's character that is progressively revealed both by the film's action and by Bauer's mise-en-scène, and it has important implications for Bauer's representation of Tina, the performer protagonist with whom Nedelin will become involved.

Thus, the film's second sequence takes place in Nedelin's study, for which Bauer constructed one of his most expressive and disturbing sets. In every respect the room resembles a gothic church or temple. Huge ornamental hinges support its heavy, arch-shaped door, and there is a desk positioned in the foreground, like an altar. The objects that fill the room enhance its aura of sanctity. A large portrait of Elena hangs like an icon in one corner, with a cloth draped across the top of the frame. Nedelin's desk is covered with lines of framed photographs of the dead woman and thus transformed into a twentieth-century iconostasis. More portraits decorate the mantelpiece. Even more suggestive, however, is Bauer's choice of *dikovinka*: towards the end of this extended sequence, the camera slowly pans to the right (the first time it has moved in the film) to reveal a glass casket containing Elena's tresses that sits in the foreground on a table of its own. Later we see that Nedelin keeps Elena's belongings as fetishes, for he also stores her clothes and necklaces in boxes and chests. Nedelin's attitude to these objects is one of possessive veneration. He frequently takes Elena's hair from its casket, reverently stroking and kissing it. Though he often picks up Elena's photo-graphs he cannot bear anyone else to touch them, not even Elena's former nurse, who is now his housekeeper. More a reliquary than a study, this set and the fetishistic objects with which Bauer fills it again reveal both Nedelin's worshipful attitude to his dead wife and his morbid, obsessive nature.

These objects also suggest another facet of Nedelin's approach to women. By their very nature, photographs offer another way of viewing the passive, objectified female. As they permit 'the possibility of a lingering look' over which the spectator is 'master',[29] Nedelin's photographs of Elena enable him to lose himself in fantasies of power and control by immortal-ising Elena in her role as spectacle, much as they provided Bauer's Viktor in the earlier *Child of the Big City* with a safe way of admiring the soci-ety *belles* he found so frightening. Nedelin's veneration of Elena's photo-graphs is more extreme than Viktor's attachment to his album, however. The deep-rooted kinship of photography and death has been noted by many writers and, as the theorist Christian Metz explains, a photograph is well-suited for use as a fetish: 'Photography [...] by virtue of the objec-tive suggestions of its signifier (stillness, again) maintains the memory of the dead *as being dead* [emphasis in original]'.[30] Drawing on Freud's study 'Mourning and Melancholia', Metz argues that photographs can therefore help those mourning the death of a loved one to accept their loss. For Freud, the successful mourner is one who learns progressively to love the person *as dead*, rather than continuing to desire his or her living pres-ence, which only prolongs the mourner's suffering.[31] Nedelin appears to have achieved the first stage of this process, for he clearly manages to love Elena as dead. His veneration of Elena's photographs far exceeds the usual practice of keeping photographs in memory of those who have died, however, and his fetishistic worship of them suggests a much more disturbing state of mind: that Nedelin loves Elena precisely *because* she is dead.

As Miriam Hansen notes, Nedelin's behaviour cannot be explained simply in terms of decadent aesthetics or personal deviance, however. It also illustrates:

> a particular configuration of male desire under patriarchal
> social conditions [detailing] the psychic mechanism, familiar

from the battle of the sexes, that the woman can only be loved as dead because in living she would be too powerful. Her death and subsequent idealization could be seen as a response to the real or imagined threat the woman poses to the male subject and the patriarchal order.[32]

The artistic representations of Elena with which Nedelin fills his study are there, then, because they are 'safe'. Likewise, the dead Elena poses no threat either to his authority or to his fantasies; her death leaves Nedelin free to imagine her as he wishes and enables him to love her. And indeed, although, since the film begins with Elena already dead, her appearances are all presented through the eyes and mind of the increasingly deranged Nedelin, there can be little doubt that Nedelin's Elena does not ring true. In the flashback sequence towards the end of the film that depicts Nedelin's memories of their marriage, she clings weakly and adoringly to her protective husband as they stroll in a deserted pastoral dreamscape, engrossed in each other in a de-eroticised way.[33] Moreover, Nedelin repeatedly uses the adjective holy/sacred [*sviataia*] to refer to Elena and, in her two appearances as a ghost, Elena is a filmic version of Aleksandr Blok's elusive and illusory Beautiful Lady [*Prekrasnaia Dama*], appearing before Nedelin only to recede and fade away again. A phantasmagoric cliché, then, Elena's image reveals more about Nedelin's social and erotic perceptions of women than it does about the real woman herself.

The reality: the living mistress

> This heart has prayed –
> Prayed and sung of you, but you are no *tsaritsa*.
> Aleksandr Blok, 21 February 1914.[34]

Having established Nedelin's morbid and deluded emotional state and demonstrated his patriarchal attitudes to women, Bauer arranges for his protagonist to encounter a living woman, the ballerina Tina Viarskaia (also played by N. Chernobaeva, for reasons that are significant, as we shall see). Bauer signals Tina's New Woman credentials from the outset by according her a foreign given name, a marker he also used in the earlier *Twilight of a Woman's Soul* and *Child of the Big City* to symbolise Vera's and Mary's rejection of the restrictive attitudes of the nineteenth-century past, and which Chardynin also adopted for his Lola in *The Love of a Councillor of State*. Other details in this sequence also stress Tina's modernity. It is significant, for example, that Nedelin first encounters her walking unaccompanied in the street (as Viktor had first met Mary in *Child of the Big City*). And it is striking that, like Mariia and Lidiia in *Children of the Age*, which was released one week before *Daydreams* on 3 October 1915, Tina is completely at home in this public domain. She is also at ease with and fully aware of her ability to attract men. A manipulator of the male gaze rather than its object, when she notices that Nedelin is following her, Tina allows her gait to become deliberately provocative; she swings her hips and throws alluring, come-hither glances over her shoulder. However, while the street along which Bauer's protagonists walk is recognisable as being in modern Moscow, it nonetheless has an eerie atmosphere, being almost entirely empty of passers-by and unnaturally still. Reflections flicker in a shop window, creating a mysterious atmosphere that reinforces the film's thematics of illusion and highlights how divorced Nedelin is from the realities of modern twentieth-century life. This ghostly street proves to be the perfect site for the playing out of Nedelin's delusions, for the grief-stricken man is drawn to Tina not because of her beauty *per se*, but because she is, in his words, 'the living portrait of Elena.'

The astounded man follows Tina in a daze to the theatre where she is appearing in a production of Giacomo Meyerbeer's *Robert the Devil* [Robert le Diable, 1831], an opera known and admired as much for the ballet that it features in Act III as for its music. Tina is cast in the ballet's central role of the deceased abbess Hélène, who is punished in death for her debauchery and wilfulness in life by being placed in thrall to the devilish Bertram. Nedelin watches the stage with increasing intensity as Tina and the other ballerinas, cast in the roles of dead nuns, emerge from the tombstones that stand in the centre of the theatre's impressive stage set. Summoned from their graves by their master, Bertram, the nuns, led by Tina, then perform a hedonistic bacchanal that is intended to seduce Robert, the opera's hero. Tina's performance also succeeds, however, in seducing Nedelin, who sees her on-stage resurrection as confirmation of his belief that the ballerina is the reincarnation of his dead Elena. His delusion is further encouraged by the fact that the character Tina is incarnating on stage is also Elena's foreign namesake (Hélène). Transfixed by this miracle and overcome by emotion, Nedelin rises from his seat and walks down the central aisle of the theatre towards the stage; as if in a trance, he is heedless of the audience's bemusement.

In the next sequence, Bauer carefully stresses the illusory nature of the stage performance that Nedelin and the viewer have just witnessed, drawing attention to its artifice by showing the stripping away of the various artificial elements out of which the performance had been constructed. Hoping to meet the ballerina, Nedelin goes backstage, where he finds himself obliged to weave a circuitous path through the many stagehands who are already dismantling the cardboard tombs that had formed part of the stage set. He pays his compliments to Tina, who is now out of her stage costume and dressed in her own modish clothes, and gives her his card. Nedelin's delusions about Tina are so extreme, however, that he is able to ignore these very clear markers of reality and to remain both unable and unwilling to distinguish between the 'real' twentieth-century woman that Bauer shows Tina to be and the nineteenth-century character he has watched her perform on stage. Seeing Tina in a role that places her passively under the absolute control of a dominant male clearly appeals to the patriarchal Nedelin, for it flatters his view of himself as a powerful man and enables him to believe that he, like Bertram, can control her. That Tina is cast in the role of Hélène also encourages Nedelin to see this confident New Woman as irredeemably 'sinful'. Indeed, both he and his friend, the artist Solskii, are incapable of responding to Tina in any other way. As they both worship Nedelin's dead wife, the 'sacred' Elena, the incarnation of inviolate purity, so they both denigrate the living mistress, Tina, the 'fallen' Elena/ Hélène; Nedelin agrees when Solskii observes that Tina is not worthy of his love.

Thus, from the moment he embarks on a relationship with this spirited woman, Nedelin is faced with a problem, for throughout the entire film, Tina refuses to compromise her individuality. She repeatedly asserts her right to be the woman she chooses, constructing her own erotic identity and refusing to conform to Nedelin's fantasies of ideal femininity, as embodied in his memories and visions of Elena. Indeed, she seems actively to enjoy shocking the conservative male protagonists by flouting their codes of acceptable feminine behaviour. She calls on Solskii, adopting a provocative pose and flirtatiously suggesting that he paint her portrait. Moreover, although prepared to try on Elena's clothes – a request that, no doubt, does not strike her as unusual since she is accustomed to donning different costumes in her professional life – Tina resists Nedelin's other attempts to remodel her in Elena's image and remains to the end an independent and assertive New Woman. This makes her murder inevitable, for by her very existence she poses an unendurable threat both to Nedelin's patriarchal authority and to his fantasies about the perfect woman. She openly mocks his cult of Elena, declaring that she is bored with hearing him speak her name, and insultingly alluding to her sexuality when she advises Nedelin to 'go and lie' with his dead wife. Sacrilegiously, she handles Elena's photograph and defiles the sacred relic of her tresses, dismissing them as a 'flea-breeding monstrosity' before wrapping them round her neck like a feather boa. At this point Nedelin can take no more; unable to cope with the 'coming down to earth' of his *Prekrasnaia Dama* and enraged beyond endurance, he strangles Tina with Elena's hair, using the fetishised body part of a woman already 'safely dead' to reduce a 'dangerous' living woman to the same unthreatening state.[35]

It is revealing, if not surprising, that most contemporary viewers shared Nedelin's and Solskii's point of view and responded to Tina in a similar vein. A reviewer writing in *Cine-Phono* described her as 'vulgar', while the commentator whose review was published in *The Projector* considered Tina to be 'evil, deceitful and a shallow creature', which is why, he continued, Nedelin murdered her.[36] As Louise McReynolds notes, 'Patriarchal impulses are self-evident in a critique that blames the woman for her own murder.'[37] It is therefore surprising that some recent commentators have joined in this condemnation of Tina. Ian Christie sees Nedelin as Tina's victim.[38] For Denise Youngblood, Tina is 'a calculating *soubrette*, [...] determined to take whatever advantage she can of Nedelin'; it is Tina who drives this 'decent man' mad and, she suggests, when Elena's ghost appears before Nedelin strangles Tina, she does so in order to offer a vision of 'her purity in sharp contrast to Tina's crassness.'[39]

These responses do not, however, reflect the objective realities of Bauer's portrayal of his ballerina. Tina does not in fact exploit Nedelin for his money. Indeed, she has no need to do so, for she has her own beautiful home and numerous fashionable outfits, which suggests that she makes a very good living from her work as a ballerina. Nor does she ask Nedelin for Elena's clothes and jewellery. Rather it is Nedelin who, obsessed with his fantasy of her as Elena's double, asks her to try them on. Moreover, although Tina flirts with Solskii, she remains faithful to Nedelin and, though she mocks Nedelin's cult of Elena, surely she is right to do so. Surely, also, it is Tina who is the victim of this deranged man: Nedelin is repeatedly violent towards Tina, beating her when she puts on Elena's pearls and half strangling her when she tells him that she is tired of hearing him speak of Elena. Nedelin's violence clearly frightens Tina, yet she seems genuinely to love him. She endures his ill treatment of her and in a letter begs him to forgive her for speaking ill of Elena, confessing that she was beside herself with jealousy.

The condemnatory tone of these responses to Tina reflects the unreliable perspective of the film's male protagonists, through whose eyes she is seen as a frightening and uncontrollable sexual force. Viewed objectively, however, Tina is shown to be a modern, independent and self-sufficient woman, a professional ballerina who works to support herself, enjoys her sexuality and wants to have a mature, adult relationship on equal terms with a man whom she loves. It is true that this New Woman is no ideal *Prekrasnaia Dama*; nor, however, is she a malevolent nineteenth-century femme fatale. Moreover, *she* is the victim, of both Nedelin's mad delusions and his patriarchal assumptions about what women should be and how they should behave.

The Dying Swan

Filmed on location near Sochi in the summer of 1916 and released on 17 January 1917, Bauer's *The Dying Swan* takes a similarly critical approach to male responses to the ballerina. This female-centred film tells the story of Gizella (played by Vera Karalli, who we remember as Lola in *The Love of a Councillor of State*), a young woman who lives alone with her father. A kindly and well-meaning man, he is inclined to be over-protective of his daughter, who is mute. Nevertheless, he allows Gizella to begin a relationship with an older man, the handsome Viktor Krasovskii (played by Vitold Polonskii), who – predictably – proves to be an unfaithful cad.[40]

On learning that Viktor has betrayed her, the heart-broken Gizella decides to devote her life to a career in ballet. She soon makes a name for herself as a ballerina of great talent and embarks on a solo tour, performing (like Pavlova) her signature role of *The Dying Swan*. Gizella's rendition of this famous dance piece brings her to the attention of the film's male protagonist, Count Valerii Glinskii (Andrei Gromov), and it is this encounter that sets in motion the film's tragic dénouement.

A decadent artist, Glinskii is obsessed with capturing the image of death on canvas. As is to be expected, Bauer conveys this obsession visually, filling the artist's studio with absurd, crudely anatomical paintings of skeletons, and choosing as *dikovinka* an actual skeleton, which remains in the foreground throughout most of the film. That this extravagant set design is intended to parody, if not to ridicule, Glinskii's obsession with death is impossible to deny.[41] The false beard that Gromov sports introduces a further note of caricature and his interpretation of the role also suggests Bauer's determination to distance himself from the point of view of this male protagonist, for, as Youngblood notes, he plays Glinskii 'in a highly negative fashion, almost as though he were a syphilitic degenerate.'[42] As he had done with Viktor and his friend Kramskoi in *Child of the Big City*, Bauer also gives the obsessive artist a foil in the person of his down-to-earth friend and on several occasions exploits the contrast between their attitudes to create humour at Glinskii's expense. Consider, for example, the pragmatic way in which his friend dismisses Glinskii's desperate confession that he despairs of ever realising his artistic aims: 'More of this nonsense. You've never shown me your pictures, but I'm sure this is all just something trivial [...] Why do you want to go searching for something and upsetting yourself?' His response to Glinskii's painting of Gizella would also create laughter, were it not for the genuine horror etched on his face and the way in which he recoils from the canvas as he passes judgement on the painting, declaring it to be 'talentless... awful!'

Despite making light of Glinskii's tortured striving, however, his friend attempts to help him, suggesting that he may find inspiration by watching the renowned ballerina Gizella Raccio perform *The Dying Swan*. The desperate artist seizes on this suggestion with enthusiasm and the performance sequence opens with a shot that shows the two men seating themselves in a theatre box. It is not only Bauer's male protagonists who are permitted to enjoy the spectacle, however; the viewer is also treated to Gizella's performance, for the camera then cuts to the stage and, for just over two and a half minutes, focuses solely on the ballerina as she dances. In this way, Bauer signals that her performance is of central importance. Indeed, a contemporary reviewer commented in *Cine-Journal* in 1917 that 'the most interesting thing in the new film is, of course, Mme Karalli's dance'.[43] This performance therefore merits full description and close analysis.

Alone on the stage and dressed in a traditional, tightly corseted tutu, the ballerina bourrés back and forth, *en pointe* throughout, making gentle and fluid fluttering movements with her extended arms until, in the final moments of the dance, she sinks gracefully to the floor and expires. In this filmed dance, woman is above all represented as beautiful, and her beauty is shown to derive primarily from the ballerina's fragile and ethereal aura, which is conveyed by many of the sequence's key features. The choreography is significant in this respect, and especially the use of *en pointe* dancing, that key symbolic element in the classical ballet tradition. The traditional costume for this dance, a tutu with frothy white tulle and lace, designed by Leon Bakst, enhances these symbolic qualities, adds the suggestion of purity and innocence and also heightens the beauty of the performing dancer. In Laura Mulvey's terminology, Gizella thus stands as the quintessential bearer of 'to-be-looked-at-ness'; she is a fragile and desirable 'woman in white', a Romantic trope.[44]

The narrative of Gizella's dance is also suggestive. It depicts the final moments in the life of a swan; considered in Greek mythology to be a mute bird who sings only once in the moment before its death, known to mate for life and to pine away if its mate dies, the swan symbolises fidelity, devotion and a certain passivity, as well as great beauty. It is therefore, it seems, the perfect vehicle through which Gizella – a young woman who lacks the power of speech – can express her pain and suffering at her lover's betrayal. The ballerina is thus represented as a helpless and fragile creature, who gradually succumbs to death – the ultimate passive state – in a way that renders death not only moving but also beautiful.

The extra-diegetic associations of the dance are also significant. As Gizella performs Pavlova's signature piece, she acquires some of Pavlova's fragile, transcendent and 'ultrafeminine' aura. Her eloquent name also, of course, links her inextricably to the heroine of one of the best-known ballets from the nineteenth-century Romantic tradition, namely *Giselle* (1841).[45] The ultimate Romantic ballet, *Giselle* tells the tale of an innocent young girl who, like Gizella, loves to dance and who is also transformed into an ethereal being, dying of a broken heart after discovering that her lover is betrothed to another. That Gizella is played by Vera Karalli, herself a famous ballet beauty and by 1917 one of the acknowledged 'Queens' of the pre-Revolutionary screen, adds another layer of resonance to the performance. Karalli had her own version of Pavlova's signature dance in her solo repertoire, and it was the enthusiastic public reception of Karalli's interpretation of this dance that gave Bauer the idea of creating a film scenario around it.[46] While Bauer's film was a great box office success in its own right, it was most popular when Karalli toured with the film, performing *The Dying Swan* live in the cinema, both before and after the showing.[47]

The cinematic construction of this lengthy sequence is also significant, especially its framing. Unusually, Bauer shuns verisimilitude and elects not to include members of either the audience or the orchestra in the frame during Gizella's performance. Instead, the camera focuses solely on the ballerina, holding its full-length shot of her throughout her dance, thereby encouraging the viewer to focus on her. As he had done more briefly in *Child of the Big City*, in the sequence featuring the oriental dancer, Bauer thus ensures that there is nothing in the frame to distract the viewer from observing the female persona, and he also contrives to suggest that Gizella's performance, while existing within the film's narrative, also stands outside it. In other words, he alerts the viewer to the fact that its motivation is both diegetic and extra-diegetic.

Only at the very end of the performance does Bauer remind the viewer that s/he is not alone in observing Gizella, when, just before the point in the dance at which the ballerina-swan 'dies', the camera cuts back to the theatre box where Glinskii sits watching with rapt attention. When, after a few seconds, the camera returns to focus on Gizella again, it cuts in even closer to her, so that as she 'dies' she is framed in medium close-up. The ballerina is therefore cast as the object of both the viewer's and the male protagonist's gaze throughout the sequence, and the gaze of the male protagonist is shown to become even more intent at the moment of her death. For, by cutting in immediately after he has shown Glinksii watching from his theatre box, Bauer suggests that the more closely framed shot replicates the death-obsessed male protagonist's point of view. Finally, the unusual way in which the original positive of Bauer's film was coloured is also note-worthy. As Tsivian has documented, a contemporary reviewer recorded that in at least some prints of the film this sequence was tinted in a 'con-stantly changing rainbow of colours'.[48] Gizella would therefore have been bathed in a magical, unearthly kaleidoscope of light as she performs her solo routine.

The cultural associations of the dance piece itself and of the actress cast in the role of the ballerina therefore combine with the way in which this sequence is filmed to present Gizella in an enchanting, but conven-tional and deeply patriarchal way. Gizella's traditional ballet costume also strengthens this representation, for, as Kant puts it: 'What the audience gets with the tutu and a pointe shoe is a whole ideology'.[49] In performing this dance, Gizella therefore becomes the embodiment of an objectified femininity that is represented as entrancingly fragile, pure and ethereal. It is an idealised, out-moded femininity that appeals to Bauer's essentially patriarchal male protagonist. Gizella's dance is therefore expressive only of male fantasies about 'perfect' femininity, and is not a means of genu-ine self-expression. For, while it enables her to convey the sorrow of unre-quited love, Gizella's dance does not allow her to express anything else. She is therefore stuck in the role of wounded but devoted lover, fragile, passive and silent female. In enacting this role on stage, she therefore remains just as mute as she is in life.

Bauer further demonstrates the way in which the ballerina's stage per-sona reduces her to the status of a voiceless object by ensuring that, from the moment that she 'dies' on stage, it is she who becomes the film's *diko-vinka*.[50] Thus, in the same way that the ballerina's body is arranged on the stage by Fokin's choreography, so it is manipulated by Glinskii when she is off stage. For, seeing in both Gizella's performance and her stage persona the embodiment of his artistic desires, and being – like Dolskii in *Twilight of a Woman's Soul* and Nedelin in *Daydreams* – unable, and unwilling, to distinguish between Gizella-the-ballerina, Gizella-the-dying-swan and Gizella-the-woman, Glinskii transfers his obsession with death from the skeleton to the ballerina and asks her to act as his model. It is telling that when Gizella attends the first sitting at Glinskii's home the skeleton has been pushed into the background; instead, as Gizella assumes her death pose on the velvet-covered, flower-decked podium that Glinskii has prepared for her, she is now the 'object' that dominates the foreground of Bauer's mise-en-scène.

In reducing Gizella so obviously to an object in this way, Bauer suggests how limited and limiting a figure the ballerina is. He also achieves this by stressing Gizella's inability to express herself in other ways, most notably by giving literal form to the ballerina's lack of a 'voice' by making Gizella mute. Thus, as the ballerina is unable to express herself on stage through her chosen dance form, so Gizella is unable to do so in words when off stage. It is striking and disturbing that, in the eyes of the film's male protagonists, this 'handicap' only serves to make Gizella more attractive. For Glinskii her 'silence' strengthens her association with death, which causes him to wax lyrical: 'How good it is that you cannot speak. I don't know whether you actually exist or whether you are part of my delirium. The most sublime thing in the world is peace, and the most sublime peace is death!' Gizella's lack of voice, both on stage and off, therefore enables Glinskii to continue to overlook the real Gizella and makes it possible for him to create his own version of the young woman and to indulge his fantasies about her to the full. Thus, when Gizella arrives at his home for the first sitting, he greets her by strewing flowers at her feet, declaring her to be a princess. Later, he kneels to kiss the hem of her dress.[51] The following day he sends her a jewel-encrusted crown.[52]

It is the hopeless ending of Bauer's film that emphasises most chillingly the impossibility of self-expression for this ballerina protagonist, however. Before Glinskii has finished his portrait of Gizella, Viktor re-enters the young woman's life with a declaration of undying love and a proposal of marriage that the ecstatic young woman loses no time in accepting. Elated, Gizella runs to Glinskii for their last sitting, but her new-found happiness threatens to ruin his masterpiece, for in her life-affirming joy she no longer embodies his ideal. To use Luce Irigaray's terms, Gizella, the mute 'object', has started to 'speak', and Glinskii's despair is palpable as he exclaims: 'Is this really the same Gizella? Where are those joyless, sad, exhausted eyes? Now her eyes blaze with a different flame… No, no, it is not Gizella'.

Gizella changes into her swan costume, but her thoughts are full of Viktor and so she finds it difficult to concentrate and retain her death pose. She fidgets repeatedly and Glinskii scolds her: 'Gizella, are you alive? That won't do at all!' When he then leaves his easel and moves slowly but deliberately towards the young woman, the viewer realises there can be only one way for him to recapture 'his' Gizella. And, indeed, he strangles the ballerina. Unlike Nedelin in the earlier *Daydreams*, this male murderer displays no awareness of the horror of his act. Instead, having returned Gizella to the desired state of beauty and peace, Glinskii calmly returns to his canvas to complete his portrait of her corpse. This shot fades out and then a close-up of the ballerina's corpse fades in, held by the camera for several seconds. By ensuring in this way that the ballerina ends the film as a to-be-looked-at object, and one, moreover, who is now 'literally' dead, Bauer stresses his contention that the ballerina is a defunct archetype.

This is not, however, the only message that the viewer extracts from the shocking ending of Bauer's film. As McReynolds has commented, 'men who feel pressured to kill because the women refuse to satisfy their demands are enacting a substantive social problem'.[53] Like Nedelin before him, Glinskii falls in love with the ballerina because he believes that, as a nineteenth-century archetype, she is 'safe' and poses no challenge to his own sense of self. When he realises that the woman he loves has a mind and desires of her own he is unable to cope with this fact. Thus this tragic ending is again shown to result from the fact that Glinskii's cultic fantasies of Gizella-the-ballerina do not coincide with the reality of Gizella-the-woman, in either sexual or social terms.

While Glinskii and the film's other male protagonists attempt to see only what they want to see in Gizella, Bauer of course makes the 'real' Gizella clear to the viewer and stresses how different she is, despite her muteness, from the outdated ballerina persona. Thus, although she is undeniably naïve, especially at the start of the film, Gizella nevertheless knows her own mind. Despite her initially being shy of Viktor, once he has declared his love Gizella takes the initiative in pursuing their affair, visiting his home uninvited on two occasions, which, ironically, results in her discovering his infidelity. She then responds to Viktor's betrayal actively, making the positive decision to leave the site and the cause of her unhappiness and pursue her dream of becoming a professional ballerina. Moreover, this is only the first of several important decisions that she will make on her own behalf; for, although Gizella, unlike Lola in Chardynin's *The Love of a Councillor of State*, does have a father, he is shown to have little say in or influence over how she lives her life. Thus it is Gizella who decides to allow Glinskii to paint her portrait and she continues to sit for him despite her father's obvious reservations. She also accepts Viktor's marriage proposal without consulting her father or seeking his approval. As Youngblood comments: 'True, Gisella [*sic*] doesn't smoke cigarettes (the tell-tale sign of the modern woman), but she has a career and wears a wristwatch (two other potent signs of female emancipation).'[54] Far from being a passive, ethereal creature then, Gizella is a twentieth-century woman.

As in his earlier films *Twilight of a Woman's Soul*, *Child of the Big City* and *Daydreams*, therefore, Bauer again reveals there to be an insurmountable disjuncture between his male protagonist's attachment to nineteenth-century female archetypes and the twentieth-century woman's rejection of such out-dated ways of being. Unlike Vera and Mary, however, both Tina and Gizella pay for this rejection with their life.

Beyond the ballerina: the early modern dancer

> [Isadora Duncan's] achievement was to protest, to raise her voice first.
>
> Anastasiia Verbitskaia, *The Keys to Happiness*.[55]

McReynolds has suggested that Bauer's intention in many of his films is not so much to celebrate female independence as to reveal 'the larger social nexus of male failure'.[56] Indeed, the fact that both Tina and Gizella elect to become ballerinas might be felt to undermine their New Woman status, for, as Ann Daly puts it: 'The ballerina, by her compliant participation in the enactment of this ceremony, in effect contributes to her own oppression and "ratifies her own subordination"'.[57] Moreover, while it is true that in films made between 1912 and 1917 not all ballerina protagonists suffer the same terrible fate as Tina and Gizella, it is also the case that those who avoid it typically do so because they are able to cast off the persona of the ballerina and embrace instead another style of dancing. As the following sections will show, women who shun ballet for other, more contemporary forms of dance are shown to have very different characters and, consequently, to have very different fates and relationships with their male counterparts from those endured by their ballerina counterparts.

Petr Chardynin's Vera Nevolina

Vera Karalli, the star of Bauer's *The Dying Swan*, was cast as a ballerina in her first film role, in Chardynin's *Chrysanthemums* [Khrizantemy], released on 4 November 1914. Although Chardynin's film also ends with the ballerina's death, this time she dies by suicide rather than at the hands of a male protagonist, and thus Chardynin manages to suggests something more positive about the female protagonist than Bauer's film would go on to do. It is striking that he does so primarily through how she is shown to dance.

At the start of the film, the ballerina, Vera Nevolina, is represented in similar visual terms to those Bauer used to represent Gizella in *The Dying Swan*. She performs in a thoroughly traditional production. Against an idyllic and idealised pastoral backdrop of meadows and silver birch trees, three ballerinas dance a brief routine before moving to the back of the stage so that Vera can move centre stage and perform her solo. When she enters the stage the camera moves from a long shot to a closer shot, emphasising that Vera is the character in whom it is interested. All four ballerinas are dressed in white tutus, and the flowers that decorate their hair and their bodices enhance the suggestion of spring and innocence created by the backdrop. The ballerina performs a routine in which *en pointe* steps feature predominantly, and her movements appear stylised and precisely coded. In fact, her jerky limbs move in time with the conductor's baton, which gives her the appearance of a puppet whose strings he is pulling. This sensation is intensified by the fact that the ballerina does not move around freely, but remains in the centre of the stage and therefore of the frame. She also faces forwards most of the time, looking and smiling at the audience, and the viewer feels that the dance is directed at him/her, performed for his/her benefit.

Like Gizella again, this ballerina is also let down by a faithless lover who, beset by financial problems, deserts her and marries a rich widow, an act of betrayal that leaves the dancer distraught. One evening, he takes his new wife to the theatre where Vera is performing. Seeing the couple in the audience from behind the stage curtain, Vera is devastated. She returns to her dressing room where she drinks a phial of poison. Before it can take effect, however, Vera is called on stage to perform. Her second and final dance performance is very different from her first, in style, mood and meaning.

163

The idyllic pastoral backdrop is gone, replaced by a plain black velvet cloth. It is no longer spring, but autumn, moving to winter: as she dances, Vera scatters chrysanthemums around the stage, flowers associated with both autumn and death. Vera's costume is also very different from the tutu she wore at the start. Now she is dressed in loose white robes and draped in a diaphanous veil. The costume appears almost shroud-like in contrast to the dark backdrop. Significantly, Vera is alone on stage for this performance and she appears engrossed in her dance, apparently performing not for the audience – she neither looks nor smiles in their direction – but for herself.[58]

The viewer is also struck by the fact that in this dance Vera's feet are bare. She is therefore unable to perform *en pointe*. At the same time, her movements are much more fluid than in her first performance and appear spontaneous and unchoreographed. Indeed, a musician seated in the front row of the orchestra looks at Vera several times during the sequence in a way that suggests bemusement or surprise, as though she is deviating from the expected routine. Vera also makes much greater use of the stage floor and in fact moves almost completely out of the frame at several points in the sequence. In this dance she is thus shown to be more mobile, more free.

Vera's last dance is emphatically not ballet. Vera alters her style of dance performance completely (a change that surprises all the more since *Chrysanthemums* is a short film, only 29 minutes long), rejecting ballet in favour of a new style of dance. This dance form, now known as 'early modern dance', came into being at the start of the twentieth century and was, as Roger Copeland stresses, 'first and foremost a repudiation of late nineteenth-century ballet'.[59] Early modern dance is associated primarily with the American dancer Isadora Duncan, who was a vociferous opponent of ballet throughout her life. In 1914, Duncan 'was not a remote, foreign idol' to Russians.[60] Peter Kurth demonstrates that articles about her began to appear in the Russian press in 1903, which meant that she was famous 'as a personality, if not a dancer', even before she first toured Russia between December 1904 and January 1905.[61] The success of her first tour was such that Duncan returned to Russia in February 1905, then in 1907–08 and again in 1909 and 1913.[62] She had a huge influence not only on Russian dance but also on early twentieth-century Russian art and culture in general, inspiring innumerable Russian poets, writers, thinkers and artists, among them Aleksandr Blok, Andrei Belyi, Fedor Sologub, Vasilii

Rozanov, Leon Bakst, Alexandre Benois and Konstantin Stanislavsky. Although Russian popular culture distilled Duncan's persona into that of a sensual and promiscuous free woman, representatives of Russian high culture took her new dance form very seriously as 'Art' and were interested in the ideas that lay behind it.[63]

The Russian thinker Vasilii Rozanov was a particularly fervent supporter of Duncan's new style of dance and, according to Henrietta Mondry, was also 'one of the first figures of modernism to condemn ballet'.[64] Mondry explains that the background to Rozanov's approach to Duncan's dance was his definition of the concept of 'naturalness' [*estestvennost´*] within his theory of sexuality. Instead of equating the concepts of 'natural' and 'sexual', Mondry states, Rozanov 'created antimonies out of them'.[65] Considering ballet 'a most unnatural art form' meant that he saw in it an emphasis on sexuality and eroticism that led him to condemn ballet as a form of dance that focussed too much on the ballerina's legs and permitted 'the pornographic exposure of the most intimate parts of a woman's body'.[66] This led Rozanov to argue that Duncan's dance form, as a more 'natural' form of movement that required no formal training, was a purer and higher form of art, and one that was not tainted by the display of female sexuality in the same way that ballet was.

As Rozanov's interpretation of her dancing style suggests, Duncan's repudiation of ballet was not merely, or even primarily, motivated by aesthetic concerns. Instead, her main objections to the ballet tradition were moral and political. As Copeland continues: 'It is essential to recognise that this repudiation is boldly feminist in character'.[67] Thus, Duncan attacked the strictures that this dance form imposed on the female body, both through the 'unnatural' physical contortions that its technical mastery demanded and also in the types of roles in which ballerinas were conventionally cast and the types of costume they were required by tradition to wear, which, Copeland says, she believed promoted 'a socially pernicious *image* of women [emphasis in original]'.[68] The condemnation of ballet as a patriarchal dance form by today's feminist dance critics is, therefore, nothing new. Indeed, Duncan's autobiography, *My Life*, reads in parts like a manifesto against the ballet tradition and it is interesting that this theme is voiced most insistently in those sections of the work that recount her first tour of Russia. While in St Petersburg, Duncan accepted invitations to ballet performances from both Matilda Kshesinskaia (Krzesińska) and Anna Pavlova. Despite admitting that she found it impossible not to applaud the ballerinas' accomplished performances, Duncan nevertheless remained 'an enemy to the ballet [that] false and preposterous art'.[69] A visit to the Imperial Ballet School in St Petersburg in 1904 left her with the following impressions:

> I saw all the little pupils standing in rows, and going through those torturing exercises. They stood on the tips of their toes for hours, like so many victims of a cruel and unnecessary Inquisition. The great, bare dancing rooms […] were like a torture chamber. I was more than ever convinced that the Imperial Ballet School is an enemy to nature and to Art.[70]

Duncan therefore wanted to develop a new language of physical expression, and she saw her own dance as being 'against the ballet' and consequently as being against the oppression of women.[71] Dance critics also talk of her style of dance as 'liberatory', when compared with ballet, and expressive of interiority. In an article written in 1913 the Russian Decadent writer Fedor Sologub used similar terms when he described Duncan's dance as a form that expressed 'internal needs' and that tried to 'liberate the individual'.[72]

Seen in its contemporary cultural context, Vera's final Duncan-esque dance in *Chrysanthemums* therefore demands to be seen as a desperate attempt to express her self and her emotions. Finding herself in an intense, highly charged situation, the dancer rejects ballet as an inadequate form of self-expression and her persona as a ballerina as inauthentic and male-defined. Instead, she chooses a newer dance form, one characterised by its naturalness and the freedom it gives to the female dancer, not only in matters of costume and movement, but also in self-expression: Duncan and her imitators choreographed their own dances, devised their own movements, designed their own costumes and – as the Salome dancers had done before them – took for themselves a creative role that the ballerina was not permitted. They could therefore construct their own personae and express their own sense of self on stage, not simply rehearse male-created and male-revered images of femininity. As Copeland notes, for Duncan and other women who embraced her style of dancing: 'A new way of moving paved the way for a new mode of being'.[73]

From literature to film: Anastasiia Verbitskaia's Mania Eltsova

By 1914, the use of the figure of the early modern dancer as a means of characterising a female protagonist as an unconventional, assertive New Woman would have been familiar to Russian cinemagoers, for – as we saw in Chapter 3 – in 1913 the best-known fictional Duncan-esque performer of this period, namely Mania Eltsova, the heroine of Verbitskaia's *The Keys to Happiness*, had made the transition from literature to film. Iakov Protazanov and Vladimir Gardin's screen adaptation of this novel, for which Verbitskaia wrote the screenplay, became the biggest Russian box office hit of the 1910s.[74] Although this film has not survived other than as a series of stills and a four-minute-long fragment,[75] we know, from the evidence of both contemporary reviews and the novel itself, that Mania's status as an early modern dancer is repeatedly used to characterise her as an unconventional, assertive New Woman and, in particular, to provide her with a means of self-expression. For, although Mania trains as a classical dancer, she performs a classical dance only once, at a concert organised by her dance tutor. In this performance she is cast as a butterfly (recalling, perhaps, Starewicz's dragonfly) and, although her technical mastery is impressive and she gives the impression that she really does have wings and is flying across the stage, the narrator notes that it is, nevertheless, a 'passionless, classical dance'.[76] It is telling that, for her debut concert and, indeed, for all subsequent performances, Mania rejects classical ballet in favour of early modern dance. Moreover, in Verbitskaia's novel the visual descriptions of Mania's dance are always interspersed with equally long passages that describe the feelings and the self that Mania seeks to convey in her dance.[77] Mania also describes her dance in these terms. When asked by an admirer if she performs character dances, Mania protests: 'No!.. No… My own…'[78] And when, later, she is again asked what she wants to convey through her dance, she replies: 'The story of my soul […]. I dream of conveying through gestures and mime everything I have experienced'.[79]

At regular intervals throughout the novel, Mania makes similar comments to many other characters. Mania's view of dance as more than entertainment is also conveyed by the title of the self-choreographed work she performs at her debut, *The Story of My Soul* [Skazka moei dushi], and by the fact that for Mania audiences are unimportant, as is fame. What matters is self-expression, and her aim in dancing, therefore, is 'to find a form through which to express in full one's individuality'.[80]

Seen in these literary, cultural and filmic contexts, then, Vera's suicide in *Chrysanthemums* is clearly much more than a simple act of despair. It is a defiantly public protest against the strictures of patriarchal values, as represented by the ballet form. In this way, her death is more a critique of oppressive patriarchal attitudes than a poeticisation of Vera's feminine weakness and dependency. Moreover, Vera's last dance is shown to succeed as a form of self-expression. Her former lover was indifferent to her grief when she expressed it verbally – when Vera challenged him face-to-face about his infidelity he denied ever having known her[81] – but, after witnessing her final dance, he feels guilt: the film's closing sequence shows him taking a bouquet of her favourite chrysanthemums to her grave.

Evgenii Bauer's Duncan-esque dancer

While Vera adopts this form of dance only at the end of Chardynin's film and then dies, the heroine of Bauer's 1916 film *Iurii Nagornyi* is cast as a Duncan-esque dancer from the outset. Unsurprisingly, this dancer protagonist (played by Emma Bauer) proves to be a very different kind of woman from Vera. Near the beginning of the film we watch her dance, viewing her performance first from backstage (Figure 6.1) and then from the wings, from the point of view of the eponymous hero, who is barely able to mask his desire as he stands watching her perform. Nagornyi, himself a singer, sets out to seduce the dancer and, despite having a husband, she appears to welcome his advances. It soon becomes clear, however, that she is motivated not by love, but by hate. When she accepts an invitation to dine with the singer, she remains sober but plies Nagornyi with alcohol, returning with him to his home and then, as he sleeps, setting fire to his room. Only towards the end of the film does the viewer learn the reason for the dancer's hatred of Nagornyi: his unfaithfulness had caused her younger sister's suicide. Having met the young girl at a ball, where he stood watching the young woman dance as he would later stand and observe her older sister's performance, he seduced her and then immediately dropped her. Distraught on discovering both her father's intention to marry her to a

Figure 6.1. The vengeful sister performs her Duncan-esque dance (Bauer, *Iurii Nagornyi*, 1916)

man she did not love and Nagornyi's callous indifference to her plight, the young girl had shot herself.

The dancer and her sister are shown to dance very differently: the older sister's new, twentieth-century Duncan-esque style is opposed to the older, nineteenth-century ballroom dancing favoured by the younger sister. And as their interaction with Nagornyi also shows, they are very different women. While the younger woman is seduced by Nagornyi, who uses the age-old male trick of alcohol to overcome her inhibitions, the Duncan-esque dancer adopts this ruse for herself, using alcohol to drug Nagornyi before setting fire to his house. Similarly, while her sister falls in love with Nagornyi, becomes his victim and kills herself, the dancer remains impervious to Nagornyi's charms and makes him her victim when she attempts to kill him. In this film, then, the male protagonist's downfall is shown to stem from the fact that when he stood in the wings watching the dancer perform he did not pay enough attention to how she danced; in other words, he did not read the 'text' of her dance accurately. Had he only watched a little how she danced, to use Elizabeth's Dempster's phrase, he might have realised that she was not the type of woman who could ever become his victim. Instead, she is shown by Bauer to have a strong sense of self and to be a determined and active character. A New Woman with a career, a mind and a life of her own, she is willing and more than able to turn the tables on the male protagonist and make him, in turn, her victim.

7

The Actress

Character and womanhood, art and nature, blend into a crucible which produces a new dimension incorporating all these
but larger than they: the permanent vitality of myth.

Nina Auerbach.[1]

While Bauer's 1913 film *Twilight of a Woman's Soul* tells the story of a woman's
progress towards becoming a stage performer, the heroine of his *After Death*
is an established actress from the outset of the film. Subtitled *Motifs from
Turgenev* [Turgenevskie motivy] and released on 29 December 1915, *After
Death* is a screen adaptation of Ivan Turgenev's 1883 story, 'Klara Milich'.
Russian directors had transposed literary texts to the screen, and particularly
the nineteenth-century Russian classics, from the earliest days of the Russian
feature film industry: we recall Drankov's 1907 adaptation of Pushkin's *Boris
Godunov*.[2] Such adaptations were frequently motivated by the film-makers'
desire to increase the social and cultural respectability of their new art form
by according it at least the appearance of an educational function. In an article published in *Pegasus* in December 1915, Petr Chardynin, who between
1909 and 1915 produced at least twelve screen adaptations of works by
canonical nineteenth-century Russian writers, argued that cinema should be
praised for providing the illiterate masses with the opportunity to become
acquainted with the great works of Russian literature.[3] Bauer's attitude to

literary adaptation was more complex than that of most of his contemporaries, however. As we have seen, Bauer was steeped in the nineteenth-century Russian literary tradition; in several films based on original scenarios (with *Child of the Big City* being the best example of this tendency) he draws freely on a broad range of classic nineteenth-century Russian texts, engaging in a ludic and often ironic dialogue with the nineteenth-century literary tradition, subverting, reversing and developing its stock protagonists, themes and concerns, a tactic that enables him to elaborate his view of the twentieth-century world. When selecting specific literary texts to adapt for the screen, however, he tended to shun the classic nineteenth-century Russian canon, preferring works by lesser-known Russian or foreign writers, and especially those not regarded as literary classics.[4] This marks *After Death* as an anomaly, for it is the only extant film from Bauer's oeuvre that is based on a nineteenth-century Russian literary classic.[5]

Film, literature and life: barbarous liberties and arbitrary alterations?

Bauer's film tells the story of an encounter between an actress and a young man. Unnaturally attached to the memory of his dead mother, Bauer's hero, Andrei Bagrov (Vitold Polonskii, in one of his first screen roles), has no romantic experience of women and little inclination to acquire any. He lives a reclusive life with his over-protective aunt Kapitolina Markovna, shunning society and spending his time reading or experimenting with photography. Andrei does have one friend, however, Tsenin, and he succeeds in persuading Andrei to accompany him to a soirée hosted by a society princess (Marfa Kassatskaia). It is there that Andrei first encounters the actress Zoia Kadmina (Vera Karalli). Her attraction to Andrei is obvious. Overcome with shyness, the young man flees the gathering without talking to her. Shortly afterwards, Andrei attends a charitable concert at which Zoia performs, but he again leaves hurriedly, declining Tsenin's offer to introduce him to Zoia. The actress then takes matters into her own hands: she writes an anonymous letter to Andrei, requesting a rendezvous. He accedes, but is horrified by her forwardness and reacts to Zoia with such prudish *froideur* that she leaves in tears.

Three months pass. One morning Andrei reads of Zoia's suicide in a newspaper report that speculates that the cause of her death was unrequited love. This causes him to fall passionately in love with the actress and he can think of nothing but her. When he travels to meet her family, Andrei obtains Zoia's diary and a photograph of her. Once he is home, his obsession grows: he dreams about Zoia and, gradually, his dreams become visions and he repeatedly sees Zoia in his bedroom. He pleads with her to forgive him and eventually the actress does so; she turns her eyes towards him and they kiss. When Andrei's aunt enters his room, she finds him on the floor in a dead faint, a lock of black hair in his hand. Finally, unable to live without Zoia, Andrei joins her in death; as his aunt weeps by his bedside, he expires.

It is unlikely that Bauer's motivation in adapting Turgenev's classic text for the screen was the desire to educate the audience in the greatness of nineteenth-century Russian literature. While Bauer's film follows the same broad diegetic line as Turgenev's text, it nevertheless deviates from its literary source in numerous ways.[6] All these differences are significant in a consideration of the film's meaning, but while some are subtle, others are immediately obvious. Thus, the viewer notices that the title of Bauer's film is not that of Turgenev's story. A further conspicuous alteration is his renaming of Turgenev's characters: in Turgenev's story the hero is named Iakov Aratov and the heroine Klara Milich, while Aratov's aunt is Platonida Ivanovna (Platosha) and his friend is called Küpfer. Also striking is the fact that Bauer modernises his screen version of the literary text, setting it in the early twentieth-century present in which it was shot.

A contemporary viewer of *After Death* was so irritated by Bauer's lack of fidelity to Turgenev's original story that she wrote to him to complain, thus:

> Would you please be so kind as to put an end to my bewilderment: why was it necessary to rechristen the universally known 'Klara Milich' in this way? [...]
>
> Why change the names and, more importantly, the characters? I should greatly appreciate your answer to this question.
>
> [...] I love cinema so much, and I find it so vexing to encounter such apparently inexplicable phenomena.[7]

This letter was published in *Pegasus* in 1916, apparently on Bauer's insistence, together with a statement from the director himself in which he acknowledged the justice of the viewer's remarks and apologised for his careless treatment of Turgenev's original, in the most humble and self-deprecatory terms:

> I agree entirely with Mme N. I., and we think that her reproofs can be extended to all pictures that illustrate Turgenev's works. In our opinion, cinema has still not found the movements and tempo required to express Turgenev's delicate poetry.
>
> Nor alas, will it find them soon, for film directors have been educated in conditions that allow them to take barbarous liberties with the authors they use. When they start out in cinema they deal only with works that are, from the literary point of view, hopeless; they have therefore become accustomed to doing as they wish, to making arbitrary alterations to the ideas, the situations and even the heroes imagined by the author.
>
> Turgenev should be approached with a different soul and with different habits.[8]

Bauer's reply is surely disingenuous, if only in part: it fails to reveal that the 'barbarous liberties' he took in renaming Turgenev's story and its protagonists were anything but 'arbitrary alterations'.[9] As Mme N. I. herself acknowledges in another paragraph of her letter, the title *After Death* is not Bauer's invention, but the one under which Turgenev originally intended his story to be published.[10] Moreover, in rechristening Turgenev's actress protagonist, Bauer contrives to allude directly to the real-life events that had provided Turgenev with the inspiration for his story, namely the dramatic staged suicide of the nineteenth-century Russian opera singer and actress Evlaliia Kadmina. On 4 November 1881, in Kharkov, Kadmina poisoned herself – using sulphur that she had scraped from the tips of some matches – while performing the title role in Aleksandr Ostrovskii's 1868 play *Vasilisa Melenteva*. When she became ill the performance was halted, and she died six days later in her hotel room.[11] Kadmina's suicide was apparently an emotional response to an unhappy love affair: on the night she killed herself Kadmina's former lover, who had recently left her to marry the daughter of a rich merchant, was in the audience, having brought his new wife to the theatre to watch Kadmina perform.[12]

Clearly, then, through his renaming of Turgenev's heroine Bauer sought to indicate that his filmic heroine should be linked not only with her immediate literary precursor, Turgenev's Klara, but also with Klara's real-life actress prototype, Evlaliia Kadmina. Through this simple alteration of his literary source Bauer therefore extends the scope of his film's reference beyond the confines of the literary text on which it was based.

Moreover, Turgenev's story was not the only nineteenth-century literary response to Kadmina's sensational death, nor, in fact, the first. On 20 December 1881, less than two months after her death, a one-act play, entitled *I Am Waiting. There is Still Time (To the Dear Memory of an Unforgettable Performer)* [Ia zhdu. Eshche est´ vremia. (Dorogoi pamiati nezabvennoi artistki)], was published anonymously in the Kiev newspaper *The Dawn* [Zaria]. A poem by S. A. Andreevskii, entitled 'The Singer' ['Pevitsa'] and dedicated to Kadmina, was published in 1883 in the same edition of the journal *Herald of Europe* [Vestnik Evropy] as Turgenev's 'Klara Milich', and that year also saw the publication of a play about Kadmina by N. N. Solovtsov entitled *Evlaliia Ramina*, which was staged the following year in Moscow and, subsequently, in Kiev, Odessa and other towns. In 1884, Nikolai Leskov, apparently directly inspired by Turgenev's story, contributed to the Kadmina theme a story entitled 'A Theatrical Character' ['Teatral´nyi kharakter']. In the season 1888–89 Kadmina's story was again transposed to the stage, in Aleksei Suvorin's four-act play, *Tatiana Repina* (1886), which premiered in St Petersburg on 11 December 1888, in Kharkov on 11 January 1889 and in Moscow on 16 January 1889, each time to sell-out audiences. Two further literary works on the Kadmina theme, both inspired by Suvorin's play, were published in 1889: Aleksandr Kuprin's story 'The Final Debut' ['Poslednii debiut'], written after Kuprin attended a performance of Suvorin's play at the Malyi Theatre in Moscow, and a one-act sketch, also entitled *Tatiana Repina*, by the young Anton Chekhov.[13] It seems likely that Bauer, one of the most culturally aware directors of this period, was familiar with some, if not, indeed, all, of these literary works.

The Kadmina legend continued to develop in the early twentieth century, spreading to other media when, in 1907, Aleksandr Kastalskii composed an operatic version of Turgenev's story, which despite being rehearsed several times in 1914 was premiered only on 11 November 1916, in Moscow.[14] Echoes of Kadmina's story first reached the Russian screen in 1914 via Chardynin's film *Chrysanthemums*.[15] While Chardynin does not explicitly link his ballerina protagonist with Kadmina, their stories coincide to a remarkable degree and it is of course significant that Vera Karalli had also played the role of Vera in *Chrysanthemums*, as we saw in Chapter 6. Finally, 1915 saw the release of screen adaptations of two different Kadmina texts, first the non-extant *Tatiana Repina*, a version of Suvorin's play produced by the Khanzhonkov studio, and, secondly, Bauer's *After Death*.[16]

These multifarious connections make *After Death* a much more complex and ambitious intertextual work than is suggested by both its subtitle, *Motifs from Turgenev*, and Bauer's own sly description of it, cited above, as a film that 'illustrates' one of Turgenev's works; it is thus an adaptation of a literary text that is itself both a creative interpretation of real-life characters and events and a catalyst text in the creation of a network of other imaginative texts that combine to create a fertile and – to use Auerbach's terms – 'permanently vital' cultural myth, the 'legend' of Evlaliia Kadmina. This background problematises the status of *After Death* in the context of the thematics of Bauer's existing oeuvre, however. As we have seen, Bauer was supremely conscious of his role as an artist working in a new medium and a new century; he was also noted for his interest in portraying the so-called New Woman of his time. Why, then, in this instance did he turn, anachronistically, to a literary text written by a classic nineteenth-century Russian author and inspired by the actions of a legendary nineteenth-century woman? This chapter aims to address these questions by proposing an analysis of Bauer's representation of his female performer protagonist that takes account of her nineteenth-century heritage. It will also consider why Bauer might have felt compelled to contribute a filmic text to the Kadmina legend and why he elected to do so by adapting Turgenev's story on this theme.

The actress as cultural stereotype

It is striking that, while the narratives of the nineteenth-century literary works inspired by Kadmina differ from each other in many respects, their representations of the central actress protagonist coincide to such a degree that it is possible to make generalised comments about them.[17]

One key feature these texts have in common is that they all represent the off-stage behaviour of their actress heroines as excessively self-dramatising and theatrical. The urge to perform is so deeply ingrained in them that it has become a way of being, and they make no distinction between the events that occur in their lives and the plots that they enact on stage. The heroine of the anonymous play *I Am Waiting...* confronts her recalcitrant lover with an outpouring of emotion that is so manneristic that it leads Julie Buckler to wonder rhetorically: 'Is he her lover or her audience?'[18] Turgenev's actress protagonist also displays this tendency: she exploits the opportunity for self-dramatization that her meeting with Aratov affords her, dressing in a black gown and mantilla and veiling her face to play the part of the mystery woman. The same point is made overtly by Leskov of his actress heroine, Piamma: she endlessly theatricalises reality, he observes, and so, of course, also shoots herself 'theatrically' on learning of her lover's death.[19] Suvorin's actress so relishes the opportunity for drama provided by her lover's betrayal that she enacts her suicide twice: once verbally in the company of her friends, and then for real while performing in Ostrovskii's *Vasilisa Melenteva* in which (in a further creative intertwining of art and life) she is cast not as the eponymous poisoner, as Kadmina had been, but as the poisoned tsarina, Anna. In Kuprin's story the actress's confusion of life and theatre is so complete that she also finds herself enacting the same role twice: once for real and in private (with her actor lover in her dressing room) and then in character and in public (on stage, opposite her real-life lover, who is cast in the role of her on-stage lover). Finally, while Chekhov's work parodies and mocks the tendency to self-dramatisation displayed by Suvorin's Tatiana Repina – Chekhov's very human 'ghost', the 'woman in black', is an embodiment of the actress's final threat to haunt her faithless lover in Suvorin's play – he does not put forward an alternative view of the female performer.

In this way, none of the nineteenth-century literary works on the Kadmina theme, Turgenev's included, looks beyond the conventional attributes of the actress's 'cultural mask' to uncover the face of the woman behind it.[20]

From Turgenev's Klara Milich to Bauer's Zoia Kadmina: the actress as real woman

In this respect Bauer's representation of his actress protagonist differs from those of his nineteenth-century precursors, for, in keeping with his reputation as a 'woman's director', Bauer *is* concerned with representing his female protagonist as a living human character. Indeed, it is striking that most of the alterations Bauer makes to Turgenev's original – even those apparently unconnected with the central female protagonist – seem intended to ensure that Zoia is presented in this way and, moreover, as a character with whom the viewer should identify and, therefore, sympathise.

Alterations, excisions and additions

The changes Bauer makes to the character of the princess, the actress's patroness, have an important impact on his representation of his actress protagonist. Turgenev's princess, although colourful and entertaining, is also depicted in negative terms as a sexual, flighty and brash woman of questionable morality and dubious social status. That Klara associates with such a woman taints her image to some extent, especially in the eyes of Turgenev's hero. Bauer completely re-imagines the princess, however: in his film she becomes, in the performance of Marfa Kassatskaia, a staid, respectable and motherly figure, more Zoia's chaperone than her patroness. No judgements are passed on her by either Bauer or his male protagonist; unlike Turgenev's Aratov, Bauer's Andrei is happy to sit beside her at the charity recital where they watch Zoia perform. The force of Bauer's alternative characterization of the princess would have been heightened for contemporary Russian cinema audiences by the fact that Kassatskaia had recently appeared in a similar screen role, in Chardynin's *The Love of a Councillor of State*, released just a month before *After Death*, where, as we have seen, she played the stodgy provincial mother of the eponymous State Councillor, who remains, throughout the film, dourly disapproving of her son's infatuation with and subsequent marriage to the music-hall dancer, Lola.

Bauer also cuts from his film all mention of the older actress whom Klara originally left home to join. We learn little about her from Turgenev other than the fact that her patron is unable to marry her because he already has a wife, and so, like the princess, she remains a stereotypical figure: the actress as compromised public woman. Klara's association with this woman leads Aratov to conclude that she cannot be morally pure or innocent, a conclusion that flies in the face of all the evidence he has of Klara's unimpeachable personality and is grounded simply in the conventional nineteenth-century view of the actress that still associated her with the prostitute and the *demi-mondaine*. Through these careful alterations and deliberate excisions, Bauer therefore ensures that none of the negative clichés Turgenev draws on in his characterization of both the older actress and the Princess are attached to Zoia's image, an attention to detail that again suggests his concern to present her both in positive terms and also as a real woman and not a cultural stereotype.[21]

Consider also how Bauer alters the nature of the first encounter between his hero and his heroine. In *After Death*, Andrei meets Zoia at the princess's soirée. In Turgenev's story, no such meeting takes place. Indeed, at no point in Turgenev's narrative of this gathering is Klara even mentioned as being present. The only hint that something unusual has occurred there comes in Turgenev's description of how it leaves Aratov with an odd impression that he finds 'oppressive' but 'significant and even disturbing' (p. 82). While he does not understand these feelings, they remain with him, but it is not until Aratov sees Klara on stage six weeks later that he remembers that she had been present at that first gathering. In this way Klara is, from the out-set of Turgenev's story, represented less as a woman and more as a bizarre but irresistible force that insinuates itself into Aratov's mind and haunts his emotions; as the poet and literary critic Innokentii Annenskii put it: 'Klara is almost absent from the action: she merely glides through the story, exactly like a Chinese shadow on a screen'.[22]

In Bauer's film, however, Zoia is from the outset a strong physical presence. Watching her arrive at the soirée with the princess, the viewer is initially struck by her shyness and modesty, for she allows her older companion to precede her into the room and hangs back, her eyes lowered. Andrei's friend introduces him to both women, before escorting the princess away. Andrei is thus left alone with Zoia, who appears unsure of what to say or do. Karalli's restrained and nuanced acting makes her character's nervousness palpable: she clasps her hands before her, perhaps in an attempt to gain control over herself, but her fingers continue to fidget and then, when she lets one arm fall to her side, they first pluck at the fabric of her skirt and then lightly trace the undulations of a cornice on an ornate pillar. Nevertheless, for all her shyness, Zoia's sexual attraction to Andrei is obvious, and she stares at Andrei, committing, in Heide Schlüpmann's words, 'an unmistakeable act of erotic choice' (Figure 7.1).[23] Bauer empha-sises Zoia's fascination with Andrei by making the camera adopt her per-spective: Andrei – who, having retired to a nearby chair, finds himself lower

Figure 7.1. Zoia makes Andrei the object of her gaze (Bauer, *After Death*, 1915)

than Zoia, who has remained standing – is shot from a slightly raised angle that replicates her point of view. His discomfort at being the object of this woman's attention is clear. Unable to bear the intent gaze of her black eyes, he shifts uneasily in his chair, lowers his eyes and then flees, as Zoia continues to watch him. In this sequence, then, in stark contrast with Turgenev, Bauer very deliberately represents his actress protagonist as a woman of flesh and blood. Indeed, it is her very physicality that makes such a strong impression on Andrei and causes his departure.

Anatomy of a cinematic sequence

The most striking addition Bauer makes to his adaptation of Turgenev's story comes just before the sequence dealing with the letter Zoia writes to Andrei. In plot terms this letter-writing sequence is immediately preceded by Zoia's recital. In cinematic terms, however, these two diegetic events are separated by a brief extra-diegetic sequence that is of central importance both to Bauer's representation of his female protagonist and to his exploration of cinematic language.

This sequence – which I shall refer to hereafter as the close-up sequence – begins when, as Zoia takes a bow after her performance, Bauer suddenly cuts in to a close-up shot of the actress's face; the camera then tracks in, moving even closer to the actress and bringing her into an extreme close-up (Figure 7.2); finally, the actress takes a slow step towards the camera, moving almost out of focus and out of the range of the light. The shot fades to black. And there this extraordinary sequence, which lasts for no more than seven seconds, comes to an end.

The meaning of this close-up sequence is difficult to unlock with certainty. In a previous analysis, I suggested that it evoked Zoia appropriating for herself the pleasure of looking, making Andrei the object of her gaze and, in so doing, asserting herself as the agent rather than the object of desire.[24] Borrowing Laura Mulvey's terminology, I suggested that Zoia was here cast as 'the bearer of the look', while Andrei was accorded the role of 'spectacle'.[25] As we have seen, this is indeed what happens in the earlier sequence when Zoia meets Andrei at the Princess's soirée. In this close-up sequence, however, this analysis is compromised by the fact that the viewpoint of the

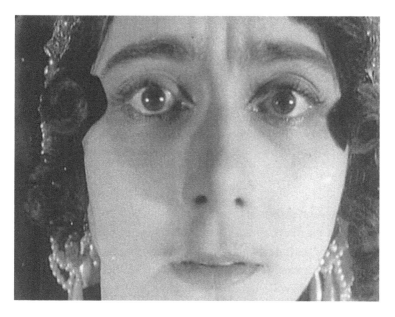

Figure 7.2. The extreme close-up of Vera Karalli as Zoia Kadmina (Bauer, *After Death*, 1915)

close-up is unclear. As Philip Cavendish has noted, it cannot be Andrei's perspective on the actress, for when this sequence occurs Andrei has already left the theatre and, more importantly, its eye-to-eye perspective does not match the view Andrei would have had of Zoia from his lower seat in the front row of the stalls.[26] The confusion about the viewpoint of this shot is made more striking by the fact that during the recital that precedes it Bauer does make his camera adopt the angled points of view that both Andrei and Zoia have of each other from their respective positions in the audience and on the stage. Thus if Bauer has left the viewpoint of this close-up sequence unclear, it can be assumed that he has done so intentionally.

In the context of his meticulously observed discussion of the poetics of camera movement in this film, Cavendish has suggested several other interpretations of this sequence: it could represent Andrei's 'memory' of the recital, or his 'projected wish-fulfilment [...] the desire for Zoia to advance physically towards him, possibly even to embrace or kiss him'.[27] Most productive, however, is his suggestion that it is 'an "objective" portrait' through which Bauer aims both to emphasise the actress's eyes (a key motif in Turgenev's original) and thereby communicate her 'mesmerizing power' and 'inner passion', and also to foreshadow her suicide by having her move symbolically from light into darkness.[28] However, while this sequence does not represent the perspective of any of the film's protagonists, this does not necessarily make it objective. Indeed, given its extra-diegetic status, this sequence could be read as Bauer's *subjective* representation of the actress: it stands as a sort of directorial aside through which Bauer seeks, self-consciously, to put forward his own view of the actress. What, though, does Bauer say about her here, and how does he contrive to say it?

The close-up
There are several aspects of the close-up with which this sequence begins that mark it as a direct, authorial mode of address. The first is its novelty in the cinema of the time. In his discussion of the origins of the close-up in early Russian cinema, Tsivian cites the memoirs of three Russian actresses who all claim to have been the first to be filmed in extreme facial close-up, in films made in 1916, the year after Bauer made *After Death*.[29] As Tsivian stresses, these memoirs are inaccurate in the sense that the facial close-up

had, in fact, often been used in Russian films made before 1916; he goes on to explain, however, that they are correct in one sense:

> Although technically the close-up had been invented years before, 1916 *was* important: it was the year when film-makers and film critics suddenly realised that, far from being just an occasional device, the close-up was turning into something dangerously central to the narrator system [emphasis in original].[30]

Bauer had obviously arrived at this realization earlier than most of his contemporaries. Indeed, in another film he made in 1915, just before *After Death*, Bauer also repeatedly framed his leading actress in close-up. It is perhaps not coincidental that this film, which has not been preserved, was Bauer's aforementioned adaptation of Turgenev's story 'The Song of Love Triumphant'.[31]

Nevertheless, the close-up was a novelty also in the context of Bauer's distinctive visual style. In Russia in the 1910s, the close-up was seen as being in opposition to the more usual long shot that privileged decorative space – the film's mise-en-scène – in the creation of meaning. As Tsivian speculates, for Bauer, who, as we have seen, had built his reputation on his genius as a set designer, 'the choice between decorative space and the close-up was an extremely difficult one to make'.[32] Indeed, although Bauer did continue to explore the expressive potential of the close-up, most notably in his 1916 film *Nelli Raintseva*, many of the films he made after 1915, such as *A Life for a Life* and *In Pursuit of Happiness*, show him still favouring long shots, medium shots and mise-en-scène over closer framing.

Clearly, then, when Bauer *does* choose to use a close-up shot, he does so for a reason. The novelty and rarity of this shot heighten the sense of its intentionality; this is true of any innovative artistic device but, as Tsivian suggests, it is especially powerful in the case of the close-up, for:

> By its very nature – 'behold!' – the close-up was seen as a deixis, the textual gesture implying direct address. The new space-free narrative mode was felt as *subjective* in contrast to the *objective* mode of the earlier space-bound narration [emphasis added].[33]

Indeed, some contemporary reviewers reacted against the use of the close-up for this very reason, feeling that it betrayed 'too much authorial presence.[34]

What does Bauer seek to say about the actress through this shot, however? In focussing on the actress's face in close-up, Bauer cuts from the frame, and therefore from the viewer's field of vision, all extraneous details such as the stage, its curtain, Zoia's costume and the audience; in other words, all the objects that signify Zoia's status as an actress. By lifting Zoia out of the context of the theatre in this way, Bauer forces the viewer to look at her as he wants her to be seen: in isolation as an individual, and not in terms of her stage persona or presence.

Indeed, this is possibly how contemporary viewers would have responded to this close-up. Tsivian has shown how the close-up began to be interpreted in Russia in the mid- to late 1910s as a means of focussing attention on the psychology of the characters. In this context he cites a contemporary Russian review of Otis Turner's 1915 film *Business is Business*, shown in Russia in 1916 under the title *The Slave of Profit* [Rab nazhivy], that praises the director's extensive use of close-up shots for precisely this reason: 'All superfluous details are removed from the viewer's field of vision, and all he sees is the actor's face. Clearly, there is no device better suited for a *psychological* picture [emphasis in original]'.[35]

It should be stressed that this interest in psychology was not, in itself, new; indeed, it was one of the most distinctive features of early Russian film, which had valued the depiction of psychology over action from its inception: as we saw in Chapter 1, the first Russian feature film, Romashkov's *Stenka Razin*, already displayed this preference in embryonic form. What does make Bauer's approach in this sequence innovative, though, is the means he adopts to convey his character's psychology. As we saw in the discussion of *The Incestuous Father-in-Law* in Chapter 2, traditionally the pace and quality of acting were seen as being fundamental to the evocation of the characters' psychology on screen: the so-called 'Russian style' of acting was defined by its adherence to a 'doctrine of immobility', a conscious aesthetic programme according to which the camera would linger at length on the actors who were required to shun action and movement in favour of inaction and near motionlessness. We recall also that such scenes became known as 'full' scenes and that they would be defined by a film theorist writing in *The Projector* in 1916 as a scene in which 'the actor is given the opportunity to depict in stage terms a specific spiritual experience, no matter how many metres it takes' and which 'aspires to *rivet* the attention of the audience on to a single image [emphasis in original]'.[36]

This perhaps explains the startling brevity of this close-up: seeking to explore the expressive possibilities of film, Bauer here challenges one of the fundamental characteristics of the established 'Russian style' that elsewhere – in *After Death* and in other films – he embraces. In so doing, he demonstrates that extended time and nuanced acting are not the only means through which a character's psychology can be conveyed; modifying space can, in itself, be just as effective. Indeed, in this sequence it is the close-up itself that ensures the impact of Bauer's portrait of Zoia. As Alyssa DeBlasio observes: 'Karalli's eyes are what connect the viewer to Bauer's on-screen psychology [...]. Because the emotion of the scene radiates from her gaping eyes and wrinkled brow, this expressive portrait could never have been accomplished without an extreme close-up'.[37]

Writing in *Cine-Gazette* in July 1918, Valentin Turkin credited Bauer with being 'the first to employ close-up shots to portray the most subtle feelings of his actors'.[38] However, while the facial close-up with which this sequence begins was almost unprecedented in Russian cinema of the time, it was not without antecedents in another, older form of visual art: the icon. In 1902, Sergei Diaghilev had, according to Rosamund Bartlett and Linda Edmondson, arranged an exhibition that for the first time presented Russian icons primarily as works of art, rather than as religious artefacts.[39] This led to an upsurge of interest in this ancient art form and the first Great Exhibition of medieval Russian art was held in Moscow in Spring 1913. The icons displayed there had been restored for the first time, revealing their extraordinary beauty, and it is perhaps, therefore, no coincidence that it was around this time that the icon first began to be studied as a work of art with distinctive *aesthetic* properties that could be analysed independently of its religious motivation and significance.[40] The success of this exhibition was such that June of the same year saw the Romanov Exhibition of Church Antiquities. The early 1910s also saw the emergence of the Russian art movement neo-primitivism, which combined elements of cubism, futurism and the paintings of Paul Cézanne with the conventions and motifs of traditional Russian art, such as the *lubok*, peasant arts and crafts and especially the icon. In 1913, Mikhail Larionov and Natalia Goncharova, the two major figures in this movement, organised an exhibition in Moscow, where they displayed their own work and that of their fellow neo-primitivists alongside more than six hundred icons and *lubki* from private collections assembled by Larionov and others.[41]

The similarities between Bauer's close-up portrait of Karalli as Kadmina and typical medieval Russian icons are both specific and general.[42] Karalli's ornately curled hair, her large, heavy-lidded, almond-shaped eyes with their prominent brows, her long nose, narrow face and her small, expressionless mouth and chin all replicate the typical facial features of ancient Russian icons.[43] Cavendish's observation that, because of the longer lens needed to film this shot, Karalli's countenance here appears 'flattened'[44] highlights another of its icon-like features. The actress's striking make-up also contributes to this effect: consider, for example, the black eyeliner that defines the contours of her eyes and especially the white face powder that, together with the 'bleaching' effect of the bright lighting, smoothes from the actress's face any lines or wrinkles that would reveal her mortality, rendering it mask-like. Her frontal pose is also that of many icons. Moreover, while this portrait disregards the principles of natural perspective, like an icon it adheres instead to those of the so-called psychological perspective, according to which the most important figure in the composition is the largest and the most centrally placed.

There are, however, crucial differences between Bauer's filmic portrait of Zoia and the icons of medieval Russia. While Bauer appropriates the expressive power of the icon to enable the viewer to relate to his screen representation of Zoia in the same way that a worshipper relates to an icon – that is, to see it not as a mere representation but as the represented itself – it is not his intention to make Zoia a (divine) object of veneration. In this respect the nature of Zoia's gaze is fundamental, for her eyes are startlingly 'real', their expression one of anxious beseeching, her furrowed brow suggestive of a deeply troubled mind.[45] Furthermore, while the serene gaze of many Russian icons seems detached, as if either turned inward, or directed past the spectator and the phenomenological world to the spiritual realm beyond,[46] Zoia's disquieted gaze is directed straight at the camera and, by extension, at the viewer. It seems, therefore, to be a deliberate attempt to connect with him or her, an example of what Tom Brown has termed 'direct address'.[47] What the viewer sees when s/he returns Zoia's gaze, however, is not the inner light of a sacred figure or the divine light of Christ, but, as Cavendish has observed, 'the dual reflections' of the two arc lights that Bauer's cameraman, Boris Zavelev, used to illuminate this portrait.[48] Thus, as an icon offers the worshipper a window beyond the 'prototype' it depicts into the realm of the divine, so Bauer's 'iconic' close-up offers the viewer a window beyond the actress's cultural mask – and the mask of her make-up – into Zoia's inner self. It also, however, allows the viewer to glimpse, beyond Bauer's character, the actress, who here represents her, the film star Vera Karalli.

The close-up shot with which this sequence begins can, therefore, be seen as Bauer's attempt to give the viewer privileged access to Zoia's psychology and to represent her as an individual, and to do so in a novel, innovative way. Moreover, as Bauer here also has Karalli break cinematic convention by staring directly into the camera, he contrives to characterise Zoia as an unconventional, confident New Woman who is able to meet the gaze not only of the central male protagonist – as she did when she first met Andrei – but also of the camera and of the viewer. In its emphasis on Karalli as Karalli, this close-up also, however, serves to 'lay bare' the very cinematic device that Bauer here exploits to such powerful emotional effect. In so doing, Bauer offers the viewer a clue to his wider concerns in this film.

The track-in

After holding the initial close-up of Zoia's face for a couple of seconds, the camera briefly tracks in towards her, bringing her face into extreme close-up. By drawing the viewer yet closer to her through this movement, Bauer again encourages the viewer to do as his camera is doing: to observe this woman more closely, to look beyond the mask-like surface of her representation as an actress. Moreover, although this may not be felt by a modern viewer, Bauer probably also intended this track-in to function as a gesture of sympathy towards Zoia and a sign of his allegiance to her. Building on a theory of camera movement in the 1910s advanced by Cherchi Usai, Tsivian suggests that Bauer frequently used the track-in – his 'favourite' camera movement[49] – as an address (which could be either sympathetic or aggressive) to the *character* rather than, or at least as well as, to the viewer.[50] As so often, Bauer is on the side of his female protagonist and he wants his viewers to be so, too.

Moving closer to the camera

What, finally, are we to make of the step that the actress takes towards the camera? Again, this action brings Zoia physically and, by extension, psychologically closer to the viewer. Moreover, like Zoia's direct gaze into the camera, in the cinematic context, this is also an unconventional action. Again, therefore, it suggests her boldness; it does not, however, make her seem threatening or intimidating – her movement is too slight and subtle for that.[51] Instead, this deliberate assault on the so-called 'fourth wall' seems to function as Zoia's address to the viewer: it is her appeal that her personal identity be recognised as being distinct from her professional identity.

The appropriateness of this interpretation of Zoia's movement is suggested by analogy with a similar scene in a different text on the Kadmina theme, Kuprin's story 'The Final Debut'. While it would doubtless be an over-interpretation to claim that Bauer is here making direct reference to this text, a comparison is, nevertheless, illuminating.

Kuprin's actress heroine, Lidiia Golskaia, finds herself in the role of spurned lover both in life and on stage; similarly, in both situations the same man, the actor Aleksandr Petrovich, plays the role of her heartless lover. Golskaia is first rejected by Petrovich for real and in the privacy of her dressing room, only moments before they are called on stage to perform the same scene in public, as part of the play they are appearing in together. Once on stage Golskaia is overcome by her emotions: she steps out of character and speaks to her lover in her own voice. If he notices, he does not react, however, and responds with the scripted words. Left alone on stage after her lover's exit, Golskaia continues to speak in her own voice, relating the story of her unhappy love affair. Suddenly she falls silent, however, and then 'slowly step[s] towards the footlights'[52] – towards the front of the stage and the audience – in a final attempt to connect with the audience, to communicate the authenticity of her emotions and to force them to see that she here speaks not as an actress in character, but for herself as a woman. Now completely calm, she drinks the poison, looks round the audience and then collapses.

Golskaia's appeal fails, however. After all, having a character move downstage in order to heighten the effect of his/her soliloquy is a long-standing theatrical convention; Golskaia's audience therefore continues to suspend disbelief, not noticing that she here both breaks character and attempts to breach the theatre's fourth wall, to shift from 'representation' to (self) 'presentation'. Thus, despite being transfixed by the intensity of what they see on stage, the people in the audience are unable to recognise its authenticity. They therefore respond to her real death as if it were a performance, with furious applause and cries of 'Bravo!'[53] By contrast, the unconventionality and the intentionality of Zoia's movement towards the camera give it enormous power; that Zoia here addresses the viewer so directly forces the viewer to engage with her as with an individual.

From Zoia's point of view

This effect is also heightened by the fact that the letter-writing sequence that immediately follows the close-up sequence continues to bring the viewer closer to Zoia, by allowing us, for the first time, access to her point of view. Zoia's lack of self-assurance is again touchingly obvious; the viewer is witness to Zoia's internal struggle – which, significantly, takes place at her home and not in the theatre – as she deliberates over taking the unconventional step of writing to Andrei to request a rendezvous. Again, this lengthy sequence – a textbook 'full' scene – represents a deliberate deviation from Turgenev's original, for at no point in his narrative does he give us access to Klara's point of view in this way. Moreover, when we look at this sequence in its historical context we again see that it reveals, through its length alone, Bauer's concern to represent his actress protagonist's psychology in a realistic fashion. As Tsivian has documented, the unrealistic speed with which letters were shown being written was one of the aspects that contemporary Russian critics focussed on when complaining about the lack of psychological realism in early Russian films. Tsivian cites an entry Aleksandr Blok made in his Notebook on 19 May 1916, in which he comments approvingly on a new tendency he has observed in Russian films: 'Much attention is paid to psychology [...]. Letters are written more slowly, etc.'[54]

Again, then, Bauer is at the forefront of his field.

Andrei's Zoia: photographs, dreams and visions

Bauer also highlights the authenticity of his representation of his actress protagonist by setting his psychologically believable female protagonist against Andrei's subjective perception of the actress. Tormented by Zoia's absence after her death, Andrei becomes fixated on attempting to revive her image and thus bring her back to life. Dissatisfied with the insubstantial memories he has of their few meetings, he turns first to photography. In the safety of his womb-like darkroom, Andrei studies Zoia's photograph obsessively. Tormented by the fact that, in this one-dimensional image, her eyes are averted from the camera, and thus from his as he gazes at her, Andrei examines the photograph through a stereoscope and enlarges it in an attempt to obtain a more pleasing image of her. As we saw in Chapter 6, in our discussion of *Daydreams*, however, 'photography [...] by virtue of the objective suggestions of its signifier (stillness, again) maintains the memory of the dead *as being dead*'.[55] Thus, the results of Andrei's photographic experiments inevitably leave him dissatisfied, for his photograph of Zoia remains an inert, lifeless image.

Andrei subsequently abandons his dark room, therefore, and instead retreats into his own mind, conjuring Zoia's presence in his dreams. Tsivian equates these two undertakings, commenting that 'Andrei's mind revives her image as photographic plates revive persons no longer present'.[56] However, while Andrei had found it impossible fundamentally to alter the appearance of the actress though the tricks of photography, his mind is not bound by such limitations and he is therefore able to re-imagine Zoia as he pleases. Predictably, the Zoia Andrei creates bears little resemblance to the unconventional, independent and modern woman Bauer has shown us. She languishes in an Arcadian cornfield, clothed in a flowing white tunic that flutters in the breeze, her loosened hair cascading down her back and her face bathed in a preternatural light that drains it of all expression and individuality – as Tsivian notes, an innovative use of a deliberately over-exposed shot.[57] Like Nedelin's remembered Elena, Andrei's dreamed Zoia is pure fantasy, an outdated icon of idealised femininity, more revealing of Andrei's attitudes to women than of Zoia herself (Figure 7.3).

In this respect it is significant that the dreams Bauer attributes to his hero are all Bauer's own invention; although Andrei – like Turgenev's

Figure 7.3. Andrei dreams of Zoia (Bauer, *After Death*, 1915)

Aratov – dreams of the actress twice, Andrei's dreams bear no resemblance
to those experienced by Turgenev's hero. In Aratov's first dream, Klara
appears as a conventionally ghostly cloud-like figure as she wanders the
barren steppe landscape that was the traditional location for the restless
spirits of suicides; in the second she comes to stand for death itself.[58]

Similarly, Bauer also alters the nature of his hero's subsequent 'visions'
of the dead actress. When Klara appears before Aratov she is dressed completely in black; when Zoia appears before Andrei, however, it is as if she
has 'descended from the canvas of his dreams',[59] for although there are subtle alterations to the arrangement of her hair or headdress each time she
appears, she is always dressed in the white robe she was wearing in his
dreams. By linking Andrei's visions to his dreams in this way Bauer identifies them as proceeding directly from either Andrei's imagination or his
unconscious and thereby downplays the possibility of their being seen as
supernatural visitations.[60]

Indeed, Bauer has prepared the viewer to see Andrei's infatuation with
the dead Zoia in psychological terms from the outset of the film, for an

early scene shows Andrei to be in thrall to the memory of another dead woman: his mother. Bauer gives this fact an emphasis that is absent from Turgenev's original, for the small portrait that Aratov has of his mother becomes in Bauer's film an almost life-size portrait of the dead woman which hangs over Andrei's fireplace and at which he gazes with undisguised adoration.[61] The psychological/sexual hold the dead (woman) has over the living (man) is a theme Bauer explored throughout his cinematic career: in 1913 he had made *Bloody Glory* in which a model commits suicide and an artist, on discovering her body, paints its portrait; similarly, in *Life in Death* [Zhizn´ v smerti, 1914], an adaptation of a story by the Symbolist writer Valerii Briusov, the male protagonist kills his beautiful wife and keeps her embalmed body in his cellar; *Daydreams* and *The Dying Swan* also explore this theme, as we saw in Chapter 6. While the male protagonists' involvement in and responses to the death of their female counterparts may vary, these men all display the same crippling inability to form a relationship with a living woman, a fact that has led many commentators to see in Bauer's films a disturbing representation of contemporary man's fear of the so-called New Woman who had begun to make her mark on Russian society at the start of the twentieth century.[62]

In this connection it is also important to note that Turgenev's male protagonist was modelled on not one but two real-life men – not only the faceless Officer T., whose abandonment allegedly drove Kadmina to suicide, but also a young St Petersburg zoologist, Vladimir Dmitrievich Alenitsyn, who, although not personally acquainted with Kadmina, fell deeply in love with her after her death and, like Bauer's Nedelin, surrounded himself with portraits of the actress and dedicated to her poetry, romances and a play, entitled *The Actress* [Aktrisa].[63] Also of relevance is the fact that the Symbolist poet Innokentii Annenskii similarly kept a portrait of Kadmina in his study.[64]

These facts perhaps explain why Bauer chose to entitle his film *After Death*, preferring Turgenev's original title, with its emphasis on the male protagonist's psychological response to the actress's death – in Turgenev's words, his 'after-death falling in love' [*posmertnaia vliublennost´*] (p. 579) – to that of the one under which his story was eventually published. In this connection, the response of Turgenev's friend Pavel Annenkov to the imposed change of title from 'After Death' to 'Klara Milich' is also significant:

I am indignant with [the publisher] for changing the title of your story. This is the most stupid thing he could have done. He didn't stop to think, the fool, that *titles with names in them* signal the author's intention to present some *type* or other, while here you don't deal in a type, but in a rare and significant psychological phenomenon [emphasis in original] (p. 578).

From staged suicide to social protest

She was a flame that consumed itself. Her tragic end was inherent in her nature.

L. A. Kupernik in his obituary 'To the Memory of Evlaliia Kadmina' ['Pamiati E. P. Kadminoi'].[65]

Like the 'real' Evlaliia Kadmina, the literary Kadminas – with the exception of Leskov's Piamma[66] – all kill themselves because they have been abandoned or betrayed by a man. Many of them also display a desire to have revenge on their faithless lovers by shaming them in public, and all of them die the way they do because their status as an actress makes such a death inevitable; their theatrical nature means that they, possibly like Kadmina herself, are unable to resist the opportunity for sensational self-dramatization that a staged suicide affords them.[67]

Like her precursors, Bauer's actress protagonist also commits suicide during a stage performance. It is impossible to dismiss Zoia's death as the hysterical posturing of a self-dramatising diva, however; this is not what Bauer shows Zoia to be either earlier in the film or during the suicide sequence itself. Again, the details Bauer adds, alters or omits in his screen rendering of the actress's suicide are significant. In Turgenev's story, we learn about Klara's suicide from two second-hand sources: a brief, factual newspaper obituary, which Bauer retains, and an enthusiastic account by Aratov's friend, Küpfer, which emphasises the 'panache' and the 'intrinsic theatricality' of her 'stagey' act.[68] Bauer, of course, dispenses with this. Tsivian highlights how lacking in conventional drama, or 'punch', Bauer's version of the suicide sequence is: 'We find no theater stage, no convulsions behind the curtain, no raving and clapping theater crowd […] nothing, aside from a brief, almost informative, flashback (backstage Klara expires surrounded by fellow actors) inserted in the story Aratov hears from Klara's sister'.[69] Tsivian suggests that Bauer downplayed Zoia's suicide scene because, as three films featuring on-stage suicides had been shown in Russia in the two years before he made *After Death* – Caserini's *Love Everlasting*, Chardynin's *Chrysanthemums* and the Khanzhonkov studio's *Tatiana Repina* – a fourth would have appeared 'self-replicating and anti-climactic', more like 'worn-out cinematic currency [...] than anything out of Turgenev'.[70] This interpretation denies the possibility of deliberate directorial intent, however. As the many other alterations Bauer makes to Turgenev's original are intentional and expressive, it seems likely that his strategy of downplaying Zoia's act is also intended, a conscious decision rather than a reaction. Moreover, in its focus on what Bauer leaves out of his suicide sequence, Tsivian's description glosses over some of the sequence's most important features. Bauer's depiction of Zoia's suicide, although indisputably lacking both melodrama and 'punch', is very specific and, in fact, lengthy: it lasts almost four minutes, which, according to DeBlasio's analysis, makes it one of the longest sequences in the film.[71] In Bauer's film the second source for details about Zoia's suicide is her sister, but the crucial deviation from Turgenev's story comes in the way in which the information she gives Andrei is relayed to the viewer: not verbally, via intertitles, as the newspaper obituary had been, but visually, as a flashback. Thus we join Zoia as she sits in costume in her dressing room and watch as, with tears streaming down her face, she deliberates over drinking the poison. In many respects, this exemplary 'full' scene recalls the earlier letter-writing sequence, and its effects are the same: to show the viewer events from Zoia's point of view, to stress the psychological reality of the female protagonist and thereby to bring viewer and female protagonist closer.

Bauer's determination constantly to represent Zoia as an authentic, sympathetic character makes it impossible to respond to her suicide with indifference or detachment, but while her death moves the viewer, it also confounds: Why does Bauer's dynamic and unconventional New Woman follow Evlaliia Kadmina and her nineteenth-century literary counterparts and respond to Andrei's rejection of her love with such a hackneyed and conventionally feminine act of self-destruction? Zoia's act is all the more puzzling when it is considered in the context of Bauer's extant oeuvre, for Zoia is a striking anomaly; she is the only one of Bauer's actress or dancer protagonists to take her own life. In other Bauer films, when the female performers are unlucky in love they not only survive – at least initially – but often flourish. Thus, Vera, in *Twilight of a Woman's Soul*, and Gizella, in *The Dying Swan*, respond to their lovers' betrayals by throwing themselves into their careers. Similarly, Tina, in *Daydreams*, does not despair when she realises her lover is still infatuated with his dead wife, but mocks his unhealthy obsession in an attempt to cure him of it. Moreover, in other Bauer films the female performers are shown to be much stronger than their male counterparts and, indeed, are more likely to inflict suffering on them than experience it themselves. Such are the *tangistka* Mary, in *Child of the Big City*, and the Duncan-esque dancer in *Iurii Nagornyi*.

However, while the fact of Zoia's suicide, if not its spirit, links her with Kadmina and her nineteenth-century literary counterparts, it also dis-tances her from another 'legendary' nineteenth-century Russian heroine. For there exists in *After Death* a further submerged reference to another key nineteenth-century Russian literary text, Pushkin's 'novel in verse', *Evgenii Onegin*. This intertext exists explicitly in Turgenev's story, for Klara chooses to declaim at her recital the bold love letter written by Tatiana to Pushkin's arrogant Onegin (p. 590) (Figure 7.4). While the identity of the text Zoia recites is not referred to explicitly in the restored version of Bauer's film, which survived without intertitles, it is such an impor-tant element of Turgenev's story that, for those who know this work, it permeates the film's subtext even without overt mention. Zoia's choice of this text explains why Andrei reacts so haughtily to her declaration of love. Although due in part to his reclusive personality, his rejection of her love is doubtless also prompted by his identification of Zoia with Tatiana: in rejecting her, Andrei, an avid reader, may feel that he is follow-ing in Onegin's glamorous footsteps. Thus, like Bauer's Dolskii in *Twilight of a Woman's Soul*, his Nedelin in *Daydreams* and his Glinskii in *The Dying Swan*, Andrei confuses his twentieth-century female counterpart with the nineteenth-century character she plays on stage before him.

However, while Zoia may indeed attempt to use both Tatiana's persona and her letter as a tool of seduction – as already discussed, the camerawork during her recital makes it appear that she is directing her performance at Andrei – in real life she is no Tatiana; she is not content to slip pas-sively into obscurity and wait patiently for her family to marry her off to a

Figure 7.4. Zoia recites Tatiana's bold love letter from Pushkin's *Evgenii Onegin* (Bauer, *After Death*, 1915)

suitable husband. Her suicide can thus be read as a deliberate act of defiance: it is her rejection of the nineteenth-century Russian literary tradition and, specifically, of Tatiana, its iconic representative of the type of saintly femininity to which Andrei, on the evidence of the nature of his dreams and fantasies of Zoia, is so firmly wedded.

In Bauer's hands, therefore, Zoia's suicide acquires greater significance, for he shows there to be more complex reasons for this act than the despair of unrequited love alone. When Zoia realises that she and Andrei are 'out of joint', suicide becomes her only option. It is a form of protest, a desperate, albeit Pyrrhic, act of rebellion against the hypocritical rules of patriarchy that allow a man sexual liberty and the active role in love but require that a woman remain chaste and patiently await marriage. As Elisabeth Bronfen has elaborated: 'Feminine suicide can serve as a trope, self-defeating as this seems, for a feminine writing strategy within the constraints of patriarchal culture'.[72] At the same time, however, such a suicide is always ambivalent, positioning a woman 'between subjectivity, self-assertion and autonomy on the one hand and a repetition of alterior signs on the other; between the construction of a personal, original and authentic autobiography and a falling prey to already existing cultural conventions, to literary precursors'.[73]

Bauer does encourage the viewer to read Zoia's suicide 'positively', as an assertion of autonomy, however, and he does so in part by expanding his range of reference beyond Kadmina and the nineteenth-century Russian literary tradition, and linking his female protagonist with two older legendary female suicides. Typically, he achieves this by exploiting the expressive potential of key aspects of the mise-en-scène, by employing carefully orchestrated lighting effects and by deviating, once again, from Turgenev's story. Turgenev is vague about Klara's final stage role; according to Küpfer she was playing a 'deceived girl' (p. 125) in a play (that does not in fact exist) by Ostrovskii. Zoia's costume, however, while not a precise indicator of the role she is playing as she dies, appears classical; the members of the cast who rush to help her when she collapses are similarly dressed in togas (Figure 7.5).

The individual details of Zoia's costume – her long white gown, her jewelled headdress, the bracelets she wears around her wrists and upper

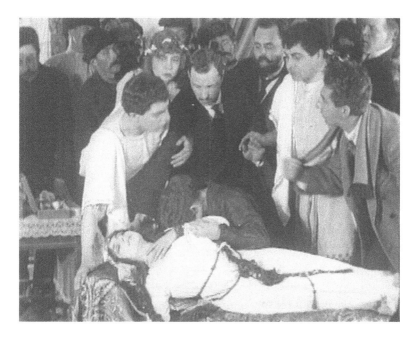

Figure 7.5. Surrounded by toga-clad actors, Zoia expires (Bauer, *After Death*, 1915).

arms, the strings of pearls that hang from them and round her neck, and her long dark plaits – thus bestow on her a resemblance to Cleopatra, the oriental queen whose life was a ceaseless struggle against men who sought to wrest power from her, and whose suicide, although in part motivated by the death of her lover, Antony, was primarily caused by her pride and her determination to avoid the shame of losing to Octavian her throne, her power and her freedom. The figure of Cleopatra would have been familiar to early twentieth-century Russian cinema audiences from Enrico Guazzoni's 1913 film, *Antony and Cleopatra* [Marcantonio e Cleopatra], which was distributed in Russia at the end of 1913 or during 1914.[74] It is striking that the headdress and ropes of pearls worn by the actress Gianna Terribili-Gonzales in the publicity poster for this film anticipate similar details of the costume Bauer designed for Zoia to wear during her final stage performance.[75] Also of relevance is the way Guazzoni's film presents Cleopatra's motive for suicide; as Maria Wyke describes it: 'At one point […] Cleopatra visualizes the coming Roman victory and reels back in horror as she watches togaed crowds jeering a procession which includes herself and her bound Egyptian subjects. It is this vision of public humiliation that compels her to suicide'.[76]

A second possible double for Zoia in this sequence is the Roman noblewoman Lucretia, wife of Lucius Tarquinius Collatinus, who also entered the annals of legend with her suicide. The Roman historian, Livy, tells how Lucretia – the quintessential virtuous wife – killed herself after she was raped by Sextus Tarquinius, the violent son of Lucius Tarquinius Superbus, the tyrant Etruscan King of Rome.[77] Again, this link is suggested visually, for here, as in other sequences in *After Death* and in many other films, Bauer derives inspiration for the staging and lighting of individual shots from the fine arts. Tsivian explores Bauer's use in *After Death* of paintings by the Dutch Renaissance artist Jan Vermeer;[78] here we see Bauer turning to a second Golden Age artist, namely Rembrandt van Rijn.[79] The shot in which we see Zoia step from behind the curtain out onto the stage just after she has taken poison recalls, in many of its details, two extraordinary portraits of Lucretia painted by Rembrandt towards the end of his life. Both entitled simply *Lucretia*, the portraits represent different moments in the tragedy of Lucretia's suicide. The first, painted in 1664, shows her just before she plunges a dagger into her breast; the second, painted in 1666, depicts the moment just after she has delivered the fatal blow.[80]

Bauer appears to include details from both of these portraits in his filmic portrait of Zoia.[81] From the 1664 *Lucretia* he borrows the pearl necklace and earrings, and from the 1666 portrait, the white gown and the braid that adorns Zoia's waist. Bauer's framing of the actress protagonist also recalls that of both of Rembrandt's portraits. In all three cases the solitary female figure is seen in a medium shot, from just below the waist to above her head, and is set against an ominously dark and featureless background. Zoia's pose and her poise are also reminiscent of those of Rembrandt's Lucretias; dignity and deep sorrow emanate from all three characters. Finally, both Rembrandt and Bauer make use of chiaroscuro (high-contrast lighting), especially on their protagonists' faces, to enhance the intimacy and the psychological expressiveness of their portraits. As Cavendish has noted, this scene demonstrates Bauer's and his cameraman, Boris Zavelev's, sophisticated approach to lighting effects, for the low-angle lighting that illuminates Zoia's face here is not only expressive, but also justified diegetically, by the demands of realism, for this scene is set on stage where she would, of course, be lit by footlights.[82] Art historians have also drawn attention to the 'theatrical' feel of the light in Rembrandt's *Lucretia* portraits, and suggested that these works may in fact depict scenes from a theatre performance; a stage version of Lucretia's tragedy was performed in Amsterdam in the mid-1660s, and Rembrandt often painted works based on scenes from contemporary theatrical performances.[83]

According to Livy, Lucretia intended through her suicide not only to assert her innocence but also to galvanise her family into acting against the man who had raped her: before stabbing herself in the presence of her father and husband, who both insisted she had no cause to die, Lucretia exacted from them an oath of vengeance. Lucretia's dead body was displayed throughout Rome, and it provided the catalyst needed to incite the Romans to rise up against the royal family and drive them out of the city, which resulted in the monarchy being replaced by the new Roman Republic.

The details of this intertextual reference remind the viewer of the socio-political context of Bauer's film – the final, chaotic years of the Tsarist regime – that Bauer stresses by 'modernising' Turgenev's story and locating the action of his film in the early twentieth-century present. Seen in this context Zoia's suicide is transformed into a strikingly contemporary act for, as is now well-documented, in Russia in the early years of the twentieth century suicide reached epidemic proportions.[84] The historian Susan Morrissey has demonstrated that the reasons for this so-called suicide epidemic were many, varied and frequently contradictory; nonetheless, she states that in Russia at the start of the twentieth century 'epidemic suicide was primarily understood as a symptom of a disease within the social body'.[85] As in so many of his films, then, Bauer here provides a bleak commentary on the social position of women and the state of gender relations in Russia in the late Imperial age.

Reviving Kadmina and updating her legend: the creation of a cinematic heroine

> Film gives back to the dead a semblance of life, a fragile semblance but one immediately strengthened by the wishful thinking of the viewer.
>
> Christian Metz.[86]

Doubtless, then, the intriguing figure of the actress heroine attracted Bauer to the Kadmina legend; with only a little updating, she makes a striking addition to his gallery of New Women. There are other features of this nineteenth-century literary legend, and of Turgenev's Kadmina text in particular, that might have engaged Bauer's interest, however.

I stated previously that none of the nineteenth-century literary works on the Kadmina theme uncovers the face of the woman behind the actress's 'cultural mask'. If they do not do this, it is in part because their interests lie elsewhere. As Buckler has commented: 'Most of these works are as much about the process by which stories are spun around an event like Kadmina's suicide as they are about Kadmina herself'.[87] For Buckler, the legend's real subject is, therefore, 'the literary imagination'[88] and, as she persuasively demonstrates, these comments are especially pertinent to Turgenev's approach to the Kadmina legend in 'Klara Milich'.[89]

Perhaps, then, this is a further reason why Bauer was drawn to transpose the legend of this nineteenth-century woman to the screen and to do so specifically through the prism of Turgenev's text. For, as Turgenev's story can be read as a text about the creation of literary images and verbal representations, so Bauer's film can be interpreted as a manifesto for the innovative and expressive representational power of the visual medium of cinema; indeed, recent critical discussions of this film invariably highlight its technical innovativeness.[90]

Privileging the cinematic

It thus becomes clear that the close-up sequence discussed previously is not only of central importance to Bauer's representation of his female protagonist. It is also revealing of his wider artistic concerns in *After Death*. Bauer's experimentation in this sequence with new ways of expressing a character's psychology – through a brief extreme close-up rather than the conventional lengthy 'full' scene – has been discussed. Moreover, as Tsivian notes in his discussion of the reception of narrative devices in early Russian cinema: 'the semantic gesture of discursive figure enlargement could be conveyed in three different ways: by the cut-in; by bringing the camera closer to the character; and by bringing the character nearer to the camera.'[91] As we have seen, the close-up sequence of Zoia demonstrates all three of these techniques. It thus seems to stand as a compendium of novel cinematic devices. Moreover, in the same way that this sequence functions literally to remove Zoia from her theatrical setting by cutting from the frame all the objects that site her on stage in a theatre, so it does this metaphorically: the close-up and the track-in were two of the key devices through which cinema freed itself from the theatrical conventions that had shaped its aesthetics in its early years. The novelty and power restored by this sequence to the long-standing theatrical convention of moving a character downstage has also been discussed. In addition to encouraging the viewer to see Zoia as a sympathetic, unconventional individual, this sequence also, therefore, emphasises her as a *cinematic* heroine. As such Zoia belongs very much to the twentieth century. She is a new icon for a new modern age: the film star.

In this respect, the key to Bauer's representation of his female protagonist is the one attribute none of her literary or theatrical predecessors could possess: endlessly repeatable visible movement. In this close-up sequence, the actress moves towards the camera and, throughout the film, she is perpetually in motion. Invariably, it is motion forwards, motion from the background to the foreground. At the princess's soirée, the location of Zoia's first appearance on screen, she walks from behind a drape out into the ballroom; at her recital she emerges from behind the thick curtains that hang at the back of the stage and walks to the front of the stage; when she arrives at the park for her rendezvous with Andrei she walks though the imposing gates seen in the very background of the frame and moves towards the foreground where Andrei awaits her. Indeed, Zoia continues to move in this way even after her death. She appears in Andrei's dreams walking towards him through a cornfield, and when she subsequently appears in his bedroom as a 'vision' she invariably moves from the back to the front of the frame. This type of movement serves not only to foreground Zoia as the film's central character, but also to characterise her as a dynamic, passionate and active figure. Moreover, as we have seen throughout this study, in early Russian cinema such high precision 'blocking' was an important 'tool of expressivity [...] an article of both necessity and pride, as clear a token of the film medium as montage would become for the next decade'.[92] Again, then, we see Bauer emphasising the cinematic specificity of his representation of his heroine.

It thus becomes clear that Bauer's choice of Turgenev's text as a way into the Kadmina legend is of fundamental importance for both his representation of his female protagonist and his wider artistic and thematic concerns. For, unlike nearly all the other nineteenth-century literary responses to Kadmina's death, Turgenev's text does not end with the actress's suicide. Instead, both story and film continue, showing how the actress's death affects the male protagonist and thereby detailing not only the male protagonist's weakness, but especially the female protagonist's power and vitality. Paradoxically, even when she is 'dead', Zoia appears more dynamic than the emotionally paralysed Andrei. Bauer conveys this not only through the way he has Zoia move within the frame, but also through declining to use semi-transparent superimposed images to represent her after her death; they would make Zoia appear spectral, but also outdated for, as Tsivian notes, by the mid-1910s such 'trick' shots were already considered old hat, 'the novelty of the previous decade'.[93] Bauer's sense of humour is also in evidence in these sequences: Zoia is a less ghostly presence than the

increasingly comic figure of Andrei's fussy aunt who, dressed like a prototypical ghost in a white nightgown and cap, obsessively scurries to her
ailing nephew's bedroom to check on him while he sleeps.

Thus, in a sense, Bauer's twentieth-century heroine is able to transcend
her suicide. By repeatedly animating Andrei's after-death dreams and
visions of Zoia, Bauer shows that he has the power endlessly to resurrect
his heroine as a dynamic human figure, for '[c]inema makes absence presence'.[94] Bauer thus succeeds where his male protagonist fails. Despite all
Andrei's efforts, his photograph of Zoia remains an inert image, for the
paradox of the photographic image is that, in Roland Barthes's words,
it 'produces Death while trying to preserve life'.[95] Bauer's film, however,
breathes new life and new motion into his actress protagonist. It also demonstrates – to use Nina Auerbach's words, cited at the head of this chapter –
'the permanent vitality of myth'.[96]

In these ways, then, Bauer brings Turgenev's story and the nineteenth-century legend of Evlaliia Kadmina into the twentieth century.
Zoia is a heroine whose representation depends on Bauer's use of devices
that were, in the context of Russia in the mid-1910s, novel, innovative
and specifically cinematic; in this way she moves beyond her nineteenth-
century predecessors, and Bauer also advances cinema's dialogue with
its artistic heritage. *After Death* can therefore be seen as Bauer's call both
for the twentieth-century woman to be seen on her own terms, and for
his twentieth-century art form, cinema, to be seen as an artistic medium
in its own right, distinct from literature, theatre and still photography,
with its own specific concerns and its own dynamic aesthetics. In May
1915, the Russian theatre director Vsevolod Meyerhold had concluded
an article on cinema with the following assessment: 'It is still too early to
say whether cinema will be an independent art or subsidiary to theatre'.[97]
Released just seven months after the publication of this article, Bauer's
film seems to exist in order to prove, once and for all, the complete independence of this remarkable new art form.

Conclusion

In his notes on Romashkov's *Stenka Razin*, prepared for its screening at the 1989 Pordenone retrospective, Carlo Montanaro suggests that this first Russian feature film is 'almost prophetic as far as the final sacrifice of the first innocent heroine is concerned'.[1] Perhaps more significant than the ultimate fate of the female protagonist, however, is the way in which this first Russian feature film concurrently signals both the weakness and the power of its only female protagonist: by casting her as a performer. For, as we have seen, when the Persian princess steps forward and begins her exotic, veiled dance, she becomes the first in a long line of female performer protagonists. The preceding chapters have examined some of the ways in which this ubiquitous female figure was exploited in the cinema of late Imperial Russia. Some general conclusions can now be made about why and how this figure was used by so many early Russian film-makers.

Performing femininity in an age of social change: the female performer as New Woman

A reviewer writing in *Pegasus* in 1915 commented that Russian films of this period offer the viewer 'a magic mirror in which [...] life in all its variety is reflected'.[2] To be sure, the use of the female performer was in part motivated by the film-makers' desire to create a realistic picture of contemporary Russian society; at the start of the twentieth century an increasing number of Russian women were carving out careers in different branches of the performing arts, one of the few spheres in which they were able to pursue a public profession that afforded them socially sanctioned visibility and gave them the opportunity to acquire financial independence. The female performer was thus a useful tool for ensuring verisimilitude and, indeed, this figure is exploited as a marker of contemporary social reality in numerous films from this period.

For early Russian film-makers, working in an era of rapid social change in which the static, rigidly defined gender roles of the past had been flung into a state of flux and uncertainty, the usefulness of this persona extended far beyond the literal and the *vraisemblable*, however. The figure of the female performer enabled them to explore in depth the complex ways in which conceptions of women and femininity were changing in early twentieth-century Russian society, for by its very nature this persona made it possible for them to cast their female protagonists in different roles, from the conventional to the unconventional, and to observe their progress through the contemporary world.

It is striking that most of the films discussed in this monograph use the relationship between the female performer and the male protagonist to suggest that the greatest obstacle to the early twentieth-century Russian woman's acquisition of independence is the early twentieth-century Russian male and, specifically, his deep-rooted and outdated attitudes to women. From the earliest Russian feature films made in the late 1900s to the sophisticated urban melodramas of the mid- to late 1910s, Russian film-makers used the figure of the female performer to reveal the male tendency to perceive women as commodities, to treat them as sexual objects and to assume that they exist to satisfy the various desires of men. However, while in Romashkov's *Stenka Razin* it is impossible to separate the reactionary views of the male protagonists from those of the male film-makers, later films – starting with Siversen's *Drama in a Gypsy Camp Near Moscow*, released just two months after *Stenka Razin* – offered less one-sided and misogynous representations of the female performer. As the 1910s progressed, Russian film-makers would devise increasingly sophisticated cinematic techniques in order to distance themselves from the points of view of their patriarchal male voyeurs, and they also began to be more direct in their condemnation. While Razin ends Romashkov's film a triumphant and patriotic hero, subsequent film-makers did not present their male protagonists so positively, but represented them either as loathsome sexual predators or as naïve, idealistic fantasists. All of them are shown to find the female performer attractive, but threatening in equal measure.

Similarly, while the earliest Russian film-makers typically used the figure of the female performer primarily in order to characterise their male protagonists and had little or no interest either in exploring her psychology or in representing her narrative perspective, from about 1910 this began to change. For, as the film-makers distanced themselves from the point of view of their male protagonists, so they became more interested in exploring the female perspective. The initial traces of an interest in the female protagonist's inner self are visible in Chardynin's *Vadim*, in which several sequences are set in Olga's bedroom, a space that, along with the performer's dressing room, would emerge as a privileged locus of female subjectivity as the decade progressed. The 1912 film *The Incestuous Father-in-Law* continued the development of this tendency and, from about 1913, the female narrative perspective would be almost entirely dominant.

The year 1912 is an important transitional year in other ways. Like the performer heroines of earlier films, Lusha, the protagonist of *The Incestuous Father-in-Law*, is an amateur dancer. Unlike them, however, Lusha takes great pleasure in dancing; it is a way to relax after a hard day's work and an outlet for the energy and *joie de vivre* that she displays in some of the film's earliest sequences. Nobody forces her to perform; she does so willingly. In this way, *The Incestuous Father-in-Law* prefigures one of the most striking changes in the way in which the female performer is represented in Russian films after 1912: the shift from the amateur performer to the professional. Bauer's *Twilight of a Woman's Soul* is the earliest extant film to feature a professional urban performer; in the years that followed, Russian film-makers invariably cast their performer heroines in this way. Thus, from 1913 it is the women themselves who choose to perform, and they usually do so in public, on a stage, before a paying audience. Their status as women who have made a career from this activity suggests that these later performers have acquired something that their amateur predecessors did not possess: a certain independence, a measure of autonomy

206

and a greater strength of purpose and of character. From 1913, therefore, the female performer would come to be seen, more than ever, as a challenging figure – in brief, as a so-called New Woman. As such, after 1912 this figure would enable Russian film-makers to explore the emergence of a new, twentieth-century female subjectivity.

Frequently, Russian film-makers would emphasise the new sense of self of their New Women protagonists by contrasting the 'real' woman – that is, the confident, independent, self-sufficient modern woman, the woman behind the performer's 'cultural mask' – with the feminine roles she enacted on stage. Invariably rooted in nineteenth-century art and culture, the roles that these twentieth-century women are shown performing include: mythic archetypes of fatal femininity (such as Salome, Cleopatra, the Carmen-esque Gypsy and the *rusalka*); the flawed and/or doomed heroines of the nineteenth-century literary, operatic and balletic traditions; and such idealised and saintly nineteenth-century roles as Aleksandr Pushkin's Tatiana. A few female performers are shown to express their new identities more emphatically, however, rejecting nineteenth-century roles in favour of new personae. Thus, Mary in Bauer's *Child of the Big City* casts herself as a *tangistka* and, following the example of Verbitskaia's Mania Eltsova, the dancer protagonists in Chardynin's *Chrysanthemums* and Bauer's *Iurii Nagornyi* both shun classical ballet in favour of early modern dance, the New Woman's art form.

Again, the male protagonists' responses to these professional performers are revealing. Too weak to face up to the challenges of the twentieth-century present, they typically insist on ignoring the 'real' woman with whom they are involved and instead relate to the female performers as though they were the nineteenth-century characters they embody on stage, seeking refuge from the new social realities of the young twentieth century by attempting to live in the familiar and comforting world of the nineteenth-century past. Thus, the male protagonists are shown to be 'out of joint' with the female performers. This clash of sensibilities sets in motion the dramatic action and tragic dénouements of these films.

Frequently, as in *Stenka Razin*, *Vadim*, *The Incestuous Father-in-Law*, Bauer's *Daydreams* and his *The Dying Swan*, the female performer suffers at the hands of the male protagonist, who resorts to violence, to rape or to murder, in an attempt to assert his control over the mind and the body of the woman with whom he is involved. Some female performers take matters into their own hands, however, turning to suicide in order to rebel against the men's patriarchal assumptions: Lusha, in *The Incestuous Father-in-Law*, kills herself in order to deny her father-in-law the pleasure of her body, while the suicides of Vera in *Chrysanthemums*, Elena in *A Ballerina's Romance* and Zoia in *After Death* can all be seen as acts of protest against the social inequalities that grant men the freedom to live as they choose and deny it to women. Other performers end the films alive and well, however, such as Olga in *Vadim*, Vera in *Twilight of a Woman's Soul*, Mary in *Child of the Big City*, Lidiia in *Children of the Age*, Lola in *The Love of a Councillor of State* and the Duncan-esque dancer in *Iurii Nagornyi*. In these films it is the male protagonist who suffers: while Chardynin's State Councillor simply experiences social humiliation, Bauer's Dolskii in *Twilight of a Woman's Soul*, his Viktor in *Child of the Big City* and the husband in *Children of the Age* all resort to shooting themselves, while the eponymous Iurii Nagornyi ends the film in a hospital bed, his handsome features maimed beyond recognition.

Thus these film-makers do not propose simple solutions to the problems encountered by the female performers. While some early Russian films subvert the melodramatic stereotypes that make women the victims of their patriarchal male counterparts, the female protagonists are still victims as often as, if not more often than, they are victors. There are therefore no clear winners, and the overriding impression created by the films considered in this study is that of a society riven by gender anxieties, in which the social problems created by modernity and changing gender roles are far from being resolved.

Performing femininity: the female performer as the embodiment of a theoretical idea

The figure of the female performer also enabled Russian film-makers to explore the broader, more timeless question of what it means to be, or to become, a woman. The most complex and ambitious films that cast their female protagonists as performers propose an idea that theorists, psychoanalysts and thinkers would not express formally in their writing until many years later, namely the view that gender is not determined by immutable, innate biological facts, but is instead a set of learnt behaviours, a social construct. Thus, they were able to demonstrate that, as Judith Butler puts it, '*gender* is not a noun, [...] gender is always a doing [emphasis in original]'.[3] In other words, 'gender proves to be performative [...] identity is performatively constituted'.[4]

As we have seen, Bauer's significantly titled *Twilight of a Woman's Soul* stands as the most sophisticated and in-depth exploration of this idea. His *Child of the Big City* also touches on it, as do other films that feature the figure of the female performer both by him and by other directors. However, the conviction that one's gender identity is constructed 'performatively', through the reiterated 'performance' of a certain mode, or modes, of behaviour, is so fundamental to Bauer's understanding that it colours the representations of all his female protagonists; those who are not cast as performers within the films' diegesis are therefore also shown by Bauer to construct their identities 'performatively', by trying on various social roles and trying out different modes of being and behaving.

It is significant, however, that unlike the female protagonists who are cast as literal performers, those who are not performers are typically shown to continue to construct their identities around the out-moded ideals of femininity revered by their patriarchal male counterparts. Thus, the little girl in Bauer's *First Love* [Pervaia liubov´, 1915], for example, is shown performing one possible version of femininity when she sneaks into her mother's bedroom and preens before her dressing table mirror, mimicking the 'feminine' gestures and poses that she has, in the previous sequence and, no doubt, on countless other occasions, watched her mother perform. Similarly, as she attempts to develop an erotic identity, Nata in *A Life for a Life* strives to adopt a mode of feminine behaviour that conforms to the ideal favoured by the man with whom she is in love, Prince Bartinskii. 'Do you believe in reincarnation?' he asks her, and his whispered fantasy about their love affair in a previous age is followed by an extravagant re-enactment of that fantasy, which transports them back in time to the classical world, where the toga-clad prince watches as Nata, dressed in long robes, drapes herself languorously over an exedra in a beautiful bower. It is an image that Nata remembers and, when she later prepares for a clandestine liaison with her lover, she dresses to please in a long white nightgown that recalls the robes she wore during the reincarnation sequence.[5] Li, the young female protagonist in Bauer's *In Pursuit of Happiness*, rehearses similar versions of femininity. Overcome by love for her surrogate father, Gzhatskii, she acts out the roles of both the classical and the romantic heroine: on holiday in Crimea she reclines in solitude by the sea, an Aphrodite born from the foam, an unfettered Andromeda awaiting her Perseus; later, posing in a secluded bower, she rejects the advances of her admirer Enrico (played by Lev Kuleshov) with the theatrical declaration: 'I am not free to love you. I have given my heart to Dmitrii Sergeevich Gzhatskii!' Predictably, like Musia in *A Life for a Life*, Li also tells her mother that, if her love for Gzhatskii remains unrequited, she will die.

This contrast again reminds us, therefore, that early Russian directors invariably used the figure of the professional performer in order to indicate that their female protagonist had become, or at least aspired to become, a New Woman.

Performing femininity in an age of artistic change: the female performer as cinematic heroine

If the portraits of women created by early Russian film-makers were new, however, so were the means of expression through which they constructed them. The early Russian film-makers' explorations of cinematic technology and their attempts to develop a specifically cinematic language through which to express their themes and to portray their protagonists were bound up with their representations of the figure of the female performer, to an extraordinary degree. Indeed, in the works of the greatest early Russian directors these two undertakings were inextricably linked. In tracing the development of the representation of the female performer this study has therefore also traced the early film-makers' development of a specifically cinematic language.

As we saw in Chapter 1, even the first filmic representation of a female performer, in Romashkov's *Stenka Razin*, is constructed 'cinematically'. In the years that followed, the specifically cinematic expressive devices employed by Romashkov and his collaborators – blocking, framing and the use of the mobile camera – would be seized upon and explored, developed and refined by other directors. For, as the 1910s progressed, so the ambition and sophistication of early Russian film-makers increased. Their understanding of the myriad expressive possibilities offered by cinematic technology grew and, as they began to exploit and explore these possibilities in their films, they were able to tell their protagonists' stories and examine their central thematic concerns in greater detail and with increasing complexity.

In particular, Bauer's *Child of the Big City* evidences how far the Russian film industry had advanced in the five and a half years since the release of the first Russian feature film. In this sophisticated film, the specifically cinematic devices, which in 1908 had been employed hesitantly by Drankov and his collaborators, are used confidently and deliberately, enabling Bauer to demonstrate that cinema is capable both of freeing itself from the theatrical traditions it had relied on in its earliest days and of developing its own unique means of artistic expression. Bauer's cinematic innovations in the use of such shots as the track-in and the close-up also made it possible for him to effect his analysis of his protagonists and his themes in greater depth and with greater sophistication, and he continued to develop his art in all his subsequent films.

Finally, then, these early film-makers also saw the figure of the female performer as a useful medium through which to express and explore their new art. After all, a performer demands to be looked at, and cinema – especially silent cinema – is all about looking. Thus, although there are no film actresses among the numerous female performers we encounter in these films, they all, nonetheless, emerge as cinematic heroines. For, in the same way that these New Women reject the nineteenth-century literary, theatrical, social and cultural values that the male protagonists attempt to impose on them, so these film-makers also cast off many of the concerns and the tactics of earlier art forms. In the same way that these women assert their twentieth-century sensibilities, so these twentieth-century artists stress that they are working in a new artistic medium, distinct from literature, theatre and still photography, with its own specific concerns and its own dynamic aesthetics. The remarkable extreme close-up of Vera Karalli in Bauer's *After Death* is perhaps the best illustration of this conviction. We recall that when the viewer looks into Zoia's eyes in this shot, what s/he

211

sees is the reflection of the two arc lights that the cameraman Boris Zavelev used to illuminate this portrait. In this way, this iconic close-up forces the viewer to look beyond Bauer's character and to contemplate also the actress who here represents her, the film star Vera Karalli. As Philip Cavendish notes, what we witness in this extraordinary shot is the beginning of pre-Revolutionary Russian cinema's star system.[6]

A new symbolic value: the female performer as an emblem of the pre-Revolutionary film industry

Ultimately, however, the importance of the figure of the female performer to early Russian cinema is suggested by the fact that, on the eve of the collapse of the industry that had made her its own, this capacious archetype was accorded a new symbolic value by the veteran director Petr Chardynin, in his two-part drama *Still, Sadness... Still...* (*A Tale of Precious Love*, 1918).[7] Produced at Dmitrii Kharitonov's Moscow studio and billed as a 'jubilee picture' [*iubileinaia kartina*], commemorating the tenth anniversary of the start of Chardynin's cinematic career, this film was conceived on a grand scale. Chardynin began working on it in late January 1918, but it would be four months before it was finished, an unprecedented length of time in an industry that typically produced films in a few weeks. Chardynin himself wrote the film's original scenario, basing it loosely on motifs from the popular romance that gave both parts of the film their titles, and he assembled a team of experienced film-makers to help him realise it: Czesław Sabiński and Viacheslav Viskovskii as co-directors, Vladimir Siversen as cinematographer and Aleksei Utkin as artistic director. Chardynin also brought together the most popular actors of the period; indeed, he had specific actors in mind when he wrote the scenario and tailored each role to showcase their talents. Vera Kholodnaia, the 'Queen' of the pre-Revolutionary screen, was cast in the lead role of Pola (another foreign name), and Chardynin surrounded her with the 'Kings' of the screen: Vitold Polonskii, Vladimir Maksimov, Osip Runich, Ivan Khudoleev and Konstantin Khokhlov; Chardynin himself also took an acting role.

While the individual details of the film's diegesis create a vast world that defies brief summation, its plot can be reduced to a series of episodes that, despite being linked to form a coherent whole, are also complete in themselves. Moreover, as Zorkaia has noted, each episode follows the same broad schematic pattern, with minor variations, for the film follows the ill-fated attempts of its young female performer to find happiness and security – with each of the film's male protagonists in turn.[8]

Thus the film's first episode introduces us to the beautiful circus performer, Pola (Kholodnaia), who is married to Lorio (Chardynin), the clown-acrobat whom she also partners in the ring. A heavy drinker, Lorio falls during a performance, injuring himself so badly that he has to leave the circus. Pola remains faithful to Lorio, rebuffing the advances of their fellow artist, the Svengaliesque hypnotist and illusionist, Olekso Presnich (Khokhlov), who promises her both love and fame. The couple eke out a meagre existence as street performers, until they are invited to perform at a bachelor party by a group of rich businessmen who have noticed Pola performing in the street and are impressed by her beauty. The men ply Lorio with wine and his weakness for alcohol enables Prakhov (Khudoleev) to begin his campaign to woo Pola. Although Pola initially rejects his advances, poverty eventually takes its toll and she moves in with him, informing Lorio by letter that she has gone for good.

Episode two shows Pola quickly adapting to her new life of luxury as Prakhov's kept woman. She soon begins to feel stifled by the older man's stolidity and his view of her as his possession, however, and tensions come to a head during an outing to see Gypsy performers, when Pola tries to perform with them for the assembled men. Prakhov objects violently and puts an end to her performance. When, after the ensuing row, Pola overhears Prakhov offer, only part in jest, to 'sell' her to his friend Telepnev, she runs from the men in outrage, straight into the arms of their friend Zaritskii (Runich).

Episode three: Pola finds some happiness with Zaritskii, but he is an inveterate gambler. Having lost a large sum of money to Telepnev, he persuades the artist Volyntsev (Maksimov) to lend him some of his mother's money, with which he pays off his debts. When he and the unwitting Pola attend a party at Telepnev's house, however, Zaritskii attempts to steal the money back. Telepnev shoots him dead and, on this cliff-hanger, Part One ends.

Although Part Two of the film has not survived, the synopsis published in *Cine-Gazette* enables us to continue the story.[9]

Episode four: Zaritskii's death forces Pola to move in with Telepnev, an unhappy arrangement from the outset. When Telepnev commissions from Volyntsev a portrait of Pola dressed as Salome, artist and model fall in love and, after Telepnev wounds Volyntsev in a duel, Pola leaves him.

Episode five: Volyntsev asks for Pola's hand in marriage, but Presnich returns and informs Volyntsev's mother of Pola's disreputable past. Horrified, Volyntseva persuades Pola to leave her son, so she accompanies Presnich, who has hypnotised her, on a foreign tour.

Episode six: Volyntsev and Lorio join forces to save Pola from Presnich. Volyntseva welcomes her as a daughter-in-law, but too late: exhausted by these trials, Pola dies, with Volyntsev and Lorio by her bedside.

Still, Sadness... Still... was a huge hit with contemporary audiences, soon becoming 'the biggest Russian box-office success'.[10] Contemporary critical responses were less positive, however. In a lengthy review, Veronin (Valentin Turkin) acknowledged that the film was diverting and skilfully produced, before cataloguing its many faults. Highlighting its 'ordinariness', the familiarity of its genre, themes, characters and settings, its overt 'theatricality' and its lack of artistic novelty, Veronin concluded that Chardynin's method had developed little during his ten-year career; the best one could say of this film was that 'it's all old, familiar and – perhaps – dear to the memory. It is well-trodden ground. It's the story of the birth and first conscious steps of film art'.[11] Veronin set the tone for subsequent critical responses. Thus, for Zorkaia, the film is 'like a catalogue, a complete compendium of all the films in which Vera Kholodnaia has previously appeared'.[12] The veracity of this observation cannot be denied, but the film's intertextual network is more extensive than Zorkaia suggests, for each relationship Pola embarks on evokes, in miniature, a relationship that not only Kholodnaia but other actresses of the period had enacted in earlier films, those of both Chardynin and other directors. In casting Pola as a circus performer, for example, Chardynin has Kholodnaia reprise both one of her most popular roles, that of the circus performer Mara Zet from *Forget About the Fire Place, the Flames Have Gone Out...* [Pozabud´ pro kamin, v nem pogasli ogni...*, 1917], and one of her most successful costumes: the most sought-after publicity postcards from this film featured

Kholodnaia wearing a daring circus outfit that anticipated the one that impresses the aristocrats in *Still, Sadness... Still....*[13] Chardynin's depiction of the beginning of Pola's relationship with Prakhov recalls that of Mariia (Kholodnaia) and Lebedev's relationship, as portrayed by Bauer in *Children of the Age*, and its unhappy progress evokes both the relationship between the actress Marianna (Kholodnaia) and the wealthy gentleman (Polonskii) in Chardynin's *Mirages* and that between the dancer Lola (Karalli) and the State Councillor in his earlier *The Love of a Councillor of State*. Pola even shares Lola's love of Gypsy roles (and almost her name), and it is an argument over their desire to continue performing that acts as the catalyst for both Pola and Lola to leave their unhappy relationships. Such parallels can be found for every episode of both parts of the film. Indeed, Chardynin even returns the viewer to the first Russian feature film: Pola, posing as Salome for Volyntsev, resembles the Persian princess from Romashkov's *Stenka Razin*.

Clearly, then, *Still, Sadness... Still...* is firmly rooted in its cinematic heritage. What neither Veronin nor Zorkaia explores in detail, however, is the idea that Chardynin actively and positively intended this hypertrophic intertextuality. Nevertheless, there are numerous reasons for seeing it as a conscious aesthetic programme. This is, after all, Chardynin's anniversary film; it is therefore neither surprising nor inappropriate that he should seek to make it a retrospective summation, or recapitulation, of his career. Indeed, the film is also a generous celebration of the careers and screen personae of the actors Chardynin helped to make stars; under his direction they produce bravura performances, remarkable in their restrained expressivity. The intertextuality might also have been motivated by Chardynin's desire to craft a paean to the Russian film industry, for 1918 was the tenth anniversary not only of Chardynin's career but also of the Russian feature film. Finally, a note of almost ironic self-consciousness also runs through the film. Consider the sequence at Prakhov's party: as Telepnev seizes Pola and kisses her passionately, in full view of the guests, Runich almost steps out of character when, pretending modesty, he holds up a tablecloth to shield the embracing couple not from the guests, who are all standing behind them, but from *the viewer*. A self-referential intertitle then fills the screen: 'In the cinema such scenes end with an iris out'.[14]

The almost obsessive intertextuality of *Still, Sadness... Still...* also confers on the film a valedictory feel, however, and for all its self-conscious celebration the film's overriding atmosphere is, as its title suggests, one of insuperable sorrow. Chardynin embedded the eponymous romance into the film's diegesis, making it Pola and Lorio's theme tune, but it is also an expressive leitmotif.[15] The romance speaks of the sorrow of unrequited love, of life's cruel indifference, of the impossibility of recapturing lost happiness and of the lyric persona's indifference to death. It therefore encapsulates in miniature the atmosphere of nostalgia, melancholy and hopelessness that accumulates as the film progresses. In this connection, the political context of its making is relevant. January 1918 saw not only the start of Chardynin's work on this film, but also the creation of a cinema subsection of the People's Commissariat of Enlightenment [Narodnyi komissariat prosveshcheniia (Narkompros)].[16] This must have been seen as a clear sign that the Russian film industry would not remain in private hands and that the days of artistic freedom were numbered.

Still, Sadness... Still... is therefore much more than a tired rehash of earlier films. Kholodnaia, for most commentators the film's 'centre and focus',[17] embodies the sorrow that weighs Pola down, and in this way both she and the character she plays – one of the last performer heroines of Russian film – also become prescient symbols of the death of the film industry over which Kholodnaia and this archetypal figure had both reigned. Indeed, Veronin described her protagonist in precisely these terms, noting: 'The only novelty [in this film] is the fact that for the first time, I think, Mme Kholodnaia has been turned into a skeleton, reminding us of the end that awaits us all and of the ephemeral nature of all beauty'.[18]

Indeed, shortly after its release, this haunting film, often described as the 'swan song' of the pre-Revolutionary film industry, would be pronounced the quintessential example of the vulgarity [*poshlost´*] and petty bourgeois nature [*meshchanstvo*] of pre-Revolutionary art.[19] It, and others like it, would be removed from the screen and consigned to the cupboards of *Gosfilmofond of Russia*, where they would remain forgotten for almost seventy years.

Coda

Beyond 1918: reversing pre-Revolutionary gender roles

As this monograph began by examining the first Russian feature film, so it will conclude by considering one of the last films made before the dismantlement of the pre-Revolutionary film industry industry, namely Komissarzhevskii and Chaikovskii's *The Stage Set of Happiness*. Released in the second half of 1918, that is ten years after Romashkov's captive Persian princess first stepped onto an oriental carpet and performed an exotic dance for the pleasure of her captors, this film stands out as a striking anomaly in the cinema of the late Imperial age. It is the exception that proves the rule, the only early Russian film with performer protagonists that shuns the typical gender roles of woman as performer and man as observer. For in this film this gender dichotomy is reversed. Thus it tells the story of Enrico, a talented and handsome dancer who earns only a meagre living performing in the street. Enrico's luck appears to change, however, when his performance and his physique catch the eye of an enigmatic countess (played by Emma Bauer). She gives him money for ballet lessons and in time Enrico becomes a famous ballet dancer. Excited by his fame, the countess has her menservants abduct Enrico. Blindfolded and captive, the dancer is driven to the countess's castle, where she seduces him. Enrico falls in love with his benefactress, but she has accepted the marriage proposal of a man from her own class and sees Enrico merely as an amusing plaything. Accordingly, she soon tires of him and, when Enrico is wrongly accused of murdering her fiancé, she refuses to provide him with an alibi, even though they had spent the night of the murder together. Enrico is wrongly found guilty of this crime and sent to prison; in the film's closing sequence he attempts to escape, but he is fired on by the prison guards and dies in the arms of his loyal sister.

Whether this telling reversal of the typical gender roles of pre-Revolutionary Russian film would have become more widespread will never be known. As the 1910s came to a close, the social concerns and gender conflicts explored by early Russian film-makers were swept to one side by more pressing and dramatic socio-political events: by Revolution. On 27 August 1919, Lenin signed a decree ordering the nationalisation of the film industry and in September of the same year the State School of Cinematic Arts [Gosudarstvennnaia shkola kinematograficheskikh iskusstv] was founded in order to train a new generation of Soviet film-makers who would make Soviet films. And thus, the New Woman of late Imperial Russian cinema was gradually replaced by a new model heroine: the New Soviet Woman.

And yet, the memory of at least one pre-Revolutionary female performer did survive on the Soviet screen, albeit in the most idiosyncratic of ways, thanks to a renegade accompanist in a Moscow cinema who would play, at any opportunity, Pola's haunting and mournful signature tune: thus, as an exasperated journalist commented in the Soviet film journal *Cinema* [Kino] in 1928: 'My eyes see on the screen a Red Army parade, but my ears hear from the piano: *Still, Sadness... Still...*'.[1]

Notes

Introduction

1 Reproduced in V. Ivanova, V. Myl'nikova, S. Skovorodnikova, Iu. Tsiv'ian and R. Iangirov (eds), *Velikii kinemo. Katalog sokhranivshikhsia igrovykh fil'mov Rossii, 1908–1919* (Moscow, 2002), p. 384. Translations from Russian are my own, unless otherwise indicated.

2 Veniamin Vishnevskii, *Khudozhestvennye fil'my dorevoliutsionnoi Rossii: fil'mograficheskoe opisanie* (Moscow, 1945).

3 Jay Leyda, *Kino. A History of Russian and Soviet Film* [1960] (Princeton, NJ, 1983).

4 Paolo Cherchi Usai, Lorenzo Codelli, Carlo Montanaro and David Robinson (eds), *Silent Witnesses. Russian Films 1908–1919*, research and co-ordination by Yuri Tsivian (London, 1989), p. 14.

5 Romil Sobolev, *Liudi i fil'my russkogo dorevoliutsionnogo kino* (Moscow, 1961).

6 Semen Ginzburg, *Kinematografiia dorevoliutsionnoi Rossii* [1963] (Moscow, 2007).

7 Georges Sadoul, *Histoire générale du cinéma. Tome III. Le cinéma devient un art – L'Avant-guerre* (Paris, 1950–1975).

8 Cherchi Usai, *Silent Witnesses*, p. 10.

9 Jean Mitry, *Histoire du cinéma. Art et industrie. Volume 1, 1895–1914* (Paris, 1967).

10 Cited in Cherchi Usai, *Silent Witnesses*, p. 10.

11 Cited ibid., p. 12.

12 Ivanova, *Velikii kinemo*.

13 Heide Schlüpmann, 'From patriarchal violence to the aesthetics of death: Russian cinema 1900–1919', *Cinefocus*, 2, 1992, 2, pp. 2–9.

14 Miriam Hansen, 'Deadly scenarios: narrative perspective and sexual politics in pre-Revolutionary Russian film', *Cinefocus*, 2, 1992, 2, pp. 10–19.

15 Richard Stites, 'Dusky images of Tsarist Russia: prerevolutionary cinema', *Russian Review*, 53, 1994, 2, pp. 285–95 (p. 294).

16 Denise J. Youngblood, *The Magic Mirror. Moviemaking in Russia, 1908–1918* (Madison, WI and London, 1999), p. 15.

17 Louise McReynolds, 'Demanding men, desiring women and social collapse in the films of Evgenii Bauer, 1913–17', *Studies in Russian and Soviet Cinema*, 3, 2009, 2, pp. 145–56.

18 Philip Cavendish, 'The hand that turns the handle: camera operators and the poetics of the camera in pre-Revolutionary Russian film', *Slavonic and East European Review*, 82, 2004, 2, pp. 201–45.

19 Natascha Drubek, *Russisches Licht. Von der Ikone zum frühen sowjetischen Kino* (Cologne, 2012).

20 Alyssa DeBlasio, 'Choreographing space, time, and *dikovinki* in the films of Evgenii Bauer', *The Russian Review*, 66, 2007, pp. 671–92.

21 Cited in T. Nikol'skaia, 'A. Blok o zhenskom tvorchestve', *Uchenye zapiski Tartuskogo gosudarstvennogo universiteta*, no. 881, *Blokovskii sbornik*, no. 10, Tartu, 1990, pp. 32–40 (p. 34).

22 Rachel Morley, 'Gender relations in the films of Evgenii Bauer', *Slavonic and East European Review*, 81, 2003, 1, pp. 32–69.

23 Catherine M. Schuler, *Women in Russian Theatre: The Actress in the Silver Age* (London and New York, 1996), p. 19.

24 Schuler shows that such personality cults were focused almost exclusively on female performers and that the theatre-going public remained largely indifferent to male performers as personalities. Ibid., pp. 20–25.

25 Louise McReynolds, *Russia at Play. Leisure Activities at the End of the Tsarist Era* (Ithaca, NY and London, 2003), p. 46.

1. The Oriental Dancer

1 Cited in Eduard Arnol'di, 'Pervenets russkoi kinematografii (k piatidesiatiletiiu vykhoda pervogo russkogo khudozhestvennogo fil'ma)', *Neva*, 1958, 12, pp. 195–99 (p. 197).

2 Aleksandr Pozdniakov, 'Nachalo. «Sten'ka Razin» («Ponizovaia vol'nitsa»), rezhisser Vladimir Romashkov', *Iskusstvo kino*, 2008, 11, pp. 5–7 (p. 5).

3 This film remained uncompleted, because at the last moment the actor cast as Godunov refused to be filmed. See Yuri Tsivian, 'Early Russian cinema: some observations' in Richard Taylor and Ian Christie (eds), *Inside the Film Factory. New Approaches to Russian and Soviet Cinema* (London and New York, 1991), pp. 7–30 (pp. 12–13 and pp. 19–24).

4 Cited in Romil Sobolev, *Liudi i fil'my russkogo dorevoliutsionnogo kino* (Moscow, 1961), p. 14.

5 Goncharov's involvement with Drankov's film was partial and complex. As Rashit Iangirov has documented, Goncharov did not intend his scenario to be made into a feature film to be released by Drankov's production company. Instead, he had conceived it as an innovative one-act stage drama that would combine theatre with film in the opening and closing scenes. Lacking the experience to

produce the filmed sequences, Goncharov engaged Drankov to do so. Drankov went behind his back, however, secretly filming the entire scenario and premiering the resulting film, *Sten´ka Razin*, in both capitals the day before Goncharov's play premiered in Moscow. Goncharov never worked with Drankov again. See Rashit Iangirov, 'Talking movie or silent theater? Creative experiments by Vasily Goncharov' in Richard Abel and Rick Altman (eds), *The Sounds of Early Cinema* (Bloomington and Indianapolis, IN, 2001), pp. 110–17 (p. 112).

6 Philip Cavendish, 'The hand that turns the handle: camera operators and the poetics of the camera in pre-Revolutionary Russian film', *Slavonic and East European Review*, 82, 2004, 2, pp. 201–45 (p. 203).

7 *Sten´ka Razin* was distributed with Ippolitov-Ivanov's score, which, cinema owners were advised, could be performed while the film was being screened by chorus, gramophone, piano or orchestra. See Jay Leyda, *Kino. A History of Russian and Soviet Film* (Princeton, NJ, 1983), p. 35. This enables Drankov to claim another 'first' for *Sten´ka Razin*: that of being the first Russian film to have a prescribed musical soundtrack.

8 Cited in B. S. Likhachev, *Kino v Rossii (1896–1926). Materialy k istorii russkogo kino. Chast´ 1. 1896–1913* (Leningrad, 1927), p. 51. For the songs' texts, see James Von Geldern and Louise McReynolds (eds), *Entertaining Tsarist Russia. Tales, Songs, Plays, Movies, Jokes, Ads and Images from Russian Urban Life 1779–1917* (Bloomington and Indianapolis, IN, 1998), pp. 41–44.

9 Leyda, *Kino*, p. 35.

10 Nikolai Anoshchenko, *Iz vospominanii*, publ. Rashit Iangirov, *Minuvshee*, 10 (Moscow, 1992), pp. 358–59.

11 Both reproduced in V. Ivanova *et al.*, (eds), *Velikii kinemo. Katalog sokhranivshikhsia igrovykh fil´mov Rossii, 1908–1919* (Moscow, 2002), p. 23.

12 Reproduced ibid., p. 22.

13 Arnol´di, 'Pervenets russkoi kinematografii', p. 199.

14 Ibid.

15 Leyda, *Kino*, p. 35.

16 Andrei Chernyshev, 'Nachalo. K 80-letiiu «Ponizovoi vol´nitsy»', *Sovetskii ekran*, 1989, 1, p. 11.

17 Anoshchenko, *Iz vospominanii*, p. 359.

18 Peter Kenez, *Cinema and Soviet Society, 1917–1953* (Cambridge, New York and Melbourne, 1992), p. 12.

19 Richard Stites, 'Dusky images of Tsarist Russia: prerevolutionary cinema', *Russian Review*, 53, 1994, 2, pp. 285–95 (p. 288).

20 Denise J. Youngblood, *The Magic Mirror. Moviemaking in Russia, 1908–1918* (Madison, WI and London, 1999), p. 116.

21 Alexander Prokhorov, 'Petr Tochilin: *Khottabych* (2006): in defense of pulp cinema and in memoriam of Aleksandr Drankov' at http://www.kinokultura.com/2007/16r-khottabych.shtml (accessed 7 July 2015).

22 Neia Zorkaia, 'Sten´ka Razin pod Peterburgom' at http://www.portal-slovo.ru/art/35956.php (accessed 16 July 2015).

23 Ibid. The idea that film is distinguished from other visual arts by its unique ability to offer a form of spectatorial experience that is not merely optical, but haptic, has been explored in recent theoretical writings. See in particular Laura U. Marks, *The Skin of the Film: Intercultural Cinema, Embodiment and the Senses* (Durham, NC, 2000) and Laura U. Marks, *Touch: Sensuous Theory and Multisensory Media* (Minneapolis, MN and London, 2002).

24 On these problems, see Tsivian, 'Early Russian cinema', pp. 8–13. On how they informed the making of *Sten´ka Razin*, see Iurii Tsiv´ian, '«Sten´ka Razin» («Ponizovaia vol´nitsa»), Rossiia (1908)', *Iskusstvo kino*, 1988, 7, pp. 93–96.

25 As Arnol´di, Stites and Youngblood have all noted, there is very little history in this so-called 'historical drama'. See Arnol´di, 'Pervenets russkoi kinematografii', p. 197; Stites, 'Dusky Images', p. 288; Youngblood, *The Magic Mirror*, p. 116.

26 Evgeny Dobrenko, *Stalinist Cinema and the Production of History. Museum of the Revolution*, translated by Sarah Young (Edinburgh, 2008), p. 22.

27 Yuri Tsivian, 'New notes on Russian film culture between 1908 and 1919' in Lee Grieveson and Peter Krämer (eds), *The Silent Cinema Reader* (London and New York, 2004), pp. 339–48 (p. 342).

28 Louise McReynolds, 'The silent movie melodrama: Evgenii Bauer fashions the heroine's self' in Laura Engelstein and Stephanie Sandler (eds), *Self and Story in Russian History* (Ithaca, NY and London, 2000), pp. 120–40 (p. 122).

29 To modern viewers, far from appearing 'specifically cinematic', this technique can seem derivatively theatrical. However, cinematic specificity is a moveable concept because each historic period has its own ideas about what constitutes cinema; those held by modern viewers are therefore necessarily different from those held by early Russian film-makers. The numerous examples of the use of blocking that we encounter in films from the 1910s and its increasing refinement by early directors prove how significant this technique was. On blocking as a cinematic means of expression in this period, see Yuri Tsivian, 'Two «stylists» of the teens: Franz Hofer and Yevgenii Bauer' in Thomas Elsaesser (ed.), *A Second Life: German Cinema's First Decades* (Amsterdam, 1996), pp. 264–76.

30 Cavendish, 'The hand that turns the handle', p. 217.

31 In his publicity material, Drankov emphasised that *Sten´ka Razin* had been 'arranged with the participation of at least 100 persons'. Cited in Leyda, *Kino*, p. 34. According to Tsivian, in reality the number was closer to 30. See Tsivian, '«Sten´ka Razin»', p. 94.

32 Ibid.

33 Ibid., p. 95.

34 Neia Zorkaia, 'Motiv persidskoi kniazhny v «Razinskom» lubochnom tsikle i v russkoi literature XIX-XX vekov' in I. E. Danilova (ed.), *Mir narodnoi kartinki: materialy nauchnoi konferentsii "Vipperovskie chteniia - 1997"* (Moscow, 1999), pp. 278–90 (pp. 288–89). On *The Boat* and its links with the legend of Sten´ka Razin, see Elizabeth Warner, *The Russian Folk Theatre* (The Hague, 1977), pp. 127–42.

35 Zorkaia, 'Sten´ka Razin'.

36 Tsiv´ian, '«Sten´ka Razin»', p. 95.

37 Zorkaia, 'Motiv persidskoi kniazhny', p. 288.

38 Laura Mulvey, 'Visual pleasure and narrative cinema' [1975] in Constance Penley (ed.), *Feminism and Film Theory* (London, 1988), pp. 57–68.

39 Ibid., pp. 59–62.

40 Ibid., p. 62.

41 Edward W. Said, *Orientalism. Western Conceptions of the Orient* [1978] (London, 1995), p. 207.

42 Ibid., p. 12.

43 Cited in Julian Graffy, *Bed and Sofa: The Film Companion* (London and New York, 2001), p. 56.

44 Zorkaia considers Razin's murder of the princess to be the legend's key motif. Zorkaia, 'Motiv persidskoi kniazhny', p. 279.

45 Ibid., p. 281.

46 Ibid., p. 279.

47 See the scenario reproduced in Neia Zorkaia (ed.), 'Rimeik', *Ekran i stsena*, 2001, 26, p. 14.

48 As Zorkaia notes, the device of the brigands' letter, which does not feature in the song, provides another example of how *Sten´ka Razin* would influence early Russian film, for in the 1910s the letter would become a common means of advancing a film's narrative. Zorkaia, 'Motiv persidskoi kniazhny', p. 288.

49 Mulvey, 'Visual pleasure', p. 64.

50 Ibid.

51 Ibid.

52 Ibid.

53 Ibid.

54 On the ways in which the film deviates from the text of the song on which it was based, see Arnol´di, 'Pervenets russkoi kinematografii', pp. 197–99.

55 Zorkaia, 'Motiv persidskoi kniazhny', p. 281.

56 Marina Tsvetaeva, *Sobranie sochinenii v semi tomakh*, volume 1, *Stikhotvoreniia*, compiled, prepared for publication and annotated by Anna Saakiants and Lev Mnukhin (Moscow, 1994), p. 344.

57 Ibid., p. 345.

58 Zorkaia, 'Motiv persidskoi kniazhny', p. 282. In this, Tsvetaeva's treatment of Razin differs markedly from that of other contemporary Russian poets, such as Velimir Khlebnikov, Sergei Esenin, Maksimilian Voloshin and Vasilii Kamenskii, who focussed on the historical Razin, the great leader and symbol of popular protest. On Tsvetaeva's treatment of the Razin legend, see Viktoria Schweitser, *Tsvetaeva*, translated from the Russian by Robert Chandler and H. T. Willets, poetry translated by Peter Norman, edited and annotated by Angela Livingstone (London, 1995), pp. 141–43.

59 Oscar Wilde, *Salomé*, translated from the French by Lord Alfred Douglas, in *The Complete Works of Oscar Wilde: Stories, Plays, Poems*, introduced by Vyvyan Holland (London and Glasgow, 1986), pp. 552–75 (p. 553).

60 According to Anthony Pym, 82 per cent of the 388 artistic, literary, theatrical and musical representations of Salome created between 1840 and 1940 date from the years 1880 to 1920. See Anthony Pym, 'The importance of Salomé: approaches to a *fin de siècle* theme', *French Forum*, 14, 1989, 3, pp. 311–22 (pp. 312–13).

61 Larry Hamberlin, 'Visions of Salome: the femme fatale in American popular songs before 1920', *Journal of the American Musicological Society*, 59, 2006, 3, pp. 631–96 (p. 631).

62 Lawrence Kramer, 'Cultural and musical hermeneutics: the Salome complex', *Cambridge Opera Journal*, 2, 1990, 3, pp. 269–94 (p. 271).

63 Ibid.

64 William Tydeman and Steven Price, *Wilde – Salome* (Cambridge, 1996), p. 58. On the Russian cult of Wilde and his influence on Russian literature, see Tat´iana Pavlova, 'Oskar Uail´d v russkoi literature (konets XIX-nachalo XX vv.)' in Iu. D. Levin (ed.), *Na rubezhe XIX i XX vekov. Iz istorii mezhdunarodnykh sviazei russkoi literatury: sbornik nauchnykh trudov* (Leningrad, 1991), pp. 77–128 and Evgenii Bershtein, 'The Russian myth of Oscar Wilde' in Engelstein and Sandler, *Self and Story*, pp. 168–88.

65 As Megan Becker-Leckrone stresses: '*It is Wilde himself who names that dance the "famous" dance of the seven veils. Its appellation simply did not exist in relation to Salome's dance before his play.* [...] The Dance of the Seven Veils – as Salome's dance – is Oscar Wilde's invention [emphasis in original]'. Megan Becker-Leckrone, 'Salome©: the fetishization of a textual corpus', *New Literary History*, 26, 1995, 2, pp. 239–60 (pp. 254–55).

66 These lines come from near the beginning of Wilde's play, which opens with the Young Syrian uttering the words: 'How beautiful is the Princess Salomé tonight!' This exchange is repeated throughout the play, until Salome's repeatedly expressed desire to kiss Jokanaan drives the Young Syrian to kill himself in a desperate, final attempt to secure her attention for himself. His attempt fails, almost comically, for neither Salome nor Jokanaan notices his death, despite

the fact that, as a stage direction indicates: 'He kills himself and falls between Salomé and Jokanaan'. See Wilde, *Salomé*, p. 552 and p. 560.

67 On these attempts to stage Wilde's *Salomé*, see especially Tydeman and Price, *Wilde*, pp. 58–66 and pp. 145–47; Toni Bentley, *Sisters of Salome* (New Haven, CT and London, 2002), pp. 137–40; Olga Matich, 'Gender trouble in the Amazonian kingdom: turn-of the-century representations of women in Russia' in John E. Bowlt and Matthew Drutt (eds), *Amazons of the Avant-Garde: Alexandra Exter, Natalia Goncharova, Liubov Popova, Olga Rozanova, Varvara Stepanova, and Nadezhda Udaltsova* (New York and London, 1999), pp 75–93 (pp. 81–84).

68 Commentators disagree about whether this performance took place. Matich, ibid., p. 82, and Bentley claim that it did not. See Bentley, *Sisters of Salome*, p. 139. However, Charles Mayer, citing Mikhail Fokin's memoirs and Irina Pruzhan's 1975 biography of Leon Bakst, insists that it did. See Charles S. Mayer, 'Ida Rubinstein: a twentieth-century Cleopatra', *Dance Research Journal*, 20, 1988, 2, pp. 33–51 (p. 47, n. 18).

69 The term 'Salomania' was coined in a *New York Times* article that poked fun at the Salome craze: 'The management [at the New Amsterdam theatre] has been exceptionally active in guarding against outbreaks of Salomania among members of the company. As soon as any chorus girl shows the very first symptoms of the disease she is at once enveloped in a fur coat – the most efficacious safeguard known against the Salome dance – and hurriedly isolated'. See 'The call of Salome: rumours that Salomania will have a free hand this season', *New York Times Magazine*, 16 August 1908, p. 4 at http://query.nytimes.com/mem/archive-free/pdf?res=9F0CEFD81631E233A25755C1A96E9C946997D6CF (accessed 10 January 2016).

70 Cited in Elaine Showalter, *Sexual Anarchy. Gender and Culture at the Fin de Siècle* (London, 1991), p. 159.

71 Bentley, *Sisters of Salome*, p. 32.

72 Wilde, *Salomé*, p. 570.

73 Some historians of the Salome dance have discerned distinct national differences among them. For an outline of critical works that identify the differences between German, French and British versions of Salome, see Hamberlin, 'Visions of Salome', p. 632, n. 3. Hamberlin himself demonstrates how early twentieth-century American musical versions of the Salome text differed from those produced in Europe.

74 A theatrical satire entitled *Salome and the Suffragettes*, staged in London in 1908, made an explicit connection between Salome's sexual voracity and women's demands for social and political equality. See Bentley, *Sisters of Salome*, p. 69.

75 Arnol´di, 'Pervenets russkoi kinematografii', p. 197.

76 The feminist economist Heidi Hartmann describes patriarchy as 'relations between men, which have a material base, and which, though hierarchical, establish or create interdependence and solidarity among them that enable them to dominate women'. Cited in Eve Kosofsky Sedgwick, *Between Men: English Literature and Male Homosocial Desire* (New York and Chichester, 1985), p. 3. I here intend the term 'homosocial' to be understood simply to refer to 'social bonds between persons of the same sex'. Ibid., p. 1.

77 Reproduced in Tsivian, 'Early Russian cinema', p. 14.

78 The responses to Mulvey's theories are too numerous to list here. For a usefully concise overview, see Shohini Chaudhuri, *Feminist Film Theorists: Laura Mulvey, Kaja Silverman, Teresa de Lauretis, Barbara Creed* (Oxford and New York, 2006).

79 Laura Mulvey, 'Afterthoughts on "Visual pleasure and narrative cinema", inspired by *Duel in the Sun*' [1981] in Penley, *Feminism and Film Theory*, pp. 69–79.

80 The princess's 'foreignness' would also have encouraged the contemporary female spectator to identify with the (Russian) male hero. For a reading that considers this, see Julian Graffy, 'The foreigner's journey to consciousness in early Soviet cinema: the case of Protazanov's *Tommi*' in Stephen M. Norris and Zara M. Torlone (eds), *Insiders and Outsiders in Russian Cinema* (Bloomington and Indianapolis, IN, 2008), pp. 1–22 (p. 2).

81 Mulvey, 'Visual pleasure', p. 59.

82 Bentley, *Sisters of Salome*, p. 19.

2. The Peasant Girl and the Boyar's Ward

1 See still reproduced in Paolo Cherchi Usai *et al.*, (eds), *Silent Witnesses. Russian Films 1908-1919* (London, 1989), p. 113.

2 Boris Palitsyn, speaking to a male guest about his young ward, Olga, in Mikhail Lermontov, 'Vadim' in G. N. Seleznev *et al.* (eds), M. Iu. Lermontov, *Polnoe sobranie sochinenii v 10 tomakh*, vol. 6, *Proza* (Moscow, 1999–2002), pp. 5–125 (p. 23).

3 Cited in V. Ivanova *et al.*, (eds), *Velikii kinemo. Katalog sokhranivshikhsia igrovykh fil'mov Rossii, 1908-1919* (Moscow, 2002), p. 45.

4 See still reproduced in Cherchi Usai, *Silent Witnesses*, p. 88.

5 Lermontov, 'Vadim', p. 25.

6 The 'tragic'/unhappy ending is one of the key defining characteristics of the early Russian cinematic tradition, often being referred to as the 'Russian ending' [*russkii final*]. See Yuri Tsivian, 'New notes on Russian film culture between 1908 and 1919' in Lee Grieveson and Peter Krämer (eds), *The Silent Cinema Reader* (London and New York, 2004), pp. 339–48 (pp. 339–42).

7 Miriam Hansen, 'Deadly scenarios: narrative perspective and sexual politics in pre-Revolutionary Russian film', *Cinefocus*, 2, 1992, 2, pp. 10–19.

8 Cited in Philip Cavendish, 'The hand that turns the handle: camera operators and the poetics of the camera in pre-Revolutionary Russian film', *Slavonic and East European Review*, 82, 2004, 2, pp. 201–45 (p. 235).

9 See those reviews reproduced in Ivanova, *Velikii kinemo*, p. 46.

10 Although *The Incestuous Father-in-Law* stands head and shoulders above most Russian films made in 1912, it has not been released commercially. For a brief consideration of the film's significance, see Rachel Morley, '1912: *The Incestuous Father-in-Law* (Snokhach)' in Julian Graffy (ed.), 'Special feature: Russian cinema centenary. A hundred years of Russian film: the forgotten and under-rated', *Studies in Russian and Soviet Cinema*, 2, 2008, 3, pp. 327–54 (pp. 331–32).

11 Mozzhukhin emigrated after the Revolution, settling in France where he soon established himself as one of the leadings stars of the 1920s French silent film industry, under the francized version of his name, Mosjoukine.

12 See still reproduced in Ivanova, *Velikii kinemo*, p. 123.

13 Denise J. Youngblood, *The Magic Mirror. Moviemaking in Russia, 1908–1918* (Madison, WI and London, 1999), p. 80.

14 Christine D. Worobec, 'Victims or actors? Russian peasant women and patriarchy' in Esther Kingston-Mann and Timothy Mixter (eds), *Peasant Economy, Culture, and Politics of European Russia, 1800–1921* (Princeton, NJ, 1991), pp. 177–206 (p. 178).

15 Hansen, 'Deadly scenarios', p. 13. As an example of this tendency, Hansen analyses the composition of a frame from the early part of the rape sequence: 'A deep space shot places the two men [Ivan and his father] with a bottle lounging in the foreground of a field, while Lusha, the narrative/emotional focus of the composition, can be seen ploughing in the background, further diminished in proportion by the horse and the unwieldy equipment'. Ibid.

16 Youngblood, *The Magic Mirror*, p. 134.

17 Henrietta Mondry, *Pure, Strong and Sexless: the Peasant Woman's Body and Gleb Uspensky* (Amsterdam and New York, 2006), p. 37. For information about the taboo practice of *snokhachestvo*, see also Rose L. Glickman, 'Women and the peasant commune' in Roger Bartlett (ed.), *Land Commune and Peasant Community in Russia. Communal Forms in Imperial and Early Soviet Society* (Basingstoke and London, 1990), pp. 321–38 (pp. 323–24) and Worobec, 'Victims or actors?', pp. 200–01. A film on the theme of *snokhachestvo* was made in the Soviet period: Ol´ga Preobrazhenskaia and Ivan Pravov's *Peasant Women of Riazan* [Baby riazanskie, 1927]. It was, however, set in the pre-Revolutionary past. For discussion of this film's treatment of the theme, see Philip Cavendish, *Soviet Mainstream Cinematography: The Silent Era* (London, 2008), pp. 111–13.

18 Heide Schlüpmann, 'From patriarchal violence to the aesthetics of death: Russian cinema 1900–1919', *Cinefocus*, 2, 1992, 2, pp. 2–9 (p. 2).

19 See still reproduced in Cherchi Usai, *Silent Witnesses*, p. 157.

20 Elisabeth Bronfen, *Over Her Dead Body. Death, Femininity and the Aesthetic* (Manchester, 1992), pp. 141–67.

21 Ibid., p. 143.

22 Ibid., p. 142.

23 Hansen, 'Deadly scenarios', p. 13.

24 Cited in Tsivian, 'New notes', p. 344.

25 Hansen, 'Deadly scenarios', p. 12.

26 Ibid., p. 13.

27 Ibid. Most nineteenth-century commentators condemned the practice of *snokhachestvo*, which in contemporary law was considered an offence punishable by fifteen to twenty lashes. However, the film-makers' 'sympathetic' approach to the phenomenon is not without precedent, for some writers did attempt to understand and justify it. For discussion of opposing nineteenth-century approaches to the practice, see Mondry, *Pure, Strong and Sexless*, pp. 33–36.

3. The Opera Singer

1 There is uncertainty about the character's surname, with some sources giving it as Dubrovskaia and others as Dubovskaia. In favouring Dubrovskaia I follow the cast list reproduced in V. Ivanova *et al.* (eds), *Velikii kinemo. Katalog sokhranivshikhsia igrovykh fil'mov Rossii, 1908–1919* (Moscow, 2002), p. 171.

2 For biographical information about Bauer, see ibid, pp. 498–500.

3 The term 'Bauer film' was used by Bauer's contemporaries. See Denise J. Youngblood, *The Magic Mirror. Moviemaking in Russia, 1908–1918* (Madison, WI and London, 1999), p. 54. Bauer is the only pre-Revolutionary Russian director who is routinely considered to be an *auteur* film-maker.

4 Simone de Beauvoir, *Le deuxième sexe I: Les faits et les mythes* [1949] (Paris, 1976), p. 11 and p. 13. Translations from French are my own, unless otherwise indicated.

5 Simone de Beauvoir, *Le deuxième sexe II: L'expérience vécue* [1949] (Paris, 1976), p. 13.

6 Monique Wittig, 'One is not born a woman' [1981] in Henry Abelove, Michèle Aina Barale and David M. Halperin (eds), *The Lesbian and Gay Studies Reader* (London, 1993), pp. 103–09 (p. 103).

7 See Rachel Morley, 'Gender relations in the films of Evgenii Bauer', *Slavonic and East European Review*, 81, 2003, 1, pp. 32–69 (pp. 38–39); Philip Cavendish, 'The hand that turns the handle: camera operators and the poetics of the camera in pre-Revolutionary Russian film', *Slavonic and East European Review*, 82, 2004,

2, pp. 201–45 (pp. 214–16); Alyssa DeBlasio, 'Choreographing space, time, and *dikovinki* in the films of Evgenii Bauer', *The Russian Review*, 66, 2007, pp. 671–92 (pp. 683–84).

8   On this aspect of Bauer's pre-film theatre career, see Viktor Korotkii, 'Evgenii Bauer: predystoriia kinorezhissera', *Kinovedcheskie zapiski*, 10, 1991, pp. 44–57; Viktor Korotkii, 'Vozvrashchaiias´ k publikatsii o Bauere, ili metodolgiia oshibki', *Kinovedcheskie zapiski*, 12, 1991, pp. 237–43; Viktor Korotkii 'A. E. Bliumental´-Tamarin i E. F. Bauer. Materialy k istorii russkogo svetotvorchestva', *Kinovedcheskie zapiski*, 56, 2002, pp. 236–71.

9   Emma Widdis describes Bauer as 'the only pre-Revolutionary Russian film-maker routinely considered to have attained a high level of innovation in set design'. See Emma Widdis, '*Faktura*: depth and surface in early Soviet set design', *Studies in Russian and Soviet Cinema*, 3, 2009, 1, pp. 5–32 (p. 9).

10 Lev Kuleshov, 'The tasks of the artist in cinema' [1917] in Richard Taylor and Ian Christie (eds), *The Film Factory. Russian and Soviet Cinema in Documents 1896–1939* (London, 1988), pp. 41–42 (p. 42). Kuleshov describes the Bauer method as follows: '[to build] cumbersome architectural structures with as many different planes and breaks in the walls as possible to create more effective lighting and thereby achieve greater depth and stereoscopic quality'. For more on Kuleshov's understanding of what he terms the 'Bauer school' of set design, see Lev Kuleshov, 'Evgenii Frantsevich Bauer (k sorokaletiiu so dnia smerti)' [1957] in his *Sobranie sochinenii v trekh tomakh*, R. N. Iurenev et al. (eds), volume 2: *Vospominaniia. Rezhissura. Dramaturgiia* (Moscow, 1988), pp. 403–09 (pp. 404–05).

11 See, for example, those reproduced in Ivanova, *Velikii kinemo*, p. 499.

12 Laura Mulvey, 'Visual pleasure and narrative cinema' [1975] in Constance Penley (ed.), *Feminism and Film Theory* (London, 1988), pp. 57–68 (pp. 59–62).

13 Aleksei Kruchenykh and Velimir Khlebnikov, 'Slovo kak takovoe' [1913] in V. Markov (ed.), *Manifesty i programmy russkikh futuristov, Slavische Propyläen*, 27 (Munich, 1967), pp. 53–58 (p. 56).

14 Yuri Tsivian, 'Video essay' on *Mad Love: Three Films by Evgenii Bauer*, BFI DVD publishing (London, 2002).

15 Aleksandra Kollontai, 'Novaia zhenshchina' [1913] in V. I. Uspenskaia (ed.), *Marksistkii feminizm. Kollektsiia tekstov A. M. Kollontai* (Tver´, 2002), pp. 154–91, (p. 187).

16 Elaine Showalter, *Sexual Anarchy. Gender and Culture at the Fin de Siècle* (London, 1991), p. 145.

17 Luce Irigaray, *Speculum of the Other Woman* [1974], translated by Gillian C. Gill (Ithaca, NY, 1985), p. 82.

18 Elizabeth Prettejohn, *Rosetti and His Circle* (London, 1997), p. 26.

229

19 Ibid. Bauer positions many of his other female protagonists before mirrors, always with the same intent: to present them as their male counterparts perceive them, as beautiful objects to be contemplated and desired. See Morley, 'Gender relations', pp. 40–41.

20 See still reproduced in Paolo Cherchi Usai et al. (eds), Silent Witnesses. Russian Films 1908–1919 (London, 1989), p. 204.

21 Tsivian, 'Video essay'.

22 Cavendish, 'The hand that turns the handle', p. 215.

23 Wittig, 'One is not born a woman', p. 103.

24 de Beauvoir, Le deuxième sexe II, p. 9.

25 Judith Butler, 'Sex and gender in Simone de Beauvoir's Second Sex', Yale French Studies, 72, 1986, pp. 35–49 (p. 36).

26 Tsivian, 'Video essay'.

27 See still reproduced in Ivanova, Velikii kinemo, p. 172.

28 Tsivian, 'Video essay'.

29 Ibid.

30 Butler, 'Sex and gender', p. 36. See also the following articles and chapters, all by Butler: 'Variations on sex and gender: Beauvoir, Wittig and Foucault' [1987] in Sarah Salih (ed. with Judith Butler), The Judith Butler Reader (Oxford, 2004), pp. 23–38; 'Performative acts and gender constitution: an essay in phenomenology and feminist theory' [1988] in Sue-Ellen Case (ed.), Performing Feminisms: Feminist Critical Theory and Theatre (Baltimore, MD and London, 1990), pp. 270–82; 'Gendering the body: Beauvoir's philosophical contribution' [1989] in Ann Garry and Marilyn Pearsall (eds), Women, Knowledge, and Reality: Explorations in Feminist Philosophy (London, 1992), pp. 253–62.

31 Moya Lloyd, Judith Butler: From Norms to Politics (Cambridge and Malden, MA, 2007), p. 39. Lloyd provides a useful critical overview of Butler's engagement with de Beauvoir. See ibid., especially pp. 30–31 and pp. 37–42.

32 Butler, 'Sex and gender', p. 36.

33 Ibid., p. 41.

34 Butler, 'Gendering the body', p. 255.

35 This phrase is used in Cavendish, 'The hand that turns the handle', p. 215.

36 Tsivian, 'Video essay'.

37 Heide Schlüpmann, 'From patriarchal violence to the aesthetics of death: Russian cinema 1900–1919', Cinefocus, 2, 1992, 2, pp. 2–9 (p. 2). On this general trend in Bauer's films, see Morley, 'Gender relations', pp. 36–37.

38 Bram Dijkstra, Idols of Perversity. Fantasies of Feminine Evil in Fin-de-Siècle Culture (New York and Oxford, 1986), p. 23. Dijkstra shows how the male cult of feminine invalidism led to a cult of feminine death, a progression that can also be traced in Bauer's films.

39 Laura Engelstein, *The Keys to Happiness: Sex and the Search for Modernity in Fin-de-siècle Russia* (Ithaca, NY and London, 1992), p. 360.

40 Neia Zorkaia, '«Svetopis´» Evgeniia Bauera', *Iskusstvo kino*, 1997, 10, pp. 77–93 (p. 85).

41 Youngblood, *The Magic Mirror*, p. 135.

42 Catherine M. Schuler, *Women in Russian Theatre: The Actress in the Silver Age* (London and New York, 1996), p. 3.

43 Ibid., p. 51.

44 Ibid., p. 29.

45 Louise McReynolds, *Russia at Play. Leisure Activities at the End of the Tsarist Era* (Ithaca, NY and London, 2003), p. 114.

46 Dijkstra, *Idols of Perversity*, pp. 120–23.

47 Ibid., p. 120.

48 Ibid.

49 Schuler, *Women in Russian Theatre*, p. 9.

50 For information about the specific texts that were available in Russian translation before 1900, see Engelstein, *The Keys to Happiness*, p. 132, n. 10.

51 Linda Edmondson, 'Women's emancipation and theories of sexual difference in Russia, 1850–1917' in Marianne Liljeström, Eila Mäntysaari and Arja Rosenholm (eds), *Gender Restructuring in Russian Studies. Conference Papers, Helsinki, August 1992* (Tampere, 1993), pp. 39–52 (p. 41).

52 Ibid., p. 46.

53 Ibid.

54 The continuing interest of Russian film-makers in this persona is evidenced by Kira Muratova giving the name Violetta to the heroine of her *Enthusiasms* [Uvlechen´ia, 1994], and having the character (played by Renata Litvinova) talk about her dead friend 'Rita Gauthier', thus linking Verdi's heroine to her prototype in Alexandre Dumas Fils's *The Lady of the Camellias* [La Dame aux camélias, 1848].

55 Catherine Clément, *Opera, or the Undoing of Women* (London, 1997), p. 6 and p. 12. Clément's arguments about the misogynist nature of nineteenth-century opera have been challenged by numerous musicologists, who have argued that in focussing on the operas' libretti Clément neglects to consider that very feature of opera that makes it opera: the singing voice. Carolyn Abbate, for example, asserts that the presence of a singing woman on stage creates a performance meaning that differs in emphasis from that of the literary plot on which the libretto is based, for the female voice creates 'a realm beyond narrative plot, in which women exist as sonority and sheer physical volume, asserting themselves outside spectacle and escaping murderous fates'. See Carolyn Abbate, 'Opera; or, the envoicing of women' in Ruth A. Solie (ed.), *Musicology and Difference: Gender and Sexuality in Music Scholarship* (Berkeley and Los

Angeles, CA and London, 1995), pp. 225–58 (p. 254). There is, of course, a very obvious difference between an operatic performance as such and the representation of the operatic performance that we get in Bauer's silent film: the lack/absence of that singing voice. Musical accompaniment was an important part of the viewing experience of early Russian films, but, as Tsivian notes, as the music was 'part of film exhibition rather than film production [...] it was the cinema proprietor who was in charge of the musical side of the business'. See Yuri Tsivian, *Early Cinema in Russia and its Cultural Reception* (Chicago, IL and London, 1994), p. 78. The cinema accompanist might, if skilful enough, have woven themes from the opera into his accompaniment at this point in the film; the proprietor could also have played a gramophone recording of the opera's closing act or hired a live singer (ibid., p. 79 and McReynolds, *Russia at Play*, p. 256). All these contemporary solutions seem unlikely in the case of Bauer's film, however, for his interest in this sequence is, like Clément's, in fact purely visual and 'literary': the actors are not shown miming the act of singing; the shot of them on stage is brief and focuses simply on the moment and the fact of Violetta's death.

56 McReynolds, *Russia at Play*, p. 127.

57 Ibid.

58 Susan Sontag, *Illness as Metaphor* (London, 1978), pp. 25–26.

59 Ibid., pp. 24–25.

60 Ibid., p. 41.

61 Ibid., pp. 20–22.

62 Ibid., p. 13.

63 Ibid., p. 25.

64 As Riviere puts it: 'Womanliness therefore [can] be assumed and worn as a mask, both to hide the possession of masculinity and to avert the reprisals expected if she [is] found to possess it'. See Joan Riviere, 'Womanliness as a masquerade' [1929] in Victor Burgin, James Donald and Cora Kaplan (eds), *Formations of Fantasy* (London and New York, 1986), pp. 35–44 (p. 35 and p. 38).

65 Ibid., p. 36

66 Butler lists numerous examples of the 'social punishments' that are meted out to people whose behaviour and/or appearance goes against society's 'gender norms'. See Judith Butler, *Undoing Gender* (New York and London, 2004), p. 55. Beth Holgrem suggests something close to this when she argues that in turn-of-the-century Russia stage actresses could increase their off-stage respectability in the eyes of the public – or, to use Holmgren's terms, could 'expiate' the 'sin' associated with being an actress – by playing on stage melodramatic roles in works that were usually moralistic and punished their transgressive heroines. See Beth Holmgren, 'The importance of being unhappy, or, why she died' in Louise McReynolds and Joan Neuberger (eds), *Imitations of Life: Two*

Centuries of Melodrama in Russia (Durham, NC and London), 2002, pp. 79–98 (pp. 84–85).

67 Mary Ann Doane, 'Masquerade reconsidered: further thoughts on the female spectator' in her *Femmes Fatales: Feminism, Film Theory, Psychoanalysis* (New York and Oxford, 1991), pp. 33–43 (p. 38).

68 Cited in Butler, *Gender Trouble*, p. 163.

69 Stephen Heath, 'Joan Riviere and the Masquerade' in Burgin *et al.* (eds), *Formations of Fantasy*, pp. 45–61 (p. 57).

70 Reprinted in V. Shcherbina (ed.), *Aleksandr Blok. Pis´ma k zhene, Literaturnoe nasledstvo*, 89 (Moscow, 1978), p. 44.

71 Butler, *Undoing Gender*, p. 48.

72 Youngblood, *The Magic Mirror*, p. 82.

73 Schuler, *Women in Russian Theatre*, p. 9.

74 Kollontai, 'Novaia zhenshchina', p. 190.

75 Anastasiia Verbitskaia, *Kliuchi schast´ia*, Volume 2 (St Petersburg, 1993), p. 482.

76 Key's writings on subjects such as human sexuality, family life, ethics, marriage, education, peace, politics and women's suffrage were hugely influential in the first decades of the twentieth century, not only in her native Sweden but also in Western Europe, America and Russia. See Thorbjörn Lengborn, 'Ellen Key (1849–1926)', *Prospects: The Quarterly Review of Comparative Education*, 23, 1993, 314, pp. 825–37 (p. 825). Key's best-known work, *The Century of the Child* [Barnets århundrade, 1900], was published in Russia under the title *Vek rebenka* in 1905 and was considered by the Russian educationalist Konstantin Venttsel´ (1857–1947) to be a central work in new education theories. See http://partners.academic.ru/dic.nsf/ruwiki/37731 (accessed 30 January 2016).

77 Cited in Louise Nyström-Hamilton, *Ellen Key: Her Life and Her Work. A Critical Study*, translated by Anna E. B. Fries (New York and London, 1913), p. 180.

78 See http://dic.academic.ru/dic.nsf/enc_literature/204/Альмквист (accessed 30 January 2016).

79 Anna Rotkirch, 'New woman with old feelings? Contrasting Kollontai's and Colette's writings on love' in Ebba Witt-Brattström (ed.), *The New Woman and the Aesthetic Opening: Unlocking Gender in Twentieth-Century Texts* (Huddinge, 2004), pp. 137–54 (p. 140).

80 Ellen Key, *Love and Marriage*, translated by Arthur G. Chater (New York and London, 1911), p. 293.

81 Cherchi Usai, *Silent Witnesses*, p. 204.

82 Louise McReynolds, 'Demanding men, desiring women and social collapse in the films of Evgenii Bauer, 1913–17', *Studies in Russian and Soviet Cinema*, 3, 2009, 2, pp. 145–56 (p. 149).

83 Kollontai, 'Novaia zhenshchina', p. 188.

4. From the Oriental Dancer to the Tango-Woman

1 Megan Becker-Leckrone, 'Salome©: the fetishization of a textual corpus', *New Literary History*, 26, 1995, 2, pp. 239–60 (p. 257).

2 Reproduced in V. Ivanova *et al.* (eds), *Velikii kinemo. Katalog sokhranivshikhsia igrovykh fil´mov Rossii, 1908–1919* (Moscow, 2002), pp. 220–21.

3 Reproduced ibid., p. 220.

4 Ibid, p. 221.

5 Ibid.

6 Ibid., p. 220.

7 Ibid., p. 221.

8 Neia Zorkaia, 'Motiv persidskoi kniazhny v «Razinskom» lubochnom tsikle i v russkoi literature XIX-XX vekov' in I. E. Danilova (ed.), *Mir narodnoi kartinki: materialy nauchnoi konferentsii "Vipperovskie chteniia – 1997"* (Moscow, 1999), pp. 278–90 (p. 278).

9 On the tango's arrival in Russia, see Yuri Tsivian, 'Russia, 1913: cinema in the cultural landscape' in Richard Abel (ed.), *Silent Film* (London, 1996), pp. 194–214 and Yuri Tsivian, 'The tango in Russia', *Experiment/Eksperiment*, 2, 1996, pp. 306–33.

10 See stills reproduced in Ivanova, *Velikii kinemo*, p. 195 and in Paolo Cherchi Usai *et al.* (eds), *Silent Witnesses. Russian Films 1908–1919* (London, 1989), p. 216 and on the book jacket.

11 On the significance of the *kabinet* as 'a liminal zone', a private space, separate from the public area of the main restaurant but still ensconced within it, that enabled guests to pursue potentially dangerous pleasures discreetly, see Louise McReynolds, *Russia at Play. Leisure Activities at the End of the Tsarist Era* (Ithaca, NY and London, 2003), pp. 203–04.

12 See Rachel Morley, '"Crime without punishment": reworkings of nineteenth-century Russian literary sources in Evgenii Bauer's *Child of the Big City*' in Stephen Hutchings and Anat Vernitski (eds), *Russian and Soviet Film Adaptations of Literature, 1900-2001: Screening the Word* (London and New York, 2005), pp. 27–43 (pp. 29–31).

13 Yuri Tsivian, *Early Cinema in Russia and its Cultural Reception* (Chicago, IL and London, 1998), p. 205.

14 For an overview of these conventions, see Philip Cavendish, 'The hand that turns the handle: camera operators and the poetics of the camera in pre-Revolutionary Russian film', *Slavonic and East European Review*, 82, 2004, 2, pp. 201–45 (pp. 204–05).

15 Ibid., p. 221.

16 Ibid., p. 220.

17 Ibid.

18 An excellent example of the significance of the 'subject' of the track-in to the meaning of the shot is the 'double wedding' sequence in Bauer's *A Life for a Life*. Here the camera tracks in past the guests to the head table, focusing on the proud but deluded mother, Khromova, as she proposes a toast to her two daughters (one biological and one adopted) and their new husbands. For analysis of this sequence and its contribution to the film's examination of the theme of maternal love (a new theme for Bauer in 1916), see Rachel Morley, 'Zhizn´ za zhizn´ / A Life for a Life' in B. Beumers (ed.), *The Cinema of Russia and the Former Soviet Union* (London and New York, 2007), pp. 13–22 (p. 19).

19 Reproduced in Ivanova, *Velikii kinemo*, p. 194.

20 Toni Bentley, *Sisters of Salome* (New Haven, CT and London, 2002), p. 70.

21 Denise J. Youngblood, *The Magic Mirror. Moviemaking in Russia, 1908–1918* (Madison, WI and London, 1999), p. 22.

22 Reproduced in Ivanova, *Velikii kinemo*, p. 195.

23 Camille Paglia, *Sexual Personae. Art and Decadence from Nefertiti to Emily Dickinson* (London and New Haven, CT, 2001), p. 16.

24 'Novaia Eva', *Sovremennaia zhenshchina*, 1914, 5, pp. 104–06 (p. 104).

25 Laura Mulvey, 'Visual pleasure and narrative cinema' [1975] in Constance Penley (ed.), *Feminism and Film Theory* (London, 1988), pp. 57–68 (p. 62).

26 Elaine Showalter, *Sexual Anarchy. Gender and Culture at the Fin de Siècle* (London, 1991), p. 146.

27 Tsivian, *Early Cinema in Russia*, pp. 204–05.

28 Ibid.

29 Ibid., p. 206.

30 Showalter writes: 'In the religious and Pre-Raphaelite art from which Beardsley drew inspiration, the full-blown rose is associated with the female body [...]. Female sexuality is [...] dangerous and impure; in the drawing of John and Salome, for example, the rosebush seems like a live thing extending its tendrils behind Salome's body to entwine John. It is full of blossoms, while all of its thorns have become giant protuberances wound in Salome's hair like a *vagina dentata*'. Showalter, *Sexual Anarchy*, pp. 153–54. Paglia's description of Beardsley's representation of Salome goes further: 'Salomé has a war-crown of tusks, thorns and lunar crescents. She seems half porcupine, half randy ram butting heads with the Baptist, who shrinks from this hectoring apparition. She is the Venus Barbata'. Paglia, *Sexual Personae*, pp. 506–07.

31 Spencer Golub, *The Recurrence of Fate: Theatre and Memory in Twentieth-Century Russia* (Iowa City, IA, 1994), p. 45. See also Nikita Lobanov-Rostovsky, 'A bargain on the Marché aux puces: the pictures of Nicolai Kalmakov' in A. Flegon (ed.), *Eroticism in Russian Art* (London, 1976), pp. 306–07 (p. 306).

32 William Tydeman and Steven Price, *Wilde – Salome* (Cambridge and New York, 1996), p. 60.
33 Oksana Bulgakova, *Fabrika zhestov* (Moscow, 2005), p. 95. Bulgakova demonstrates the pervasiveness of this fashionable pose by citing examples taken not only from early Russian film, but also from literary works by such diverse early twentieth-century writers as Anna Akhmatova, Lidiia Zinov´eva-Annibal, Anastasiia Verbitskaia and Benedikt Livshits. Ibid., pp. 95–96.
34 While no director had previously made such sustained and significant use of the tango in an acted feature film, Mary's tango performance is not the dance's first appearance in Russian cinema. At least three earlier Russian films had featured the tango: Vladimir Kas´ianov's *Drama in the Futurist Cabaret No. 13* [Drama v kabare futuristov No. 13], released in January 1914, included two unconventional tango performances, and in February 1914 two 'tango films' were released: Iakov Protazanov's five-minute short, *Tango*, which featured the dancers Potopchina and Kuznetsov, and Władysław Starewicz's comedy, *Everyone is Dancing the Tango in the Land of Russia* [Vse tantsuiut tango v strane Rossii] in which the main characters were animated tangoing frogs. On these films, which have not survived, see Tsivian, 'The tango', pp. 306–33 (pp. 310–11).
35 Tsivian, 'Russia' 1913', p. 204.
36 Tsivian gives a detailed account of the key speeches delivered at these events in 'The tango', p. 311.
37 Cited and translated ibid., pp. 313–14.
38 Cited and translated ibid., p. 315. Homo Novus was the pseudonym of Aleksandr Kugel´, the noted St Petersburg theatre critic, the founder of the St Petersburg theatre *The Crooked Mirror* [Krivoe zerkalo] and, between 1897 and 1918, the editor of the journal *Theatre and Art* [Teatr i iskusstvo].
39 Cited and translated ibid., p. 309.
40 Tsivian, 'Russia, 1913', p. 208.
41 Dominique Nasta, 'Setting the pace of a heartbeat: the use of sound elements in European melodramas before 1915' in Richard Abel and Rick Altman, *The Sounds of Early Cinema* (Bloomington and Indianapolis, IN, 2001), pp. 95–109 (p. 106).
42 Ibid., pp. 106–07.
43 Maiia Turovskaia, 'Zhenshchina-ubiitsa v russkom i sovetskom nemom kino', *Iskusstvo kino*, 1997, 5, pp. 108–13 (p. 111).
44 This text comes from one of the film's original intertitles, which have not survived, as cited in a review published in the journal *Cinema* [Kinema] in 1914. Reproduced in Ivanova, *Velikii kinemo*, p. 195.
45 Tsivian, 'The tango', p. 308, n. 12. For discussion of how Mary's body language changes throughout the film, see Bulgakova, *Fabrika zhestov*, pp. 72–71. Bulgakova argues that, as Mary goes up in the world, she gradually sheds the vulgar physical gestures and mannerisms that Viktor had read as a sign of her

unspoilt nature, adopting in their place, at least while in public, 'the accepted forms of body language of a higher social class'. Ibid., p. 72. When she is alone, or caught off guard, however, she reverts to using the type of gestures that in the film's early scenes had marked her as 'uncultured'. In this way, Bulgakova suggests, the viewer is never allowed to forget Mary's lower-class origins. Ibid., pp. 71–72. For an English translation of excerpts from Bulgakova's discussion of this film, see Oksana Bulgakova, 'The Scheherezade of the boulevard novel: a piquant mix of the vulgar and the proper' in Rimgaila Salys (ed.), *The Russian Cinema Reader. Volume One: 1908 to the Stalin Era* (Boston, MA, 2013), pp. 61–63.

46 A. Ando, U. Yasuo and T. Mochizuki (eds), *A Concordance to Dostoevsky's 'Crime and Punishment'*, vol. 2, Sapporo, 1994, pp. 760–61.

47 Fedor Dostoevskii, *Polnoe sobranie sochinenii v tridtsati tomakh*, vol. 6: *Prestuplenie i nakazane*, V. V. Vinogradov (ed.) (Leningrad, 1973), p. 199. All references to this novel will be to this edition. Henceforth, page references will be given in parentheses in the text.

48 As Bram Dijkstra and Elaine Showalter have both demonstrated, many other turn-of-the-century (male) artists working in other media and other cultures also emphasised the timeless universality of the Salome theme in similar ways. See Bram Dijkstra, *Idols of Perversity. Fantasies of Feminine Evil in Fin-de-Siècle Culture* (New York and Oxford, 1986), pp. 387–401 and Showalter, *Sexual Anarchy*, pp. 149–68.

49 Miriam Hansen, 'Deadly scenarios: narrative perspective and sexual politics in pre-Revolutionary Russian film', *Cinefocus*, 2, 1992, 2, pp. 10–19 (p. 14).

50 Many of Bauer's weak male protagonists seek refuge from the real women with whom they are involved in this way. For discussion of this tendency, see Rachel Morley, 'Gender relations in the films of Evgenii Bauer', *Slavonic and East European Review*, 81, 2003, 1, pp. 32–69 (pp. 55–58).

51 See still reproduced in Morley, ' "Crime without punishment"', p. 30.

52 The density and range of the nineteenth-century literary and cultural allusions contained in this film are such that full discussion of this aspect of Bauer's method is beyond the scope of the present study. For further discussion of this, see ibid.

53 Nikolai Gogol´, *Sobranie sochinenii v deviati tomakh*, vol. 3: *Povesti*, E. S. Smirnova (ed.) (Moscow, 1994), p. 12 and p. 24. All references to this story will be to this edition. Henceforth, page references will be given in parentheses in the text.

54 Neia Zorkaia, 'Kinorezhisser Evgenii Bauer. Serebrianye deviat´sot desiatye', *Slovo. Obrazovatel´nyi portal* at http://www.portal-slovo.ru/art/35960.php (accessed 6 July 2015).

55 Paglia, *Sexual Personae*, p. 397.

56 These observations are not intended to disparage Lina Bauer's screen presence or her performance of this role. She would go on to act in many of Bauer's films to considerable contemporary critical acclaim. Usually, however, she performed

comic roles and some commentators have even suggested that she was the driving force behind the creation of the light-hearted strand of Bauer's work that comprises films such as the 1914 farces *Her Heroic Feat* [Ee geroiskii podvig], *Only Once a Year* [Tol´ko raz v godu] and *Cold Showers* [Kholodnye dushi], the comedy *The Thousand and Second Ruse* [Tysiacha vtoraia khitrost´, 1915] and the so-called 'Lina' farces: *Lina's Adventure in Sochi* [Prikliuchenie Liny v Sochi, 1916] and *Lina Under Examination, Or the Turbulent Corpse* [Lina pod ekspertizoi, ili Buinyi pokoinik, 1917], in which she also appears as a dancer. See Neia Zorkaia, '«Svetopis´» Evgeniia Bauera', *Iskusstvo kino*, 1997, 10, pp. 77–93 (p. 85) and Romil Sobolev, *Liudi i fil´my russkogo dorevoliutsionnogo kino* (Moscow, 1961), p. 101 and pp. 158–59. While Bauer would go on to cast his wife in serious dramatic roles, he would not do so until the end of 1915 and Lina appears in only two extant Bauer dramas: *Iurii Nagornyi* (1916), in which she is again cast as a dancer, and *The King of Paris* [Korol´ Parizha, 1917]. She also took a serious role in Komissarzhevskii and Chaikovskii's *The Stage Set of Happiness* (1918).

57 Turovskaia, 'Zhenshchina-ubiitsa', p. 111.

58 Zorkaia, '«Svetopis´»', p. 85.

59 Oscar Wilde, *Salomé*, translated from the French by Lord Alfred Douglas, in *The Complete Works of Oscar Wilde: Stories, Plays, Poems*, introduced by Vyvyan Holland (London and Glasgow, 1986), pp. 552–75 (p. 561).

60 Cited in Louise McReynolds, '"The incomparable" Anastasiia Vial´tseva and the culture of personality' in Helena Goscilo and Beth Holmgren (eds), *Russia. Culture. Women* (Bloomington, IN, 1996), pp. 273–94 (p. 275).

61 Contemporary commentators concurred that the tango seemed somehow to encapsulate early twentieth-century life in Russia. Mikhail Bonch-Tomashevskii, for example, commented that 'after many years this dance will serve as evidence of the way we felt and loved in the first half of the twentieth century'. Cited and translated in Tsivian, 'The tango', pp. 313–14. While Homo Novus felt that 'the tango has no spark of youth, as there is no youth in this century. [...] The tango has no smile. The smile is banished. A smile would ruin the very character of the tango, the dance manifesting the grave submission to necessity, to the solemn rhythm of cultural rites'. Cited and translated ibid., p. 315.

62 Cited and translated ibid., pp. 307–08.

63 Ibid., p. 308

64 Cited and translated ibid., pp. 308–09.

65 In Part 4, Chapter 4, Raskolnikov tells Sonia that when she became a prostitute she committed moral suicide: 'You too have stepped over [...] were capable of stepping over. You've laid hands on yourself, you've destroyed a life – your own life (it's all the same!)' (p. 252).

66 Bauer's refusal to approach the actions of his female protagonists from a moral
perspective can be observed in most of his films. For a discussion of his 'amorality', see Hansen, 'Deadly scenarios' and Heide Schlüpmann, 'From patriarchal violence to the aesthetics of death: Russian cinema 1900–1919', *Cinefocus*,
2, 1992, 2, pp. 2–9. For a summary of their arguments, see Jane Gaines,
'Revolutionary theory/prerevolutionary melodrama', *Discourse*, 17, 1995, 3, pp.
101–18 (pp. 105–06).

67 Tsivian, 'The tango', p. 324.

68 Semen Ginzburg, *Kinematografiia dorevoliutsionnoi Rossii* [1963] (Moscow,
2007), pp. 281–83. Ginzburg's synopsis appears in English in Jerry Heil, 'Russian
Futurism and the cinema: Majakovskij's film work of 1913', *Russian Literature*,
19, 1986, 2, pp. 178–79. Drawing on Ginzburg's work and on the unpublished
research of the Estonian scholar Rein Kruss, Tsivian produces his own synopsis
in 'The tango', pp. 323–26 and 'Russia, 1913', pp. 209–11.

69 Ibid., pp. 209–10. It is possible that the grotesque and decadent dwarfs who
tango on a food-laden table in Sergei Eizenshtein's 1924 film *The Strike* [Stachka]
were inspired by this sequence.

70 Tsivian, 'Russia, 1913', p. 210.

71 On Kriuger's career, see Georgii Kovalenko, 'Elza Kriuger', *Experiment/
Eksperiment*, 2, 1996, pp. 334–57.

72 Tsivian, 'The tango', p. 318. The so-called 'reincarnation' sequence in Bauer's *A
Life for a Life* in which Nata and her lover, Prince Bartinskii, re-enact Bartinskii's
fantasy that their ill-starred affair is predetermined by fate, also bears the hallmarks of tango choreography, as does the sequence in *Child of the Big City* when
Mania and Viktor share their first kiss.

73 Ibid. Tsivian also explores the idea that the so-called 'Russian style of acting' –
one of the several features of the early Russian cinematic tradition that differentiate it from the early film traditions of other countries – derives from the
rhythm of the tango, specifically in its 'bias towards a slow tempo bordering on
immobility'. See ibid., pp. 319–20. For a revealing comparison of the contrasting body language employed by Kriuger in her portrayal of the aristocratic
Ellen and by Dora Chitorina, the actress cast in the role of the maid, Nastia,
see Bulgakova, *Fabrika zhestov*, pp. 56–58 and pp. 66–68.

74 Tsivian, 'The tango', p. 309.

75 Only one of the film's five reels has survived. A contemporary synopsis of the
film, published in *Screen World* [Mir ekrana] in 1918, is reproduced in Ivanova,
Velikii kinemo, p. 467.

76 On the song, see Anton Iani, *Vera Kholodnaia. Pervaia liubov' rossiiskogo kinozritelia* (St Petersburg, 2012), p. 106.

77 Ivanova, *Velikii kinemo*, p. 468.

78 On this event, see B. B. Ziukov (ed.), *Vera Kholodnaia. K 100-letiiu so dnia rozh-deniia* (Moscow, 1995), pp. 66–67 and p. 96. On the making of this film and the shooting of the final dance sequence, see Elena Prokof′eva, *Koroleva ekrana. Istoriia Very Kholodnoi* (Moscow, 2001), pp. 108–14.

79 The appropriateness of this reading is bolstered by the fact that films made during the early Soviet period would often also use both the tango dancer and her forebear, the oriental dancer, as convenient shorthand indicators of the amoral decadence and political torpor of the pre-Revolutionary period. The tangoing dwarfs in Eizenshtein's *The Strike* have been mentioned. Consider also the prologue of Grigorii Kozintsev and Leonid Trauberg's *The Youth of Maksim* [Iunost′ Maksima, 1934], in which the thoughtless gaiety of the upper classes is evoked most strikingly by the figure of a woman who, dressed in oriental costume, gyrates wildly in a sleigh as it speeds through the snowy streets of St Petersburg on New Year's Eve, as 1909 gives way to 1910; a still from this sequence is reproduced in John Riley, *Dmitri Shostakovich: A Life in Film* (London and New York, 2005), p. 27. Her drunken celebrations are contrasted with the sobriety of Natasha and Polivanov, who spend their evening engaging in underground Revolutionary activity. Although a Soviet cult of the tango would develop in the mid-1930s, in Grigorii Aleksandrov's first musical comedy *The Jolly Fellows* [Veselye rebiata, 1934] tango music is similarly used to ridicule the social and erotic aspirations of the bourgeoise, uncultured and un-Soviet Elena as, carrying an over-sized parasol and over-dressed in a fashionable trouser suit and high-heeled shoes, she teeters along the stony beach in pursuit of the famous Paraguayan conductor and 'maestro', Costa Fraschini.

5. The Gypsy Dancer

1 See Angus Fraser, *The Gypsies* (Oxford and Cambridge, MA, 1992), p. 205 and David M. Crowe, *A History of the Gypsies of Eastern Europe and Russia* (London and New York, 1995), pp. 154–55 and pp. 162–63.

2 On Gypsy entertainment in nineteenth-century Russia, see ibid., pp. 164–65; Vladimir Bobri, 'Gypsies and Gypsy choruses of Old Russia', *Journal of the Gypsy Lore Society*, 40, 1961, 3–4, pp. 115–18; T. Shcherbakova, *Tsyganskoe muzykal′noe ispolnitel′stvo v Rossii* (Moscow, 1984); Louise McReynolds, *Russia at Play. Leisure Activities at the End of the Tsarist Era* (Ithaca, NY and London, 2003), pp. 200–01.

3 Fraser, *The Gypsies*, p. 205.

4 This was true even of the songs performed by Orlov's choir. See Dmitrii Oleinikov, 'Pesnia russkoi Karmen', *Rodina*, 7, 2004, pp. 96–97 (p. 96).

5 On the careers of Panina and other early twentieth-century 'Gypsy' singers, such as Anastasiia Vial'tseva and Nadezhda Plevitskaia, see Richard Stites, *Russian Popular Culture. Entertainment and Society Since 1900* (Cambridge, 1992), pp. 13–14. For biographical information about Vial'tseva and consideration of what the audience's reception of this performer suggests about the changing roles of women at the start of the twentieth century, see Louise McReynolds, ' "The incomparable" Anastasiia Vial'tseva and the culture of personality' in Helena Goscilo and Beth Holmgren (eds), *Russia. Culture. Women* (Bloomington, IN, 1996), pp. 273–94.

6 Between 1827 and 1892, *The Gypsies* inspired no less than six opera libretti, including one by Mikhail Lermontov. See Leighton Brett Cooke, 'Pushkin and the *femme fatale*. Jealousy in *Cygany*', *California Slavic Studies*, 14, 1992, pp. 99–126 (p. 102). On the prevalence and significance of the figure of the Gypsy in nineteenth-century Russian literature, thought and culture, see Alfred E. Hamill, 'Gypsies in and about Russian literature', *Journal of the Gypsy Lore Society*, 22, 1943, 1–2, pp. 57–58; Crowe, 'Russia', pp. 165–69; Z. G. Mints and Iu. M. Lotman, '«Chelovek prirody» v russkoi literature XIX veka i «tsyganskaia tema» u Bloka' in Z. G. Mints, *Aleksandr Blok i russkie pisateli*, St Petersburg, 2000, pp. 343–88.

7 Elisabeth Bronfen, *Over Her Dead Body. Death, Femininity and the Aesthetic* (Manchester, 1992), p. 189.

8 On the fraught question of influence between these three works, including consideration of the possibility that Pushkin's *poema* inspired Mérimée's novella and that Meilhac and Halévy used not only Mérimée's 'Carmen', but also his translation of Pushkin's *The Gypsies* [*Les Bohémiens*, 1852] as a basis for their libretto for Bizet's opera, see Cooke, 'Pushkin and the *femme fatale*', pp. 102–05; David A. Lowe, 'Pushkin and *Carmen*', *Nineteenth-Century Music*, 20, 1996, 1, pp. 72–76; A. D. P. Briggs, 'Did *Carmen* really come from Russia (with a little help from Turgenev?)' in Joe Andrew, Derek Offord and Robert Reid (eds), *Turgenev and Russian Culture. Essays to Honour Richard Peace* (Amsterdam and New York, 2008), pp. 83–102.

9 Reproduced in V. Ivanova *et al.* (eds), *Velikii kinemo. Katalog sokhranivshikhsia igrovykh fil'mov Rossii, 1908–1919* (Moscow, 2002), p. 16.

10 Ibid.

11 Ian Christie, Sleeve note to *Drama in A Gypsy Camp Near Moscow, Early Russian Cinema*, volume 2, *Folklore and Legend*, London, 1992.

12 Paolo Cherchi Usai *et al.* (eds), *Silent Witnesses. Russian Films 1908–1919* (London, 1989), p. 46.

13 Semen Ginzburg, *Kinematografiia dorevoliutsionnoi Rossii* [1963] (Moscow, 2007), p. 72. Later in this work, Ginzburg describes this film more appropriately as 'one of the first Russian acted films'. Ibid., p. 149.

14 Denise J. Youngblood, *The Magic Mirror. Moviemaking in Russia, 1908–1918* (Madison, WI and London, 1999), p. 91.

15 According to Ginzburg, the contemporary running time of the film was seven minutes. See Ginzburg, *Kinematografiia*, p. 149. The surviving version of the film lasts only a little over two and a half minutes.

16 Reproduced in Ivanova, *Velikii kinemo*, pp. 15–16.

17 Ibid., p. 16.

18 Ibid.

19 Prosper Mérimée, 'Carmen' [1846] in Jean Decottignies (ed.), *Prosper Mérimée. Les Ames du purgatoire. Carmen* (Paris, 1973), pp. 105–69 (p. 164). Although Pushkin's Zemfira does not dance, it is her song – another form of performance – that alerts Aleko to her defiant infidelity, as it had previously alerted the old man to that of her mother, Mariula.

20 Reproduced in Ivanova, *Velikii kinemo*, p. 16.

21 Ibid.

22 Ginzburg, *Kinematografiia*, pp. 149–50.

23 Ibid., p. 150.

24 Cavendish, 'The hand that turns the handle: camera operators and the poetics of the camera in pre-Revolutionary Russian film', *Slavonic and East European Review*, 82, 2004, 2, pp. 201–45 (p. 217).

25 Aleksandr Pushkin, 'Tsygany' in *Pushkin: Selected Verse*, with introduction and prose translations by John Fennell (London, 1995), pp. 77–109 (pp. 106–07).

26 Cooke, 'Pushkin and the *femme fatale*', p. 99.

27 Ibid., pp. 99–100.

28 McReynolds, *Russia at Play*, p. 271.

29 Reproduced in Ivanova, *Velikii kinemo*, p. 71.

30 Ibid., pp. 70–71.

31 Ginzburg, *Kinematografiia*, pp. 145–46.

32 Veniamin Vishnevskii, *Khudozhestvennye fil´my dorevoliutsionnoi Rossii: fil´mograficheskoe opisanie* (Moscow, 1945), p. 51.

33 Alyssa DeBlasio, 'Choreographing space, time, and *dikovinki* in the films of Evgenii Bauer', *The Russian Review*, 66, 2007, pp. 671–92 (p. 689).

34 Lev Kuleshov, 'Evgenii Frantsevich Bauer (k sorokaletiiu so dnia smerti)' [1957] in his *Sobranie sochinenii v trekh tomakh*, R. N. Iurenev *et al.* (eds), volume 2: *Vospominaniia. Rezhissura. Dramaturgiia* (Moscow, 1988), pp. 403–09 (p. 406).

35 For analysis of Bauer's use of the *dikovinka* in *In Pursuit of Happiness* [Za schast´em, 1917] (also known by the English title *For Luck*), *Daydreams* [Grezy, 1915] and *The Dying Swan* [Umiraiushchii lebed´, 1917], see Rachel Morley, 'Gender relations in the films of Evgenii Bauer', *Slavonic and East European Review*, 81, 2003, 1, pp. 32–69 (pp. 45–46, pp. 55–58 and pp. 59–60, respectively) and DeBlasio, 'Choreographing space', pp. 674–83.

36 Louise McReynolds, 'Demanding men, desiring women and social collapse in the films of Evgenii Bauer, 1913–17', *Studies in Russian and Soviet Cinema*, 3, 2009, 2, pp.145–56 (p. 152).

37 Anastasiia Verbitskaia, *Kliuchi schast'ia*, Volume 2 (St Petersburg, 1993), p. 25.

38 The figure of the *tsyganka* recurs throughout Blok's oeuvre. She is not a static persona, however, but, as Mints and Lotman have demonstrated in detail, one to whom Blok accords significantly different symbolic values at different stages in his poetic career. See Mints and Lotman, '«Chelovek prirody»'.

39 Aleksandr Blok, 'K muze' in V. N. Orlov, A. A. Surkov and K. I. Chukovskii (eds), *Aleksandr Blok. Sobranie sochinenii v vos'mi tomakh*, vol. 3, *Stikhotvoreniia i poemy, 1907–1921* (Moscow and Leningrad, 1960), pp. 7–8 (p. 8).

40 Aleksandr Blok, *Karmen*, ibid, pp. 227–39 (p. 239). All subsequent references *Karmen* will be to this edition, with page references given in parentheses in the text. *Karmen* was inspired by Blok's obsession with the opera singer Liubov' Del'mas, who, between October 1913 and March 1914, performed the role of Carmen in St Petersburg. On Blok's relationship with Del'mas and her influence on this cycle, see Anatolii Gorelov, 'Aleksandr Blok i ego Karmen' in his *Groza nad solov'inym sadom. Aleksandr Blok* (Leningrad, 1973), pp. 556–604.

41 Youngblood goes further than this, suggesting: 'It may be that Lebedev has somehow entrapped Lidiia as well'. Youngblood, *The Magic Mirror*, p. 85.

42 Laurie Bernstein suggests that the source of this trope is Nikolai Chernyshevskii's 1863 novel *What Is To Be Done?* [Chto delat'?], in which two prostitutes abandon their trade when given the opportunity to join a sewing cooperative. See Laurie Bernstein, *Sonia's Daughters. Prostitutes and Their Regulation in Imperial Russia* (Berkeley and Los Angeles, CA and London, 1995), pp. 212–13. For a survey of this theme, see Arnold McMillin and Svetlana McMillin, 'Sex, speech and sewing machines: whores' voices and useful occupations in Russian literature', *Slovo*, 11, 1999, pp. 121–39.

43 Bauer also draws on this trope in his earlier *Child of the Big City*, using it to indicate Mary's moral fall as she moves from seamstress to kept woman and, ultimately, to high-class courtesan. He also uses it to emphasise Viktor's outdated approach to women, showing him to believe, naively (and again like Gogol''s Piskarev before him), that Mary will be happy to begin a new life of work and modest living. Thus, like her namesake Mary, Mariia journeys from poverty to wealth, from innocent seamstress to corrupt kept woman, thereby reversing the path of many nineteenth-century Russian literary heroines. In this way she too becomes a true child of the new age of the twentieth century. For further discussion of Bauer's treatment of the trope of sewing in *Child of the Big City*, see Rachel Morley, '"Crime without punishment": reworkings of nineteenth-century Russian literary sources in Evgenii Bauer's *Child of the Big City*' in Stephen Hutchings and Anat Vernitski (eds), *Russian and Soviet*

Film Adaptations of Literature, 1900–2001: Screening the Word, London and New York, 2005, pp. 27–43 (pp. 29–36).

44 Aleksandr Blok, 'V restorane' in Orlov *et al.* (eds), *Stikhotvoreniia i poemy, 1907–1921*, p. 25.

45 Reproduced in Ivanova, *Velikii kinemo*, p. 238.

46 On the contemporary reception of these introductory portraits, see Yuri Tsivian, *Early Cinema in Russia and its Cultural Reception* (Chicago, IL and London, 1994), pp. 186–88. For an example of this convention, see the opening credits of Bauer's *Twilight of a Woman's Soul*, in which the actors are, as was usual, introduced in their own clothes, as themselves, and not in costume as the characters they play in the film.

47 See the reviews reproduced in Ivanova, *Velikii kinemo*, pp. 257–60.

48 While it is Mariula whom the old man directly likens to a freedom-loving bird in Pushkin's *The Gypsies* (l. 414), Zemfira is also associated with this creature, not only through her resemblance to her mother, but also through the song about the allegorical 'God's little bird' (ll. 104–19). The narrator explicitly contrasts Aleko with this bird (ll. 120–29); implicitly, however, he links Zemfira with it, for, like the bird, she is truly carefree and happy to move from place to place, she takes pleasure in the moment and expresses herself through song. Bizet's Carmen echoes Pushkin's image of the *tsyganka* as a bird when she sings, in the Habañera in Act 1, of her belief that 'love is a rebellious bird. Love is a Gypsy's child. It has never known any laws'.

49 Reproduced in Ivanova, *Velikii kinemo*, p. 260.

50 In this connection it is interesting that Lola, like so many of the female performers in films from this period, has no father, the person who would usually have made decisions about marriage.

51 Cited in a review published in *Theatre Review* [Obozrenie teatrov] in 1915 and reproduced in Ivanova, *Velikii kinemo*, p. 258.

52 The review indicates that von Brück utters these words: 'at a party at his house'. Ibid.

53 This song was apparently inspired by the bad behaviour of students from the St Petersburg Imperial Legal Academy, situated on the Fontanka. They wore green and yellow uniforms, making them look like siskins, and were reputed to relax after classes by drinking at a local tavern. The song is very widely known in Russia and appears in numerous literary and musical texts, including Anton Chekhov's 1887 drama *Ivanov* (Act 1, Scene V11), Vladimir Nabokov's translation of Lewis Carroll's *Alice in Wonderland* [Ania v strane chudes, 1923] (as the basis for Nabokov's rendition of the Mad Hatter's song 'Twinkle, Twinkle, Little Bat') and Dmitrii Shostakovich's Five Satires (Pictures from the Past, 1960) op. 109.

54 Reproduced in Ivanova, *Velikii kinemo*, p. 259.

55 'Polka. History of Dance' at http://www.centralhome.com/ballroomcountry/polka.htm and 'Polka!' at http://www.bratwurstpages.com/polka.html (both accessed 10 January 2016).

56 Reproduced in Ivanova, *Velikii kinemo*, p. 259.

57 Ibid.

58 Cherchi Usai, *Silent Witnesses*, p. 274.

59 Ibid.

60 Youngblood, *The Magic Mirror*, p. 85.

61 Reproduced in Ivanova, *Velikii kinemo*, p. 259.

62 Osip Mandel´shtam, 'Barsuch´ia nora (A. Blok: 7 avgusta 1921 g. – 7 avgusta 1922 goda)', *Sobranie sochinenii v dvukh tomakh*, volume 2, *Stikhotvoreniia. Proza* (New York, 1966), pp. 312–17 (p. 315).

6. From the Ballerina to the Early Modern Dancer

1 Anastasiia Verbitskaia, *Kliuchi schast´ia*, Volume 2 (St Petersburg, 1993), p. 151.

2 Ann Kodicek (ed.), *Diaghilev. Creator of the Ballets Russes. Art. Music. Dance* (London, 1996), p. 34. On the differences between European and Russian attitudes to classical ballet in the early twentieth century, see also Marion Kant 'The soul of the shoe' in Marion Kant (ed.), *The Cambridge Companion to Ballet* (Cambridge and New York, 2007), pp. 184–97 (p. 193).

3 Cited in Natalia Roslavleva, *Era of the Russian Ballet* (London, 1966), p. 187.

4 Dance historians disagree about when this piece was choreographed and premiered. For discussion of the different versions of its genesis and performance history, see Keith Money, *Anna Pavlova. Her Life and Art* (London, 1982), p. 71.

5 Sally Banes, *Dancing Women. Female Bodies on Stage* (London and New York), 1998, p. 168.

6 Roger Copeland, 'Towards a sexual politics of contemporary dance', *Contact Quarterly*, 7, 1982, pp. 45–50 (pp. 47–48).

7 Before he acquired a movie camera, Shiriaev had experimented with recording choreography by producing two-dimensional moving images: he made little sketches of each of the individual positions that made up a dance piece on strips of paper 45mm wide and then animated them, using a rotating mechanism and mirror prisms in a praxinoscope. See Birgit Beumers, '1909: *Harlequin's Jest* [Shutka Arlekina]' in Julian Graffy, 'Special feature: Russian cinema centenary', *Studies in Russian and Soviet Cinema*, 2, 2008, 3, pp. 327–54 (pp. 329–30). See also Birgit Beumers, Victor Bocharov and David Robinson (eds), *Alexander Shiryaev: Master of Movement* (Gemona, 2009), pp. 43–46. Some of these paper films are animated in Bocharov's documentary *A Belated Premiere* [Zapozdavshaia prem´era, 2003].

8 Created in Brighton in 1899 by Alfred Darling, the Biokam was one of the earliest amateur cameras and an incredibly versatile piece of equipment. It could be used as a movie or stills camera, and as a projector, printer and enlarger. It used 17.5mm film with central perforations between frames. Shiriaev also used a 17.5mm Ernemann Kino camera. Developed in Germany in 1903 by Ernemann AG, this was Germany's first small-gauge camera for amateurs. See Martina Roepke, 'Tracing 17.5mm practices in Germany (1902–1908)', *Film History*, 19, 2007, 4, pp. 344–52 (p. 344).

9 Bocharov, *A Belated Premiere*.

10 This last category of films rewrites another accepted fact of early Russian film history, namely that which identifies Władysław Starewicz as the 'father' of Russian animation and the inventor of narrative stop-frame animation. Starewicz made his first films starring animated beetles and other insects in 1911; Shiriaev's animations thus pre-date Starewicz's by more than two years.

11 Elizabeth Dempster, 'Women writing the body: let's watch a little how she dances' in Susan Sheridan (ed.), *Grafts. Feminist Cultural Criticism* (London and New York, 1988), pp. 35–54, (p. 39).

12 Susan Leigh Foster, *Reading Dancing: Bodies and Subjects in Contemporary American Dance* (Berkeley, CA, 1986).

13 Dempster, 'Women writing the body', p. 37.

14 Ibid., p. 35.

15 Cited in ibid.

16 Ibid, p. 41.

17 See also Ann Daly, 'The Balanchine woman: of hummingbirds and channel swimmers', *The Drama Review*, vol. 31, no. 1, 1987, pp. 8–22 and Christy Adair, *Women and Dance. Sylphs and Sirens* (New York, 1992).

18 Dempster, 'Women writing the body', p. 39.

19 One contemporary reviewer described the dragonfly as 'a famous barefoot-dancer' [*znamenitaia bosonozhka*], thus linking her to the American dancer Isadora Duncan. Reproduced in V. Ivanova *et al.* (eds), *Velikii kinemo. Katalog sokhranivshikhsia igrovykh fil'mov Rossii, 1908–1919* (Moscow, 2002), p. 118. However, there is nothing in the film itself to justify this characterization. On the contrary, as Mikhail Iampol'skii and Rimgaila Salys have both noted, her visual representation is clearly based on the many female roles in nineteenth-century romantic ballets that cast ballerinas as butterflies, or other delicate insects, and dress them in winged costumes. See M. B. Iampol'skii, 'Starevich: mimika nasekomykh i kul'turnaia traditsiia', *Kinovedcheskie zapiski*, 1, 1988, pp. 84–90 and Rimgaila Salys, 'The Cameraman's Revenge' in Rimgaila Salys (ed), *The Russian Cinema Reader. Volume One. 1908 to the Stalin Era* (Boston, MA, 2013), pp. 48–51 (p. 50).

20 Reproduced in Ivanova, *Velikii kinemo*, p. 119.

21 Ibid.

22 For a fascinating discussion of how early Russian viewers received the moving image, apprehended the status of the screen and its relationship to the image, and understood what 'happened' to visual images when they 'disappeared' from the cinema screen, see Yuri Tsivian, *Early Cinema in Russia and its Cultural Reception* (Chicago, IL and London, 1994), pp. 135–61. For a revealing contemporary response that addresses these issues, see Maxim Gorky, 'The Lumière cinematograph (extracts)' [4 July 1896] in Richard Taylor and Ian Christie (eds), *The Film Factory. Russian and Soviet Cinema in Documents 1896–1939* (London and New York, 1994), pp. 25–26.

23 This film has survived only partially. The following discussion therefore draws on contemporary reviews and synopses of the film, reproduced in Ivanova, *Velikii kinemo*, pp. 350–51.

24 Camille Paglia, *Sexual Personae, Art and Decadence from Nefertiti to Emily Dickinson* (London and New York, 1999), p. 9.

25 Cited in Dempster, 'Women writing the body', p. 52.

26 Paolo Cherchi Usai *et al.*, (eds), *Silent Witnesses. Russian Films 1908–1919* (London, 1989), p. 256.

27 Bram Dijkstra, *Idols of Perversity. Fantasies of Feminine Evil in Fin-de-Siècle Culture* (New York and Oxford, 1986), pp. 37–63.

28 Helena Goscilo, 'Playing dead: the operatics of celebrity funerals, or, the ultimate silent part' in Louise McReynolds and Joan Neuberger (eds), *Imitations of Life: Two Centuries of Melodrama in Russia* (Durham, NC and London, 2002), pp. 283–319 (p. 291).

29 Christian Metz, 'Photography and fetish' [1985] in Carol Squiers (ed.), *The Critical Image. Essays on Contemporary Photography* (London, 1991), pp. 155–64 (p. 155).

30 Ibid., p. 158.

31 Ibid., p. 159.

32 Miriam Hansen, 'Deadly scenarios: narrative perspective and sexual politics in pre-Revolutionary Russian film', *Cinefocus*, 2, 1992, 2, pp. 10–19 (p. 14).

33 This sequence also connects Nedelin with Viktor in the earlier *Child of the Big City*, for it recalls his daydream in which Mary expresses her love for him 'innocently', by seeking protection in his embrace and resting her head on his chest.

34 Aleksandr Blok, 'Nu, chto zhe? Ustalo zalomleny slabye ruki…' in V. N. Orlov, A. A. Surkov and K. I. Chukovskii (eds), *Aleksandr Blok. Sobranie sochinenii v vos´mi tomakh*, vol. 3, *Stikhotvoreniia i poemy, 1907–1921* (Moscow and Leningrad, 1960), p. 46.

35 'Safely dead' is Dijkstra's term. Dijkstra, *Idols of Perversity*, p. 63.

36 Reproduced in Cherchi Usai, *Silent Witnesses*, p. 256.

37 Louise McReynolds, 'Demanding men, desiring women and social collapse in the films of Evgenii Bauer, 1913–17', *Studies in Russian and Soviet Cinema*, 3, 2009, 2, pp. 145–56 (p. 149).

38 Ian Christie, sleeve note to *Daydreams, Early Russian Cinema*, volume 7, *Evgenii Bauer*, London, 1992.

39 Denise J. Youngblood, *The Magic Mirror. Moviemaking in Russia, 1908–1918* (Madison, WI and London, 1999), pp. 95–96.

40 Vitol´d Polonskii, an actor with the Malyi Theatre who had entered cinema in 1915 and had quickly become one of the 'Kings' of the pre-Revolutionary screen, was often cast in the role of the faithless upper-class lover, particularly after his memorable performances as the callous Dymov in Petr Chardynin's *Mirages* [Mirazhi, 1915] and the immoral Prince Bartinskii in Bauer's *A Life for a Life*.

41 Philip Cavendish has suggested that Bauer may have intended Glinskii to be 'a barely disguised parody' of the contemporary Russian writer, artist and photographer Leonid Andreev: Andreev's work, in all media, is similarly focused on 'death-obsessed themes', Glinskii resembles Andreev physically, and Andreev 'lost his wife (in 1906) and mourned her death for years afterwards'. See Philip Cavendish, 'Yesterday' (13 October 2015). Online. Email: p.cavendish@ucl.ac.uk Indeed, the decadence of the set design for Glinskii's studio is so exaggerated that one also wonders whether Bauer, who explored the theme of the psychological/sexual hold a dead (woman) has over a living (man) throughout his cinematic career, may not also have intended to introduce of a note of self-parody into this film, made towards the end of the First World War when the extent of Russia's massive losses would have been becoming known.

42 Youngblood, *The Magic Mirror*, p. 137.

43 Reproduced in Ivanova, *Velikii kinemo*, p. 356.

44 Marion Kant notes that the nineteenth-century trope of the 'woman in white' can be traced 'in novels, paintings, operas, poems, but above all in ballets'. See Kant, 'The soul of the shoe', p. 190.

45 Petipa revived and revised *Giselle* for the Imperial Ballet many times between 1884 and 1903, when Anna Pavlova performed the title role.

46 Yuri Tsivian, 'Video essay' on *Mad Love: Three Films by Evgenii Bauer*, BFI DVD publishing, London, 2002.

47 Ibid. Karalli was the mistress of Grand Duke Dmitrii Pavlovich of Russia, a co-conspirator, with Felix Iusupov, in the plot that led Grigorii Rasputin to his death at the Moika Palace in St Petersburg in December 1916. It has been suggested that, because of her beauty and her fame, Karalli was used, unawares, to lure Rasputin to his death. See Edvard Radzinsky, *Rasputin. The Last Word* (London, 2000), pp. 620–22 and Gennadii Kagan, *Vera Karalli – legenda russkogo baleta* (St Petersburg, 2009), pp. 191–99.

48 Tsivian, 'Video essay'.

49 Marion Kant, 'The soul of the shoe', p. 197. Some dance historians have argued that *The Dying Swan* is not as traditional as its outward signs of tutu and *bourrées en pointe* suggest. For example, Elizabeth Souritz summarises Vera Krasovskaia's view that *The Dying Swan* displays 'an improvisational quality', which she likens to Isadora Duncan's dancing. She also cites Kay Bardsley, who likewise finds elements of Duncan's style in *The Dying Swan*, commenting that it 'may possibly owe its [...] origin (certainly the portion which relates to the arms and upper torso) to the movements set forth by Isadora Duncan in the Chopin Prelude no. 20, op. 28'. See Elizabeth Souritz, 'Isadora Duncan and prewar Russian dancemakers' in Lynn Garafola and Nancy Van Norman Baer (eds), *The Ballets Russes and its World* (New Haven and London, 1999), pp. 97–115 (pp. 111–12). Indeed, Fokin himself stressed that he had intended his choreography to be innovative: '*The Dying Swan* is the transition from the old ballet to the new. Here I make use of the technique of the old, so-called classical dance, and the traditional costume of the ballet. But it contains all the elements from which the new Russian Ballet has been created. [...] This is a dance of the whole body – not a dance of the limbs only – such as in the old ballet dances. For instance, here the movement of the arms is equally, if indeed not more, important than the movement of the legs'. See Michel Fokine, *Choreographic Compositions by Michel Fokine: 'The Dying Swan': Thirty-six Photographs from Poses by Vera Fokina: Detailed Description of the Dance by Michel Fokine: Music by C. Saint-Saens* (New York, 1925), p. 4. However, while individual details of the choreography may not be wholly conventional from a dance specialist's point of view, for the general viewer the associations evoked by its screen representation are overwhelmingly traditional. As Marion Kant notes: 'By the twentieth century, ballet costume and pointe shoes had been publicly accepted as symbols of the art as a whole. They carried all the representational implications for the female body'. See Kant, 'The soul of the shoe', p. 194.

50 For an alternative discussion of the swan/ballerina as *dikovinka* in this film, see Alyssa DeBlasio, 'Choreographing space, time, and *dikovinki* in the films of Evgenii Bauer', *The Russian Review*, 66, 2007, pp. 671–92 (pp. 677–79).

51 See still reproduced in Ivanova, *Velikii kinemo*, p. 356.

52 Viktor also makes it clear that he finds Gizella's muteness attractive. Indeed, throughout Bauer's oeuvre his male protagonists, even those less extreme in their behaviour than Glinskii, often choose to love women with some flaw or shortcoming that detracts from their power in the male protagonists' eyes. See Rachel Morley, 'Gender relations in the films of Evgenii Bauer', *Slavonic and East European Review*, 81, 2003, 1, pp. 32–69 (p. 60).

53 McReynolds, 'Demanding men', p. 151.

54 Youngblood, *The Magic Mirror*, p. 99.

55 Anastasya Verbitskaya, *Keys to Happiness: A Novel*, translated and edited by Beth Holmgren and Helena Goscilo (Bloomington and Indianapolis, IN, 1999), p. 163.

56 McReynolds, 'Demanding men', p. 149.

57 Cited and summarized in Dempster, 'Women writing the body', p. 39.

58 See still reproduced in Cherchi Usai, *Silent Witnesses*, p. 249.

59 Copeland, 'Towards a sexual politics', p. 47.

60 Laura Engelstein, *The Keys to Happiness: Sex and the Search for Modernity in Fin-de-siècle Russia* (Ithaca, NY and London, 1992), p. 414.

61 Peter Kurth, *Isadora. The Sensational Life of Isadora Duncan* (London, 2001), p. 151.

62 On Duncan's reception in Russia, see ibid., pp. 143–55, pp. 173–78 and pp. 221–27.

63 On Duncan's impact on Russian dance and culture, see Engelstein, *The Keys to Happiness*, pp. 414–20 and Souritz, 'Isadora Duncan', pp. 97–115.

64 Henrietta Mondry, 'Performing the paradox: Rozanov and the dancing body of Isadora Duncan', *Essays in Poetics*, 24, 1999, pp. 91–116 (pp. 93–94).

65 Ibid., p. 98.

66 Ibid., pp. 98–99.

67 Copeland, 'Towards a sexual politics', p. 47.

68 Ibid.

69 Isadora Duncan, *My Life* [1927] (London, 1996), p. 120.

70 Ibid., p. 121.

71 Ibid., p. 120.

72 Cited in Engelstein, *The Keys to Happiness*, p. 418.

73 Copeland, 'Towards a sexual politics', p. 47.

74 In the film, Mania was played by the ballerina Ol´ga Preobrazhenskaia. On the film's popularity, see Youngblood, *The Magic Mirror*, pp. 57–60 and Denise J. Youngblood, 'The return of the native: Yakov Protazanov and Soviet cinema' in Richard Taylor and Ian Christie (eds), *Inside the Film Factory. New Approaches to Russian and Soviet Cinema* (London and New York, 1991), pp. 103–23 (p. 103, p. 107).

75 The film was thought lost until 2007, when a short clip was discovered in the Lenfil´m studio, edited into a 1940 film made in homage to Vladimir Gardin, one of the film's directors. See http://www.cinetecadibologna.it/ evp_Preobrazhenskaya_Pravov/programmazione/app_5085/from_2013-06-30/h_1015 (accessed 9 January 2016).

76 Anastasiia Verbitskaia, *Kliuchi schast´ia*, Volume 2 (St Petersburg, 1993), p. 42.

77 For the best examples of this technique, see ibid, pp. 43–45 and p. 101, and Anastasiia Verbitskaia, *Kliuchi schast´ia*, Volume 1 (St Petersburg, 1993), pp. 18–19, pp. 156–57 and pp. 504–06.

78 Ibid., p. 136.
79 Ibid., p. 500.
80 Verbitskaia, *Kliuchi schast'ia*, Volume 2, p. 126.
81 Although this film survives without intertitles, contemporary reviews enable us to reconstruct the original titles. One reviewer cites the intertitle from the scene in which Vladimir dismisses Vera's confrontation of his infidelity as reading: 'I do not know you'. Reproduced in Ivanova, *Velikii kinemo*, p. 226.

7. The Actress

1 Nina Auerbach, 'Victorian womanhood and literary character' in her *Woman and the Demon. The Life of a Victorian Myth* (Cambridge, MA and London, 1982), pp. 185–217 (p. 211).
2 For a selective list of pre-Revolutionary Russian films based on literary sources, see Veniamin Vishnevskii, *Khudozhestvennye fil'my dorevoliutsionnoi Rossii: fil'mograficheskoe opisanie* (Moscow, 1945), pp. 157–60.
3 Chardynin's untitled article is cited in Denise J. Youngblood, *The Magic Mirror. Moviemaking in Russia, 1908–1918* (Madison, WI and London, 1999), p. 68. On the perceived educational function of literary adaptations, see also Neia Zorkaia, *Na rubezhe stoletii: U istokov massovogo iskusstva v Rossii 1900–1910 godov* (Moscow, 1976), pp. 99–111.
4 For a list of extant film adaptations of literary works directed by Bauer, see Rachel Morley, '"Crime without punishment": reworkings of nineteenth-century Russian literary sources in Evgenii Bauer's *Child of the Big City*' in Stephen Hutchings and Anat Vernitski (eds), *Russian and Soviet Film Adaptations of Literature, 1900–2001: Screening the Word*, (London and New York, 2005), pp. 27–43, (pp. 42–43, n. 3).
5 In 1915 Bauer also adapted another late Turgenev story, 'The Song of Love Triumphant' ['Pesn' torzhestvuiushchei liubvi', 1881]. This film has not survived.
6 For concise synopses of Turgenev's story, see Yuri Tsivian, 'The invisible novelty: film adaptations in the 1910s' in Robert Stam and Alessandra Raengo (eds), *A Companion to Literature and Film* (Oxford, 2004), pp. 92–111 (p. 94) and Otto Boele, '*After Death*, the movie (1915) – Ivan Turgenev, Evgenii Bauer and the aesthetics of morbidity' in Robert Reid and Joe Andrew (eds), *Turgenev: Art, Ideology, Legacy* (Amsterdam and New York, 2010), pp. 253–268.
7 Reproduced in V. Ivanova *et al.* (eds), *Velikii kinemo. Katalog sokhranivshikhsia igrovykh fil'mov Rossii, 1908–1919* (Moscow, 2002), pp. 270–71. In 1918, the viewing board of the Cinema Committee of the People's Commissariat of Enlightenment [Kinematograficheskii Komitet Narodnogo Komissariata Prosveshcheniia], which was set up after the Revolution to assess the artistic and

ideological value of pre-Revolutionary films, similarly criticised the film for its lack of fidelity to Turgenev's story, concluding: 'This screen version of the story does not at all convey the story's meaning, and in several places even distorts in its own way introductory episodes that do not occur in the story. The setting does not at all evoke the story's period, the actors are dressed in contemporary suits and have different names from in the story. Resolution: change the title of the film'. Ibid., p. 271.

8 Ibid.

9 Tsivian feels that 'the humble note' Bauer strikes in this reply is 'no doubt sincere'. See Tsivian, 'The invisible novelty', p. 97. While it is certainly possible that Bauer intended some of his comments to be taken at face value, this cannot be true of the entire statement, for if the *obvious* alterations he makes to Turgenev's original are far from arbitrary, the other, more subtle, alterations that can be discerned in the film are doubtless also intentional.

10 Turgenev changed the title to 'Klara Milich' on the insistence of the publisher, who judged 'After Death' to be 'too lugubrious'. See Ivan Turgenev, 'Klara Milich' in his *Polnoe sobranie sochinenii i pisem v dvadtsati vos´mi tomakh*, 13 (Moscow and Leningrad, 1967), text pp. 76–134 and commentary pp. 575–90 (p. 578). Henceforth, all references to this story will be to this edition, with page references given in parentheses in the main body of the text.

11 For biographical information about Kadmina, see Boris Iagolim, *Kometa divnoi krasoty. Zhizn´ i tvorchestvo Evlalii Kadminoi* (Moscow, 1970). For a critical interpretation of her biography, see Julie Buckler, 'Her final debut: the Kadmina legend in Russian literature' in Andrew Baruch Wachtel (ed.), *Intersections and Transpositions. Russian Music, Literature and Society* (Evanston, IL, 1998), pp. 225–52.

12 Kate Sealey Rahman presents Kadmina's suicide as a carefully pre-meditated act of revenge addressed to her former lover when she notes that it was Kadmina herself who was responsible for his presence in the audience that evening, as she had '[i]n a final macabre touch, [...] sent front row tickets for the performance to her former lover and his new spouse'. See Kate Sealey Rahman, 'Ostrovskii on the British stage: 1894–1928', *Toronto Slavic Quarterly: Academic Electronic Journal in Slavic Studies*, 9, 2004 at http://www.utoronto.ca/tsq/09/rahman09.shtml (accessed 11 January 2016). John Racin also states that Kadmina sent tickets to the newly married couple. See John Racin (ed.), *Tatyana Repina. Two Translated Texts by Alexei Suvorin and Anton Chekhov* (Jefferson, SC and London, 1999), p. 15. Neither Iagolim nor Buckler mentions this, however; Iagolim conjectures that it was the shock of unexpectedly seeing them together in public that provoked Kadmina's suicide. See Iagolim, *Kometa divnoi krasoty*, pp. 132–33.

13 Chekhov's work was originally intended neither for publication nor performance but rather as a gift for his friend, Suvorin. On the connections between the two plays, see Racin, *Tatyana Repina*, pp. 13–73.

14 Svetlana Zvereva, *Alexander Kastalsky: His Life and Music*, translated by Stuart Campbell (Aldershot, 2003), pp. 104–07 and p. 257.

15 Tsivian suggests that Chardynin based his film on Mario Caserini's *Love Everlasting* [Ma l'amor mio non muore, 1913] in which a singer commits suicide on stage to save the man she loves from disgrace. Tsivian, 'The Invisible Novelty', p. 97.

16 The Kadmina legend continues to develop: in 2002 the director Kira Muratova added to this network her film *Chekhovian Motifs* [Chekhovskie motivy], an ingenious reworking of both Chekhov's 1886 story 'Difficult People' ['Tiazhelye liudi'] and his *Tatiana Repina*. For an analysis of Muratova's film that considers its dialogic status, see Julian Graffy, 'Difficult people: Kira Muratova's cinematic encounter with Chekhov', *Essays in Poetics: Chekhov Special Issue 2*, 31, 2006, pp. 180–212.

17 For critical synopses of most of the nineteenth-century Kadmina texts mentioned here, see Buckler, 'Her final debut', pp. 237–44.

18 Ibid., p. 238.

19 Nikolai Leskov, 'Teatral´nyi kharakter', *Teatral´nyi mirok*, 1888, pp. 11–14 (p. 14).

20 I take this term from Svetlana Boym, who uses it in her discussion of the life and work of Marina Tsvetaeva. Svetlana Boym, 'The death of the poetess' in her *Death in Quotation Marks: Cultural Myths of the Modern Poet* (Cambridge, MA, 1991), pp. 192–240.

21 For further delineation of the alterations Bauer makes to the social setting of Turgenev's story and for discussion of the effect this has on his representation of Zoia *as an actress*, see Boele 'After Death, the movie'.

22 I. F. Annenskii, 'Umiraiushchii Turgenev: *Klara Milich*' [1906] in N. T. Ashimbaeva, I. I. Podol´skaia and A. V. Fedorov (eds), *I. F. Annenskii: Knigi otrazhenii* (Moscow, 1979), pp. 36–43 (p. 40).

23 Heide Schlüpmann, 'From patriarchal violence to the aesthetics of death: Russian cinema 1900–1919', *Cinefocus*, 2, 1992, 2, pp. 2–9 (p. 8).

24 Rachel Morley, 'Gender relations in the films of Evgenii Bauer', *Slavonic and East European Review*, 81, 2003, 1, pp. 32–69 (pp. 49–50).

25 Ibid.

26 Philip Cavendish, 'The hand that turns the handle: camera operators and the poetics of the camera in pre-Revolutionary Russian film', *Slavonic and East European Review*, 82, 2004, 2, pp. 201–45 (pp. 222–23).

27 Ibid., p. 223.

28 Ibid.

29 Yuri Tsivian, *Early Cinema in Russia and its Cultural Reception* (Chicago, IL and London, 1994), pp. 192–93. Tsivian does not mention this close-up sequence in *After Death* in his discussion of the development and reception of the close-up, but refers to it briefly only as an example of a track-in. See ibid., p. 205.

30 Ibid., p. 193.
31 The actress in this film was Vera Kholodnaia, the 'Queen' of the pre-Revolutionary screen and the only major star of this period to begin her acting career in the cinema, in this Bauer film. For discussion of Bauer's use of the close-up in *The Song of Love Triumphant* and of the 'legend' that Kholodnaia's extraordinary beauty and notoriously weak acting ability contributed to its 'invention', see ibid., pp. 192–93.
32 Ibid., p. 194.
33 Ibid., p. 195.
34 Ibid.
35 Ibid., p. 194.
36 Cited ibid.
37 Alyssa DeBlasio, 'Choreographing space, time, and *dikovinki* in the films of Evgenii Bauer', *The Russian Review*, 66, 2007, pp. 671–92 (p. 685).
38 Cited in Romil Sobolev, *Liudi i fil'my russkogo dorevoliutsionnogo kino* (Moscow, 1961), p. 101.
39 Rosamund Bartlett and Linda Edmondson, 'Collapse and creation: issues of identity and the Russian *fin-de-siècle*' in Catriona Kelly and David Shepherd (eds), *Constructing Russian Culture in the Age of Revolution: 1881–1940* (Oxford, 1998), pp. 165–224 (p. 188).
40 See George Heard Hamilton, 'Icon-painting' in his *The Art and Architecture of Russia* (Harmondsworth, 1975), pp. 67–110 and Hans Belting, 'The rediscovery of the icon in Russia' in his *Likeness and Presence. A History of the Image before the Era of Art*, translated by Edmund Jephcott (Chicago, IL and London, 1994), pp. 19–21.
41 Anthony Parton, *Mikhail Larionov and the Russian Avant-Garde* (Princeton, NJ, 1993).
42 See in particular the twelfth-century icon 'The Archangel with the Golden Hair'. Still reproduced in Rachel Morley, 'Performing femininity in an age of change: Evgenii Bauer, Ivan Turgenev and the legend of Evlaliia Kadmina' in Reid and Andrew (eds), *Turgenev*, pp. 269–316 (p. 285).
43 For discussion of the defining features of medieval Russian icons, see Hamilton, 'Icon-painting', pp. 67–110.
44 Cavendish, 'The hand that turns the handle', p. 224.
45 DeBlasio similarly draws attention to the contrast between Zoia's 'static', mask-like face and her powerfully expressive gaze. DeBlasio, 'Choreographing space', p. 685.
46 On the changes in and significance of the expression of the eyes in Russian icons, see Hamilton, 'Icon-painting', p. 83.
47 Tom Brown, *Breaking the Fourth Wall. Direct Address in the Cinema* (Edinburgh, 2012).

48 Cavendish, 'The hand that turns the handle', p. 224.

49 Tsivian, *Early Cinema in Russia*, p. 205.

50 Ibid., pp. 205–06.

51 In a discussion of early film-makers' exploration of the expressive possibilities of film, which emphasises as a characteristic of 1910s cinema its lack of 'international uniformity' and singles out early Russian films as demonstrating, more than other early national cinemas, a distinctive national style, Kristin Thompson describes how, from D. W. Griffith's 1912 film *The Musketeers of Pig Alley* onward, in early American films the device of having a character move toward the camera while staring into the lens was invariably used 'to create a sense of menace'. See Kristin Thompson, 'The international exploration of cinematic expressivity' in Lee Grieveson and Peter Krämer (eds), *The Silent Cinema Reader* (London and New York, 2004), pp. 254–69 (p. 259).

52 Aleksandr Kuprin 'Poslednii debiut' [1889] in A. I. Kuprin, *Sobranie sochinenii v deviati tomakh*, volume 1 (Moscow, 1964), pp. 43–49 (p. 49).

53 Ibid.

54 Tsivian, *Early Cinema in Russia*, p. 190.

55 Christian Metz, 'Photography and fetish' [1985] in Carol Squiers (ed.), *The Critical Image. Essays on Contemporary Photography* (London, 1991), pp. 155–64 (p. 158).

56 Yuri Tsivian, 'Video Essay' on *Mad Love: Three Films by Evgenii Bauer*, BFI DVD publishing, London, 2002.

57 Ibid. and Tsivian, 'The invisible novelty', p. 100.

58 For further discussion of these differences and an alternative interpretation of their motivation and significance, see ibid., pp. 97–100.

59 Tsivian, 'Video essay'.

60 Turgenev also suggests rational interpretations of some of the apparently 'supernatural' events of his story, but he does so in different ways from Bauer. For example, the narrator comments that the mysterious lock of black hair that Platosha finds in Aratov's hand could have come from between the pages of Klara's diary.

61 See still reproduced in Boele, '*After Death*, the movie', p. 263.

62 See especially: Heide Schlüpmann, 'From patriarchal violence to the aesthetics of death: Russian cinema 1900–1919', *Cinefocus*, 2, 1992, 2, pp. 2–9; Miriam Hansen, 'Deadly scenarios: narrative perspective and sexual politics in pre-Revolutionary Russian film', ibid., pp. 10–19; Morley, 'Gender relations'; Michele L. Torre, 'Filtering culture: symbolism, modernity and gender construction in Evgenii Bauer's films' in John Fullerton (ed.), *Screen Culture: History and Textuality* (Eastleigh, 2004), pp. 99–112.

63 Turgenev had met Alenitsyn through some mutual friends, although he did not know him well. He had also seen Kadmina perform once, but was not acquainted

with her. On Alenitsyn, see Iagolim, *Kometa divnoi krasoty*, pp. 141–42 and Buckler, 'Her final debut', p. 251, n. 50.

64 Ibid. For a description of this portrait, see Annenskii, 'Umiraiushchii Turgenev', p. 41.

65 Cited in Iagolim, *Kometa divnoi krasoty*, p. 135.

66 In Leskov's story, a Romeo and Juliet style misunderstanding lies at the root of the lovers' deaths: the heroine is persuaded by her lover's mother to end their affair; her lover then shoots himself, and Piamma follows suit.

67 Buckler speculates that Kadmina's decision to commit suicide on stage was also motivated by the opportunity it afforded her to upstage her professional rival, the actress Ponizovskaia, who was playing the role of Anna, the tsarina whom Kadmina's Vasilisa poisons in Ostrovskii's play: as the performance had to be stopped when Kadmina became unwell, Ponizovskaia was denied the chance to play her big death scene, and Kadmina thus stole the limelight. Buckler, 'Her final debut', p. 236.

68 Tsivian, 'The invisible novelty', p. 95.

69 Ibid., pp. 95–96. Tsivian refers to Bauer's characters by the names Turgenev gave to them throughout his article.

70 Ibid., p. 97.

71 DeBlasio, 'Choreographing space', p. 682.

72 Elisabeth Bronfen, *Over Her Dead Body. Death, Femininity and the Aesthetic* (Manchester, 1992), p. 142.

73 Ibid., p. 143.

74 Maria Wyke, *Projecting the Past. Ancient Rome, Cinema and History* (New York and London, 1997), pp. 84–85.

75 Reproduced ibid., p. 87.

76 Ibid., pp. 85–86.

77 Livy, 'Book one: Rome under the kings' in his *The Early History of Rome* (Harmondsworth, 1960), pp. 33–101 (pp. 97–101).

78 Tsivian, 'The invisible novelty', pp. 101–08.

79 For discussion of the innovative nature of Bauer's cinematic pictorialism, or so-called 'Rembrandtism', see Mikhail Iampolski, 'Russia: the cinema of anti-modernity and backward progress' in Valentina Vitali and Paul Willemen (eds), *Theorising National Cinema* (London, 2006), pp. 72–87 (pp. 77–79). Iampolski sees Bauer's exploitation of Renaissance art in his innovations in lighting, staging and set design as evidence of his 'archaising inclination' and, following Tynianov, applies to him the term 'archaist-innovator'. Ibid., p. 79. Bauer's tendency to borrow from the fine arts and the experimental nature of this undertaking are also discussed illuminatingly by Tsivian, with reference to sequences from *The Dying Swan*, in his 'Two «stylists» of the teens: Franz Hofer and Yevgenii Bauer' in Thomas Elsaesser (ed.), *A Second Life: German Cinema's First Decades* (Amsterdam, 1996), pp. 264–76.

80 See stills reproduced in Morley, 'Performing femininity', pp. 298–99.

81 See still reproduced ibid., p. 296.

82 Cavendish, 'The hand that turns the handle', p. 228 n. 65.

83 Arthur K. Wheelock Jr. and George Keyes, *Rembrandt's Lucretias* (Washington, DC, 1991).

84 See Susan K. Morrissey, *Suicide and the Body Politic in Imperial Russia* (Cambridge, 2006) and Irina Paperno, *Suicide as a Cultural Institution in Dostoevsky's Russia* (Ithaca, NY and London, 1997), pp. 75–104. The suicide epidemic of 1906–1914 was the second to hit Russian society; Evlaliia Kadmina's death occurred during the first, which ran from the 1860s into the 1880s.

85 Morrissey, *Suicide*, p. 345.

86 Metz, 'Photography and fetish', p. 158.

87 Buckler, 'Her final debut', p. 232.

88 Ibid., p. 243.

89 Ibid., pp. 239–40.

90 See especially: David Robinson, 'Evgenii Bauer and the cinema of Nikolai II', *Sight and Sound*, 59, 1989–90, 1, pp. 51–55 (p. 55); Tsivian, 'The invisible novelty'; Cavendish, 'The hand that turns the handle', pp. 222–24; DeBlasio, 'Choreographing space', p. 685; Tsivian, *Early Cinema in Russia*, p. 205.

91 Ibid., p. 199.

92 Tsivian, 'Two «stylists»', p. 274.

93 Tsivian, 'The invisible novelty', p. 99.

94 Susan Hayward, *Cinema Studies. The Key Concepts* (London and New York, 2006), p. 3.

95 Roland Barthes, *Camera Lucida. Reflections on Photography*, translated by Richard Howard (London, 2000), p. 92.

96 Auerbach, 'Victorian womanhood', p. 211.

97 Cited and translated in Richard Taylor and Ian Christie (eds), *The Film Factory. Russian and Soviet Cinema in Documents 1896–1939* (London and New York), 1994, p. 39.

Conclusion

1 Paolo Cherchi Usai *et al.*, *Silent Witnesses. Russian Films 1908–1919* (London, 1989), p. 56.

2 Cited and translated in Denise J. Youngblood, *The Magic Mirror. Moviemaking in Russia, 1908–1918* (Madison, WI and London, 1999), p. v.

3 Judith Butler, *Gender Trouble. Feminism and the Subversion of Identity* (New York and London, 1999), p. 33.

4 Ibid.

5 For further discussion of this film and its use of classical tropes, see Rachel Morley, 'Zhizn´ za zhizn´ / A Life for a Life', in Birgit Beumers (ed.), *The Cinema of Russia and the Former Soviet Union* (London and New York 2007), pp. 13–22.

6 Philip Cavendish, 'The hand that turns the handle: camera operators and the poetics of the camera in pre-Revolutionary Russian film', *Slavonic and East European Review*, 82, 2004, 2, pp. 201–45 (p. 225).

7 See Rachel Morley [Reichl Morli], '*Molchi, grust´, molchi...* (1918)' in Ekaterina Vasil´eva and Nikita Braginskii (eds), *Noev kovcheg russkogo kino. Ot 'Sten´ki Razina' do 'Stiliag'* (Vinnitsa, Ukraine, 2012), pp. 32–38.

8 Neia Zorkaia, 'Pervaia russkaia kinozvezda' in B. B. Ziukov, *Vera Kholodnaia. K 100-letiiu so dnia rozhdeniia* (Moscow, 1995), pp. 251–78 (p. 272).

9 'Skazka liubvi dorogoi («Molchi, grust´, molchi!..»). Iubileinaia kartina P. I. Chardynina', *Kino-gazeta*, 1918, 20, pp. 4–7 (pp. 6–7) reproduced in *Early Russian Cinema Online (BrillOnline Primary Sources)*, advisor R. Yangirov, Leiden and Boston, 2005 at http://primarysources.brillonline.com/browse/early-russian-cinema (accessed on 13 January 2016), access provided by University College London. The section of this article that outlines the plot of Part One of the film is reproduced in V. Ivanova *et al.*, *Velikii kinemo. Katalog sokhranivshikhsia igrovykh fil´mov Rossii, 1908–1919*, pp. 451–52. The section that provides a synopsis of Part Two is not included, however.

10 Iurii Tsiv´ian, *Istoricheskaia retseptsiia kino. Kinematograf v Rossii, 1896–1930* (Riga, 1991), p. 108.

11 Reproduced in Ivanova, *Velikii kinemo*, pp. 452–54 (p. 454).

12 Zorkaia, 'Pervaia russkaia kinozvezda', p. 271.

13 Elena Prokof´eva, *Koroleva ekrana. Istoriia Very Kholodnoi* (Moscow, 2001), p. 98.

14 In early cinema, an iris out was a shot in which an iris (or diaphragm) was positioned in front of the camera lens and gradually closed to mask the image. To the early viewer, it appeared that the image was held in a circle, surrounded by a black frame, and that the circle containing the image gradually contracted as the black frame expanded, until, at the end of the shot, the screen was completely black. The iris out was a common transitional device, used and received as a form of punctuation that, among other effects, enabled film-makers to conclude a scene with the suggestion that there was more to come that could not (for reasons of delicacy, perhaps) be shown; in other words, it was similar to the use of ellipsis in a written text, an invitation to the viewer to imagine what might come next. By 1918 concluding a scene featuring a kiss with an iris out would have been considered rather clichéd.

15 Yuri Tsivian, *Early Cinema in Russia and its Cultural Reception* (Chicago, IL and London, 1998), p. 92.

16 Peter Kenez, *Cinema and Soviet Society, 1917–1953* (Cambridge, New York and Melbourne, 1992), p. 31.

17 Kseniia Mar, 'Vera Kholodnaia – Pola («Skazka liubvi dorogoi»)' [1918] in Ziukov, *Vera Kholodnaia*, pp. 133–34 (p. 134).

18 Reproduced in Ivanova, *Velikii kinemo*, p. 453.

19 Prokof´eva, *Koroleva ekrana*, p. 108.

Coda

1 Cited in Iurii Tsiv´ian, *Istoricheskaia retseptsiia kino. Kinematograf v Rossii, 1896–1930* (Riga, 1991), p. 109.

Bibliography

Abbate, Carolyn, 'Opera; or, the envoicing of women' in Ruth A. Solie (ed.), *Musicology and Difference: Gender and Sexuality in Music Scholarship* (Berkeley and Los Angeles, CA and London, 1995), pp. 225–58.

Adair, Christy, *Women and Dance. Sylphs and Sirens* (New York, 1992).

Ando, A., Yasuo, U. and Mochizuki, T. (eds), *A Concordance to Dostoevsky's 'Crime and Punishment'*, vol. 2 (Sapporo, 1994).

Annenskii, Innokentii F., 'Umiraiushchii Turgenev: *Klara Milich*' [1906] in N. T. Ashimbaeva, I. I. Podol'skaia and A. V. Fedorov (eds), *I. F. Annenskii: Knigi otrazhenii* (Moscow, 1979), pp. 36–43.

Anoshchenko, Nikolai, *Iz vospominanii*, publ. Rashit Iangirov, *Minuvshee*, 10 (Moscow, 1992), pp. 358–59.

Arnol'di, Eduard, 'Pervenets russkoi kinematografii (K piatidesiatiletiiu vykhoda pervogo russkogo khudozhestvennogo fil'ma)', *Neva*, 1958, 12, pp. 195–99.

Auerbach, Nina, 'Victorian womanhood and literary character' in her *Woman and the Demon. The Life of a Victorian Myth* (Cambridge, MA and London, 1982), pp. 185–217.

Banes, Sally, *Dancing Women. Female Bodies on Stage* (London and New York, 1998).

Barthes, Roland, *Camera Lucida. Reflections on Photography*, translated by Richard Howard (London, 2000).

Bartlett, Rosamund and Edmondson, Linda, 'Collapse and creation: issues of identity and the Russian *fin-de-siècle*' in Catriona Kelly and David Shepherd (eds), *Constructing Russian Culture in the Age of Revolution: 1881–1940* (Oxford, 1998), pp. 165–224.

Becker-Leckrone, Megan, 'Salome©: the fetishization of a textual corpus', *New Literary History*, 26, 1995, 2, pp. 239–60.

Belting, Hans, 'The rediscovery of the icon in Russia' in his *Likeness and Presence. A History of the Image before the Era of Art*, translated by Edmund Jephcott (Chicago, IL and London, 1994).

Bentley, Toni, *Sisters of Salome* (New Haven, CT and London, 2002).

Berger, John, *Ways of Seeing* (London, 1972).

Bernstein, Laurie, *Sonia's Daughters. Prostitutes and Their Regulation in Imperial Russia* (Berkeley and Los Angeles, CA and London, 1995).

Bibliography

Bershtein, Evgenii, 'The Russian myth of Oscar Wilde' in Laura Engelstein and Stephanie Sandler (eds), *Self and Story in Russian History* (Ithaca, NY and London, 2000), pp. 168–88.

Beumers, Birgit, '1909: *Harlequin's Jest* (Shutka Arlekina)' in Julian Graffy (ed.), 'Special feature: Russian cinema centenary. A hundred years of Russian film: the forgotten and under-rated', *Studies in Russian and Soviet Cinema*, 2, 2008, 3, pp. 327–54 (pp. 329–30).

Beumers, Birgit, Bocharov, Victor and Robinson, David (eds), *Alexander Shiryaev: Master of Movement* (Gemona, 2009).

Blok, Aleksandr, 'K muze' in V. N. Orlov, A. A. Surkov and K. I. Chukovskii (eds), *Aleksandr Blok. Sobranie sochinenii v vos′mi tomakh*, vol. 3, *Stikhotvoreniia i poemy, 1907–1921* (Moscow and Leningrad, 1960), pp. 7–8.

_____ *Karmen* in V. N. Orlov, A. A. Surkov and K. I. Chukovskii (eds), *Aleksandr Blok. Sobranie sochinenii v vos′mi tomakh*, vol. 3, *Stikhotvoreniia i poemy, 1907–1921* (Moscow and Leningrad, 1960), pp. 227–39.

Bobri, Vladimir, 'Gypsies and Gypsy choruses of Old Russia', *Journal of the Gypsy Lore Society*, 40, 1961, 3–4, pp. 115–18.

Boele, Otto, '*After Death*, the movie (1915) – Ivan Turgenev, Evgenii Bauer and the aesthetics of morbidity' in Robert Reid and Joe Andrew (eds), *Turgenev: Art, Ideology, Legacy* (Amsterdam and New York, 2010), pp. 253–268.

Boym, Svetlana, 'The death of the poetess' in her *Death in Quotation Marks: Cultural Myths of the Modern Poet* (Cambridge, MA, 1991), pp. 192–240.

Briggs, A.D.P., 'Did *Carmen* really come from Russia (with a little help from Turgenev?)' in Joe Andrew, Derek Offord and Robert Reid (eds), *Turgenev and Russian Culture. Essays to Honour Richard Peace* (Amsterdam and New York, 2008), pp. 83–102.

Bronfen, Elisabeth, *Over Her Dead Body. Death, Femininity and the Aesthetic* (Manchester, 1992).

Brown, Tom, *Breaking the Fourth Wall. Direct Address in the Cinema* (Edinburgh, 2012).

Buckler, Julie, 'Her final debut: the Kadmina legend in Russian literature' in Andrew Baruch Wachtel (ed.), *Intersections and Transpositions. Russian Music, Literature and Society* (Evanston, IL, 1998), pp. 225–52.

Bulgakova, Oksana, *Fabrika zhestov* (Moscow, 2005).

_____ 'The Scheherezade of the boulevard novel: a piquant mix of the vulgar and the proper' in Rimgaila Salys (ed.), *The Russian Cinema Reader. Volume One: 1908 to the Stalin Era* (Boston, MA, 2013), pp. 61–63.

Butler, Judith, 'Sex and gender in Simone de Beauvoir's *Second Sex*', *Yale French Studies*, 72, 1986, pp. 35–49.

_____ 'Performative acts and gender constitution: an essay in phenomenology and feminist theory' [1988] in Sue-Ellen Case (ed.), *Performing Feminisms: Feminist Critical Theory and Theatre* (Baltimore, MD and London, 1990), pp. 270–82.

Bibliography

_____ 'Gendering the body: Beauvoir's philosophical contribution' [1989] in Ann Garry and Marilyn Pearsall (eds), *Women, Knowledge, and Reality: Explorations in Feminist Philosophy* (London, 1992), pp. 253–62.

_____ *Bodies that Matter. On the Discursive Limits of 'Sex'* (New York and London, 1993).

_____ *Gender Trouble. Feminism and the Subversion of Identity* (New York and London, 1999).

_____ 'Variations on sex and gender: Beauvoir, Wittig and Foucault' [1987] in Sarah Salih (ed., with Judith Butler), *The Judith Butler Reader* (Oxford, 2004), pp. 23–38.

_____ *Undoing Gender* (New York and London, 2004).

Cavendish, Philip, 'The hand that turns the handle: camera operators and the poetics of the camera in pre-Revolutionary Russian film', *Slavonic and East European Review*, 82, 2004, 2, pp. 201–45.

_____ *Soviet Mainstream Cinematography: The Silent Era* (London, 2008).

Chaudhuri, Shohini, *Feminist Film Theorists: Laura Mulvey, Kaja Silverman, Teresa de Lauretis, Barbara Creed* (Oxford and New York, 2006).

Cherchi Usai, Paolo, Codelli, Lorenzo, Montanaro, Carlo and Robinson, David (eds), *Silent Witnesses. Russian Films 1908–1919*, research and co-ordination by Yuri Tsivian (London, 1989).

Chernyshev, Andrei, 'Nachalo. K 80-letiiu «Ponizovoi vol´nitsy»', *Sovetskii ekran*, 1989, 1, p. 11.

Christie, Ian, Sleeve note to *Drama in A Gypsy Camp Near Moscow*, *Early Russian Cinema*, volume 2, *Folklore and Legend*, London, 1992.

_____ Sleeve note to *Daydreams*, *Early Russian Cinema*, volume 7, *Evgenii Bauer*, London, 1992.

Clément, Catherine, *Opera, or the Undoing of Women* (London, 1997).

Cooke, Leighton Brett, 'Pushkin and the *femme fatale*. Jealousy in *Cygany*', *California Slavic Studies*, 14, 1992, pp. 99–126.

Copeland, Roger, 'Towards a sexual politics of contemporary dance', *Contact Quarterly*, 7, 1982, pp. 45–50.

Crowe, David M., *A History of the Gypsies of Eastern Europe and Russia* (London and New York, 1995).

Daly, Ann, 'The Balanchine woman: of hummingbirds and channel swimmers', *The Drama Review*, 31, 1987, 1, pp. 8–22.

_____ 'Dance history and feminist theory: reconsidering Isadora Duncan and the male gaze' in L. Senelick (ed.), *Gender in Performance. The Presentation of Difference in Performing Arts* (Hanover, NH, 1992), pp. 239–59.

de Beauvoir, Simone, *Le deuxième sexe I: Les faits et les mythes* [1949] (Paris, 1976).

_____ *Le deuxième sexe II: L'expérience vécue* [1949] (Paris, 1976).

Bibliography

DeBlasio, Alyssa, 'Choreographing space, time, and *dikovinki* in the films of Evgenii Bauer', *The Russian Review*, 66, 2007, pp. 671–92.

Dempster, Elizabeth, 'Women writing the body: let's watch a little how she dances' in Susan Sheridan (ed.), *Grafts. Feminist Cultural Criticism* (London and New York, 1988), pp. 35–54.

Dijkstra, Bram, *Idols of Perversity. Fantasies of Feminine Evil in Fin-de-Siècle Culture* (New York and Oxford, 1986).

Doane, Mary Ann, 'Masquerade reconsidered: further thoughts on the female spectator' in her *Femmes Fatales: Feminism, Film Theory, Psychoanalysis* (New York and Oxford, 1991), pp. 33–43.

_____ 'Melodrama, temporality, recognition: American and Russian silent cinema', *Cinefocus*, 2, 1991, 1, pp. 13–26.

_____ 'Film and the masquerade: theorizing the female spectator' in Mandy Merck (ed.), *The Sexual Subject. A 'Screen' Reader in Sexuality* (London and New York, 1992), pp. 227–43.

Dobrenko, Evgeny, *Stalinist Cinema and the Production of History. Museum of the Revolution*, translated by Sarah Young (Edinburgh, 2008).

Dostoevskii, Fedor, *Polnoe sobranie sochinenii v tridtsati tomakh*, vol. 5: *Povesti i rasskazy, 1862–1866*, E. I. Pokusaev (ed.) (Leningrad, 1973).

_____ *Polnoe sobranie sochinenii v tridtsati tomakh*, vol. 6: *Prestuplenie i nakazane*, V. V. Vinogradov (ed.) (Leningrad, 1973).

Drubek, Natascha, *Russisches Licht. Von der Ikone zum frühen sowjetischen Kino* (Cologne, 2012).

Duncan, Isadora, *My Life* [1927] (London, 1996).

Edmondson, Laura, *Feminism in Russia: 1900–1917* (London, 1984).

_____ 'Women's emancipation and theories of sexual difference in Russia, 1850–1917' in Marianne Liljeström, Eila Mäntysaari and Arja Rosenholm (eds), *Gender Restructuring in Russian Studies. Conference Papers, Helsinkii, August 1992* (Tampere, 1993), pp. 39–52.

Engelstein, Laura, *The Keys to Happiness: Sex and the Search for Modernity in Fin-de-siècle Russia* (Ithaca, NY and London, 1992).

Fokine, Michel, *Choreographic Compositions by Michel Fokine: 'The Dying Swan': Thirty-six Photographs from Poses by Vera Fokina: Detailed Description of the Dance by Michel Fokine: Music by C. Saint-Saens* (New York, 1925).

Foster, Susan Leigh, *Reading Dancing: Bodies and Subjects in Contemporary American Dance* (Berkeley, CA, 1986).

_____ 'The Ballerina's Phallic Pointe' in S. L. Foster (ed.), *Corporealities: Dancing, Knowledge, Culture and Power* (London, 1996), pp. 1–24.

Fraser, Angus, *The Gypsies* (Oxford and Cambridge, MA, 1992).

Gaines, Jane, 'Revolutionary theory/prerevolutionary melodrama', *Discourse*, 17, 1995, 3, pp. 101–18.

Bibliography

Garafola, Lynn, 'Soloists abroad: the pre-war careers of Natalia Trouhanova and Ida Rubinstein', *Experiment/Eksperiment*, 2, 1996, pp. 9–40.

Ginzburg, Semen, *Kinematografiia dorevoliutsionnoi Rossii* [1963] (Moscow, 2007).

Glickman, Rose L., 'Women and the peasant commune' in Roger Bartlett (ed.), *Land Commune and Peasant Community in Russia. Communal Forms in Imperial and Early Soviet Society* (Basingstoke and London, 1990), pp. 321–38.

Gogol´, Nikolai, *Sobranie sochinenii v deviati tomakh*, vol. 3, *Povesti*, E. S. Smirnova (ed.) (Moscow, 1994).

Golub, Spencer, *The Recurrence of Fate: Theatre and Memory in Twentieth-Century Russia* (Iowa City, IA, 1994).

Gorelov, Anatolii, 'Aleksandr Blok i ego Karmen' in his *Groza nad solov´inym sadom. Aleksandr Blok* (Leningrad, 1973), pp. 556–604.

Gorky, Maxim, 'The Lumière cinematograph (extracts)' [4 July 1896] in Richard Taylor and Ian Christie (eds), *The Film Factory. Russian and Soviet Cinema in Documents 1896–1939* (London and New York, 1994), pp. 25–26.

Goscilo, Helena, 'Playing dead: the operatics of celebrity funerals, or, the ultimate silent part', in Louise McReynolds and Joan Neuberger (eds), *Imitations of Life: Two Centuries of Melodrama in Russia* (Durham, NC and London, 2002), pp. 283–319.

Graffy, Julian, *Bed and Sofa: The Film Companion* (London and New York, 2001).

_____ 'Difficult people: Kira Muratova's cinematic encounter with Chekhov', *Essays in Poetics: Chekhov Special Issue 2*, 31, 2006, pp. 180–212.

_____ 'The foreigner's journey to consciousness in early Soviet cinema: the case of Protazanov's *Tommi*' in Stephen M. Norris and Zara M. Torlone (eds), *Insiders and Outsiders in Russian Cinema* (Bloomington and Indianapolis, IN, 2008), pp. 1–22.

Hamberlin, Larry, 'Visions of Salome: the femme fatale in American popular songs before 1920', *Journal of American Musicological Society*, 59, 2006, 3, pp. 631–96.

Hamill, Alfred E., 'Gypsies in and about Russian literature', *Journal of the Gypsy Lore Society*, 22, 1943, 1–2, pp. 57–58.

Hamilton, George Heard, 'Icon-painting' in his *The Art and Architecture of Russia* (Harmondsworth, 1975), pp. 67–110.

Hansen, Miriam, 'Deadly scenarios: narrative perspective and sexual politics in pre-Revolutionary Russian film', *Cinefocus*, 2, 1992, 2, pp. 10–19.

Hayward, Susan, *Cinema Studies. The Key Concepts* (London and New York, 2006).

Heath, Stephen, 'Joan Riviere and the masquerade' in Victor Burgin, James Donald and Cora Kaplan (eds), *Formations of Fantasy* (London and New York, 1986), pp. 45–61.

Heil, Jerry, 'Russian Futurism and the cinema: Majakovskij's film work of 1913', *Russian Literature*, 19, 1986, 2, pp. 175–91.

Holmgren, Beth, 'The importance of being unhappy, or, why she died' in Louise McReynolds and Joan Neuberger (eds), *Imitations of Life: Two Centuries of Melodrama in Russia* (Durham, NC and London, 2002), pp. 79–98.

Iagolim, Boris, *Kometa divnoi krasoty. Zhizn´ i tvorchestvo Evlalii Kadminoi* (Moscow, 1970).

Iampol´skii, Mikhail, 'Starevich: mimika nasekomykh i kul´turnaia traditsiia', *Kinovedcheskie zapiski*, 1, 1988, pp. 84–90.

_____ [Iampolski, Mikhail], 'Russia: the cinema of anti-modernity and backward progress' in Valentina Vitali and Paul Willemen (eds), *Theorising National Cinema* (London, 2006), pp. 72–87.

Iangirov, Rashit, 'Talking movie or silent theater? Creative experiments by Vasily Goncharov' in Richard Abel and Rick Altman (eds), *The Sounds of Early Cinema* (Bloomington and Indianapolis, IN, 2001), pp. 110–17.

Iani, Anton, *Vera Kholodnaia. Pervaia liubov´ rossiiskogo kinozritelia* (St Petersburg, 2012).

Irigaray, Luce, *Speculum of the Other Woman* [1974], translated by Gillian C. Gill (Ithaca, NY, 1985).

Ivanova, V., Myl´nikova, V., Skovorodnikova, S., Tsiv´ian, Iu. and Iangirov, R. (eds), *Velikii kinemo. Katalog sokhranivshikhsia igrovykh fil´mov Rossii, 1908–1919* (Moscow, 2002).

Kagan, Gennadii, *Vera Karalli – legenda russkogo baleta* (St Petersburg, 2009).

Kant, Marion, 'The soul of the shoe' in Marion Kant (ed.), *The Cambridge Companion to Ballet* (Cambridge and New York, 2007), pp. 184–97.

Kenez, Peter, *Cinema and Soviet Society, 1917–1953* (Cambridge, New York and Melbourne, 1992).

Key, Ellen, *Love and Marriage*, translated by Arthur G. Chater (New York and London, 1911).

Kherroubi, A. (ed.), *Le Cinéma russe avant la révolution* (Paris, 1989).

Kodicek, Ann (ed.), *Diaghilev. Creator of the Ballets Russes. Art. Music. Dance* (London, 1996).

Kollontai, Aleksandra, 'Novaia zhenshchina' [1913] in V. I. Uspenskaia (ed.), *Marksistkii feminizm. Kollektsiia tekstov A. M. Kollontai* (Tver´, 2002), pp. 154–91.

Korotkii, Viktor M., 'Evgenii Bauer: predystoriia kinorezhissera', *Kinovedcheskie zapiski*, 10, 1991, pp. 44–57.

_____ 'Vozvrashchaiias´ k publikatsii o Bauere, ili metodolgiia oshibki', *Kinovedcheskie zapiski*, 12, 1991, pp. 237–43.

_____ 'A. E. Bliumental´-Tamarin i E. F. Bauer. Materialy k istorii russkogo svetotvorchestva', *Kinovedcheskie zapiski*, 56, 2002, pp. 236–71.

Kosofsky Sedgwick, Eve, *Between Men: English Literature and Male Homosocial Desire* (New York and Chichester, 1985).

Bibliography

Kovalenko, Georgii, 'Elza Kriuger', *Experiment/Eksperiment*, 2, 1996, pp. 334–57.

Kramer, Lawrence, 'Cultural and musical hermeneutics: the Salome complex', *Cambridge Opera Journal*, 2, 1990, 3, pp. 269–94.

Kruchenykh, Aleksei and Khlebnikov, Velimir, 'Slovo kak takovoe' [1913] in V. Markov (ed.), *Manifesty i programmy russkikh futuristov, Slavische Propyläen*, 27 (Munich, 1967), pp. 53–58.

Kuleshov, Lev V., 'The tasks of the artist in cinema' [1917] in Richard Taylor and Ian Christie (eds), *The Film Factory. Russian and Soviet Cinema in Documents 1896-1939* (London and New York, 1994), pp. 41–42.

_____ 'Evgenii Frantsevich Bauer (k sorokaletiiu so dnia smerti)' [1957] in his *Sobranie sochinenii v trekh tomakh*, R. N. Iurenev *et al.* (eds), volume 2: *Vospominaniia. Rezhissura. Dramaturgiia* (Moscow, 1988), pp. 403–09.

Kuprin Aleksandr, 'Poslednii debiut' in A. I. Kuprin, *Sobranie sochinenii v deviati tomakh*, volume 1 (Moscow, 1964), pp. 43–49.

Kurth, Peter, *Isadora. The Sensational Life of Isadora Duncan* (London, 2001).

Lemon, A., *Between Two Fires. Gypsy Performance and Romany Memory From Pushkin to Postsocialism* (Durham, 2000).

Lengborn, Thorbjörn, 'Ellen Key (1849–1926)', *Prospects: The Quarterly Review of Comparative Education*, 23, 1993, 314, pp. 825–37.

Lermontov, Mikhail, 'Vadim' in G. N. Seleznev *et al.* (eds), M. Iu. Lermontov, *Polnoe sobranie sochinenii v 10 tomakh*, vol. 6, *Proza* (Moscow, 1999–2002), pp. 5–125.

Leskov, Nikolai, 'Teatral´nyi kharakter', *Teatral´nyi mirok* (1888), pp. 11–14.

Lévi-Strauss, Claude, *La Pensée sauvage* (Paris, 1962).

Leyda, Jay, *Kino. A History of Russian and Soviet Film* [1960] (Princeton, NJ, 1983).

Likhachev, B. S., *Kino v Rossii (1896-1926). Materialy k istorii russkogo kino. Chast´ 1. 1896-1913* (Leningrad, 1927).

Livy, 'Book one: Rome under the kings' in his *The Early History of Rome* (Harmondsworth, 1960), pp. 33–101.

Lloyd, Moya, *Judith Butler: From Norms to Politics* (Cambridge and Malden, MA, 2007).

Lobanov-Rostovsky, Nikita, 'A bargain on the marché aux puces: the pictures of Nicolai Kalmakov', in A. Flegon (ed.), *Eroticism in Russian Art* (London, 1976), pp. 306–07.

Lowe, David A., 'Pushkin and *Carmen*', *Nineteenth-Century Music*, 20, 1996, 1, pp. 72–76.

McMillin, Arnold and McMillin, Svetlana, 'Sex, speech and sewing machines: whores' voices and useful occupations in Russian literature', *Slovo*, 11, 1999, pp. 121–39.

McReynolds, Louise, '"The incomparable" Anastasiia Vial´tseva and the culture of personality' in Helena Goscilo and Beth Holmgren (eds), *Russia. Culture. Women* (Bloomington, IN, 1996), pp. 273–94.

_____ 'Reading the Russian romance: what did the keys to happiness unlock?', *Journal of Popular Culture*, 31, 1998, 4, pp. 95–108.

_____ 'The silent movie melodrama: Evgenii Bauer fashions the heroine's self' in Laura Engelstein and Stephanie Sandler (eds), *Self and Story in Russian History* (Ithaca, NY and London, 2000), pp. 120–40.

_____ 'Home was never where the heart was: domestic dystopias in Russia's silent movie melodramas' in Louise McReynolds and Joan Neuberger (eds), *Imitations of Life: Two Centuries of Melodrama in Russia* (Durham, NC and London, 2002), pp. 127–51.

_____ *Russia at Play. Leisure Activities at the End of the Tsarist Era* (Ithaca, NY and London, 2003).

_____ 'Demanding men, desiring women and social collapse in the films of Evgenii Bauer, 1913–17', *Studies in Russian and Soviet Cinema*, 3, 2009, 2, pp. 145–56.

Mandel´shtam, Osip, 'Barsuch´ia nora (A. Blok: 7 avgusta 1921 g. – 7 avgusta 1922 goda)', *Sobranie sochinenii v dvukh tomakh*, volume 2, *Stikhotvoreniia. Proza* (New York, 1966), pp. 312–17.

Mar, Kseniia, 'Vera Kholodnaia – Pola («Skazka liubvi dorogoi»)' [1918] in B. B. Ziukov, *Vera Kholodnaia. K 100-letiiu so dnia rozhdeniia* (Moscow, 1995), pp. 133–34.

Marks, Laura U., *The Skin of the Film: Intercultural Cinema, Embodiment and the Senses* (Durham, NC, 2000).

_____ *Touch: Sensuous Theory and Multisensory Media* (Minneapolis, MN and London, 2002).

Marsh, Rosalind, 'Anastasiia Verbitskaia reconsidered' in Rosalind Marsh (ed.), *Gender and Russian Literature. New Perspectives* (Cambridge, 1996), pp. 184–205.

Matich, Olga, 'Gender trouble in the Amazonian kingdom: turn-of the-century representations of women in Russia' in John E. Bowlt and Matthew Drutt (eds), *Amazons of the Avant-Garde: Alexandra Exter, Natalia Goncharova, Liubov Popova, Olga Rozanova, Varvara Stepanova, and Nadezhda Udaltsova* (New York and London, 1999), pp 75–93.

Mayer, Charles S., 'Ida Rubinstein: a twentieth-century Cleopatra', *Dance Research Journal*, 20, 1988, 2, pp. 33–51.

Mérimée, Prosper, 'Carmen' [1846] in Jean Decottignies (ed.), *Prosper Mérimée. Les Ames du purgatoire. Carmen* (Paris, 1973), pp. 105–69.

Metz, Christian, 'Photography and fetish' [1985] in Carol Squiers (ed.), *The Critical Image. Essays on Contemporary Photography* (London, 1991), pp. 155–64.

Mints, Z. G. and Lotman, Iu. M., '«Chelovek prirody» v russkoi literature XIX veka i «tsyganskaia tema» u Bloka' in Z. G. Mints, *Aleksandr Blok i russkie pisateli* (St Petersburg, 2000), pp. 343–88.

Mitry, Jean, *Histoire du cinéma. Art et industrie. Volume 1, 1895–1914* (Paris, 1967).

Mondry, Henrietta, 'Performing the paradox: Rozanov and the dancing body of Isadora Duncan', *Essays in Poetics*, 24, 1999, pp. 91–116.

_____ *Pure, Strong and Sexless: the Peasant Woman's Body and Gleb Uspensky* (Amsterdam and New York, 2006).

Money, Keith, *Anna Pavlova. Her Life and Art* (London, 1982).

Morley, Rachel, 'Gender relations in the films of Evgenii Bauer', *Slavonic and East European Review*, 81, 2003, 1, pp. 32–69.

_____ ' "Crime without punishment": reworkings of nineteenth-century Russian literary sources in Evgenii Bauer's *Child of the Big City*' in Stephen Hutchings and Anat Vernitski (eds), *Russian and Soviet Film Adaptations of Literature, 1900–2001: Screening the Word* (London and New York, 2005), pp. 27–43.

_____ 'Zhizn' za zhizn' / A Life for a Life' in B. Beumers (ed.), *The Cinema of Russia and the Former Soviet Union* (London and New York, 2007), pp. 13–22.

_____ '1912: *The Incestuous Father-in-law* (Snokhach)' in Julian Graffy (ed.), 'Special feature: Russian cinema centenary. A hundred years of Russian film: the forgotten and under-rated', *Studies in Russian and Soviet Cinema*, 2, 2008, 3, pp. 327–54 (pp. 331–32).

_____ 'Performing femininity in an age of change: Evgenii Bauer, Ivan Turgenev and the legend of Evlaliia Kadmina' in Robert Reid and Joe Andrew (eds), *Turgenev: Art, Ideology, Legacy* (Amsterdam and New York, 2010), pp. 269–316.

_____ [Morli, Reichl], '*Molchi, grust'*, molchi... (1918)' in Ekaterina Vasil'eva and Nikita Braginskii (eds), *Noev kovcheg russkogo kino. Ot 'Sten'ki Razina' do 'Stiliag'* (Vinnitsa, Ukraine, 2012), pp. 32–38.

Morrissey, Susan K., *Suicide and the Body Politic in Imperial Russia* (Cambridge, 2006).

Mulvey, Laura, 'Visual pleasure and narrative cinema' [1975] in Constance Penley (ed.), *Feminism and Film Theory* (London, 1988), pp. 57–68.

_____ 'Afterthoughts on "Visual Pleasure and Narrative Cinema", inspired by *Duel in the Sun*' [1981] in Constance Penley (ed.), *Feminism and Film Theory* (London, 1988), pp. 69–79.

Nasta, Dominique, 'Setting the pace of a heartbeat: the use of sound elements in European melodramas before 1915' in Richard Abel and Rick Altman (eds), *The Sounds of Early Cinema* (Bloomington and Indianapolis, IN, 2001), pp. 95–109.

Nikol'skaia, T., 'A. Blok o zhenskom tvorchestve', *Uchenye zapiski Tartuskogo gosudarstvennogo universiteta*, no. 881, *Blokovskii sbornik*, no. 10 (Tartu, 1990), pp. 32–40.

'Novaia Eva', *Sovremennaia zhenshchina*, 1914, 5, pp. 104–06.

Nyström-Hamilton, Louise, *Ellen Key: Her Life and Her Work. A Critical Study*, translated by Anna E. B. Fries (New York and London, 1913).

Oleinikov, Dmitrii, 'Pesnia russkoi Karmen', *Rodina*, 7, 2004, pp. 96–97.

Paglia, Camille, *Sexual Personae. Art and Decadence from Nefertiti to Emily Dickinson* (London and New Haven, CT, 2001).

Paperno, Irina, *Suicide as a Cultural Institution in Dostoevsky's Russia* (Ithaca, NY and London, 1997).

Parton, Anthony, *Mikhail Larionov and the Russian Avant-Garde* (Princeton, NJ, 1993).

Pavlova, Tat´iana, 'Oskar Uail´d v russkoi literature (konets XIX-nachalo XX vv.)' in Iu. D. Levin (ed.), *Na rubezhe XIX i XX vekov. Iz istorii mezhdunarodnykh sviazei russkoi literatury: sbornik nauchnykh trudov* (Leningrad, 1991), pp. 77–128.

Pozdniakov, Aleksandr, 'Nachalo. «Sten´ka Razin» («Ponizovaia vol´nitsa»), rezhisser Vladimir Romashkov', *Iskusstvo kino*, 2008, 11, pp. 5–7.

Prettejohn, Elizabeth, *Rosetti and His Circle* (London, 1997).

Prokhorov, Alexander, 'Petr Tochilin: *Khottabych* (2006): in defense of pulp cinema and in memoriam of Aleksandr Drankov' at http://www.kinokultura.com/2007/16r-khottabych.shtml (accessed 7 July 2015).

Prokof´eva, Elena, *Koroleva ekrana. Istoriia Very Kholodnoi* (Moscow, 2001).

Pushkin, Alexander, 'Tsygany' in *Pushkin: Selected Verse*, with introduction and prose translations by John Fennell (London, 1995), pp. 77–109.

Pym, Anthony, 'The importance of Salomé: approaches to a *fin de siècle* theme', *French Forum*, 14, 1989, 3, pp. 311–22.

Racin, John (ed.), *Tatyana Repina. Two Translated Texts by Alexei Suvorin and Anton Chekhov* (Jefferson, SC and London, 1999).

Radzinsky, Edvard, *Rasputin. The Last Word* (London, 2000).

Riley, John, *Dmitri Shostakovich: A Life in Film* (London and New York, 2005).

Riviere, Joan, 'Womanliness as a masquerade' [1929] in Victor Burgin, James Donald and Cora Kaplan (eds), *Formations of Fantasy* (London and New York, 1986), pp. 35–44.

Robinson, David, 'Evgenii Bauer and the cinema of Nikolai II', *Sight and Sound*, 59, 1989–90, 1, pp. 51–55.

Roepke, Martina, 'Tracing 17.5mm practices in Germany (1902–1908)', *Film History*, 19, 2007, 4, pp. 344–52.

Roslavleva, Natalia, *Era of the Russian Ballet* (London, 1966).

Rotkirch, Anna, 'New woman with old feelings? Contrasting Kollontai's and Colette's writings on love' in Ebba Witt-Brattström (ed.), *The New Woman and the Aesthetic Opening: Unlocking Gender in Twentieth-Century Texts* (Huddinge, 2004), pp. 137–54.

Sadoul, Georges, *Histoire générale du cinéma. Tome III. Le cinéma devient un art – L'Avant-guerre* (Paris, 1950–1975).

Said, Edward W., *Orientalism. Western Conceptions of the Orient* [1978] (London, 1995).

Bibliography

Salys, Rimgaila, 'The Cameraman's Revenge' in Rimgaila Salys (ed), *The Russian Cinema Reader. Volume One. 1908 to the Stalin Era* (Boston, MA, 2013), pp. 48–51.

Schlüpmann, Heide, 'From patriarchal violence to the aesthetics of death: Russian cinema 1900–1919', *Cinefocus*, 2, 1992, 2, pp. 2–9.

Schuler, Catherine M., *Women in Russian Theatre: The Actress in the Silver Age* (London and New York, 1996).

Schweitser, Viktoria, *Tsvetaeva*, translated from the Russian by Robert Chandler and H. T. Willets, poetry translated by Peter Norman, edited and annotated by Angela Livingstone (London, 1995).

Sealey Rahman, Kate, 'Ostrovskii on the British stage: 1894–1928', *Toronto Slavic Quarterly: Academic Electronic Journal in Slavic Studies*, 9, 2004 at http://www.utoronto.ca/tsq/09/rahman09.shtml (accessed 10 January 2016).

Shcherbakova, T., *Tsyganskoe muzykal'noe ispolnitel'stvo v Rossii* (Moscow, 1984).

Shcherbina, V. (ed.), *Aleksandr Blok. Pis'ma k zhene, Literaturnoe nasledstvo*, 89 (Moscow, 1978).

Showalter, Elaine, *Sexual Anarchy. Gender and Culture at the Fin de Siècle* (London, 1991).

Simonson, M., '"The Call of Salome". American Adaptations and Re-creations of the Female Body in the Early Twentieth Century', *Women and Music. A Journal of Gender and Culture*, 11, 2007, pp. 1–16.

'Skazka liubvi dorogoi («Molchi, grust'... molchi...»). Iubileinaia kartina P. I. Chardynina', *Kino-gazeta*, 1918, 20, pp. 4–7, reproduced in *Early Russian Cinema Online (BrillOnline Primary Sources)*, advisor R. Yangirov (Leiden and Boston, 2005) at http://primarysources.brillonline.com/browse/early-russian-cinema (accessed on 13 January 2016), access provided by University College London.

Sobolev, Romil, *Liudi i fil'my russkogo dorevoliutsionnogo kino* (Moscow, 1961).

———— 'Aleksandr Drankov' in *Migaiushchii sinema. Rannie gody russkoi kinematografii. Vospominaniia, dokumenty, stat'i*, compiled and introduced by M. I. Volotskii (Moscow, 1995), pp. 77–94.

Sontag, Susan, *Illness as Metaphor* (London, 1978).

———— *On Photography* (London, 1979).

Souritz, Elizabeth, 'Isadora Duncan and prewar Russian dancemakers' in Lynn Garafola and Nancy Van Norman Baer (eds), *The Ballets Russes and its World* (New Haven, CT and London, 1999), pp. 97–115.

Stites, Richard, *Russian Popular Culture. Entertainment and Society Since 1900* (Cambridge, 1992).

———— 'Dusky images of Tsarist Russia: prerevolutionary cinema', *Russian Review*, 53, 1994, 2, pp. 285–95.

Taylor, Richard and Christie, Ian (eds), *The Film Factory. Russian and Soviet Cinema in Documents 1896–1939* (London and New York, 1994).

Thompson, Kristin, 'The international exploration of cinematic expressivity' in Lee Grieveson and Peter Krämer (eds), *The Silent Cinema Reader* (London and New York, 2004), pp. 254–69.

Torre, Michele L., 'Filtering culture: symbolism, modernity and gender construction in Evgenii Bauer's films' in John Fullerton (ed.), *Screen Culture: History and Textuality* (Eastleigh, 2004), pp. 99–112.

Tsivian, Yuri [Tsiv'ian, Iurii], '«Sten'ka Razin» («Ponizovaia vol'nitsa»), Rossiia (1908)', *Iskusstvo kino*, 1988, 7, pp. 93–96.

_____ 'Les pionniers. Le premier film' in A. Kherroubi (ed.), *Le Cinéma russe avant la révolution* (Paris, 1989), pp. 26–31.

_____ *Istoricheskaia retseptsiia kino. Kinematograf v Rossii 1896–1930* (Riga, 1991).

_____ 'Early Russian cinema: some observations' in Richard Taylor and Ian Christie (eds), *Inside the Film Factory. New Approaches to Russian and Soviet Cinema* (London and New York, 1991), pp. 7–30.

_____ 'Early Russian Cinema and its Public', *Historical Journal of Film, Radio and Television*, 11, 1991, 2, pp. 105–20.

_____ 'Portraits, mirrors, death: on some decadent clichés in early Russian films', *Iris*, 14–15, 1992, pp. 67–83.

_____ *Early Cinema in Russia and its Cultural Reception*, translated by Alan Bodger, edited by Richard Taylor, with a foreword by Tom Gunning (Chicago, IL and London, 1994).

_____ 'Russia, 1913: cinema in the cultural landscape' in Richard Abel (ed.), *Silent Film* (London, 1996), pp. 194–214.

_____ 'The tango in Russia', *Experiment/Eksperiment*, 2, 1996, pp. 306–33.

_____ 'Two «stylists» of the teens: Franz Hofer and Yevgenii Bauer' in Thomas Elsaesser (ed.), *A Second Life: German Cinema's First Decades* (Amsterdam, 1996), pp. 264–76.

_____ 'Video Essay' on *Mad Love: Three Films by Evgenii Bauer*, BFI DVD publishing (London, 2002).

_____ 'New notes on Russian film culture between 1908 and 1919' in Lee Grieveson and Peter Krämer (eds), *The Silent Cinema Reader* (London and New York, 2004), pp. 339–48.

_____ 'The invisible novelty: film adaptations in the 1910s' in Robert Stam and Alessandra Raengo (eds), *A Companion to Literature and Film* (Oxford, 2004), pp. 92–111.

Tsvetaeva, Marina, *Sobranie sochinenii v semi tomakh*, volume 1, *Stikhotvoreniia*, compiled, prepared for publication and annotated by Anna Saakiants and Lev Mnukhin (Moscow, 1994).

Bibliography

Turgenev, Ivan S., 'Klara Milich' in his *Polnoe sobranie sochinenii i pisem v dvadtsati vos´mi tomakh*, vol. 13 (Moscow and Leningrad, 1967), text pp. 76–134 and commentary pp. 575–90.

Turovskaia, Maiia, 'Zhenshchina-ubiitsa v russkom i sovetskom nemom kino', *Iskusstvo kino*, 1997, 5, pp. 108–13.

Tydeman, William and Price, Steven, *Wilde – Salome* (Cambridge, 1996).

Verbitskaia, Anastasiia, *Kliuchi schast´ia* [1910–1913], volumes 1 and 2 (St Petersburg, 1993).

_____ *Keys to Happiness: A Novel*, translated and edited by Beth Holmgren and Helena Goscilo (Bloomington and Indianapolis, IN, 1999).

Vishnevskii, Veniamin, *Khudozhestvennye fil´my dorevoliutsionnoi Rossii: fil´mograficheskoe opisanie* (Moscow, 1945).

Von Geldern, James and McReynolds, Louise (eds), *Entertaining Tsarist Russia. Tales, Songs, Plays, Movies, Jokes, Ads and Images from Russian Urban Life 1779–1917* (Bloomington and Indianapolis, IN, 1998).

Warner, Elizabeth, *The Russian Folk Theatre* (The Hague, 1977).

Weaver, Warren, *Alice in Many Tongues: The Translations of Alice in Wonderland* (Madison, WI, 1964).

Wheelock Jr., Arthur K. and Keyes, George, *Rembrandt's Lucretias* (Washington, DC, 1991).

Widdis, Emma 'Faktura: depth and surface in early Soviet set design', *Studies in Russian and Soviet Cinema*, 3, 2009, 1, pp. 5–32.

Wilde, Oscar, *Salomé*, translated from the French by Lord Alfred Douglas, in *The Complete Works of Oscar Wilde: Stories, Plays, Poems*, introduced by Vyvyan Holland (London and Glasgow, 1986), pp. 552–75.

Wittig, Monique, 'One is not born a woman' [1981] in Henry Abelove, Michèle Aina Barale and David M. Halperin (eds), *The Lesbian and Gay Studies Reader* (London, 1993), pp. 103–09.

Worobec, Christine D., 'Victims or actors? Russian peasant women and patriarchy' in Esther Kingston-Mann and Timothy Mixter (eds), *Peasant Economy, Culture, and Politics of European Russia, 1800–1921* (Princeton, NJ, 1991), pp. 177–206.

Wyke, Maria, 'Augustan Cleopatras: female power and poetic authority' in Anton Powell (ed.), *Roman Poetry and Propaganda in the Age of Augustus* (London, 1992), pp. 98–140.

_____ *Projecting the Past. Ancient Rome, Cinema and History* (New York and London, 1997).

Youngblood, Denise J., 'The return of the native: Yakov Protazanov and Soviet cinema' in Richard Taylor and Ian Christie (eds), *Inside the Film Factory. New Approaches to Russian and Soviet Film* (London, 1994), pp. 103–23.

_____ *The Magic Mirror. Moviemaking in Russia, 1908–1918* (Madison, WI and London, 1999).

Ziukov, B. B., *Vera Kholodnaia. K 100-letiiu so dnia rozhdeniia* (Moscow, 1995).

Zorkaia, Neia, *Na rubezhe stoletii: U istokov massovogo iskusstva v Rossii 1900–1910 godov* (Moscow, 1976).

_____ 'Pervaia russkaia kinozvezda' in B. B. Ziukov, *Vera Kholodnaia. K 100-letiiu so dnia rozhdeniia* (Moscow, 1995), pp. 251–78.

_____ '«Svetopis´» Evgeniia Bauera', *Iskusstvo kino*, 1997, 10, pp. 77–93.

_____ 'Kinorezhisser Evgenii Bauer v poiskakh «iskusstva svetopisi»' in B. I. Zingerman et al (eds), *Mir iskusst. Al´manakh* (Moscow, 1997), pp. 270–85.

_____ 'Prolog. Serebriannyi vek russkogo kino' in N. Zorkaia, *Krutitsia, vertitsia shar goluboi... Desiat´ shedevrov sovetskogo kino* (Moscow, 1998), pp. 7–23.

_____ 'Motiv persidskoi kniazhny v «Razinskom» lubochnom tsikle i v russkoi literature XIX-XX vekov' in I. E. Danilova (ed.), *Mir narodnoi kartinki: materialy nauchnoi konferentsii "Vipperovskie chteniia – 1997"* (Moscow, 1999), pp. 278–90.

_____ (ed.), 'Rimeik', *Ekran i stsena*, 2001, 26, p. 14.

_____ 'Kinorezhisser Evgenii Bauer. Serebrianye deviat´sot desiatye', *Slovo. Pravoslavnyi obrazovatel´nyi portal* at http://old.portal-slovo.ru/rus/art/964/5888/ (accessed 6 July 2015).

_____ 'Sten´ka Razin pod Peterburgom' at http://www.portal-slovo.ru/art/35956.php (accessed 16 July 2015).

Zvereva, Svetlana, *Alexander Kastalsky: His Life and Music*, translated by Stuart Campbell (Aldershot, 2003).

Filmography

This filmography lists all the films referred to in the text, in alphabetical order by director. The list includes the following information: director, translated title, Russian title (if different), alternative titles (if applicable), name of studio or production company, country of production (if not Russia), year of production, date of release (if known). Films that have not survived are identified as non-extant. Films whose director is unknown are given at the end of the filmography, in alphabetical order by title.

Aleksandrov, Grigorii, *The Jolly Fellows* [Veselye rebiata], Moskovskii kinokombinat, 1934; 25 December 1934.

Bauer, Evgenii, *Twilight of a Woman's Soul* [Sumerki zhenskoi dushi], Kinofabrika 'Star' (A. Khanzhonkov and Pathé Frères), 1913; 26 November 1913.

_____ *Child of the Big City* [Ditia bol'shogo goroda] (*Girl from the Street* [Devushka s ulitsy]), A. Khanzhonkov & Co., 1914; 5 March 1914.

_____ *Silent Witnesses* [Nemye svideteli], A. Khanzhonkov & Co., 1914; 29 April 1914.

_____ *Only Once a Year* [Tol'ko raz v godu] (*The Road to Hell* [Doroga v ad]), A. Khanzhonkov & Co., 1914; 1 October 1914.

_____ *Life in Death* [Zhizn' v smerti], A. Khanzhonkov & Co., 1914; 6 August 1914 in the provinces and 24 October 1914 in Moscow [non-extant].

_____ *Cold Showers* (also known by the English title *Frigid Souls*) [Kholodnye dushi], A. Khanzhonkov & Co., 1914; 11 November 1914.

_____ *Her Heroic Feat* [Ee geroiskii podvig], A. Khanzhonkov & Co., 1914; 29 November 1914.

_____ *The Thousand and Second Ruse* [Tysiacha vtoraia khitrost'], A. Khanzhonkov & Co., 1915; 29 May 1915.

_____ *First Love* [Pervaia liubov'], A. Khanzhonkov & Co., 1915; 1 August 1915.

_____ *The Song of Love Triumphant* [Pesn' torzhestvuiushchei liubvi], A. Khanzhonkov & Co., 1915; 22 August 1915 [non-extant].

_____ *Children of the Age* [Deti veka], A. Khanzhonkov & Co., 1915; 3 October 1915.

_____ *Daydreams* [Grezy] (*Deceived Dreams* [Obmanutye mechty]), A. Khanzhonkov & Co., 1915; 10 October 1915.

_____ *After Death* [Posle smerti] (*Motifs from Turgenev* [Turgenevskie motivy]), A. Khanzhonkov & Co., 1915; 29 December 1915.

_____ *Iurii Nagornyi* (*The Seducer* [Obol´stitel´]), A. Khanzhonkov & Co., 1915; 16 January 1916.

_____ *A Life for a Life* [Zhizn´ za zhizn´] (*A Tear for Every Drop of Blood* [Za kazhduiu slezu po kaple krovi] and *The Rival Sisters* [Sestry-sopernitsy]), A. Khanzhonkov & Co., 1916; 10 May 1916.

_____ *Lina's Adventure in Sochi* [Prikliuchenie Liny v Sochi], A. Khanzhonkov & Co., 1916; 10 September 1916.

_____ *Nelli Raintseva*, A. Khanzhonkov & Co., 1916; 13 December 1916.

_____ *The Dying Swan* [Umiraiushchii lebed´], A. Khanzhonkov & Co., 1916; 17 January 1917.

_____ *Lina Under Examination, Or the Turbulent Corpse* [Lina pod ekspertizoi, ili Buinyi pokoinik], A. Khanzhonkov & Co., 1917; 10 February 1917.

_____ *In Pursuit of Happiness* [Za schast´em] (*For Luck* [K schast´iu]), A. Khanzhonkov & Co., 1917; 3 September 1917.

Bauer, Evgenii and Brianskii, Vitalii, *Bloody Glory* [Krovavaia slava] (*From the Life of One Female Student* [Iz zhizni odnoi kursistki]), Fabrika 'Star', Pathé Frères, 1913; 7 October 1913 [non-extant].

Bauer, Evgenii and Rakhmanova, Ol´ga, *The King of Paris* [Korol´ Parizha], A. Khanzhonkov & Co., 1917; 6 December 1917.

Bocharov, Victor, *A Belated Premiere* [Zapozdavshaia prem´era], Kinokompaniia 'Miris', 2003.

Bonch-Tomashevskii, Mikhail, *The Mother-in-Law in the Harem* [Teshcha v gareme], P. Perskii, 1915.

Caserini, Mario, *Love Everlasting* [Ma l'amor mio non muore], 1913 (Italy); 1 December 1913.

Chaikovskii, Boris, *A Ballerina's Romance* [Roman baleriny] (*A Ballerina's Diary* [Dnevnik baleriny] and *The Romance of the Ballerina Elena Lanskaia* [Roman baleriny Eleny Lanskoi]), A. Khanzhonkov & Co., 1916; 2 November 1916.

Chardynin, Petr, *Vadim* (*A Tale from the Times of Pugachev* [Povest´ iz vremen Pugacheva] and *The Boyar Palitsyn* [Boiarin Palitsyn]), A. Khanzhonkov, 1910; 2 November 1910.

_____ *Chrysanthemums* [Khrizantemy] (*The Tragedy of a Ballerina* [Tragediia baleriny] and *A Ballerina's Romance* [Roman baleriny]), A. Khanzhonkov & Co., 1914; 4 November 1914.

_____ *Gypsy Romances* [Tsyganskie romansy] (*The Tragedy of a Gypsy's Soul* [Tragediia tsyganskoi dushi] and *The Tragedy of a Gypsy Girl* [Tragediia tsyganki]), Khanzhonkov & Co., 1914; 6 December 1914.

_____ *Tat´iana Repina*, A. Khanzhonkov & Co., 1915; 25 July 1915 [non-extant].

Filmography

_____ *The Love of a Councillor of State* [Liubov´ statskogo sovetnika], A. Khanzhonkov & Co., 1915; 10 November 1915.

_____ *Mirages* [Mirazhi] (*The Tragedy of a Beautiful Girl* [Tragediia krasivoi devushki]), A. Khanzhonkov & Co., 1915; 3 January 1916.

_____ *Still, Sadness... Still...* [Molchi, grust´... molchi...], D. Kharitonov, 1918; 14 May 1918.

_____ *A Tale of Precious Love* [Skazka liubvi dorogoi], D. Kharitonov, 1918; 21 May 1918) [non-extant].

Eizenshtein, Sergei, *The Strike* [Stachka], Goskino (First Factory) and Proletkul´t, 1924; 28 April 1925.

Goncharov, Vasilii, *Vanka the Steward* [Van´ka-kliuchnik] (*A True Story from C17th Russia* [Russkaia byl´ XVII stoletiia]), A. Khanzhonkov, 1909; 1 November 1909.

_____ *The Water Nymph* [Rusalka], A. Khanzhonkov, 1910; 30 March 1910.

Goncharov, Vasilii, Hansen, Kai, Gash, Moris and Novikov, Mikhail, *The Dashing Merchant* [Ukhar´-kupets], Pathé Frères, 1909; 29 September1909.

Griffith, D. W., *The Musketeers of Pig Alley*, Biograph Company (USA), 1912; 31 October 1912.

Guazzoni, Enrico, *Antony and Cleopatra* [Marcantonio e Cleopatra], Società Italiana Cines (Italy), 1913; December 1913.

Hansen, Kai, *Coppélia*, Pathé Frères, 1913; 20 October 1913 [non-extant].

Ivanov-Gai, Aleksandr and/or Chardynin, Petr, *The Incestuous Father-in-Law* (also known by the English title *The Daughter-in Law's Lover*) [Snokhach], A. Khanzhonov & Co., 1912; 29 September 1912.

Kas´ianov, Vladimir, *Drama in the Futurist Cabaret No. 13* [Drama v kabare futuristov No. 13], production company unknown, 1913; January 1914 [non-extant].

Komissarzhevskii, Fedor and Chaikovskii, Boris, *The Stage Set of Happiness* [Dekoratsiia schast´ia], A. Khanzhonkov & Co. (Ialta), 1918.

Kozintsev, Grigorii and Trauberg, Leonid, *The Youth of Maksim* [Iunost´ Maksima] (*The Bolshevik* [Bol´shevik]), Lenfil´m, 1934; 27 January 1935.

Libkin, Grigorii, *Sten´ka Razin*, Grigorii Libkin (Iaroslavl´), 1914; 5 December 1914.

Maître, André, *The Gypsies* [Tsygane], Pathé Frères, 1910; 7 December 1910.

Muratova, Kira, *Enthusiasms* [Uvlechen´ia], Nikola-fil´m, with Komitet rossiiskoi federatsii po kinematografii and Rossiiskoe televidenie, 1994.

_____ *Chekhovian Motifs* [Chekhovskie motivy], Nikola-fil´m, Sluzhba kinematografii Ministerstva kul´tury Rossiiskoi Federatsii, Ministerstvo kul´tury i iskusstva Ukrainy, Odesskaia kinostudiia khudozhestvennykh fil´mov, 2002.

Preobrazhenskaia, Ol´ga and Pravov, Ivan, *Peasant Women of Riazan* [Baby riazanskie], Sovkino (First Factory), 1927; 13 December 1927.

276

Protazanov, Iakov, *Moment musical* [Muzykal´nyi moment], P. Timan and F. Reingardt, 1913; 19 February 1913.

_____ *A Chopin Nocturne* [Noktiurn Shopena], P. Timan and F. Reingardt, 1913; 12 September 1913.

_____ *Tango (Modnyi tanets tango)*, Russian Golden Series, 1914; 24 February 1914 [non-extant].

Protazanov, Iakov and Gardin, Vladimir, *The Keys to Happiness* [Kliuchi schast´ia], Timan and Reingardt, 1913; 7 October 1913 and 28 October 1913 [only a fragment survives].

Reinol´s, Robert, *Baldy among the Gypsies* [Lysyi u tsygan], A. Drankov, 1916 [non-extant].

_____ *Baldy in Love with the Dancer* [Lysyi vliublen v tantsovshchitsu], A. Drankov, 1916.

Romashkov, Vladimir, *Sten´ka Razin* (*Brigands from the Lower Reaches* [Ponizovaia vol´nitsa] and also known by the English title *Free Men of the Volga*), Drankov, 1908; 15 October 1908.

Sabiński, Czesław, *The Living Corpse* [Zhivoi trup], 1918 [non-extant].

Shiriaev, Aleksandr, *The Artist Pierrots* [P´ero-khudozhniki], 1906/07.

Shukhmin, N., *Prince Serebrianyi* [Kniaz´ Serebrianyi], Drankov, 1907 [non-extant].

Shuvalov, I., *Boris Godunov* (*Dmitrii Samozvanets* and *Scenes from Boyar Life* [Stseny iz boiarskoi zhizni]), Drankov, 1907 [non-extant].

Siversen, Vladimir, *Drama in a Gypsy Camp Near Moscow* [Drama v tabore podmoskovnykh tsygan] (*Drama Near Moscow* [Drama pod Moskvoiu]), A. Khanzhonkov and E. Osh, 1908; 20 December 1908.

Soifer, Iosif, *Aziade* (*In the Harem Against Her Will* [Nevol´nitsa garema]), K. Abramovich (Titan), 1918.

Starewicz, Władysław, *The Cameraman's Revenge* [Mest´ kinematograficheskogo operatora], A. Khanzhonov & Co., 1912; 27 October 1912.

_____ *Everyone is Dancing the Tango in the Land of Russia* [Vse tantsuiut tango v strane Rossii], production company unknown, 1914 [non-extant].

Turner, Otis, *Business is Business*, Universal Film Manufacturing Company, 1915 (USA); 13 September 1915.

Ural´skii, A. and Larin, Nikolai, *The Tercentenary of the Rule of the House of Romanov, 1613–1913* [Trekhsotletie tsarstvovaniia doma Romanovykh 1613–1913], Aleksandr Drankov and A. Taldykin, 1913; 16 February 1913.

Viskovskii, Viacheslav, *The Last Tango* [Poslednee tango] (*Beneath the Burning Sky of Argentina* [Pod znoinym nebom Argentiny]), D. Kharitonov, 1918; 31 May 1918.

Films Whose Director Is Unknown

Aza the Gypsy [Tsyganka Aza], D. Kharitonov (Odessa), 1919 [non-extant].

Forget About the Fire Place, the Flames Have Gone Out... [Pozabud´ pro kamin, v nem pogasli ogni...], 1917 [non-extant].

The Funeral of Vera Kholodnaia [Pokhorony Very Kholodnoi], production studio unknown, 1919.

The Song of Persia [Pesn´ Persii], production studio unknown, 1919 [non-extant].

Index

279

Index

Index

Index

Index

Index

Lightning Source UK Ltd.
Milton Keynes UK
UKHW021839030821
388225UK00010B/241